1981

Goethe and Lessing:
The Wellsprings of Creation

By the same author *(in preparation)*:

Schiller's Drama: Talent and Integrity

*Schiller: A Master of the Tragic Form –
His Theory in His Practice*

Ilse Graham

GOETHE
AND
The Wellsprings of Creation
LESSING

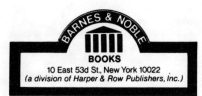

BARNES & NOBLE
BOOKS
10 East 53d St., New York 10022
(a division of Harper & Row Publishers, Inc.)

Published in the U.S.A. 1973 by
HARPER & ROW PUBLISHERS, INC.
BARNES & NOBLE IMPORT DIVISION

First Published 1973 by Elek Books Limited London

ISBN 06-492509-9

Printed in Great Britain

du hol-de Kunst,—ich dan - ke dir!

Contents

Author's Note

Lessing's works are referred to throughout in the Lachmann-Muncker Ausgabe, 3rd Edition (Stuttgart, 1886-1924). Unless otherwise stated, Goethe's works are referred to throughout in the Artemis Gedenkausgabe der Werke, Briefe und Gespräche (Zurich, 1949-60), here abbreviated as AGA. Where references are to the Hamburger Ausgabe, the abbreviation used is HA. Works which do not appear in either edition are referred to in the Weimarer Ausgabe, here abbreviated as WA. Chapters 3 and 4 refer to the Text of the Akademie-Ausgabe of Goethe's works (Berlin, 1958), here abbreviated as Ak.

In quoted passages heavy (medium) type, as distinct from italic, indicates the author's emphasis.

The German letter ß is throughout rendered as *ss*.

Author's Acknowledgements

I should like to acknowledge the permission granted by the editors and publishers of *German Life and Letters* and *Euphorion* to make use of materials previously published in those periodicals.

My most grateful thanks go to Mary E. Gilbert and Tom W. Eason who proved to be untiring listeners and unfailingly constructive critics; to Professor John Watkins of the London School of Economics, who kindly checked the correctness of the syllogistic exposition in Chapter 10; also to my editor, Antony Wood, who took an active part in the last stages of getting this book ready for the press far in excess of his official function; last but not least to my family, Gerald, Nina and Martin, for their forbearance and, even, interest.

Introduction

The following pages owe their existence to a single sentence in a single letter – a letter addressed by Goethe to Herder in July 1772. They record the stages of a journey of discovery undertaken to find out what Goethe meant when he wrote of the play he had just completed – it was the first version of his *Götz* – that it was 'alles nur gedacht'; adding *'Emilia Galotti ist auch nur gedacht'* and bringing it under the same condemnation. The whole of this book, and above all its central conception, have sprung from this single point of growth. I was led first to find in what sense Goethe's *Urgötz* and Lessing's *Emilia Galotti* could possibly lie open to the same charge; then the direction the young Goethe took to transcend what he felt to be his play's creative defect, and where his development subsequently led him; and also to consider the parallel yet plainly distinct course of Lessing's development as a creative artist in the light of this same stricture.

As sometimes happens in criticism, the journey has taken me to fields wider and far more remote than I envisaged when I first set out on it. As I continued to explore the two writers' work I realised how trenchant Goethe's *aperçu* had been. Not in the sense that what was a creative defect for him was necessarily one for Lessing too, nor indeed that his way of coming to terms with the demands of his own prodigious genius was indicative of the way in which Lessing's more limited talent could best come to fruition. Goethe's *aperçu* was true, rather, in that he divined how deeply, in the case of both plays, the experience of the fashioning process itself had entered into the heart of the works and shaped their import and structure alike. Whatever their subject-matter, they were also and crucially 'about' their own production.

The further afield I ventured in Goethe's work and Lessing's, the more I marvelled how seminal Goethe's insight had been. Wherever I tried to grasp the import and organisation of one of their works, I found, to my own surprise, I was also taking a reading of the creative pulse that had beat at the heart of its life. I based my further course on this discovery. To penetrate to the creative matrix of each work, to the point where in it I might discern those energies which had in the first place seized upon materials congruent to themselves to shape them into symbolic structures expressive of themselves henceforth became the method and aim of my investigation.

The patterns of creativity thus revealed were often different from work to work, and very different indeed as between Lessing and Goethe. Nevertheless I gradually found landmarks enabling one to trace, in each poet, the configuration of internal and external factors which would allow him to exploit his creative potential to the fullest. Most prominent were certain symbolisms concerned more directly than others with articulating the artist's relation to his own nascent product. Of such symbolisms – I propose to call them 'operational symbolisms' – I would mention, first and foremost, the human hand, mediating between mind and world; then erotic arousal and fulfilment, food and its digestive cycle, water in circulation, the cycle of the seasons, journeying and homecoming, trading, the handling and possession of money, the gift and loss of rings. All these are symbols of circulation and directed movement, and all are variations on a single theme which is the cycle of organic life, the rhythmical alternation of systole and diastole, giving out and taking in, flowing out to what is not the self and thence returning to the self.

Such a view of the rhythms of organic life as pulsing, so to speak, equally throughout artistic and intellectual creation, is as old as Plato's conception of creative Eros. What seemed new, and exciting, was the discovery that this creative heartbeat should be discernible in artists as different in almost every other respect as are Lessing and Goethe; that, long before the aesthetic preoccupations of the late nineteenth and the present century, I should find two writers of such plainly different metal, though nurtured in the same intellectual climate, for whom the cycle of completion – the cycle of the painter's vision for instance, from the eye to the heart to the hand, to the very fingertips – should be an analogue of the creative cycle by which their works themselves were brought forth and which they themselves symbolised. To a greater or lesser extent, these two sons of the Age of Enlightenment anticipated the trend towards that poetic self-awareness which has become the hallmark of contemporary writing, from Proust and Joyce to Mann and Benn and Grass. Already in the objective Lessing, and to an incomparably greater degree in Goethe, whose genius defies all traditional divisions into the objective and the subjective mode, the experience of the making of a work of art remained active, and resonant, in its meaning, endowing it with a plurality of imports capable of reflecting and even symbolising one another. And paradoxically it is the personal, psychosomatic experience of the self-in-the-process-of-creation which, entering into the very mould and meaning of a work of art and blending with them, imbues it with its most universal imports and lends it its most persistent organic overtones. When the act of creation and the result of creation are so closely intertwined, 'How can we know the dancer from the dance?'

London, October 1970

Part One

CLOSED ROADS

Anaxagoras actually claims that through having hands man is the
most rational of animals; one could equally argue that it is through
his being the most rational that he comes by hands. For hands are
an instrument . . .

(Aristotle: *Parts of Animals*)

Die Charakterisierung des Menschen, als eines vernünftigen
Tieres, liegt schon in der Gestalt und Organisation seiner *Hand,*
seiner *Finger und Fingerspitzen,* deren teils Bau, teils zartes Gefühl,
dadurch die Natur ihn nicht für Eine Art der Handhabung der
Sachen, sondern unbestimmt für alle, mithin für den Gebrauch
der Vernunft geschickt gemacht, und dadurch die technische-
oder Geschicklichkeitsanlage seiner Gattung, als eines *vernünftigen*
Tieres, bezeichnet hat.

(Kant: *Anthropologie in pragmatischer Hinsicht*)

dextra mihi deus
(Virgil: *Aeneid*)

1

Emilia Galotti: The Vision and the Way

Heard melodies are sweet, but those unheard
  Are sweeter; therefore, ye soft pipes, play on;
Not to the sensual ear, but, more endear'd,
  Pipe to the spirit ditties of no tone.

(Keats: *Ode on a Grecian Urn*)

I

The episodic in literature – the incident, the anecdote, the *ad hoc* conversation – always deserves our attention. For whilst life is full of irrelevancies, art is not, least of all an art form as selective as is drama. All its materials are equally relevant, the seemingly incidental no less than those which evidently further the development of plot or character. Perhaps even more so. For, because it stands clear of the pull and thrust of the dramatic action, the episode may well be used as a symbolic structure concentrating the drama's deeper import by reflecting it as it were on the small surface of a convex mirror.

To assign any such function to the opening scenes of *Emilia Galotti* – the scenes taken up by the conversation between the Prince and the painter – at first sight seems far-fetched and unconvincing. True, this conversation motivates the ensuing action in that it affords us some insight into the Prince's disturbed condition and thus prepares us for his violent reaction to the news that the object of his passion, Emilia, is to be married that very day. But what wider bearing could this lighthearted *causerie* about fashionable aesthetic topics conceivably have upon a tragedy as stark as that which is about to begin? Indeed, the action about to be precipitated is as remorseless as any on the German stage, and by mere contrast with it the poet's stance here, in these opening scenes, appears to be so casual that one is inclined to regard them as a preliminary skirmish permitting the dramatist, and his audience, to warm up to the slaughter that lies ahead.

What is more, our initial impression of waywardness is strengthened by the fact that the most searching observations of the artist – his reflections on the questionableness of art, and not just his art but of all art *per se* – fall on deaf ears and seem designed, principally, to highlight the Prince's indifference to all but his clandestine passion. For he simply does not hear the thesis Conti develops and it is only when Conti insists on some answer that he is roused from his dreams. Thus the painter's provocative remarks fall by the wayside, unheard, undeveloped and, so it appears, forgotten, by the Prince, by us and by the poet.

In fact, the outsider's chance remarks, brushed aside because of more pressing concerns, go on echoing throughout the play. Indeed in Conti's aesthetic reflections, the poet for the first time sounds the poetic theme which is to be developed, fully and broadly, in the main body of his tragedy. The theme of discourse that runs through this opening conversation is the tragic disparateness of mind and medium, of the vision and the way in art and the hint of an even greater dichotomy in life. It is a miracle of a conversation, combining a rigorous pursuit of its theme with expositional and dramatic elements without ever losing the appearance of complete flexibility of movement and artless improvisation.

'Guten Morgen, Conti. Wie leben Sie? Was macht die Kunst?' (I, 2), the Prince exclaims on seeing the painter. The form of his question is significant. The Prince separates the outer man from his inner vocation. There is the merest suggestion of a fissure between the two, and this is presently deepened by the painter's reply: 'Die Kunst geht nach Brodt,' he says, and goes on to complain how easy it is for the artist to prostitute his art when he is pressed by need. The conversation now takes a more personal turn; Conti produces the portrait of Orsina, the Prince's former mistress, only to meet with blank indifference on the part of her erstwhile lover. But all the while the argument is carried forward. If before the poet had hinted that art is imperilled by the objective economic sphere in which the artist is placed, we are now being told of another adversary, nearer home. Art is endangered by the imponderables which enter into its making and its taking. As Conti uncovers Orsina's portrait, he begs the Prince to remember 'die Schranken unserer Kunst' (I, 4). He knows as well as his patron that his interpretation flatters the sitter. The real Orsina is older and uglier. But he also knows that this shortcoming is inevitable. The painter is up against the imperfection of the physical medium in which his object – the true Orsina – is embodied; not only against the accidental imperfections of her aging body which make his vision appear dated even now: he is up against the inherent defectiveness of matter as such. So defective indeed is the medium of physical reality – and here Conti rallies the big guns of Plotinian metaphysics in his defence – that Nature herself, in descending into matter in the act of creation, has forfeited the purity of her original vision. Never, not even in her prime, did the real Orsina, the embodied woman, match her image in the mind of the 'plastische Natur' *(ibid.)*. Thus the artist, like nature, is defeated by the deficiency of the medium in which his object is embodied, by the 'Abfall, welchen der widerstrebende Stoff unvermeidlich macht', by the 'Verderb, mit welchem die Zeit dagegen an kämpfet' *(ibid.)*. Inevitably, then, the connection between his immaterial vision and the material reality to which it has reference is precarious. And strangely enough, this problem has its precise counterpart in the relation between the artistic vision and its recipient. The rapport between Conti's artistic vision and the Prince who sees it is as precarious as the connection of this vision with Orsina who sat for it, and for the same reason. The artist comes up against the same variability and lability of the human medium with which he has vainly contended in the act of creation. Conti is defeated by the unsteadiness of the Prince whom he had counted upon to be the same that he was when he ordered the picture. But the Prince is no longer the man that commissioned the portrait, just as Orsina is no longer the woman who sat for her portrait to be painted. His soul is a fickle medium. He confesses that he carries in it 'ein anderes Bild, das mit andern Farben, auf einen andern Grund gemalet ist' (I, 3). At either end of the creative process, at its reception as well as at its conception, the connection between the artist's vision and the human sphere to which it has reference is threatened. As his vision becomes real, it is obsolescent.

When, after this debacle, Conti produces Emilia's portrait, the conversation shifts to the heart of the aesthetic matter; to the problem of vision and realisation, of mind and medium in the creative act. 'Ha! dass wir nicht unmittelbar mit den Augen malen!' the painter exclaims, ignoring the Prince's praise of his achievement and pondering its distance from his vision:

> Auf dem langen Wege, aus dem Auge durch den Arm in den Pinsel, wie viel geht da verloren! – Aber . . . dass ich es weiss, was hier verloren gegangen, und wie es verloren gegangen, und warum es verloren gehen müssen: darauf bin ich eben so stolz, und stolzer, als ich auf alles das bin, was ich nicht verloren gehen lassen. Denn aus

jenem erkenne ich, mehr als aus diesem, dass ich wirklich ein grosser
Maler bin: dass es aber meine Hand nur nicht immer ist. – Oder meynen
Sie, Prinz, dass Raphael nicht das grösste malerische Genie gewesen
wäre, wenn er unglücklicher Weise ohne Hände wäre geboren worden?
Meynen Sie, Prinz? (I, 4)

From the lips of a creative artist, and a plastic artist at that,
these are startling words.[1] For the adversaries of artistic vision so
far encountered – the shortcoming of material reality, and the
shortcoming of those on the periphery of the aesthetic process –
are harmless compared to the enemy that is now named: the
artist's own hands. His vision is spoilt even before it reaches the
'other', the material world that is to receive its imprint. It is
vitiated by his own hands, the tools and material organs of his
spirit. Can it be that, being material, they are the enemy's agents
inside the camp, corrupting the vision on its short way from the
centre to the skin, from the eyes to the paintbrush? Can it be that
the poet, through the lips of the painter, articulates a split
between mind and medium so deep that it runs through the
centre of the personality, dividing not merely the person from the
external world but the mind from its embodied self?

It is a desperate aesthetic that the painter expounds to the Prince
of a fine morning. And the gravity of the thesis he develops, as
well as the logical rigour with which he pursues it, make it
impossible to brush this conversation aside lightly and to interpret
it as a chatter on fashionable topics thrown out by Lessing with
a sidelong wink at his audience. This is not the stuff of which
patter is made, however erudite or courtly. It is much more likely
the stuff of which tragedy is spun. And indeed, the painter's words
are the nucleus from which the verbal finestructure of the drama
is developed. 'Auf dem langen Wege, aus dem Auge durch den
Arm in den Pinsel, wie viel geht da verloren . . .' Every word
here: *lang, Weg, Auge, geht* – yes, even *geht* – *verloren,* and of course
Hand, the thrice repeated keyword of the passage – every single
word sustains an imagistic web whose threads run through the
play and combine to weave its poetic theme. And the straightest
of threads runs from the sense of inevitable loss the painter voices
here, in the aesthetic sphere, to Emilia's final acknowledgment
'dass alles verloren ist; – und dass wir wohl ruhig seyn müssen'
(V,7).

This reading may claim the authority of no less a critic than
Goethe. For did he not, in his own novel *Werther,* perceive a
connection between the art motif sounded at the beginning of
Lessing's tragedy and the motif of death in which it culminates,
and did he not exploit this link for his own purposes? 'Ich könnte

jetzt nicht zeichnen, nicht einen Strich,' Werther writes in the second letter of the book, 'und bin nie ein grösserer Maler gewesen als in diesen Augenblicken.' It is generally accepted that these words echo Conti's extraordinary claim 'dass ich wirklich ein grosser Maler bin; dass es aber meine Hand nur nicht immer ist'[2] (I, 4). And, as if to match this beginning, we read on the last page of the novel: 'Emilia Galotti lag auf dem Pulte aufgeschlagen.' This piece of information furnishes the last glimpse we get into Werther's mind. Clearly, the very place assigned to these allusions lends them the highest significance[3]. They are as it were the frame in which we are invited to perceive the hero's career, from his obdurately deluded beginnings to his catastrophic end, and they suggest an equally meaningful link between the art motif sounded at the outset of *Emilia Galotti* and the heroine's violent death.

Let us then follow Lessing's lead and Goethe's, and pursue the symbolism which is introduced so casually to the point where the whole tragic action and import of *Emilia Galotti* may be seen to have flowed from it.

II

Take the eye first, and very briefly. The painter's curious exclamation: 'Ha! dass wir nicht unmittelbar mit den Augen malen!' suggests that the eye is a spiritual organ close to the seat of vision. There is much in the play to support that suggestion, as for instance when Conti says to the Prince: 'Ihre Seele . . . war ganz in Ihren Augen. Ich liebe solche Seelen, und solche Augen.' (I,4). The eye is the mirror of the soul and transparently expresses its promptings. But it not only expresses what is inside the person. It also receives impressions from the outside; indeed, the mediation of the external world through perception is its principal function. And as soon as perception is employed in this, its sensory function, it diverges from the inner vision and its truth.

One need only recall to what extent the movement of the plot hinges on the act of seeing and its consequences. For the longest time, the Prince's relation to Emilia is one of seeing. He falls in love with her when he first sees her at a social gathering, and he goes on seeing her intermittently at Mass. Then he sees her portrait. This fresh impact on his senses becomes an event of the greatest consequence. In every sense, it marks the beginning of the end. Not only does he look at the portrait greedily – there are four lengthy stage directions to this effect – and repeatedly; with Conti, after his dismissal, and then again after dismissing

Marinelli, his chamberlain; what is more important is that each renewed seeing leads more directly into action and disaster. He looks and feels love-sick. He looks again and half formulates thoughts of seduction. He looks and gives Marinelli *carte blanche* to engineer a plot. He looks once more and rushes to church to see Emilia, thereby in advance spoiling Marinelli's scheme and bringing about its discovery, a turn of events which precludes a conciliatory solution and precipitates Emilia's death. Thus perception, so near the spiritual source of vision, by the exercise of its sensuous function loses itself in remote regions and engenders chaos and ultimate catastrophe.

But if perception loses sight of vision, how much more distant from its truth is the hand which the painter so readily disowns! So long indeed is the way from the mind to the hand that to say it belongs to its owner is to make an altogether problematic statement. This is already evident in the beginning, when Conti distinguishes between the I and its hand, arguing 'dass ich wirklich ein grosser Maler bin; dass es aber meine Hand nur nicht immer ist.' (I,4). This dichotomy becomes deepened later in the play. Looking for a gun with which to kill the Prince, and finding himself unarmed, Emilia's impetuous father, Odoardo, exclaims: 'Wunder, dass ich aus Eilfertigkeit nicht auch die Hände zurück gelassen!' (IV,7). The association of hands with gun establishes the tenor of the image: hands are henceforth felt to be as detached and as dangerous as a fire-arm.

It is an ominous beginning when the Prince seizes Emilia's picture with the words: 'Aber dieses bleibt hier. Mit einem Studio macht man so viel Umstände nicht: auch lässt man das nicht aufhängen; sondern hat es gern bey der Hand.' (I,4.) For all his studied carelessness there is ruthlessness in these words – in the note of command they strike, in the summary dismissal of 'viele Umstände' and in the contrast they offer between his treatment of the two pictures: Orsina's is kept at a distance, framed and hung on the wall of a picture gallery; Emilia's, snatched from the realm of disinterested pleasure where it belongs, is drawn into the real world of will and hot desire. Ruthlessness and cynicism increase with every occurrence of the image; when Marinelli advises the Prince to seduce Emilia after her marriage, saying 'Waaren, die man aus der ersten Hand nicht haben kann, kauft man aus der zweyten . . . um so viel wohlfeiler . . . Freylich, auch um so viel schlechter' (I,6); and when he asks the Prince to give him 'freye Hand' *(ibid.)* to remove the bridegroom. Tinged with such associations, the symbol of the hand is introduced in the context of actual violence, and henceforth its occurrence marks the successive phases in the process of destruction. As Emilia's hand is seized by the Prince in church, she knows that she is seized by her doom. And Appiani seals his, when he takes the hand of Marinelli urging him to duel straightaway. Within minutes Emilia's bridegroom is murdered in a contrived 'Handgemenge' with Marinelli's hirelings, and the brutality of the deed is topped by the cynicism of Marinelli's comment on its execution: 'Pfuy, Angelo! Das heisst sein Handwerk sehr grausam treiben; – und verpfuschen.' (III,2.)

No – hands in this play are sinister tools,[4] associated not with creating and caressing, but with guns and daggers and pins; never used to nurse the vision of the spirit into the ripeness of reality, but to betray it, insidiously or violently, by corruption or destruction. Thus when Odoardo tells Emilia of the Prince's intention to keep her with him – 'Du bist, du bleibst in den Händen deines Räubers' (V,7) – the mere word suffices to harden Emilia's resolve to die, and to make her decision self-explanatory. Her fourfold reiteration of the word – 'in seinen Händen' – tells us more eloquently of her dread now, and of the horrors she foresees, than does her florid story of the temptations she had experienced at the dubious gathering where she had first set eyes on the Prince. To be delivered into a pair of human hands has come to mean to be delivered to corruption or, at best, destruction. Thus, at the end, the hand that merely destroys her is the benign hand. 'Lassen Sie mich sie küssen, diese väterliche Hand' *(ibid.)*, Emilia says as her father's hand stabs to death his own creation.[5]

He destroys a lovely girl in order to save the vision she embodies. It is the vision of virginal beauty, of the unravaged rose, which she once more invokes to incite him to the deed. It is her vision and his, the Prince's and the painter's and the vision of her that Appiani had cherished. Odoardo must destroy Emilia to save this vision from corruption. In a hostile world, it could not come true. Can we wonder when even the skilled hands of the painter could not woo it into reality in his chosen medium? When even the hands of Nature had fumbled in the act of creation? 'Das Weib wollte die Natur zu ihrem Meisterstücke machen. Aber sie vergriff sich im Thone; sie nahm ihn zu fein.' (V,7.)[6] In the end, it is not enough to say that the vision of virginal beauty could not come true in a hostile world. It cannot live in the medium in which Nature erroneously embodied it. Thus, the split between mind and medium does run through the centre of the personality. It divides not only the person from the world, but the mind from its embodied self. In the final analysis, the union is untenable. To be faithful to itself, the mind must sever its connection with its body.

How right Goethe was to suggest an inner connection between

Emilia's suicide and the painter's reflections. And how superbly right
he was in using Lessing's tragedy poetically to pattern his own
Werther's tragic drift to dissociation and to death. For Conti's words
do in fact formulate a dichotomy which, once its full implications are
developed, inevitably means dissociation and death. 'Auf dem langen Wege, aus dem Auge durch den Arm in den Pinsel, wie viel geht
da verloren! . . . ' (I,4.) We know the answer. It is, in Emilia's own
words, 'dass alles verloren ist' (V,7).

III

But we must yet take note of the strange awareness of time that is
expressed in these words. Why should the painter feel as long, indeed
as disastrously long, the passage of experience through the body, a
passage which for most of us is unconscious yet enriching, and for
none more so than for the creative artist?[7] What vision indeed can a
painter be said to possess outside the knowledge that resides in his
hand, which permeates his every thought and feeling, informing his
every movement and directing the use he makes of his media? What
inspiration can a dancer be said to have that is not in terms of the
kinaesthetic experience of his – or her – body projected into a felt
space? It is important to realise that this is the phase of the creative
process on which the painter's words focus attention. He is not
concerning himself with the later problems of articulating a vision in
a physical medium which has been experienced in the viscera and in
the muscles. Colour and canvas and questions of execution are never
so much as mentioned by Conti. His words point to an earlier, more
rudimentary phase of the creative process: he is concerned with the
immediate transmission of a psychic content to a bodily level of
experiencing. This transmission, his image tells us, is disrupted.
Psychic experience is arrested in its passage through the body, before
ever it becomes a physically felt reality, capable of being projected
outward, into an external medium.

It is this disruption of a continuum of experiencing which finds
expression in the intervening consciousness of time; and Lessing
has articulated this stalling of internal communication in the overall
poetic symbol of the play, the spatio-temporal symbol of *der lange Weg*.
Again and again this tragedy asks the same question: if even the short
and sheltered way of the vision through the bloodstream to the finger
tips is too long, what distance can be small enough, and what time
sufficiently short, to keep vision intact once it enters the alien medium
of the world? And he answers this question as he must, given the
painter's premiss: however small the distance between the vision and

realisation, however near the place, however short the way, it is longer than the way from the mind to the hand, and infinitely less protected. Where the passage of the vision through the body is disrupted, its passage into the world must of necessity be barred.

On every level of the outer and inner action, we come upon instances of a vision separated by an arm's length from fulfilment and spoilt on the way. One day and one short ride separate Appiani from marriage and happiness, but the day is too long and the ride is too far and he is murdered by the wayside. A minute separates him from seeing Emilia as he first saw her and continued to see her in his mind's eye, and from embracing this vision in reality. 'Eine kleine Geduld, und ich stehe so vor Ihnen da!' she says. (II,7.) These are her last words to him. He never sets eyes on her again. The short way to church turns out to be fatal, for both Emilia and the Prince. Odoardo knows that she should not have gone 'die wenigen Schritte' (II,2) for 'Einer ist genug zu einem Fehltritt' *(ibid.)*, a foreboding taken up by Appiani when he muses on the very threshold of fulfilment: 'Noch Einen Schritt vom Ziele, oder noch gar nicht ausgelaufen seyn, ist im Grunde eines' (II,8) – Emilia knows it too, darkly, already before the outward consequences of her action are brought home to her. For even before the Prince interrupts her worship, she experiences a loss of inner vision, for no other reason than that she found herself 'weiter von dem Altare, als ich sonst pflege, – denn ich kam zu spät' (II,6). Even that slight distance between her and the 'Allerreinste' is fatal. Consciousness intervenes, and in the anxiety 'dass eines andern Andacht mich in meiner stören möchte' *(ibid.)* her own experience is destroyed.

The Prince, too, knows that the way defeats the vision. He had sat down to work, only to find that he no longer feels like working, the moment the first document hits his eye. He had felt like a ride only to discover that this impulse has gone too, by the time that Marinelli appears. He had ordered Orsina's portrait, only to brush it aside when it comes. Her image in his heart has been replaced by another. And will not his vision of Emilia be mocked before the day is out, by the sight of her disfigured body, and her memory be overlaid by other memories, as the memory of Orsina had been dispelled by Emilia? The Prince's flightiness is only a variation on the all-pervading theme of the tragedy – the flight of a vision which is all but reached yet never grasped, because the time and the way into reality, however short, are too long.

This crippling experience of time is shared by all and verbalised by Appiani, as he stands on the brink of supposed happiness and actual disaster: 'Ja, wenn die Zeit nur ausser uns wäre! – Wenn eine Minute am Zeiger, sich in uns nicht in Jahre ausdehnen könnte! – ' (II,8).

Appiani's words confirm at the centre of the tragedy what the words of the painter have told us at the outset: time, in the universe of discourse of this tragedy, is an inner experience, and its disastrousness has its roots deep within the person. The actual minute that is measured by the clock is short enough, as short as the passage of the hand over the face of the clock, from one painted stroke to the next. But in us it can grow into years, an eternity signifying the cessation of communication from mind to medium, from heart to hand, from conscious to unconscious, and the death of the vision in a divided self. This is the meaning of the words *zu spät* which echo through the tragedy like a funeral knell. They do not really tell us of events in time. They tell us, rather, of the advent of time, of its intrusion into consciousness. They mourn the disruption of an organic, timeless cycle of experiencing. Once that is broken, once the clock begins to tick and time and consciousness intervene, everything is 'too late'.

It is this inward experience of time – an extravagantly subjective one – rather than any punctilious concern for dramatic conventions which accounts for Lessing's strict adherence to the unities in this drama. By curtailing clock-time to an absolute minimum, the poet underscores as effectively as he could possibly do the demoniacal role of time as a psychological force. Inside the person, the fleeting moment is in danger of expanding into an unconquerable infinity. In fact, time, in this tragedy, is progressively unmasked as the ultimate antagonist, and it is in the handling of this invisible presence rather than of characters and their motives that the poet develops his subtlest mastery. As a study of time *Emilia Galotti* is compelling, in the gradual transition it traces from the characters' initial awareness, and fear, of clock-time – its briefness and the terror of its passing – to an annihilating awareness of their own time – its cessation and the terror of discontinuity. In the measure in which time itself is experienced as a frantic rush grinding to a halt, haste gives way to mesmerised inactivity in the face of the Inevitable. And what is not inevitable when, transfixed, it will no longer pass? With the flow of time, the flow of life itself is frozen into motionlessness by minds incapable of enduring the threat of either.[8]

In the universe of discourse of this tragedy, the mind is disinherited. It has no corporeal home, neither in its own body nor in the external world. It has no choice beside purity or prostitution, destruction or corruption. It is a tragic world, and one which in the final analysis fills one with uneasiness and misgivings: a world where integrity means exile, where vision rots in the body, where virginity is preferred to marriage and maturity, and where a plastic artist repudiates his hand and dreams of painting, contactless, with his eyes – *un-mittel-bar*: a world of insubstantial minds without medium.

In this world, tragedy is absolute. There is no figure and no level of discourse which is exempt from the dichotomy the poet articulates and from the crippling experience of time which springs from such duality. And indeed, does the work as a whole transcend its theme? Is it not deeply inarticulate for all the chiselled sharpness of its speech, and do not its words fail the poet at every crucial point? Does not Emilia herself – embodiment of loveliness doomed to die – remain a construct of the poet's mind rather than a fully embodied creature of his imagination? Does not the painter's eulogy of her beauty read like a catalogue of 'points' and her own confession of sensuality remain cerebral and academic? 'Auch meine Sinne, sind Sinne' (V,7) – it is our mind that spells out the ambiguity of these words. They do not speak sensuously to our senses. We shall be concerned with such questions in a later chapter.[9] What we may say now, however, is this: had Lessing been able to let Emilia speak of herself and the painter speak of her in poetic utterance rich with sensuous resonance, the problems of interpretation of her character and motive which have exercised critical minds for so long would have resolved themselves as effortlessly as they do vis-à-vis the first unconscious stirrings of Gretchen's love in the room that Faust has entered.

In the last resort, Lessing's tragedy is the soliloquy of an artist who knows himself to be in precarious touch with his medium and his creativeness. The gulf between mind and medium, between the vision and the way is not only its inner theme. It is its author's unresolved artistic problem: and that is why it is here experienced as absolute.[10]

2

Philotas: A Price for Purity

So must pure lovers' soules descend
  T'affections, and to faculties,
Which sense may reach and apprehend,
  Else a great Prince in prison lies.

                 (Donne: *The Exstasie*)

'Philotas ist der erste glaubwürdige Jüngling des deutschen Dramas,' a critic has recently written[1] and persuasively argued that Lessing's tragedy, written in 1759, some ten years before the actual onset of the *Sturm und Drang,* unmistakably adumbrates the mood of the movement. 'Es ist ein Trauerspiel der Jugendleidenschaft,' the same critic writes – 'ein im aufgeklärten Deutschland unerhörtes Thema.'[2] Here is a youth in all his impetuosity, with a youth's thirst for perfection and a youth's extravagant elations and depressions: one whose violent temperament may justly be summed up in the words addressed to him by Strato, his captors' general: 'Fasse dich, lieber Prinz! Es ist der Fehler des Jünglings, sich immer für glücklicher, oder unglücklicher zu halten, als er ist.' (I,2.) And indeed, this strange play sends the mind forward to the extreme subjectivism of a Werther – Philotas after all, too, commits suicide for no clear-cut external reasons but because of a malaise which, on closer inspection, eludes ready definition.[3] Nor are our thoughts arrested there. They run on to later, and uncannier, figments of the romantic imagination: to Kleist's *Amphitryon* with its shifting identities, to the dream-like blend of tenderness and ferocity we find in *Penthesilea* and *Käthchen von Heilbronn,* and, most of all perhaps, to that sleep-walking warrior, Prinz Friedrich von Homburg. Our thoughts are carried even beyond those horizons, to Heine's *Doppelgänger,* to Müller's *Nebensonnen* (immortalised in Schubert's song-cycle *Die Winterreise*), to the works of E. T. A. Hoffmann or even to late Van Goghs where rival suns whirl side by side in darkened skies. But do not such associations, with the suggestions they evoke of doubled vision and blurred perspectives, appear aeons removed from the clarity and simplicity that seem to prevail in Lessing's tragedy? We must reserve judgment.

It is an archaic world in which the action is set; pointing back to a more hoary age than that suggested by the Greek nomenclature: to the world of Abraham and Isaac perhaps, a world of fathers and sons, close-knit in tribal groups, where love and hate as yet lie mingled in the womb of darkest unconsciousness, where begetter and begotten enact initiation rites of barbaric solemnity, and the beloved son trembles at the blade of an axe wielded by his father in a sacrificial act, at once ferocious and tender; a world where kings are patriarchs who love and sacrifice their subjects as they love and sacrifice their sons. Two fathers in this drama, Aridäus and Parmenio, the young prince's paternal friend, contemplate the sacrifice of their sons. Two kings share a biblical vision of their people's welfare; their public deeds and private dreams are tinged with an aura of the numinous; and their souls are moist as yet with religious awe. In this masculine world women play no part. Wives and mothers are not so much as mentioned. Only as concubines and as the inflictors of love-bites do they flit across the horizons of the characters' imaginations. It is a world of men, and all the deeper passions, those kindled by love and hate, and by honour and disgrace, are shared between men, and, most of all, between fathers and sons.

In such an atmosphere the poet has set a plot of archaic simplicity. A young prince, taken prisoner during the first battle he sees, discovers that the opponent king's son, too, has been captured and is held prisoner by his own father. After a shortlived period of relief he realises that the advantage his father might have derived from his precious spoil is cancelled out by the fact that he himself will now have to be ransomed: thus, so as not to compromise his father's chances of exploiting the luck of battle to the full, he decides to kill himself.

A straightforward plot if any, strictly contained within the unities of time and place, and above all, sustaining the inner unity of an action which permits of no secondary interest and which, without so much as a sidelong glance, channels all its momentum into the figure of the hero whose intrepid reasoning and burning idealism carry all before him. In one flash of inner vision Philotas conceives the idea that he has it in him to tip the scales of fortune, acts on what he has perceived and dies. This headlong race of a boy to the autonomy of manhood and extinction is what the tragedy is about, and the sequence of inner events takes scarcely longer than it takes the mind of Philotas to recognise that his specific case is an instance of a universal law and to implement what he has thus perceived.[4]

And yet, when we look at the structure of this work embodying an action so seemingly unilateral and pivoted upon a centre so seemingly unequivocal, we begin to wonder. To enter into its organisation is like entering into a gallery of mirrors, where every presence and configuration is reflected doubly, triply or even fourfold, until, at the end, we ask ourselves in confusion which is original and which reflection, or even whether, amongst these manifold mirror images, there is one that is incontestably real. There are two kings and two only sons, Philotas and Polytimet, both equally cherished, and now both 'gefangene Prinzen', each in his opponent's hand. At their kings' side there are two generals, Aristodem at the court of Philotas's father, and Strato, the general of Aridäus. Strato too has a son, a youth just like Philotas and Polytimet; so much like them, in fact, that Aridäus, cheated of his hostage and foreseeing the death of his son, turns to Strato, saying: 'Strato, ich bin nun verwaiset, ich armer Mann! – Du hast einen Sohn; er sey der meinige! – Denn *einen* Sohn muss man doch haben.' (VIII.) And there is Parmenio, soldier and Philotas's fellow prisoner, chosen by his Prince as the emissary who is to arrange for the exchange of the two hostages. Parmenio too has a son, loving and beloved, and it is this son who becomes the stake in the cruel pledge Philotas elicits from his ambassador to delay the exchange of the captives by a day.

The kings, we hear, were the closest of friends in their youth – 'das seelige Alter, da wir uns noch ganz unserm Herzen überlassen durften' (III) – until the early bond of love was severed by the cares and rivalries of kingship. But even now Aridäus feels moved as he perceives in the youth before him the likeness of his once-loved father. 'O welcher glücklichen Tage erinnert mich deine blühende Jugend! So blühte die Jugend deines Vaters!' he exclaims. 'Ich umarme deinen jüngern Vater in dir.' *(ibid.)* This indeed is the response the youth receives from all those he encounters in the enemy's camp. Strato, the King's general, goes out towards the captive Prince as though he were his own flesh and blood and as though he recognised his own youth in the fierce grace of the boy. 'Ich bin unwillig,' he murmurs at the end of Philotas's story of courage and disaster; 'du hättest mich nicht so bewegen sollen. – Ich werde mit dir zum Kinde – '. (II.) The King himself clearly does not treat him as an enemy, Philotas muses as he first looks about him and sees the comfort of the tent in which he is kept: 'auch sein König muss mich für ein Kind, für ein verzärteltes Kind halten' (I). Even the soldier who had thrown him off his horse had been moved by his youthfulness. 'Er nannte mich:' – Philotas indignantly recalls – 'Kind!' *(ibid.)*. Parmenio, himself the father of a son only a little older than the captive Prince and, like him, of the fiercest temperament, calls him 'mein lieber, kleiner Freund' and 'mein lieber frühzeitiger Held' and warns him: 'Du bist noch Kind! Gieb nicht zu, dass der rauhe Soldat das zärtliche Kind so bald in dir ersticke.' (V.) To this solicitude Philotas responds and, to make amends for his own overweening ways, he says to him: 'Murre nicht, Alter! Sey wieder gut, alter Vater!' *(ibid.)*

This world of fathers and sons, an austere men's world, is yet filled with a reticent tenderness. For in the figure of the child, the father perceives the image of himself as he once was, in the purity of youth, unblemished as yet by the scars of life. The child is the father's promise of a better world, his hope of immortality. This is the way that these three fathers feel about their sons; it is the way also in which they feel about the subjects under their rule: 'Was ist ein König, wenn er kein Vater ist!' Aridäus says to the captive youth. 'Was ist ein Held ohne Menschenliebe!' (VII.) And this love, the same love which Philotas's father bears to his son, the three fathers – Aridäus, Strato and Parmenio, enemies and compatriot alike – feel for the young stranger in their midst. He is child, blossom, the graceful earnest of a better future. In him they see their own inner regeneration and the regeneration of a world that has become scarred by evil and by time. Parmenio is willing to pledge his son's life and his own to the service of the Prince: ' . . . Nur deswegen, um dich auf dem Throne zu sehen, um dir zu dienen, möchte ich – was ich sonst durchaus nicht möchte – noch einmal jung werden – Dein Vater ist gut; aber du wirst besser.' (V.) And Aridäus embraces in the sombre youth not only 'das seelige Alter, da wir uns noch ganz unserm Herzen überlassen durften'; in him he embraces the hope of peace for his peoples and those of Philotas, and, most of all, the renewed faith in a Providence which, in delivering two sons into the power of two fathers each of whom singly might have yielded to his baser impulses, has bound their hands and recalled them to their better selves. To Aridäus and Strato, as well as Parmenio, Philotas is as precious as their own sons; as the welfare of their subjects; as precious as the integrity of their own hearts, capable still of feeling the sanctity of life. In every deeper sense, Philotas is the child of those he encounters in the enemy's camp: of friend and foe alike. He is 'das Kind des Hauses'; and to borrow this phrase Schiller was to coin more than thirty years later is by no means to be guilty of an anachronism: for Lessing, in this fiercely masculine and melancholy tragedy, has endowed the concept of the child with that aura of tenderness and even reverence which we have come to associate with Schiller's use of it; a depth of resonance which stems not only from a man's nostalgic attachment to what he was bound to lose in order to become a man, but, more deeply, from the poet's recognition that the child, in any age and in any individual, embodies a wholeness of being, an innate goodness of impulse and instinct which must be preserved or retrieved in any member of humanity that is worthy of its name, if maturity is not to be a mockery.

Thus the three characters whom Philotas encounters in the short course of his career as warrior may all say, in the words of Wallenstein: 'denn er stand neben mir wie meine Jugend . . .'.

It is part of the construction and, I think, the overall plan of the drama that we only perceive this paternal tenderness held out to Philotas by figures who are no more his actual begetters than he is their actual son. What little we know of Aridäus's relation to his own son Polytimet we learn from what he says in the presence of Philotas, and thus our impression of this relationship becomes coloured by the enigmatic attraction the King feels towards the sombre youth. The real blood bond has, as it were, become the reflection of the one that is presented on the stage, within the camp of the enemy. The obverse is true of the relation that holds between Philotas and his own father. It is King Aridäus, Strato and Parmenio who in turn interpret it for us, and thus again it appears, not as the primary, but as the reflected reality. Aristodem, the general of Philotas's father, is brought to life, both as a person and in relation to his young charge, through the Prince's response to the corresponding personage at Aridäus's court, Strato. (And how alike their names are!) 'Du kennst ihn, den Aristodem' Philotas tells Strato as he recounts how the general helped him persuade his father, the King, to let him go into battle – 'er ist meines Vaters Strato' (II). Through this reflected relation we do indeed get to know Aristodem: but, again, the reflection is more real than reality itself. And it is not the King, his own begetter, whom we hear Philotas call by the sacred name of father. It is Parmenio he addresses thus, and Parmenio, in his turn, who is prepared to sacrifice his own son's life to the irresistible majesty of Philotas, addresses the stranger in words of an extravagant and slightly heady tenderness which, although originally felt in relation to his own flesh and blood, it took the powerful presence of the youth before him to draw from the old warrior's lips. '. . . Wüsste ich,' Parmenio says to Philotas,

dass sich der junge Wildfang nicht in allen Augenblicken, die ihm der

Dienst frey lässt, nach seinem Vater sehnte, und sich nicht so nach ihm sehnte, wie sich ein Lamm nach seiner Mutter sehnet: so möchte ich ihn gleich – siehst du! – nicht erzeugt haben. Itzt muss er mich noch mehr lieben, als ehren. Mit dem Ehren werde ich mich so Zeit genug müssen begnügen lassen; wenn nehmlich die Natur den Strom seiner Zärtlichkeit einen andern Weg leitet; wenn er selbst Vater wird. (V)

In these words Parmenio is formulating two important, and interconnected, truths which hold good in the universe of discourse of this play: to be a father and roughly and possessively to love are synonymous; such love, on the other hand, is not fixed in the object of its reference. It passes from generation to generation, or it may be transferred from one father's son to that of another. It is a collective phenomenon. Indeed, the image of water used by Parmenio here with which we shall be extensively concerned in a later chapter,[5] is particularly well fitted to give expression to the fluidity and ubiquity that is inseparable from the primitive life of feeling.

Thus, although the action of the play hinges on four figures of equal importance – the two kings and their two sons each of whom is now a hostage in the hands of the enemy – only two of these figures are *dramatis personae* in a play which is, in its entirety, set in the camp of Philotas's adversary. This means, as we have seen, that Philotas's father remains a shadowy figure outside the bounds of the action, so much so, in fact, that we do not hear his name. As a person, in his attitudes and in his relationship to his son he is wholly represented by the figure of King Aridäus, the Prince's captor. It also means – and this is perhaps more important still – that King Aridäus's son, Prince Polytimet, remains beyond the fringe of the enacted plot, and is represented by his counterpart, Prince Philotas. Indeed, of all the characters that figure in the action, on-scene or off-scene, it is of Polytimet that we know least. A pivotal figure, he is an all but total blank. We know no more than what Aridäus tells Philotas: 'dass mein Sohn deines Vaters Gefangener ist, wie du meiner' (III); this and the circumstances of his capture which Strato adds for the information of the young Prince: 'Eben dasselbe Geschwader, dem du zu hitzig entgegen eiltest, führte Polytimet', he explains, 'und als dich die Deinigen verloren erblikten, erhob sie Wuth und Verzweiflung über alle menschliche Stärke. Sie brachen ein, und alle stürmten sie auf den einen, in welchem sie ihres Verlustes Ersetzung sahen. Das Ende weisst du'. *(ibid.)*

This event is the pivot on which the action hinges, and the words in which it is related are vital, too. For they establish a

precise yet oddly surrealist symmetry between two separate oc-
currences, making it appear as if they were in truth two halves of
one as yet not clearly comprehended whole. This impression finds
us by no means unprepared. For the poet has embedded this
crucial piece of exposition in a poetic structure which in every one
and all of its configurations has something of the symmetry, the
veiled correspondences, that are characteristic of the dream-life.
He has put before us a fabric of figures who have no separate faces
as it were, and of relationships which are abstract patterns
without fixed terms of reference. In this play a Strato could be an
Aristodem, an Aridäus could be the father of the Prince he holds
captive and a Parmenio is exchangeable with either of these. The
poet has overlaid a design of geometrical precision and constancy
by a curiously nebulous weave of figures and configurations;
dissolving, doubling and coalescing again, like clouds drifting past
the unseeing gaze of a day-dreamer, or after-images grouping and
regrouping themselves on the retina of eyes that have been exposed to an overpowering light.

Indeed, is it not a dreamer par excellence who forms the
centrepiece of such a setting? For Philotas *is* in a dream, and not
only in the opening monologue of the play when, dashed from the
heights to which he had soared in his imagination, he feels as
deeply uncertain as his younger brother, Prinz Friedrich von
Homburg, of what is the truth – his vision or the common reality;
he is a youth who, with his eyes open but unseeing, lives in an
inner world woven of fantasy and dreams, however much he
seems to move about in the world of reality; one gifted with the
dangerous gift of youth

> In dem andern [zu] sehn, was er nie war,
> Immer frisch auf Traumglück auszugehen
> Und zu schwanken auch in Traumgefahr.[6]

Philotas had reached out for a 'Traumglück' when, donning his
manly toga and dashing into the encounter with life, he had
hoped to bring himself back untouched by experience. Similarly
he is now living through the distortions of a 'Traumgefahr'.
Surrounded though he is by fatherly figures who treat him with
every tenderness and care, he sees himself ringed by implacable
enemies, the villains of his imagination. This delusion becomes
only too patent when, presented, at his request, with a sword so
that he may meet and conquer the hearts of Aridäus's nobles, he
hits around him in a frenzy, crying: 'Wieder umringt? – Entset-
zen! – Ich bin es! Ich bin umringt! Was nun? Gefährte! Freunde!
Brüder! Wo seyd ihr? Alle todt? Ueberall Feinde? Ueberall – Hier

durch, Philotas! Ha! Nimm das, Verwegner – Und du das! Und du das!' (VIII.)

And had the young *Schwärmer* not shown the same danger of derangement when he had been asked to pick a fellow prisoner as an emissary to his father, one of his own compatriots upon whom **he and the King could equally rely?** 'So willst du, dass ich mich **vervielfältiget*** verabscheuen soll? In jedem der Gefangenen werde ich mich selbst erblicken,' he had answered. 'Schenke mir diese Verwirrung.' (III.)

It is this youth – a youth like others who does not see those around him for what they really are and instead surrounds himself with the hosts bred by his teeming imagination – who is captured by the enemy in the precise fashion and at the precise moment when the other Prince is captured by his own father's armies. A coincidence, for sure, the factual reality of which is beyond all doubt. The event is the lever of the action and it is witnessed and reported by impartial observers. But does this reality exhaust its significance for a play which is the strangest fabric of figures and their reflections, of configurations and their reflections? Or indeed for the inner life of a character who sees foes where there are none but friends and multiplies them in his fertile mind? The Prince, charging and thrown off his horse, is shown to himself, as it were, riding into a mirror: and there, in the mirror, he meets another Prince, also charging and thrown off his horse. This other Prince, to be sure, is Polytimet, the son of Aridäus. But is he not also the double of Philotas, the youth who sees himself multiplied in every other prisoner, as Aridäus is the double of Philotas's father, as Strato is the double of Aristodem, and as Parmenio is the double **of them all? The King's first reference to the twin occurrence, no** less than Strato's subsequent recounting of the event, emphasises its abstract symmetry, the constancy of the pattern rather than the singularity of the protagonists who make up its weave. After **the bare mention of the fact** 'dass mein Sohn deines Vaters Gefangener ist, wie du meiner', Aridäus muses: 'So wollt' es das Schicksal!' and continues: 'Aus gleichen Wagschalen nahm es auf einmal gleiche Gewichte, und die Schalen blieben noch gleich.' (III.) The image is derived from the realm of physics, a science **exclusively concerned with the measurable, and the thrice-**repeated operative word is 'gleich': equal. The pattern is all.

The Prince himself reinforces the impression of an abstract symmetry governing his own fortune and that of his counterpart. The equality is complete but for one incredible possibility which

---

* Here and throughout, bold type indicates author's emphasis in quotations.

occurs to him as he perceives the balance in which the scales of their destinies are suspended. It is a possibility expressed by the addition of a single word; and that single word, translated into reality, will decisively tilt the balance in his father's favour: '... Mein Vater hätte ... einen gefangenen Prinzen ... und der König, sein Feind, hätte – den **Leichnam** eines gefangenen Prinzen . . . ' (IV).

The other Prince in whom Philotas sees himself and his misfortune mirrored is his self experienced as it were from the outside, as outside, as a self embodied. And what he thus sees as 'the other' he repudiates. For his experience of self is essentially one of **disembodied inwardness.** The outward reflection of himself he glimpses teaches him that he prefers his disembodied mind to the embodied self of 'the other' – that is, to himself as others experience him. It is this illumination of what he is, and what he will not be, which determines the choice he will eventually make.

The true nature of the Prince's predicament is borne in on us, steadily and relentlessly, from the opening lines of the play. Not for a moment does the poet allow us to think that Philotas makes his choice to secure peace for his peoples or material gains for his father. He protests the former, it is true; but in fact his father will reap the hatred that his son has sown; and Aridäus's last words make it clear that the blood that has been shed was shed in vain and that more blood will now have to flow for his captive son's sake. And as for material gain – how could an idealist possessed of a contempt so burning for the things of this world give his life for so base a goal? No, Philotas dies for another and more radical reason. He dies not in order to realise any earthly goods, but rather because he detests whatever belongs to physical reality and because he shrinks from contact with it as though it were a contagious disease. He abhors women and bodily comforts: 'In was für ein Zelt hat er mich bringen lassen! Aufgeputzt, mit allen **Bequemlichkeiten** versehen! Es muss einer von seinen Beyschläferinnen gehören. Ein ekler Aufenthalt für einen Solda-ten!' (I.) He detests material goods: 'Unseliges Gold, bist du denn immer das Verderben der Tugend!' (VI). He shrinks from the aura of softness that surrounds childhood; and not only, and understandably, because he himself is barely more than a child, but because he denies the gentler feelings wheresoever he en-counters them: 'Männer, König, müssen kein Kind bewundern,' (VII) he admonishes Aridäus; and Parmenio's warning words to him: 'Gieb nicht zu, dass der rauhe Soldat das zärtliche Kind so bald in dir ersticke. Man möchte sonst von deinem Herzen nicht zum besten denken' (V) suggest that this denial is not so much a passing phase but a trait that has its roots deep in his character. Most importantly, he abhors his own youthful grace. He is not ignorant or bashful of it, as might befit the chastity of youth. He knows it and feels defiled by it. When Strato, taken aback by the fierceness of Philotas's sense of humiliation, says to him: 'Prinz, deine Bildung, voll jugendlicher Anmuth, verspricht ein sanftres Gemüth', Philotas snaps in return: 'Lass meine Bildung unver-spottet! Dein Gesicht voll Narben ist freylich ein schöners Gesicht – .' (II.) Unwittingly, Strato has added insult to injury. For grace springs from the felicitous union of body and mind, and to the spirit of this youth the very thought of such a union is degrading. To him the body is the 'dross', not the 'alloy' of the spirit, and to enter into partnership with it is to court corruption.

Has Philotas not already experienced the treachery of the body, when his hand, slovenly minister of his mind's vision, betrayed him on his first sally into the world he had meant to conquer? When the road to victory led him to captivity? The first words and scenes of this drama sound the motifs of the hand and the long way without return which Lessing was to take up again, nearly a dozen years later, in *Emilia Galotti*,[7] motifs to which, as we shall see in later chapters, he was to resort again and again, in *Minna von Barnhelm* and in *Nathan der Weise*.[8] Philotas, like Tellheim, has an injured hand, a hand that has spoilt the vision of his spirit in the act of transmitting it to reality; a bungling hand, like that of Conti the painter, of the Prince, of Marinelli and of Odoardo. And like these figures, he dissociates himself from the faulty tool Nature has given to him, material itself and by necessity bound to desecrate the spirit in its enforced dealings with a material world. Philotas hates his hand; and already here, in this early drama, the rift between mind and hand which the young hero so forcibly protests in his opening monologue betokens that dichotomy between self and non-self which is familiar to us from the later tragedy. Here as there it is a split which not only divides the person from the world but which runs straight through the centre of the embodied being. 'Wenn ich sie nicht sähe, nicht fühlte, die Wunde, durch die der erstarrten Hand das Schwerd entsank!' Philotas soliloquises: 'Man hat sie mir wider Willen verbunden . . . Sie ist nicht tödtlich, sagte der Arzt, und glaubte mich zu trösten. – Nichtswürdiger, sie sollte tödtlich seyn! – Und nur eine Wunde, nur eine! – Wüsste ich, dass ich sie tödtlich machte, wenn ich sie wieder aufriss, und wieder verbinden liess, und wieder aufriss!' (I.) How could the will of the spirit towards dissociation from the material medium in which it is embedded – a will which is of necessity bound to lead to disembodiment and death – be more uncompromisingly sounded than here, at the very outset of the tragedy?[9]

The Prince's sally into the world was to have been a brief one, as brief and innocuous as Emilia's way to Mass and Appiani's way to his wedding. The young warrior was only to roam the hills, 'um den Weg nach Cäsena „offen zu halten." ' Yet like Emilia's few steps to church it ended in captivity, and like Appiani's short ride to his wedding it will end in death. As towards the close of the tragedy he intimates to the King that his career, only just begun, will shortly end, he says: 'Oder vielleicht war auch dieses meine Meynung, dass ich noch einen weiten und gefährlichen Weg zum Throne habe. Wer weiss, ob die Götter mich ihn vollenden lassen? – Und lass mich ihn nicht vollenden, Vater der Götter und Menschen, wenn du in der Zukunft mich als einen Verschwender des Kostbarsten, was du mir anvertrauet, des Blutes meiner Unterthanen, siehest!' (VII.) It is the same plaint we have heard from the lips of Conti the painter: 'Auf dem langen Wege, aus dem Auge durch den Arm in den Pinsel, wie viel geht da verloren!' But whereas Emilia confirms the painter's pessimism at the close of a tragedy in which vision is squandered and corrupted on the road of no return, the hero of this early tragedy makes the *a priori* judgment 'dass alles verloren ist.'

But what in fact has he lost that is irreparable? The gods and men seem to smile on Philotas whilst, step by step, an evil spell draws the figures in *Emilia Galotti* towards a disaster none can avert. The young Prince's injured hand will heal, so the doctor assures him, and his captivity, it soon turns out, will be more shortlived even than his injury; for the two royal hostages, one as valuable as the other, will be exchanged within a matter of hours and safely returned to their homes. Indeed, there is every promise that the Princes' homecomings, so far from signifying loss of honour or any other penalty, will be happier events than their outgoings. As Aridäus invites the Prince to meet his generals ('sie brennen vor Begierde, dich zu sehen und zu bewundern') he hints at the 'glückliche Folgen' which are likely to spring from the re-opening of frozen channels, adding: 'Liebenswürdige Kinder sind schon oft die Mittelspersonen zwischen veruneinigten Vätern gewesen' (VII). The two warring kings and their countries will be reunited and peace, the cessation of bloodshed which Philotas himself avows to be his most sacred goal, will finally be achieved.

What is more, even the shortlived captivity to which this young hero is subjected is anything but ignominious. We have seen that he is treated, not as a foe, not even as a cherished guest or friend, but as a son showered with every sign of tenderness and care. His

captors have become the captives of his wild and sombre grace.
He has conquered the hearts of all. He does not suffer 'the slings
and arrows of outrageous fortune.' He merely suffers the slings
and arrows of loving involvement with the world.

This triumph of his grace is the ultimate disgrace. For it means
the experience which this proud spirit dreads most of all: the
experience of contact, of involvement with what is not spirit and,
thus, degrading. It means entering into collusion, despite himself,
with his own body; entering into collusion with other embodied
beings whom, despite himself, his charm seduces into tenderness.
It means contamination everywhere for the spirit that prizes none
but itself.

This, then, is the true nature of his captivity: the captivity of
the spirit in a body which, against his will, entangles him in a
physical world as corrupt as its agent, his own hand, had proven
it to be. The radical and inward nature of his predicament dawns
on him at the precise moment when he is adjudged to be the equal
of one who seems his exact likeness: the other 'gefangenen Prinzen'. In the mirror image which reflects back to him how he
appears – the mirage of a noble and gentle youth longing to get
back to his father – he discovers, by a sudden illumination, his
own nature and identity. He has found his inalienable self. And
instantaneously he tips the scales of the balance, disproving the
notion that the weights they contain are equal, and precluding
any possibility of a happy end brought about by the exchange of
two hostages, one as precious as the other. The 'other', ostensibly
his equal, the one he sees in the mirror, is a healthy young man
in the bloom of his life. He himself is pure spirit. If he withdraws
this spirit from the body he despises, his opponent's scale will fly
up emptied of its treasure. It will contain only 'den Leichnam
eines gefangenen Prinzen,' whilst his own father's scale will be
depressed by the greater weight of its content. For it will contain
a captive spirit, 'einen gefangenen Prinzen'. A content of greater
weight or of greater value? That is the question.

To the King and his counsellor the question of value, at first,
does not even remotely suggest itself. Their reverence for life
extends to the reverence, and piety, towards the dead body of one
so recently alive, and loved. Aridäus would not dream of anything
but to exchange the dead youth he cherished for his living son.
But Philotas teaches him otherwise. He teaches him to despise the
body of his enemy 'den er – müsste begraben oder verbrennen
lassen, wenn er ihm nicht zum Abscheu werden sollte' (IV); so
that in the end, desperate to have his own son back and desperate
at being mocked and cheated by Philotas, he exclaims: 'Ich will

ihn doch wieder haben! Und für dich! – Oder ich will deinem
toden Körper so viel Unehre, so viel Schmach erzeigen lassen!—' at
which Philotas raps out the icy reply: 'Den toden Körper! – Wenn
du dich rächen willst, König, so erwecke ihn wieder! – ' (VIII.)
More than this, he teaches the King to despise his own humanity
and his love, to despise the choice his heart compels him to make.
Philotas forces his friends to be not only his enemies, but the
enemies of their own better selves. By his savage spirituality he
forces them on to their knees, compelling them, against their
instinct and their will, to cede victory to the disembodied mind
and to despise themselves for the greater good they have brought
back from a degrading barter: life. 'Da zieht er mit unserer Beute
davon, der grössere Sieger,' King Aridäus says as Philotas dies.
'Komm! Schaffe mir meinen Sohn! Und wenn ich ihn habe, will
**ich nicht mehr König seyn. Glaubt ihr Menschen, dass man es
nicht satt wird?'**[10] These are the final words of the play. The
'grösserer Sieger' is the pure spirit who, for fear of corruption, has
refused to have truck with humanity, an inhuman spirit which –
tragic irony of unparalleled bite – by the overpowering charm he
exercises upon those around him has seduced them into despising
their most sacred values and tarnished their humanity.

For let it be understood, the King has not only lost his faith in
the oneness of body and mind; nor only his faith in the goodness
of human beings. He has lost the overarching faith that is supported by these twin pillars, and in turn supports them; he has
lost his belief in the goodness of Providence. To this, his belief in
the Theodicy, he had given utterance when he had seen the hand
of divinity in the miraculous symmetry of misfortunes, a benign
symmetry cancelling out his own misfortune and that of his
enemy and promising extravagant returns from a hostile encounter with the world: 'Die Götter – ich bin es überzeugt' – so
he had prefaced the revelation that both Princes are hostages –

[Die Götter] wachen für unsere Tugend, wie sie für unser Leben
wachen. Die so lang als mögliche Erhaltung beyder, ist ihr geheimes,
ewiges Geschäft. Wo weiss ein Sterblicher, wie böse er im Grunde ist,
wie schlecht er handeln würde, liessen sie jeden verführerischen
Anlass, sich durch kleine Thaten zu beschimpfen, ganz auf ihn
wirken? – Ja, Prinz, vielleicht wäre ich der, den du mich glaubst;
vielleicht hätte ich nicht edel genug gedacht, das wunderliche
Kriegesglück, das dich mir in die Hände liefert, bescheiden zu nützen;
vielleicht würde ich durch dich ertrozt haben, was ich zu erfechten
nicht länger wagen mögen; vielleicht – Doch fürchte nichts; allen
diesen Vielleicht hat eine höhere Macht vorgebauet; ich kann deinen

Vater seinen Sohn nicht theurer erkaufen lassen, als – durch den meinigen. (III)

For a moment Philotas too is very much overawed by the spectacle of powers who mysteriously interlace the fortunes of body and soul and match virtue and reward. 'In tiefe Anbetung der Vorsicht verloren – ' the youth murmurs, only to be awakened to reality and – to himself, by the King's rejoinder; a down to earth rejoinder which might equally well have sprung from Minna's or Nathan's lips: 'Die beste Anbetung, Prinz, ist dankende Freude. Ermuntere dich! Wir Väter wollen uns unsere Söhne nicht lange vorenthalten. Mein Herold hält sich bereits fertig; er soll gehen, und die Auswechselung beschleunigen.' (ibid.)

But what does the prospect of being exchanged and returned to life mean to one like Philotas who is not a youth like any other but a spirit bent on repudiating his embodied self? How can such a spirit be beholden to powers whose secret and eternal business it is to balance the fortunes of body and mind and to safeguard both alike? How can such a spirit feel the joys which spring from that union of body and mind, of inner and outer: the joys of living and of loving? All this complicated artifice of faith, faith in the goodness of the embodied self, faith in a world deserving to be loved, and faith in the powers that balance spiritual and material gains, is foreign to one who rejects matter as a worthy partner of spirit; and his own answer, the answer that is appropriate to his new-found self, is contained in the words he will speak to Parmenio: 'Das Glück, weisst du wohl . . . ist blind. Blind, Parmenio;' (V.) In the universe of discourse of a Lessing, a world in which bitterness and belief, the will to love and the instinct to distrust are for ever poised on a knife-edge, such words are nothing short of blasphemous. They cut the precarious bond between mind and matter on the religious plane as Philotas cuts it when he looks down on his young body and in ecstatic contemplation extols the vision of his lifeless frame, 'gestreckt auf den Boden, das Schwerd in der Brust' (VI), as he will finally cut it when, in the end, he thrusts his sword into his heart.

No more appropriate assessment of Philotas is given than that of the soldier who unseated him and who, shortly before the close of the play, says: 'Der Prinz ist ein kleiner Dämon' (VIII), that is to say a disembodied spirit whose laws are incommensurable with those of human beings, one who may well become evil when his path crosses with the paths of mortals. The laws of organic life are not binding on a demon and, to him, its joys are immaterial. What does he know of the sweetness of youth, the sweetness of

coming to fruition, the sweetness even of seeing the cycle of his
own life repeated in that of another generation? What does he
know of the returns that life holds in store for him who embraces
it in trust and love? Contemplating his bodily extinction, Philotas
may truthfully say: 'Ich werde bey diesem Tausche nichts
verlieren' (VIII). For what he is forfeiting in this barter means less
than nothing to one who rejects matter on every possible level of
experience. But to the others, unlike him embodied spirits, the loss
of an answering echo from what is not spirit – the denigration of
the body in which the spirit lives, the denial of the return that
comes from a loving encounter with the world, the denial of an
ultimate harmony between mind and matter ordained by
Providence – means nothing less than the destruction of every
sanction by which mortals may live.

   'Auf dem langen Wege . . . wie viel geht da verloren?'
Nothing, in the world of this early and starkest of Lessing's
tragedies, need have been lost but for the mischievous intervention
of a young demon. Given time and love, the two matrices of
organic life, the road would have been wide open and the returns
would have warranted the most extravagant faith in the goodness
of the world. But Philotas, the purest *Schwärmer* in German
literature, has no use for love or time. All the time he needs is time
enough in which he may learn to die: 'Wer zehn Jahr gelebt hat,
hat zehn Jahr Zeit gehabt, sterben zu lernen; und was man in
zehn Jahren nicht lernt, das lernt man auch in zwanzig, in
dreissig und mehrern nicht.' (IV). All the time the pure spirit
needs to fulfil his destiny is time enough for the pure intellect to
apprehend it. And that is not a long organic process, a slow
ending of 'the heartache and the thousand natural shocks that
flesh is heir to,' because he does not live, and learn, through his
flesh any more than he loves through it. To immolate his body
takes no longer than it takes for his mind to intuit the self-evident
truth of a syllogism:[11] 'Jedes Ding, sagte der Weltweise, der mich
erzog, ist vollkommen, wenn es seinen Zweck erfüllen kann. Ich
kann meinen Zweck erfüllen, ich kann zum Besten des Staats
sterben: ich bin vollkommen also, ich bin ein Mann. Ein Mann,
ob ich gleich noch vor wenig Tagen ein Knabe war.' (IV.)
Philotas races from boyhood to the autonomy of manhood and
thence to extinction in the few minutes that it takes the intelligence to subsume the minor premiss – the assessment of his
condition here and now – under the major premiss to which his
spirit adheres, the commonwealth of minds 'wo . . . alle Tapfere
Glieder *Eines* seligen Staates sind' (VIII). To a disembodied spirit
the abstraction from the accidents of his particular life comes as

easy as the act of abstraction from life itself. There is no call for a swan-song, or even for a farewell.

Because his essential existence is out of time, the organic images, such as *Keim, Knospe, Blüte* and *Frucht* by which time and again Philotas refers to his earthly span, are incongruous, and even malicious, in that by using them he confounds others as to his true convictions and intentions.[12] Again we are reminded of Emilia Galotti's dying words: 'Eine Rose gebrochen, ehe der Sturm sie entblättert.' But Emilia had initially wanted to live; it is Time that is the secret antagonist of the later tragedy; an inner experience of time which, on the brink of fulfilment, becomes an abyss which no vision is strong enough and no road long enough to bridge. Philotas, more life-hating than any figure in any later play, rejects time *a priori*, and with it he rejects development, fruition, and life itself. He would lacerate the wound of his hand if only he could be certain that, by doing so, he could make it fatal; and to make sure that there *is* no way back into life, and no return coming to him from it, he charms his emissary into delaying the exchange until he has had time to kill himself. 'Denn ist es nicht eine wahre Kleinigkeit meinem Vater zu sagen, ihn zu **überreden, dass er mich nicht eher als morgen auswechsle? Und wenn er ja die Ursache wissen will; wohl, so erdenke dir unter** Weges eine Ursache.' (V.)

In the end, the idealistic *Schwärmer* turns out to be, not only a little demon, but a veritable devil. A luciferic figure, he dies, still dazzling and seducing those whose sanctuary he has wrecked by his fall: including, I believe, even the poet, his charmed creator.

3

Götz von Berlichingen's Dead Hand[1]

> Grow, hands, into those living
> Hands which true hands should be
> By making and by giving
> To hands you cannot see.
>
> (W. H. Auden: *Precious Five*)

I

The winter of the year 1771-72 saw the composition of one of the most perfectly constructed dramas in the German tongue, terse and architectonic throughout: Lessing's *Emilia Galotti*. During the same months a young man, urged by his sister Cornelie 'Mich nur nicht immer mit Worten in die Luft zu ergehen, sondern endlich einmal das, was mir so gegenwärtig wäre, auf das Papier festzubringen',[2] set about giving dramatic shape to a subject of the German past that had long fascinated him, and within a few weeks produced his *Geschichte Gottfriedens von Berlichingen mit der eisernen Hand dramatisirt,* one of the most diffuse and sprawling of dramas in modern German literature.

These events occurred independently of one another and indeed they seem to be profoundly unconnected, both in the history that led up to them and in their final outcome. And yet Goethe, in the letter he wrote to Herder in July 1772, bracketed both dramas, and for good reason: for by an astonishing literary coincidence *Emilia Galotti* and *Gottfried von Berlichingen* have, at their centre, one and the same poetic symbol: the symbol of the hand.

We have seen that hands, in Lessing's tragedy – and indeed in the earlier *Philotas* – are visualised as destructive things detached from the mind whose executors they are, and inevitably construing the miscarriage of its vision in the material world.

Such is the hand of Odoardo which stabs his daughter to preserve her virtue, the hands of Marinelli and his hirelings which destroy Appiani and his vision of the good life, the hand of Emilia which at a touch of the Prince betrays her integrity, the hand of the Prince which seizes hold of Emilia as he seizes hold of her ideal likeness and drags her from her sheltered innocence to destruction. Such is the hand of the painter which so distorts the vision of his mind that he comes to think of artistic genius as residing in the mind alone and conceives the fantastic idea of a Raphael born without hands; and such is the hand of Nature herself who in the act of creation erroneously compounded mind with defective matter, whose hand fumbled when she fashioned the innocence of woman in the yieldingness of clay.

The hand, in Lessing's tragedy, is the overall poetic symbol of that tragic discontinuity of experience which is enunciated time and again by the characters within the play and which constitutes its inner theme. And in the final analysis – it had suggested itself – it is a cypher for a deep-seated reticence on the part of the poet himself vis-à-vis his own medium, signifying the faltering of the creative vision on its way to embodiment and words.[3]

The suggestion that the iron fist of Goethe's rough and ready hero may have any significance that is remotely comparable would seem to border on the absurd. And yet it is rewarding to examine its import; partly because of its crucial formal as well as thematic significance for Goethe's drama, and partly because a full grasp of its meaning for the play is needed to appreciate Goethe's subsequent attitude to his firstborn. For in the heart-searchings occasioned by the *Urgötz* and by Herder's reception of it, the hand once again assumes cardinal importance. What did the hand mean to Goethe, in the *Urgötz* and later on, when he had gained some distance from this strange conception? We may hope that an illumination of the central poetic structure of this drama may pave the way towards a more precise understanding of those artistic insights and intentions which it precipitated in the young poet and enable us to appraise the aims and achievement of the final version in which these insights were to be embodied.

Undoubtedly it was the iron hand that first attracted Goethe to his subject, the downfall of the last champion of personal freedom, the *freier Ritter* exercising his *Faustrecht,* in a feudal system in the process of disintegration. 'What great eyes the Philistines will make at the Knight with the Iron-hand! That's glorious – the Iron-hand!' he is supposed to have told his mother according to the account of H. C. Robinson,[4] and this is the first remark recorded on the subject. Indeed the motif is already firmly established in the first draft. Apart from two important additions relating, however, not to Götz but to Weislingen, the revised version confirms the existing pattern, pruning an outcrop here and there that obstructs its contour and in turn adding a few references to strengthen it.

The commanding statement occurs early on in the play, in Götz's conversation with Brother Martin. Offering him his left hand, Götz explains to him that the other hand is missing.

> Meine Rechte obgleich im Kriege nicht unbrauchbaar, ist gegen den Druck der Liebe unempfindlich. Sie ist eins mit ihrem Handschuh, ihr seht er ist Eisen. (I, p. 22)

But significantly, it is to Weislingen that Götz himself first mentions the loss of his hand. Recalling the intimacy of their youth, Götz reproachfully says:

> Ah! wie mir vor Nürnberg diese Hand weggeschossen ward . . . Da hofft ich Weislingen wird künftig deine Rechte Hand seyn. (I, p. 45)

In fact, Weislingen has gone his own way. He has left Götz, left his friend's sister, his betrothed, to join the entourage of the Bishop of Bamberg. In the words of the second version, he has become 'des Bischofs rechte Hand' (I, p. 3). These words are profoundly significant and their significance is enhanced by their position: they are the first reference to Weislingen in the play.[5] It is in this final version too that Götz, seeing his erstwhile friend as the associate of his enemies, sums up the situation in the image that Martin had earlier on used of him: 'Und du Weislingen bist ihr Werkzeug!' (I, p. 50).

When eventually their friendship is restored and Weislingen declares his love for Götz's sister Maria, Goethe again resorts to the image of the hand. All three, Maria and the friends, link hands and Götz recounts a dream that is patently symbolic:

> Ich träumt heute Nacht ich gäb dir meine rechte eiserne Hand, und Du hieltest mich so fest, dass sie aus den Armschienen ging wie abgebrochen. Ich erschrak und wachte drüber auf. Ich hätte nur fortträumen sollen, da würd ich gesehen haben, wie du mir eine neue lebendige Hand ansetztest. (I, p. 68)

But the dream is truer than reality, and Götz comes to understand its message when Weislingen has finally betrayed him. Outlawed, deceived by a false promise of free retreat, captured and attacked at Heilbronn, his being is at its lowest ebb, and his friend Sickingen's plans for the future leave him despondent. When the latter tells him that he counts upon his 'Faust' in his schemes, Götz looks at his maimed hand and says:

> Oh, das deutete der Traum den ich hatte als ich Tags drauf, Marien

an Weislingen versprach. Er sagte mir Treu zu, und hielt meine rechte Hand so fest, dass sie aus den Armschienen ging wie abgebrochen. Ach! Ich binn in diesem Augenblick wehrloser, als ich war da sie mir vor Nürenberg abgeschossen wurde. Weisl[ing] Weis[ling]. (IV, p. 195)

At the nadir of his life, incarcerated and close to death, Götz sums up his condition once more, and once again it is in terms of the symbol of the hand:

Sie haben mich nach und nach verstümmelt meine Hand meine Freyheit, Güter, und guten Nahmen. Das schlechste haben sie zuletzt aufbehalten, meinen Kopf, was ist der ohne das andre. (V, p. 261)

This is the bare outline of the pattern, and from it the general nature of the relation that holds between Götz and Weislingen will have become apparent. The two characters are not merely closely related in any ordinary meaning of the words. They are not wholly separate. They share a hand, and the emotion-charged reiteration of this configuration throughout Götz's career at its most crucial points suggests that Götz's destiny at any rate is bound up with it. Before going into this, however, it may be useful to consider a few more instances in which the image of the hand is significantly used, and to examine what it is to which our attention is thereby being directed.

A good deal of importance attaches to the fact that Götz's most faithful friend, Selbitz, is one-legged, as Götz himself is one-handed. What might otherwise be regarded as fortuitous gains significance from such a reiteration, and our association of Götz, and what he stands for, with the lack of a limb is strengthened. When Weislingen is discovered to have gone back to the Bishop, and Selbitz exclaims: 'Ich wollte lieber mein ander Bein dazu verliehren als so ein Hundfut seyn!' (II, p. 118), we are covertly reminded that the loss of Weislingen, for Götz, means the loss of a vital limb. And this too is the effect of the Emperor's words at the beginning of Act III, when Weislingen tries to inveigle him into declaring open war on Götz:

Heiliger Gott! Heiliger Gott! Was ist das? Der eine hat eine Hand der andre nur ein Bein, wenn sie denn erst zwo Händ hätten und zwo Bein was wolltet ihr denn tuhn. (III, p. 128)

In the thick of the fight with the imperial troops sent out to capture Götz, Selbitz exclaims: 'Mir nach. Sie sollen zu ihren Händen rufen, multiplizirt euch' (III, p. 152). The irony of this is patent. For the next moment Selbitz, the one-legged, is wounded and Götz, the one-handed, is surrounded and in immediate danger of his life. It is they, evidently, that need to produce more limbs for their cause to flourish. But another effect, already prepared by the instances quoted, is that the number of limbs ceases to be strictly determinate. People have one or two as the case may be, and, being unstable, their number may conceivably be multiplied. The Emperor's comment on the merchants' complaint contributes to that impression, even though he does not use the word *Hände*, but the cognate form *Händel*: ' . . . wieder neue Händel,' he says. 'Sie wachsen nach wie die Köpfe der Hydra' (III, p. 128).

Perhaps most significant, however, is the incident Götz recalls at the very beginning of the encounter with Weislingen which culminates in the full statement of his dependence on his friend (and for that matter, of Weislingen on Götz) and ends in their renewed intimacy. Götz recalls being received with a handshake by Weislingen's Bishop who had evidently not recognised his enemy. To pique him, Götz says loudly to a bystander: 'Der Bischoff hat mir die Hand geben, ich wett er hat mich nicht gekannt.' Hearing this remark the Bishop approaches Götz and says: 'Wohl weil ich euch nicht kannt gab ich euch die Hand'; to which Götz replies: 'Herr ich merckts wohl dass ihr mich nicht kannt habt, Da habt ihr sie wieder' (I, p. 37f). (The second version takes the point more neatly, saying: 'Und hiermit habt ihr eure Hand wieder.') Taken by itself, this incident seems insignificant enough. But placed as it is just before Götz lays claim to Weislingen's right hand, it attunes us to the idea that hands can not only change numbers, but can also change owners. They are separate entities which may pass from one person to another and back again. This is precisely what happens between Götz and Weislingen. The latter is a hand which passes between the Bishop and Götz. First, in the youthful phase of their friendship, he is Götz's right hand, then he becomes the right hand of the Bishop. Then, captured by Götz and captivated by his sister, he becomes Berlichingen's right hand once more: and it is at this point, and here alone, that the reunited hand is referred to as a 'lebendige Hand'. Weislingen then becomes 'bundbrüchig', attaches himself to the Bishop and Adelheid, the magnetic centre of his court, and Götz's mutilation becomes final.

This strange configuration is borne out by Weislingen's own statements as well as by the statements of others about him. When he muses under the first impact of his reunion with Götz: 'Ich binn nicht mehr ich selbst, und doch binn ich wieder ich selbst,' and continues 'Der kleine Adelbert der an Gottfrieden hing wie an seiner Seele' (I, p. 43), when, having attached himself to Götz and Maria, he sums up his ambiguous situation in the single word: 'Abzuhängen!' (I, p. 71) – what else is he saying but that he knows that as a separate entity he is not himself, and that he becomes himself only when he is attached to Götz as a small part to a whole, almost an appendage? He himself knows that this is his destiny, and he formulates it in a speech that is the formal equivalent to the one in which Götz recounts his dream and adds that Weislingen is now attaching a 'neue lebendige Hand' to his stump. In that speech Götz had observed: 'Du siehst nicht ganz frey. Was fehlt dir.' (I, p. 68.) In his monologue Weislingen echoes this question and confirms Götz's interpretation of their relationship from his own side:

> O warum binn ich nicht so frey wie du! Gottfr[ied] Gottfr[ied]! vor dir fühl ich meine Nichtigkeit ganz. Abzuhängen! Ein verdammtes Wort, und doch scheint es als wenn ich dazu bestimmt wäre. (I, p. 71)

The words *hängen, abhängen* recur with remarkable frequency to describe Weislingen's relation both to Götz and to the Bishop and Adelheid, and so do images suggesting that he attaches himself to others as a severed part attaches itself to the body: by the growth of a fine fibrous tissue. This impression is confirmed by the frequency of words like *reissen, ausreissen, herausbrechen,* used to describe the violence it takes for him to detach himself. 'Und wenn er sich losreisen will verblutet er,' as Adelheid's maid has it (II, p. 94).

Furthermore there is a steady stream of suggestions creating, on the imaginal plane, an impression of Weislingen's smallness – he is 'der kleine Adelbert', he has a small nose, he is 'gewachsen wie eine Puppe'; he is called a 'Weisfisch' with a significant play on his name. Having just recalled his former hope that Weislingen would be his right hand, and pondering his actual attachment to the Bishop, Götz asks his friend: 'Wolltet ihr wohl in einen scheuslichen bucklichen Zwerg verwandelt seyn' (I, p. 46).

At the end of the play, all these suggestions are gathered up in an explicit statement of Weislingen's relationship to Götz in terms of the dominant symbol, which is the precise counterpart of Götz's opening statement. Weislingen too has a dream:

> Die vorige Nacht begegnete ich Gottfrieden im Walde. Er zog sein Schwerdt und forderte mich heraus. Ich hatte das herz nicht, nach meinem zu greifen, hatte nicht die Kraft. (V, p. 270)

(Here the second version reads, more neatly: 'Ich fasste nach meinem, die Hand versagte mir.')

> Da sties ers in die Scheide, sah mich verächtlich an, und ging vorbey. *(Ibid.)*

We know why Weislingen is impotent against Götz. He is a part of him, a member of his body; he is Götz's right hand, and the hand cannot rise against the master.

II

What is it that Götz has lost with his hand which is embodied in Weislingen? 'Meine Rechte', he says to Martin, 'obgleich im Kriege nicht unbrauchbar, ist gegen den Druck der Liebe unempfindlich.' Götz's hand is not an organ of contact. A 'todtes Werckzeug' as Brother Martin has it, and severed from his mind and heart, it can neither communicate his feelings to others nor indeed their feelings to him: it is 'gegen den Druck der Liebe unempfindlich.' Thus, in losing his live hand, Götz has lost the capacity for relatedness through touch; and with it, he has become cut off from the knowledge, the sustenance and the wholeness that is born of the fertilising contact between the mental and the physical worlds. For in the loving reciprocity of touch – the 'Druck der Liebe' – the mental and the bodily, the inner and the outer, the self and the non-self light up and enhance one another and utterly fuse in a single experience. What we touch from without, we know from within through our own answering response; and the experience of the other, so intimately felt, merges with our own and multiplies it. And as we experience with the whole of ourselves, with hand and heart in unison, so we perceive wholeness and harmony about us, between matter and mind, between world and self.

It is this intercourse with the world that is denied to Götz's hand, and the drama portrays with terrifying insight the maiming of an active, vital and good man as his mind is cut off from living contact with what is outside it. Götz uses his iron hand, it is true, and he uses it 'belebt durch des edelsten Geistes Vertrauen auf Gott' (I, p. 22). Nevertheless, it is not a 'lebendige Hand', but a 'todtes Werckzeug', a tool that, at best, is 'nicht unbrauchbar' for his rough calling. The words 'nicht unbrauchbar' confirm what the image of the tool suggests: Götz uses his hand as a means to an end. At first it seems that, given integrity of intention, such

pragmatic activity may be creative. After his loss Götz prays to
God – 'Und wenn ich zwölf Händ hätte und deine Gnad wollt mir
nicht was würden sie mir **fruchten,** so kann ich mit einer' (I, p.
23)[6] – and the impression that Götz uses his hand creatively is
strengthened by the juxtaposition of his activity with the indolent
holiness of the 'wohltätige Kind' which goes about performing
miracles by laying on its right hand. But the drama tells us otherwise.
At the beginning of the fourth act, after his reverse and capitulation,
Götz says – and significantly this is added in the second version:

> Ich komme mir vor wie der Böse Geist, den der Capuziner in einen
> Sack beschwur. Ich arbeite mich ab und fruchte mir nichts. (IV, p.
> 179)

And when, at his death, he refuses to see his only son again,
saying:

> An unserm Hochzeittag Elis[abeth] ahndete mirs nicht, dass ich so
> sterben würde – Mein alter Vater seegnete uns, und eine
> Nachkomm[en]schafft von edlen tapfern Söhnen quoll aus seinem
> Gebet. – Du hast ihn nicht erhört, und ich binn der letzte. (V, p. 292)

does not the bitter knowledge of the barrenness of his life cut all
the deeper since on the physical level his words are so patently
untrue?

Götz's iron hand signifies, then, that for all his vitality he is not
creative; that in some fundamental way he is not 'in touch' with
life. And indeed, is he not 'out of touch' with the world by the
very calling **'zu** dem er verstümmelt ist,' as the poet has it, with
a most telling ambiguity of the preposition 'zu'? For the *freier
Ritter* exercising his *Faustrecht* is a survival of a former age and a
bygone order. Clinging to this outmoded ideal, Götz is in fact an
outsider in his own time and society. He does not know or understand the world that surrounds him, and his assessment of its
movements and motives becomes progressively more incorrect and
jaundiced. And how could he know a world he has no organ to
explore, only to attack? His contact with the outside is restricted
to hostile sallies, and from these encounters he returns with no
booty, except once, when he captures Weislingen. On the contrary, he is impoverished step by step, as he loses his men in
battle, then retreats to his castle, exhausting all his ammunition
and victuals in its defence, then capitulates, leaving behind what
is left, finally endeavours to save his possessions by joining forces
with the peasants, only to end his life in prison. There is no
increase here, no replenishing of resources as there is in the loving

assimilation of the 'other'. The only replenisher in this drama is Georg – time and again he retrieves what is lost and more – and he dies before his master. And that, indeed, is the mortal blow for Götz.

As Götz is shorn of his possessions – the intermediate zones of contact with the outside world – and hostile forces converge on him from all sides, references to his sense of inner constriction – his *Enge* – crowd in thick and fast; gradually the world ceases to be a medium that could be moulded by his intentions and ideals. It becomes an alien and corrupt place from which his mind withdraws into an inwardness that becomes ever more complete. 'Ich lasse dich in einer nichtswürdigen Welt' (V, p. 292), the dying Götz says to his wife, and he goes on to use an image expressing an extreme of constriction and withdrawal from contact with what is without. 'Verschliesst eure Herzen sorgfältiger als eure Truhen', he warns her. (The second version reads 'Thore', calling to mind the beleaguerment of Götz's castle, which marks the beginning of his gradual retreat.) But it is in Götz's last words that his development comes full circle and its tragic irony becomes apparent. 'Freyheit, Freyheit' he cries as he dies, and his wife adds: 'Nur droben droben bey dir. Die Welt ist Gefängniss.' This is the language of Werther when he dies, and indeed it is the language of *Emilia Galotti*. In this drama it is the language of Maria and of the holy child whose other-worldliness has been contrasted with Götz's sturdy grasp on life. Coming at the end of a long process of enforced retreat, Götz's last words do not signify the triumph of his spirit; on the contrary, they betoken its final dispossession: it has no medium and no earthly home. Götz's last words cede victory to the iron hand.

As the world ceases to be a medium for him, his activity first takes on a morally dubious quality and finally comes to a complete standstill. The association of this good and gentle man with the brutality of the peasant rising is by no means as extraneous as has been supposed.[7] The hand that is degraded to being a mechanical executor of the mind may well grow estranged from its intentions and become brutalised.[8]

In the *Kerkerszene,* close to the end, Götz himself sums up the process of his decline:

> Sie haben mich nach und nach verstümmelt meine Hand meine Freyheit, Güter, und guten Nahmen. Das schlechste haben sie zuletzt aufbehalten, meinen Kopf, was ist der ohne das andre. (V, p. 261)

The double use of 'verstümmeln' – which is cognate with *stumpf,* blunt – first in a literal sense referring to his hand, and then in a metaphorical sense with reference to his other losses, has a twofold effect: it invests the mutilation of his hand with symbolic significance and, simultaneously, lends his other losses a terrible concreteness: creating a haunting image of a once whole man who is dismembered, limb by limb, until all zones and organs of contact are obliterated and he is left stripped, a sentient and suffering stump.

If Götz must perish without Weislingen, the more so must Weislingen perish without Götz. For he is only part of a larger whole – Götz's right hand. Supremely *empfindlich gegen den Druck der Liebe,* this labile lover cannot flourish in a separate existence from Götz. For Götz is his body and soul, and without him he loses life, integrity and even identity. He is the chameleon, the traitor, a thing torn this way and that by the spirits that in turn possess him, now by his 'Schutzgeist' and now by 'feindselige Mächte'; and time and again he is called 'ein Schatten'. Only once is his hand called a 'lebendige Hand': when he attaches himself to the whole to which he belongs, which alone can sustain his life. Before that he is a 'Werckzeug' and after it he fails Adelheid by his 'todten Umarmungen'. It is not for nothing that there is much play on his fish name: for the fish is both a cold-blooded creature and a phallic symbol.

Weislingen dies because, apart from Götz, he is not viable. The little remnant of life that he has without Götz ebbs away. *Matt, elend, schwach* are the words associated with him. The first version is perhaps psychologically truer than the second in the motivation of his death. There is no external agency administering the poison. His life is simply and mysteriously drained away by 'geheime verzehrende Mittel'.

It is only in the light of the central symbol of the hand that the true connection between the lives and destinies of the protagonists becomes fully apparent. It has been asserted that although Goethe succeeded to some degree in integrating the figure of Weislingen with the main action in the early acts of the final version, he completely failed to do so in the closing acts of the tragedy.[9] If we compare the two versions with our eyes sharpened to the true mode of connection between Weislingen and Götz, it will, on the contrary, be found that virtually all the changes – the shifting of scenes and the addition of verbal links – are undertaken to illuminate, by juxtapositions and mirrorings, the symmetry of the protagonists' decline. It is to this end that all scenes diverting the attention from this parallel process are eliminated and that the order of the remaining scenes has been changed. It is patently to

this end that Weislingen's sickness to death, his 'elendes Fieber',
now echoes Götz's 'schleichendes Fieber', and that Götz now
reiterates the very words of Weislingen: 'Meine Kraft sinkt nach
dem Grabe' (V, p. 291).

                                    III

One question still remains: for what reason and by what necessity
is Götz's hand maimed? What is it that he must not touch? This
question is neither explicitly asked nor answered in the drama; in
all probability because its author was not conscious of it.
Therefore we must tread carefully. But sometimes the formal
relations obtaining in a work of art may indicate an import that
altogether exceeds the conscious intention and knowledge of the
artist. This is the case here, and since the import thus revealed
throws light on meaning and structure of the drama itself, it is
rewarding to press this enquiry a little farther.
    The key to the answer lies in the image pattern of the hand. If
Weislingen is Götz's hand – and the configuration of the images
permits no doubt of this – then it follows that whatever
Weislingen reaches out for is that which is denied to the hand of
Götz. And Weislingen reaches out for Maria, the sister.
    Such an intimation of an unconscious erotic bond between brother
and sister does not, of course, come as a surprise in Goethe's work. We
find it, in far more open form, in *Die Geschwister* and it still
reverberates in the recognition scene of *Iphigenie* and in the much
quoted lines to Charlotte von Stein:

            Ach, du warst in abgelebten Zeiten
            Meine Schwester oder meine Frau.[10]

In this early work, however, this aspect of the relationship
between brother and sister is in no wise implemented on the level
of action and barely intimated on the verbal plane. It is merely
implied in the formal relations set up by the dominant image
pattern. If this suggests, as I think it does, that the poet himself
was largely unconscious of an aspect of the relation between his
characters of which they themselves are certainly unaware, it is
none the less interwoven into the overt pattern of relationships
with considerable psychological acumen. For the relationship
between Elisabeth and Götz, although warm and close, is a
companionship of spirits rather than a love relation. As Elisabeth
has it, with a significant ambiguity of gender: '[Ich] . . . binn . . .

mit Cartoffeln und Rüben erzogen, das kann keine zarte Gesellen machen' (I, p. 29). The existence of an unconscious erotic bond between brother and sister is further confirmed by the fact that Weislingen, being a part of Götz, cannot go through with the love relationship with Maria.[11] Götz's sister literally cannot be touched. 'Könnt ihr nicht reden ohne mich anzurühren' (I, p. 64), she says as she withdraws her hand from her betrothed.

Inhibited in this relation, Weislingen is driven further afield. The second time he reaches out for Adelheid, and the love relation that has proved impossible with the figure of the sister becomes a reality with the stranger in a strange setting. The poet has created, in and around Adelheid, a world that seems entirely disconnected from that of Götz, and it has been a stock in trade of criticism that Goethe, falling in love with his own creation, forgot his Götz and forfeited the unity of an action centred in his figure. And indeed, Goethe himself tells us so in *Dichtung und Wahrheit*.[12] But again we must ask whether the seeming disconnectedness of these two figures and their worlds in fact holds true on every level of the play and whether it can be accounted for, as has lately been done, by saying 'dass die Welt jener Zeit, dass der Raum selbstherrlich geworden ist und als fast eigenwertige Strukturschicht sich neben die der Konzeption nach tragende gelagert hat.'[13]

All the material so far presented argues that a connection between Götz and Adelheid is in fact entailed by the formal configuration of the dominant image pattern: through Weislingen, Götz's right hand, Götz himself stands in an oblique relation to Adelheid as well as Maria. And indeed there is a good deal of additional evidence to support this view. It is borne out by the characterisation of Weislingen in this love relation. Throughout it he is characterised as part of Götz, and this is the reason why he fails Adelheid as a lover. It is because he is a severed part of Götz that his hand, too, becomes a 'todtes Werckzeug' and can only dispense those 'todte Umarmungen' of which Adelheid grows weary; that, drained of vitality, he appears to her as a 'Schatten' rather than a proper man. 'Und mann nennt dich einen Mann', she says to him (II, p. 112), and instances of similar taunts could be multiplied. She is fully alert to his diminutive stature and his dependence on Götz: 'Frisst nicht die magerste Aehre seines Wohlstandes deine fettsten', she asks. 'Indem sie ringsumher verkündet, Adelbert wagt nicht mich auszureissen. Sein Daseyn ist ein Monument deiner Schwäche.' (II, p. 112.) Indeed she seems to be as preoccupied with the man who dwarfs her lover as she is with Adelbert himself. She certainly knows that in taking him on, she has taken on Götz as well!

This oblique connection is reinforced by yet another pattern of relationships: Sickingen's love relation with Adelheid. The second brother-in-law of Götz, Sickingen is Götz's closest companion in arms. He is also his coarsened mirror image. He uses his 'Faust' ruthlessly where Götz suffers from the impairment of his sensitivity. In the *Urgötz*, Sickingen's career as a lover is identical with that of Weislingen. He succeeds him, first with Maria, and then as the lover of Adelheid. This coincidence is most striking. There is no similarity between these two disparate figures that would furnish a motive for such symmetry of grouping. The only point of likeness between them is the intimate relation in which both are placed to Götz, one as part, the other as parallel. I would suggest that the principal function of Sickingen's love relation with Adelheid in the first version of the drama is precisely to underscore once again the implied connection between Götz and Adelheid which, completely suppressed on the level of the action, has already been intimated through Weislingen's connection with her. Goethe very properly deleted the love relation between Sickingen and Adelheid in the revised version, as its function is barely discernible, and thus left us with a tantalising image of two dynamic figures, a match in stature and vitality, both head and shoulders above all others, both narrowly missing fulfilment and yet living worlds apart.

Such an image begins to crystallise as soon as Adelheid is introduced. When Franz, in his first description of her, exclaims: ' . . . um dich Adelheid ist eine Atmosphäre von Leben, Muth, tähtiges Glück!' (I, p. 76), do not these words recall the Götz of the early scenes? When Adelheid upbraids Weislingen for being a fretful old maid 'statt des acktiven Manns' (II, p. 110) she had expected to find, is it not to Götz that our thoughts gravitate?

More important, Adelheid and Götz are connected by an extremely telling formal link. Both are associated with the giving and taking of physical enjoyment in a way that sets them apart from all other figures in the play. Götz, when Brother Martin laments his calling which condemns 'die besten Triebe, durch die wir werden wachsen und gedeyen' (I, p. 19) and contrasts his lot with the naturalness of Götz's life:

Wenn ihr Wein getruncken habt seyd ihr alles doppelt was ihr seyn sollt, noch einmal so leicht denckend, noch einmal so unternehmend, noch einmal so schnell ausführend. (I, p. 16f)

to which Götz replies: 'Wie ich ihn trincke, ist es wahr.' Adelheid,

when Franz describes the effect of seeing her, which he compares
to the effect of – drinking wine:

Das letztemal dass ich sie sah, hatt ich nicht mehr Sinnen als ein
Trunckener . . . Alle Sinne stärcker, höher, vollkommner . . . (I, p.
74)

She gives in the way that Götz takes; and the stuff she gives and
the stuff he takes is a strong potion which doubles the strength of
the drinker.

Yet the fact remains that Adelheid's giving and Götz's taking,
so perfectly attuned that it cries out to be united in the reciprocity
of love, is squandered, separately, and on substitutes: on an
adolescent boy and drink; for the simple reason that on the level
of the action, the two figures remain disconnected. The two never
meet face to face. Why has the poet inhibited a connection that
is clearly intended by the drama itself on every level bar that of
the action: implied in the dominant verbal pattern, and reinforced by the formal grouping of relationships as well as by the
gravitation of the characters themselves towards it? The answer is
that Goethe has inhibited the relationship between Götz and
Adelheid by the same token by which he has given Götz a hand
that is 'gegen den Druck der Liebe unempfindlich', and thus
unable to receive what she can give. This is as far as we can go,
and it does not answer the question: it merely staves it off. Both
facts, the dissociated hand and the dissociation of the two figures
that 'ought' to be connected, are *données* of the drama the ultimate
explanation of which lies beyond the work itself, in the psychology
of the dramatist.

IV

The question suggests itself whether these two *données* are themselves significantly connected. Clearly they illuminate each other
psychologically. The inhibition of a fructifying love relation
between Götz and Adelheid is psychologically entailed in the fact
that Götz is denied a live hand that can function as an organ of
contact. But does not the connection between these two facts
illuminate yet another aspect of the work – its form? Does not the
separation of Götz's hand from himself betoken a taboo so deep
as to light up the dissociation of Adelheid's world from his own?
The denial of touch expressed in the symbol of the severed hand
is so radical that it is hardly surprising that Adelheid, the object

of that touch, should be insulated from Götz as completely as is
ever possible. And separated from Götz she is well and truly. The
poet has placed her in a world apart, divided off from that of Götz
by the multiple barriers of physical distance, a different social and
political climate and an ultimate incongruence of values. More
than that: within that alien world he has ringed Adelheid by a
throng of figures so vividly conceived, so much seen in the round,
that they create the illusion of being set in a surrounding space of
their own. Thus Adelheid is distanced from Götz by every conceivable device, and the much discussed spread of epic and
episodic elements in that part of the drama which is dominated
by her must be seen in the light of this underlying 'intention' to
be properly appraised. Such poetic luxuriance springs, not from
any slackening of tension, but on the contrary from a tension so
unmanageable as to threaten the cohesion of the whole to the
point of disconnectedness, stylistically as well as structurally. In
other words, the split enunciated in the central symbol extends
through the dramatic structure in its entirety and on every level.
The centrifugality of structure – the *Gestalt* of the drama – is fully
determined by the experience of dissociation – its *Gehalt*. The
resultant 'Raumstruktur', as it has been called, may be an artistically unsatisfactory form; but it is a true and felt 'inner' form
none the less, and to see in it no more than the poet's youthful
exuberance and lack of artistic discipline[14] is sadly to miss the
point.

And is not the same true of the 'Zeitstruktur' of the play?
Critics have repeatedly observed that, whilst the actual events of
the dramatic action take up no more than a few months in all, we
are yet under an illusion that a lifetime has elapsed between the
beginning and end of the tragedy.[15] This time-span, moreover, sees
not only the deterioration of Götz from the prime of manhood to
old age and decrepitude, but the eclipse of the whole epoch to
which he belongs: the decline of the Empire and the Emperor's
death. Thus the unity of time, like that of place, seems attenuated
to the point of disruption; yet nothing has been said that might
explain this curious double perspective.

Indeed, so far from explaining it, critics have in turn adduced
the time-structure to explain the biggest 'unknown' in the tragedy,
the death of Götz.[16] We are told variously that Götz and his
friends die 'weil ihre Zeit um ist',[17] because 'der Geist der Zeit' is
against him,[18] because – somewhat cryptically – 'die Zeit, die Götz
vertritt . . . Natur geworden und in ihren Herbst getreten [ist].'[19]
But to argue thus is to explain one unknown by reference to
another, and, worse still, to explain the lesser unknown in terms

of one that is of major importance. Götz, it has been seen, dies for
the most personal and least public of reasons. He dies because he
is 'gegen den Druck der Liebe unempfindlich'. 'Out of touch' with
his environment and his own bodily self, his life is severed from
the vital springs that feed it; and thus unreceived and
unreplenished, it drains away.[20] The symbol of the mutilated hand
marks the beginning of this process of attrition, the metaphor of
truncation its inevitable end; an end, however, of which the
young Goethe himself only became gradually aware. For this
crucial metaphor was added in the final version of the play.
'Meine Wurzeln sind abgehauen', he says, 'meine Kraft sinkt nach
dem Grabe' (second version, V, p. 291). The remorselessness of
this process is perfectly expressed in statements which surprise us
only as long as we look for their motivation on the level of the
external action. There is nothing on that plane to account for a
condition so inward and so radical as that implied in Elisabeth's
words: 'du verglühst in dir selbst' (V, p. 260) or in Götz's own
'meine Wunden verbluten' (V, p. 250). But such statements – and
there are many, most of them added in the second version – make
sense as soon as we understand, in the light of the central symbol,
that for all his mighty vitality Götz is from the very beginning
bleeding to death because he is unable to replenish his life by
creative contact.[21]

It is because this process gradually cuts off and destroys a whole
organism that the illusion of a biological time-span is created
which imperceptibly overlays our awareness of the actual time
gone by. And it is because Götz's ebbing life is the secret pulse of
the tragedy that time itself seems to expire when he dies.[22] The
time of the drama is *his* time and the sickness of the time *his*
sickness. The times are out of joint because Götz is out of joint,
not vice versa. That the play moves thus – from the centre to the
circumference – becomes abundantly clear from the metaphor in
which Götz himself sums up his relation to the historical forces
about him, to the Emperor and the State. Toasting his Emperor,
he says:

Ich lieb ihn, denn wir haben einerley Schicksaal . . . Er muss den
Reichsständen die Mäuse fangen, inzwischen die Ratten seine
Besitztümer annagen. Ich weiss, er wünscht sich manchmal lieber
Todt, als länger die Seele eines so krüplichen Körpers zu seyn. Ruft
er zum Fuse Marsch, der ist eingeschlafen, zum Arm heb dich, der ist
verrenckt, Und wenn ein Gott im Gehirn säs, er könnt nicht mehr
tuhn als ein unmü[n]dig Kind, die Speculationen und Wünsche
ausgenommen, um die er nur noch schlimmer dran ist. (III, p. 172f)

What is this if not the magnified projection of Götz's impairment, and Selbitz's?

Thus the length and looseness of the time sequence in this drama is no more accidental than the width and looseness of its spatial structure. Indeed, the disruption of the 'unities' in this tragedy and the diffuseness of its dramatic form are not only determined by the irreparable disunity of Götz's hand and heart but directly symbolise it. Both, theme and structure, coincide in the formulation of a single ultimate import: a wholeness threatened by a powerful centrifugal drive towards dissociation. And who would doubt that such tensions, pervading the play on every level, so hidden as yet and so gravely impairing the evolving form, were tensions that threatened the young Goethe himself? We cannot gainsay the probability that the iron hand, symbol of dissociation within the drama, came to encompass for its creator the precariousness of his own condition in much the same way in which the hand in *Emilia Galotti,* for him as well as for Lessing, became a metaphor of the unresolved creative problems of its maker.

The accusers of the secret court that sit in judgment at the end of the play ritualistically reiterate the need for 'reine Herzen' and 'reine Hände'.

Mein Herz ist rein von Missetaht und meine Hände von unschuldigen Blut. Verzeih mir Gott böse Gedancken, und hemm den[en] den Weg zum Willen. (V, p. 280)

In no figure and no relationship was the young Goethe ready as yet to embody an integrity springing from wholeness of being and informing hand and heart alike. He could not do so in a drama form and import of which were alike blighted by the experience of dissociation which had made him choose his subject in the first place. And yet, there were underground currents moving him toward a new sense of integrity. These currents were to rise to the surface within months or even weeks of finishing the first draft of *Götz,* at first in his letters and, soon afterwards, in the 'Künstler-gedichte' written in 1773 and 1774. In a later chapter we shall watch the process of self-discovery and liberation as it expresses itself in these documents.[23] But first we must turn to the revision of the *Urgötz* which Goethe undertook in the spring months of 1773. For here, too, we may discern a groundswell, a subtle and sub-terranean process of knitting together what had been divided, a movement toward organic wholeness of experiencing and creating which transforms Goethe's language and thence, almost imperceptibly, changes the complexion of his drama in its entirety. It is to these timid but telling manifestations of an epoch-making change that we must now give our attention, in a comparison of the two versions of *Götz*.

4

From *Urgötz* to *Götz* : A Torso Grown Whole?

> Who would have thought my shrivel'd heart
> Could have recover'd greennesse? It was gone
>   Quite under ground; as flowers depart
> To see their mother-root, when they have blown;
>   Where they together
>   All the hard weather,
> Dead to the world, keep house unknown.
>
> (George Herbert: *The Flower*)

I

Ever since the spring of 1773 when, after some weeks of furious work, Goethe's *Götz von Berlichingen mit der eisernen Hand* saw the light of the day, the question has been asked: was this drama in its final form the result of a hasty revision, of a tidying up and pruning of the excesses Herder had criticised, or was it a rebirth in the true sense of the word?[1] Goethe himself gave an unequivocal answer. Already the letter to Herder which accompanied his manuscript of the *Urgötz* shows that he knew just what was needed: 'Denn ich weiss doch,' he writes at the beginning of 1772, 'dass alsdann radicale Wiedergeburt geschehen muss, wenn es zum Leben eingehn soll.'[2] His reply to Herder's strictures on the *Urgötz* confirms such intentions, if indeed it is possible to speak of intentions where a return to the matrix of the unconscious is at issue. 'Genug, es muss eingeschmolzen, von Schlacken gereinigt, mit neuem edlerem Stoff versetzt und umgegossen werden. Dann soll's wieder vor Euch erscheinen', he writes to his candid older friend.[3] And if the metallurgic image might seem to indicate changes of a different nature and less total than those implied in the organic image of rebirth, the last paragraph of the letter leaves no doubt that the young Goethe is anticipating a transformation that will take root and shape in the depths of his unconscious being. He alludes to intimations of new things 'im Grunde der Seele' and to the hope that 'wenn Schönheit und Grösse sich mehr in dein Gefühl webt, wirst du Gutes und Schönes thun, reden und schreiben, ohne dass du's weisst, warum.'[4]

As we shall see, the analogy between art-making and biological procreation and birth is a favourite one with Goethe in these early years; and we may assume that he is giving expression to a sense of successful creative paternity when, within a few weeks of finishing the rewriting, he writes to Kestner: 'Und nun meinen lieben Götz! Auf seine gute Natur verlass ich mich, er wird fortkommen und dauern. Er ist ein Menschenkind mit viel Gebrechen und doch immer der besten einer.'[5] Just about a year later, in a letter containing some of his most astute reflections on the nature of his poetic activity, the young poet refers to his previous creations in the identical vein: 'Was red ich über meine Kinder, wenn sie leben; so werden sie fortkrabeln unter diesem weiten Himmel.'[6] Years later, in *Dichtung und Wahrheit*, the poet confirms his assessment in distant retrospect. He recalls setting about rewriting his *Urgötz* 'mit solcher Tätigkeit, dass in wenigen Wochen ein ganz erneutes Stück vor mir lag.'[7]

At first sight it would seem that there can be no question of that 'radicale Wiedergeburt' which the poet had predicted. Goethe's original conception had been a strangely ambiguous one: the figure of a great and vital nature declining and, unaccountably, perishing in an epoch of decadence. We have seen in the previous chapter that this pessimistic trend cannot be attributed to the influence of Herder's philosophy of history, but that it has its roots deep in the poetic conception.[8] For what first attracted Goethe to his subject was the iron hand of his hero, which duly became the commanding symbol of his play; and it is in the ambiguous admixture, within this symbol, of vitality and depletion that we must seek the explanation for Götz's tragic career and for the blending of bright and gloomy tones which informs the portrait of the man and the times.

Doubtless the iron hand did not at first impress itself as a symbol of impairment, neither on the young poet who gloried in its strength,[9] nor on his contemporaries for whom the appearance of the drama heralded the dawn of a new age. To a generation longing for release from the mundaneness of the Rococo and the slick eudaemonism of the Enlightenment, the rough-hewn figure from the German past must have come as a symbol of spiritual regeneration, an embodiment of that simplicity, sincerity and strength they were themselves aspiring to achieve. There was nothing smooth about this image of heroic impairment. Indeed, Götz's blunt iron hand must have especially endeared him to the young who in every age tend to oppose *Schein* to *Sein,* who rate bluffness of expression as an earnest of a pure intent and who suspect sincerity in the garb of urbanity and grace. Here was a perfect symbol of rugged integrity uncontaminated by a world it was so patently unable to woo. For Götz has lost his live hand of flesh and blood: 'Sie ist eins mit ihrem Handschuh, ihr seht er ist Eisen' (I, p. 22). The instrument he wields is a mechanical executor of his ideals in the medium of the world, insensitive to its seduction and exempt from treason. His mental vision is as cut off from living touch with the material world as a castle without drawbridge – and as immune to its contagion.

For an artist as fine-grained as Goethe it was impossible not to tumble sooner or later to the problematic implications – aesthetic, emotional and philosophical – of his chosen symbolism. The very activity of fashioning his idealistic conception in his verbal medium would forcibly bring home to him the sterility of a view elevating the ideal, mental aspect of experience to the detriment of its material pole. And so, whilst the iron fist remained the symbol of rugged integrity and strength for his public, it inevitably became a symbol of dissociation for a poet struggling to achieve wholeness in his life and art. Imperceptibly it became the cypher of the hero's tragic unviability, for all his prodigious vitality. For the robber-knight with the iron fist is, as we have seen, unable to live in a relation of creative reciprocity with his environment, replenishing his resources through regenerating contact with what is outside him and in turn enriching reality with his vision.

'Amputate a sculptor's hand,' writes a modern aesthetician, 'and you will gradually blind him.'[10] No words more fitting could be found to describe the destiny of Götz, the least artistic of Goethe's characters. For by some ultimate tragic irony – of which the young poet shows himself fully aware – the loss of the hand, the executive organ of the mind, in the last resort means not only progressive biological mutilation, but the mutilation also of that very vision which had seemed so safely tucked away in the recesses of the hero's mind. In the final scenes of the drama Götz fails to recognise himself in the man whose image has become sullied by the atrocities committed in his name: 'Sie haben mich nach und nach verstümmelt,' he reflects in prison, 'meine Hand, meine Freyheit, Güter und guten Namen.' (V, p. 288).

Explicit though the poet is about his hero's tragic depletion, we only become aware of its full extent through the figure of

Weislingen, Götz's *alter ego* and right hand. What Weislingen reaches out for and enjoys defines the area from which Götz, because of his impairment, remains cut off: the mundane eroticism of the Bishop's court and, more specifically, Adelheid. So strong is the taboo expressed in the central symbol of the play – the hand that may not touch – that, as has been shown in the previous chapter, this sphere remains totally separated off from the main area of the drama dominated by Götz. Thus, the centrifugal structure of the play is determined by the dissociative force of the commanding symbol and the feeling-import that has accrued to it.

Already the mellow scenes of Götz's dying towards the close of the *Urgötz* suggest that Goethe was beginning to outgrow the spell of a symbolism which from the first had marred his conception of a vital and viable human nature; perhaps he was doing this in the very process of fashioning his vision in the material of his linguistic medium. The letter referred to above, written only a few months after the completion of the *Urgötz* in reply to Herder's strictures of it, shows that his eyes had meanwhile been opened to the necessity and possibility of achieving oneness, in the sphere of both life and art.[11]

Thus there is evidence to suggest that by the spring of 1773, when Goethe set about rewriting his *Urgötz*, his conception of a vital character and a viable way of life had begun to change. But it is equally clear that there were formidable obstacles barring the way to that 'radicale Wiedergeburt' of the drama he had envisaged. For what was he to do with his material such as it was? There he was, saddled with a hero who had a mutilated hand, powerful symbol of dissociation and the pivot of the poetic conception as a whole, of its structure no less than its theme. He could not dream to the end the unfinished dream of his hero; the dream which, in a moment of hope, Götz confides to Weislingen: 'Ich hätte nur fortträumen sollen, da würd ich gesehen haben, wie du mir eine neue lebendige Hand ansetztest.' (I, p. 68). All the poet could do – and he did it – was to strengthen the symbolism of the hand which connects the principal figures, and to throw into relief, by a rearrangement of the relevant scenes, the strict symmetry of their destiny, and thus to suggest that biological interdependence of the protagonists which both have forfeited at their peril.[12] But then again, what remedy was there against a dissociation of structure which was the inevitable consequence of the central import of the play? None. As long as Götz was denied a live hand, the poet could not force together the ends of his drama, which strained asunder centrifugally. Adelheid was bound to remain dissociated from Götz, insulated in a world of her own. The schism between her world and his, between their ways, their values and conventions, was bound to remain in force because it is the reflection of the schism within the figure of Götz. Again, all the poet could do – and he did it – was to curb the temptation of which he tells us in *Dichtung und Wahrheit*:[13] to cease usurping his hero in vicarious erotic enjoyment of Adelheid by pruning those ramifications of the drama in which he followed her into the intricacies of her love life regardless of their irrelevance to Götz, and to redirect the poetic energy thus retrieved into channels more directly nourishing the main conception.[14]

Thus cursory reflection would suggest that Goethe was wrong. His torso could not be reborn, whole. His portrait of a vital nature was flawed by a tendency towards dissociation marring import and poetic organisation alike, and no artistic operation could hope to remove these marks of imperfection without at the same time severing the life nerve of the work. By what right can a revision which had to stop short of touching vital portions of the drama – portions most evidently in need of improvement – be called a rebirth? A rebirth in a qualitative, if not a quantitative sense?

The following reflections endeavour to answer this question. From the foregoing observations it will have become clear that a total recasting of the work in quantity was out of the question. All that the poet could hope to accomplish was a tuning up of its poetic quality. Let us then single out those portions of the drama in which a transformation of the overall poetic quality is evident. Such a tuning up of the poetic pitch one would expect to find in sections which occupy a commanding position within the total structure, viz., the beginning and the end. It is thus with the opening and the closing scenes of the *Urgötz* and *Götz* respectively – sections to which Goethe did in fact devote much attention in the process of revision – that this chapter will concern itself in especial detail.

II

The first scene of the *Urgötz* is set at an inn and during its course Berlichingen's men, commissioned to ambush Götz's erstwhile friend Weislingen, overhear a chance conversation revealing his whereabouts. It is thus the birth of a plot within the plot we witness, and on it hangs the action of the drama and, in the last analysis, its catastrophe: for all the subsequent events turn on Weislingen's *rapprochement* with Götz which is prepared here, and on his eventual defection. No wonder that the mechanics of getting the ambush under way are handled with every care. The whole scene is devoted to this aim. Götz's men report that Weislingen did *not* arrive at his destination along the direct route where they had awaited him. Presently two peasants are heard recounting that a nobleman got stuck on a secondary and bad road leading to the same destination, and wondering why he should have chosen such a detour. The nobleman, we presently learn, was none other than Weislingen. This information is overheard by Götz's men who are duly off to catch their victim.

This simplified account gives an inadequate impression of what an ingenious piece of expositional engineering this first scene is. For the two groups of speakers interact in such a fashion that the one group comes up with a set of answers which exactly fit the set of questions asked by the other group, so that both together combine to give a coherent picture of Weislingen's moves and motives. To give Götz's men such a briefing is the evident purpose of the scene, and the poet has spelt out the relevant facts in circumstantial detail. With every other aspect of the situation he has dealt in a cavalier fashion: the characters involved in the conversation have no individual features and, until just before the end, no individual names. They appear on stage to fulfil their appointed task and depart when this purpose is accomplished.

But *one* characteristic does emerge in this scene: and this is the pragmatic temper shared by all its participants. As Götz's men feel frustrated that their catch has escaped them, so the coachman and the peasant feel exploited, both by the nobleman they met and by nobility in general; and each argues his view with that same explicit cogency with which they and the horsemen had previously charted out Weislingen's moves. The protagonists themselves, before they have appeared, are infected with the dominant temper of the scene. 'Unser Herr wird wild seyn, und ich binn's selbst', says one of Götz's men, and the other retorts: 'Du schickst dich fürtrefflich zu deinem Herrn . . . Ihr fahrt den Leuten gern durch den Sinn und könnt nicht wohl leiden dass euch was durch fährt.' (I, p. 5f). Analogously, the other party speculates that Weislingen had his intentions in choosing the devious route: 'Seine Ursachen hat er', the peasant says with an emphatic inversion, 'denn er ist für einen pfiffigen Kerl bekannt.' (I, p. 8).

This pragmatic mood persists through Götz's first appearance – his short monologue. As his men have anticipated, he frets at the apparent miscarriage of his plot. He worries about his men and tries to recall the arrangement they have made. He tries to envisage Weislingen's next move and the countermove that he might make. He comforts himself with the hope of spoil. 'Ich muss dich haben Weislingen, und deinen schönen Wagen Güter dazu.' (I, p. 11). He thinks that his plot may have been given away and he gnashes his teeth at the thought. This is a man who is geared to the immediate practical situation of which he gives us a very coherent picture. His sole concern is the furtherance of his plan – which is the poet's plan in that Götz's ambush is the hinge of the external action – and to this plan he clings as though his life hung upon its outcome. And so in a sense it does. For in this scene at least Götz has no life apart from the purpose he serves. He is a tool in the poet's hand, endowed with just as much life as is required for us to understand the situation of which he is the main agent and for him to further the action; no more.

This preoccupation of the hero with his schemes still persists into the main part of the scene in which Götz marks time chatting with his young charge Georg. Clearly, the scene is interpolated to illuminate the relation between the boy and him, and so it does, within the limits of the older man's practical concerns. True, we can glean the contours of the relation between boy and hero: the solicitude of the older man and the boy's liveliness and devotion. It is all there, in the incidents which Georg recounts and in the sparing comments they prompt: Georg playing at soldiers, unobserved; imagining himself in the thick of fighting, at the side of his hero; and ingeniously getting the latest battle news. All these things Georg relates *en bloc,* in big chunks of virtually unbroken narrative. Or is 'relates' the right word to use? If the expression suggests that the telling itself may constitute an act of relatedness over and above that which is being told, then it is ineptly chosen. For Georg merely *reports* these incidents. They are left to testify to the character of his relation to Götz indirectly, symptomatically as it were. Nor are Götz's responses more immediately revealing. When the boy appears in his grown-up armour, Götz, putting two and two together, punctiliously observes: 'Darum kamst du nicht wie ich rief'; and Georg himself concludes his account with the corroborating remark 'Wie ihr rieft konnt ich nicht alles geschwind weg werfen.' (I, p. 12). It is the same all along. Georg's stories are never permitted to insinuate themselves into the atmosphere and to steal the show. They are reeled off hurriedly, and insulated on every side by references to the practical situation which keep them in their place, firmly. The poetry of the relationship stands no chance against the prevailing temper of the scene. For the poet has little time for relatedness. He is much too busy engineering his plot and having Götz catch Weislingen. To him and his misfired ambush the hero's thoughts return time and again, and with a somewhat tedious pedantry he punctuates Georg's stories with the request 'Geh – sags deinem Vater und Hansen!' (I, pp. 13 and 15). And the end of the scene sees him precisely where he was at the beginning: worrying over his men and about the counterplot that Weislingen may be hatching.

To return from these scenes to the opening of *Götz* is to witness something of a revelation. We want to exclaim, as Goethe did more than twenty years later, when he watched the creatures of the sea on the lagoons near Venice: 'Was ist doch ein Lebendiges für ein köstliches herrliches Ding! Wie abgemessen zu seinem Zustande, wie wahr, wie seiend!'[15] Gone is the obsession with their plots and schemes which all the characters shared, and gone the tone of ill humour which overlaid them all alike as with a shroud through which we could barely discern their differentiated forms and contours. A new liberality has set in in which the characters are free to come and go, to brawl and drink and chat, darting from one topic to another, instead of arguing to the point as they had done before. References to their physical situation abound, and even where they speak of general topics, they now do so in a language that is saturated with allusions to immediate and concrete bodily experience.[16] In the genialness of this atmosphere the protagonists emerge as individuals: Götz, the 'Getreuherzige', is generous to a fault; Weislingen is not a schemer either, nor indeed the opposite, but something different altogether: he is 'des Bischofs rechte Hand'. This epithet contributes nothing to the psychology of the character; it operates on the formal plane alone. For in the 'rechte Hand', the one that is missing in Götz, we recognise the central poetic structure of the drama which here emerges in nucleus.

And what of the betrayal of Weislingen's whereabouts which had caused such a lot of to-do in the first version of the play? It is dealt with in a quiet and casual fashion, taking up a mere fraction of the scene. The fact that he is nearby is simply learned through a chance question asked by Götz's men as they come in. That is all. There is none of the jigsaw of facts of the first draft: the account of the way that Weislingen did *not* take, from Nersheim via Crailsheim to the Winsdorfer Wald, and the route the stranger *did* take, to Rotbach and Mardorf for which destination he ought, by rights, to have taken the Crailsheim road. And there is none of the intellectual excitement accompanying the piecing together, from these data, of the picture of Weislingen's movements. All we hear, and all we need to hear, is: 'Sagt ich dir nicht er wär daher? Hätten wir dort drüben eine Weile passen können. Komm Veit.' (I, p. 8.) Surely a superbly vague bit of

plotting, this! In the first version the inn scene had seemed
contrived, because the facts that were brought to light in it were
too complicated and changed hands too cleverly to permit of any
sense of true coincidence. Logical coherence born of the poet's
preoccupation with his plot had killed the imponderables of the
situation and, therewith, its life-likeness. If this slipping out of the
news through a haphazard meeting in a tavern convinces us in the
second version, it is in a large measure due to the waywardness
with which the poet has handled a once central event.

The same waywardness impresses itself on us in Götz's
monologue. Here as in the opening scene, the physical facts of the
situation have come to the fore. Götz is seen fighting sleep and
walking to and fro to keep himself awake, musing, drinking,
calling and musing again. And here as in the opening scene, there
is none of the toothgnashing determination of the first draft, and
there are none of the intricacies of the ambush that had filled his
mind to the exclusion of anything else.[17] True, he is out to catch
Weislingen, and even the idea of having him seems to excite him
pleasantly; but now, while he is waiting, Goethe projects the
image of a being without a nameable purpose, aimless, cradled
between despondency and cheer, drowsiness and wakefulness,
between strong gusts of bodily awareness and effortless thought
which ranges far beyond his immediate plight.

What is more, Götz's thinking itself is suffused with his intimate
awareness of his bodily condition; and therein lies the charm of
the scene. Everything he has to say about his situation in general
– about freedom, about Weislingen and the Bishop – is conceived
in the terms of his physical situation here and now: his tiredness,
his thirst and his satisfaction when it is quenched. It is a man
whose throat is parched and whose very body rebels against
sleeplessness who says: 'Es wird einem **sauer** gemacht, das bissgen
Leben und Freyheit.' (I, p. 11). Having Weislingen means the end
of protracted strain; and this anticipation of ease is faithfully
projected in the benignness of his exclamation: 'Wenn ich dich
habe Weislingen, will ich mirs **wohl** seyn lassen.' (ibid.) The
thought of that satisfaction merges with the immediate satisfaction of the draught of wine he drinks, and both are included in
the image: 'So mag denn dein lieber Weislingen die Zeche
bezahlen' (ibid.). The refreshment which the drink has given him
at once revives his 'frischen Muth', and thus revived he avows his
readiness to deal with all the intrigues that Weislingen and the
other nobles may be spinning against him, in the simple
statement: 'Ich bin wach.' (ibid.)

The same shift of emphasis from purposive thinking and doing to vegetative being is perceptible in the third scene, the conversation between Georg and his master. The poet seems to be obsessed with sleep: Götz asks Georg whether he has slept; is told by Georg that he got his armour from Hans who took it off because he wanted some sleep; retorts 'Er ist bequemer als sein Herr' and a little later asks again 'Schläft Hanns?' (I, p. 12). All this is new, and so is Götz's repeated mention of wine, both at the beginning when he also asks for a glass to be brought to Hans, and again at the end of the scene.

This new awareness of the physical aspect of being is all the while supported by the way in which the poet handles his dialogue.[18] In the first draft of the scene Götz has asked Georg two questions in all: 'How do you come by the armour you are wearing?' ('wie kommst du dazu.') and 'How do you know that I lost my bow at my last encounter?' ('wie weisst du das.') (I, pp. 12 and 14). Ordinary questions, these, revealing interest in the boy and genuine ignorance of his little ways. In the revised version Götz asks six questions instead of the original two, and what is more, these questions have undergone a marked change of character. The original 'wie kommst du dazu' has been replaced by the rhetorical question 'Es ist Hannsens Küras?' (I, p. 11). Similarly, the end of Georg's adventure, which had been previously reported by the boy himself, now comes as an informed guess from the lips of Götz. 'Und hiebst um dich herum?' – he surmises – 'Da wirds den Hecken und Dornen gut gegangen seyn' (I, p. 12). Again, later on Götz asks Georg what in the first version Georg had told Götz; 'Erzählen dir das meine Knechte' (I, p. 14). These questions do not drive at anything. In a sense, they are redundant in that they answer themselves. In truth, however, through that very fact they have become important instruments for expressing relatedness over and above the relatedness expressed in overt behaviour and reported incident. For both the act of asking and the intuitive knowledge contained in the question reveal Götz's receptiveness to the boy. These are the knowing questions of one who is in touch with the other. And the dialogue is handled in a corresponding manner on Georg's side. Only one of Götz's enquiries does the boy answer directly. For the rest he carries on with his own story, all the time lightly aware of Götz and in touch with his mood. As Götz anticipates the boy's phantasies and actions, so Georg anticipates his master's needs. The horses for which Götz asks are fed, saddled and ready to go. Götz's tenderly proud 'Weisst du das?' (I, p. 14) – what a change from the pedestrian 'Wie weisst du das' of the earlier version! – finds its echo in Georg's tenderly proud 'Gelt ich weiss' (ibid.).

Both reach deep into the territory of the other's mind and, by word or action, anticipate thoughts and needs before they have been expressed or even consciously formulated by the other.

Through such a flexible form of dialogue, the poet achieves two objects: in the first place, he delineates a large marginal area of implicit understanding between his characters. Paradoxically, dialogue has become a mode of achieving relatedness on a deep, non-verbal level. Secondly, and more basically, by suggesting such an area of non-verbal relatedness, the poet intimates the existence of a depth dimension to his figures, the habitat as it were of those non-verbal and unconscious processes that are plying between them.

The importance of this free and associative handling of dialogue[19] cannot be overstressed. Its effects may once more be seen from the consideration of another scene that received considerable attention during the rewriting of the play: the *Kerkerszene* in its earlier and later form. In the earlier draft the statements are lengthier in themselves and firmly cemented with their respective responses. Götz's central statement: 'Sie haben mich nach und nach verstümmelt . . . ' follows immediately upon his wife Elisabeth's reference to his wounds and is logically elicited by it. Similarly, her next statement: 'welch eine muthlose Finsterniss! Ich finde dich nicht mehr' (V, p. 261), draws from him the question: 'Wen suchtest du. Doch nicht Gottfrieden von Berlichingen. Der ist lang hin.' *(ibid.)* In the second version Elisabeth, after her opening reference to Götz's wounds, continues: 'In der muthlosen Finsterniss erkenn ich dich nicht mehr', to which Götz replies: 'Suchtest du den Götz? Der ist lang hin.' (V, p. 288). The original 'finden' – logical correlative to Götz's 'suchen' – has been replaced by 'erkennen'; and the logical uncoupling of statement and response which is thereby achieved is made complete by the omission of the intermediate link expressed in 'Wen suchtest du?' Thus, when Götz speaks, saying 'Suchtest du den Götz?', his words seem to come as from some great distance. The associative loosening up of statement and response has opened up a depth of space which previously the tight interlocking of the edges of the dialogue had not permitted to unfold. His reference to himself as 'den Götz' helps to create this effect. He sees his familiar image from a long way off as it were, as though he, too, had become estranged from it. It is at this point that the shattering statement of mutilation follows, by way of an abrupt juxtaposition of his old self with his present disfigurement in which he is recognisable neither to himself nor to his wife; not as before by way of a direct and logical response to Elisabeth's mention of his 'Wunden'. And yet his forlorn question, by its sensitive perception of what goes on in his wife's mind, evinces much more relatedness to her than did his earlier, more literal 'wen suchtest du?' What a responsive instrument dialogue has become! By the slightest increase of the distance between these two voices which nevertheless move in concert the poet, without adding a word, has projected both the relatedness of man and wife and, beyond it, the depths of loneliness and the speechless despair into which Götz has sunk at the nadir of his life.

III

All this amounts to saying that, by comparison with the second version, the idiom of the *Urgötz* – for all its *Würfe und Sprünge* and its appearance of spontaneity – is predominantly discursive in character. A paraphrase of the conversation between Götz and Georg in the first version, for instance, would offer no real difficulty. A paraphrase of the scene in its final form would have to make explicit all those implicit meanings created by the form of the dialogue itself. And it is the same everywhere. Once the discursive character of the early idiom is granted, Goethe's own impatient comparison of the *Urgötz* with its contemporary, Lessing's *Emilia Galotti,* begins to appear in an altogether new light. And it is to this comparison that we may now turn. For in Lessing's tragedy, too, under the guise of a naturalistic idiom, a relentless – indeed, a much more relentless – intelligence is at work. Lessing's sharp-edged verbal duels, full of nervous energy, of hard-driving definitions, repetitions and antitheses, illuminate as with a searchlight a precise area of intellectual exchange, bounded at either end by sharply delineated centres of consciousness. They fail to suggest what only a less logically controlled, more associative idiom could intimate: surrounding areas of non-verbal contact into which the intellectual encounter shades off, and, therewith, beings in depth not themselves made of thought, in which those non-verbal aspects of relationship that are brought into play could be anchored. If we keep unprofitably guessing at Emilia's deeper feelings and motives as we do, if nearly two hundred years after the publication of the drama yet another study has appeared dealing with the 'mystery' of *Emilia Galotti,*[20] it is not because the poet has created the illusion of a person in depth whose most intimate promptings elude analysis. It is, on the contrary, because he has failed to project, through the evocative power of his idiom, a depth dimension beneath her intelligence to

which any unconscious motives whatever can properly be attached.[21] But is not precisely this failure to project such a depth
dimension of being the flaw which mars the idiom of the *Urgötz?*

Again: as a consequence of the unusually ratiocinative
character of his idiom, the mature Lessing is forced to resort to an
indirect technique in the presentation of passion. As the character
of his idiom forbids him to portray passion directly, he does so
by tightening up even further the logical processes of his
characters, revealing their compulsiveness through their excessive
ratiocination and the ensuing faultiness of their reasoning. This is
so in *Emilia Galotti,* the only play in which, after *Miss Sara Sampson,*
the problem of presenting passion between the sexes arises in
earnest. It is the fallacious syllogisms of an Orsina and the logical
short-circuits of an Odoardo which are the secret of their powerful
presences and of the life which they – and they alone – communicate to the drama as a whole. This technique could not be
employed in the case of Emilia herself, because her role as an
innocent young girl forbade any marked emphasis on her intellectual powers as a foil for her passion.

Something very similar goes on in the pages of the *Urgötz,* and,
to isolate more precisely what it is, it is worthwhile returning once
more to the *Kerkerszene.* Clearly the object of that scene had been,
from the beginning, to present Götz in that state of gloom which
the final version evokes so beautifully through Götz's abstracted
words – 'Suchtest du den Götz? Der ist lang hin.' We know the
poet's intention all too plainly, from four long passages in the
Urgötz which came to be deleted in the final draft and which are
in their entirety devoted to creating just this mood of despondency.
Elisabeth makes direct references to Götz's 'tiefe Verzweiflung' in
her first speech; his metaphor of the ruined castle 'worinn der
Geist seines Alten Besitzers ächzend herumgleitet' (V, p. 261)
expresses his own sense of desolation. His obliviousness of the good
news of the coming of Lersee, his loyal comrade in arms, which
Elisabeth had brought him the day before – 'Ich weis nichts
davon' he says, 'Du merckst nicht auf wenn ich rede' (V, p. 262)
she rejoins – serves to enact his abstraction in dramatic terms.
And this brooding despair is once again reflected in the final
speech of Götz in which he diagnoses the secret connection
between his misfortunes with the dispassionate detachment of an
outside observer.

For all their diversity these four passages have two things in
common: firstly they all bear, all too openly, the mark of the poet's
intention. It is only too easy to see the reason why they were
introduced and, eventually, dropped. Secondly – and this is more

important in the context of the comparison with Lessing's technique – the characters in every single one of these passages are themselves aware of a purposive agency at work which however defeats itself in the end. Elisabeth has an avowed purpose in looking at Götz's wounds: she wants to take him out of himself and occupy his mind. The peasants in Götz's morose imagination cart away the stones from the edifice of his spirit in order to build their own houses from the rubble. Elisabeth has arranged for Lersee's discharge so that he may comfort her husband. Götz, finally, perceives purpose in the concatenation of his misfortunes: 'Dann fühlt man den Geist der sie zusammen bewegt.' (V, p. 263).

All this display of purposeful thinking and acting points up the prevailing mood of meaninglessness. It is this sense of futility which informs Götz's despair and gives it its bitter edge; this which goes into the coining of the desolate image of the 'Wintermitternächtlichsten' hour (V, p. 263). Elisabeth knows that whatever hope she may kindle in Götz is a false hope. The peasants' industry underscores the fact that a nobler structure is being destroyed. Lersee, Götz bitterly observes, will come when it is too late. And the assumption of an apparent purpose animating the forces that destroy Götz only emphasises his sense of futility in the face of total extinction and his terror at the thought of it. Even the central statement of mutilation which has survived into the final version in the lovely limpid form – 'Mein Kopf was ist an dem?' (V, p. 288f) – in the earlier version smacks of a purposiveness gone awry: 'Das schlechste haben sie zuletzt aufbehalten, meinen Kopf, was ist der ohne das andre.' (V, p. 261).

What a rationalistic procedure, and how reminiscent of Lessing! To project the despair born of the meaninglessness of life, the poet piles purpose upon purpose only to collapse his teleological edifice like a house of cards. This is exactly the same technique as that used by Lessing: the promptings of passion in his characters are revealed by an excess of ratiocination which in the end defeats itself. The young author of the *Geschichte Gottfriedens von Berlichingen mit der eisernen Hand dramatisirt* is still as unable as the creator of *Emilia Galotti* to give full-throated utterance to experiences stemming from the depth of our being rather than from the top levels of our intellect. As Lessing resorts to logic to create an analogue of passion, so the Goethe of 1771 resorts to teleological constructs to wrest from their negation an analogue of sheer creature suffering.[22]

And so, we remember, the young poet dealt with that other, objective, imponderable of human existence – the imponderable of chance: ignoring its essential intractableness and the absence in it of all design, and, instead, substituting a complex configuration of events which interlock so perfectly as to preclude any semblance of true coincidence.

How right Goethe was when, in his letter to Herder, he coupled his *Urgötz* with Lessing's *Emilia* in one inclusive judgment: 'Es ist alles nur gedacht.' How right he was when he amplified this criticism of his own work in his further comment on *Emilia*: 'Emilia Galotti' – he writes – 'ist auch nur gedacht, und nicht einmal Zufall oder Caprice spinnen irgend drein. Mit halbweg Menschenverstand kann man das Warum von jeder Scene, von jedem Wort, mögt' ich sagen, auffinden.'[23] For if the purposive thinking of the characters in the *Kerkerszene* is, admittedly, a special device to underpin their underlying sense of futility, it is also a special instance of that preoccupation with conscious purpose which we have found in a number of other scenes of the play: whether we take the opening scene, Götz's monologue, his conversation with Georg or indeed the *Kerkerszene,* in every case we have found strenuous argumentation going hand in hand with concern for purposive action.[24] The Plan, the Plot, the Purpose seem the be-all and the end-all of these characters. It is the stuff of which they are made, the substance of their being; and the idiom they speak – a discursive idiom for all its seeming ebullience – is in keeping with the pragmatic temper they all share. Once we know their intent we can indeed tell the why and wherefore of every scene, almost of every word. It rigorously governs character and dialogue as well as action. And because this pragmatic temper of the characters overrides all individual differences it is not difficult to perceive in it the prevailing temper of the young poet himself. If they are so busy arguing and scheming and plotting, it is because they are the executors of the plotter-in-chief who is concerned to keep his action moving and to define his historical perspectives, and who keeps the noses of his characters to the grindstone doing just those things for him. It is in fact the poet's Plan, his Plot, his Purpose, which is the be-all and the end-all of those characters. His cogitating is the stuff of which they are made, which constitutes their being. And if their being as yet lacks poetic density and substance, it is the paucity of the creative processes that have gone into their making – their consciousness and intellectuality – which we must hold responsible. From such head-work only a discursive idiom could spring which in turn could only project beings made of thought. We must not be deflected from this estimate by the extravagances of behaviour and diction which are characteristic of this manifesto of the *Sturm und Drang*; by the frequent gusts of rage or frustration, such as when Götz gnashes his teeth at the thought of Weislingen having escaped his grasp or has bitter things to say about Lersee's coming and about life in general. Such emotional posturing does not reflect a true exuberance of vitality on the part of the dramatist. In the storm and stress of this as of every other age, it is much more likely to reflect anxiety and doubt as to whether there is enough vitality and depth of feeling. In the *Urgötz* at least, the impetuousness, the angers and rages bear witness to the shallowness of creative processes that as yet project an image of life in the straitjacket of a purpose and are fed by the meagre emotions derived from its fulfilment or frustration.[25]

In the second version of *Götz* this intellectual purposiveness is amazingly relaxed. As a result of this relaxation action naturally grows out of character and character, in the sense of psychophysical being in depth, naturally grows out of the poetic idiom. For in the final version Goethe has achieved an idiom capable of projecting being in depth, has achieved, in short, that supreme quality of art which time and again strikes the reader in the consideration of the revised version and which may be now named: its semblance of life. It is the overall absence of this quality in the first draft, as well as the paucity of the creative processes that went into its making, which Goethe had in mind when he condemned it, for all its promise and for all the passionate emotion it occasioned, saying 'Es ist alles nur gedacht.' And it is the presence of this quality in the revised version which made Goethe speak of its hero as though he were one of his physical children and which makes us adjudge it a true product of the poetic imagination.

The figure of Götz, it has been seen, could not be reborn. It was too indelibly marred from the first ever to become an adequate symbol of organic life; and indeed the overall form of the drama was bound to remain fragmented. But a symbol may lose force in the course of a poet's development, and new imports may create for themselves new symbolisms. This is what happened in Goethe's *Götz*. What was in fact reborn in the months of self-discovery which preceded the rewriting of the drama was the equivalent of a hero with a new hand: it was a poetic idiom itself capable of projecting the semblance of organic life. It is our task in the pages that follow to trace the emergence of that idiom and to indicate the processes by which it structured itself until the forms of language itself became the analogue of that organic life which the mutilated figure of Götz failed to be. It is here, on the primordial level of the verbal organisation, that we must seek for the precipitate of that unconscious 'Schönheit und Grösse' which,

Goethe felt, was beginning to weave itself into his soul, a new wholeness of being which, he dared to hope, would find expression in the good and beautiful things he was going to do, to say and to write, 'ohne dass du's weisst, warum.'

IV

The nuclei of the new poetic language appear early on in the final draft. The poet's awareness of the physical aspects of the being of his characters has already been noted.[26] Not only does it find expression in their overt behaviour, in their drinking, sleeping, coming and going, and brawling: it saturates their diction when they touch on broader and more general issues. This is already marked in the opening scene, and it becomes more striking in Götz's monologue. In the short lines of this monologue in which physical and mental experience have merged with one another, the three principal image patterns of the drama are beginning to exfoliate, almost imperceptibly. Imperceptibly, because they are very homely images indeed, denoting the most primordial activities of a sentient being: *trinken, essen* and *schlafen* – the activities by which it takes in sustenance from its environment and spontaneously regenerates its resources; *mutig* or *brav sein* – the activity of giving out strength to the environment; and *wohlsein* – the basic pleasurable awareness of a sentient organism. These motifs fuse to create the conception of an organism – the later Goethe would have spoken of an entelechy or monad – whose well-being, and indeed whose well-doing, is rooted, precisely, in this double rhythm of intaking and outgiving in a ceaselessly pulsating activity.

Indeed, the conception of such organic well-being had already played a large part in the earlier version of the drama. It was all there, in the conversation between Götz and Brother Martin, in which Götz's natural and active way of life is juxtaposed to the self-denying weakness of the 'Mann der heiligen Ruhe' (I, p. 15), and the monk's holy orders to the mundane order of Knighthood, 'den Orden . . . den mein Schöpfer selbst gestifftet hat' (I, p. 19). Food and drink, sleep, valour and well-being in this scene in turn become explicit themes of discourse, and we are left in no doubt that the denial of the natural appetites – 'die besten Triebe, durch die wir werden, wachsen und gedeyen' (I, p. 19) – goes hand in hand with an ineffectual piety which in this play is termed holiness, and that, on the other hand, Götz's active goodness springs from a sense of physical well-being and a vigorous assertion of his natural instincts. The closest connection between well-being and well-doing – 'Wohlsein' and 'Wohlthun' – is established and maintained, both here and elsewhere, by a number of characters in a variety of independent contexts. Götz readily accepts the fact that 'Essen und trincken . . . ist des Menschen Leben' (I, p. 16) – 'Wohl,' he says in reply to the monk's nostalgic observation. 'Wohl euch', says Brother Martin, 'dass ihr's nicht versteht' (I, p. 16) when he begins to expound his own fear of the senses, and again 'Wohl dem, der ein tugendsam Weib hat!' (I, p. 21), and we must not overlook the fact that the thrice-repeated 'Wohl', in such a vital context, subtly contributes to the dominant image pattern of well-being and virtue, in that it expresses moral approbation of Götz as well as praise of his good fortune. Götz himself later on concurs with Martin's judgment when, finally at home after long exertion, he recalls his conversation in the forest and reflects: 'Die Bequemlichkeit wird mir **wohl thun,** Bruder Martin du sagtest recht' (I, p. 36) – a significant opening to the encounter between the protagonists.

The connection between vitality and goodness and, alternately, between a weak natural endowment and 'holiness' had already been driven home in the two conversations between Elisabeth and Maria in the first and second acts of the *Urgötz*. The first of these conversations is occasioned by the 'heiligem Müsiggang' (I, p. 30) of the child whose 'Wohltätigkeit' (I, p. 26) consisted in having no appetite for his breakfast; the second one arises à propos of a discussion concerning the monastic destination of Carl, Götz's spineless offspring; and here again it is the man whose initial appetites are feeble – who is too lazy to reach for the apple on the table before him – who will be weak and indolent in all things: a Weislingen or a Carl. Again, Adelheid is obsessed with the notion of vital goodness. Hence her disappointment with Weislingen who has turned out to be an effete Romantic 'statt des acktiven Manns' she had imagined him to be (II, p. 110). And there is much unconscious irony in the comment with which she greets his resolve to challenge his great opponent: 'Mich däucht ich sehe einen auferstandnen verklärten Heiligen in dir.' (II, p. 114). The conception of goodness allied to vitality receives its most drastic formulation from Elisabeth who declares that 'Wohltätigkeit . . . ist nur das Vorrecht starcker Seelen' (I, p. 28), adding that, when it is practised by the weak who cannot help being good, it is nothing but mental incontinence.

But in all these passages – every one of which was to be deleted – the governing idea is operative as a concept rather than as an image, as a theme itself discursively defined and in turn in-strumental in defining characters through the attitude they take towards it. In the final version it emerges as a series of pure images growing out of the poet's perception of his characters in their psychosomatic wholeness, and articulating the pattern of vitality which pertains to Götz and those close to him: Georg, Elisabeth, Selbitz and Lerse (as the name is spelt in the second version).

It is in the nature of such homely verbal materials that they give rise to poetic structures which are unassuming in the extreme and tend to elude the attention of the reader as well as any attempt at critical enumeration. References, as often literal as metaphorical, to food and drink and sleep and to valour and well-being pervade the fabric of the final *Götz*, often in seemingly insignificant, factual contexts, often in idiomatic turns of phrase to which we might well hesitate to ascribe any special significance; and even the purpose of an added reference here and there, taken by itself, might remain open to doubt. Yet pattern and significance there is. It impresses itself in the beginning scenes in which the new imagery is given an intensive launching,[27] and becomes firmly established in Götz's opening monologue where, for the first time, the separate image strands converge to form one encompassing pattern: 'Wenn ich dich habe Weislingen, will ich mirs **wohl seyn lassen. (Schenkt ein)** . . . So langs daran nicht mangelt, und an **frischem Muth,** lach ich der Fürsten Herrschsucht und Ränke.' (I, p. 11.) From then on, this pattern emerges from intermittent obscurity in every climactic scene of the drama, like a planetary constellation peeping out through the clouds: the three images appear interwoven in the encounter between Götz and Martin where the quality of goodness which is allied to the vitality articulated in the opening scenes of the drama is first defined. The triad appears again in the encounter between Götz and Weislingen, when Götz recalls the happiness of their young days spent at one another's side and says: 'Wir hielten immer redlich zusammen als **gute brave** Jungens, dafür erkennte uns auch jedermann' – then *pours out wine and offers it to his friend* and continues: 'Castor und Pollux! **Mir thats immer im Herzen wohl,** wenn uns der Margraf so zutrank' (I, p. 44f). And indeed the confluence of images here, at the reunion of the protagonists, tells us what the course of the action only gradually confirms: the full measure of their interdependence. Only together can they be a healthy organism and be vital as well as good: 'Gut **und** brav'. Again, the constellation of images appears in the 'last supper' scene before the evacuation of the castle, where drinking and solemn toasting interweave with the nostalgic vision of an organic society in which alone it would be possible for the individual to live well *and* valorously, fulfilling himself through being part of the larger whole.[28] The images finally converge in the last scene of the play where Götz, out in the open, for the last time experiences a sense of well-being, recalls the valour of Georg and the other 'Edlen' who have gone before him, takes a draught of water and dies. And now, at the end, we realise how much the pattern itself has metamorphosed and how much it has contributed to the transmutation of mood and meaning that is revealed in those final scenes.

For these scenes, in the second version, have an unearthly quality about them, a transparence and serenity on which critics have remarked with admiration. Indeed the emergence of this new quality – it has often been called religious – has been compared to the transcendence of the real at the end of *Egmont*, and has been recognised as an early instance of that poetic intensification – 'Steigerung' – which, many years later, Goethe was to formulate in morphological terms when he described the structural law of his *Novelle*.[29] And rightly so. There are many elements that go into the making of this metamorphosis, and many have been described. But none seems to be more primary in creating the mellowness of these dying scenes than the transmutation – one feels inclined to say transfiguration – that the basic image patterns have undergone. For if at the beginning of the drama they denoted physical activities – physical intake of food, physical prowess, physical vitality and well-being – they have now come to denote activities and awarenesses of a highly sublimated nature. This change has been carefully prepared in the earlier portions of the drama, and it is in the preparing of it that the second version subtly differs from the first.

In the scene preceding the communal meal (III, p. 167) in the first version, for instance, the question of victuals had been introduced on a factual level. Anticipating the beleaguerment of the castle, Elisabeth has had provisions brought up from the cellar all through the night; but too much had to be abandoned there and she is annoyed to think of it falling into the enemy's hands. In the second version Götz explains the shortage by lack of time to make provisions, to which his wife adds: 'Und die vielen Leute die ihr zeither gespeisst habt. Mit dem Wein sind wir auch schon auf der Neige' (III, p. 167). The pragmatic orientation which we have so often remarked in the first draft has gone, and with it the grossly physical character of the reference.[30] Bodily sustenance is now being invested with a new meaning: it is becoming a symbol of giving as well as of taking; of a shared spiritual experience as well as a private, physical one. Thus prepared, the meaning of the 'last supper' scene becomes unequivocally established (III, p. 171).

Götz insists on sharing with his friends the last bottle of wine which Elisabeth had kept for him, saying: 'Sie brauchen Stärkung, nicht ich, es ist ja meine Sache.' (III, p. 172). And the last draught they take becomes a giving in that it is likened to the last drops of blood they are preparing to sacrifice for their cause. 'Es geht just noch einmal herum,' Götz says as he pours out the wine; 'Und wenn unser Blut anfängt auf die Neige zu gehen, wie der Wein in dieser Flasche erst schwach, dann tropfenweise rinnt, (*er tröpfelt das letzte in sein Glas*) Was soll unser letztes Wort seyn?' (III, p. 173). In the communion of the shared meal giving and taking have fused. It is a symbolic act, a sacramental act, in which the whole person, body and soul, is involved.

The end of the final version draws on these new meanings and further strengthens them. Götz refuses the food that his wife offers him. Material sustenance is no longer what he needs. As he dies, he drinks a draught of water – purest of substances; but he has drawn the strength to spend himself in death from other sources. He asks to be allowed out into the garden, 'dass ich der lieben Sonne genösse, des heitern Himmels und der reinen Luft.' (V. p. 289). The partitive genitives and the word 'genösse' make it clear that Götz is partaking of these ethereal goods and drawing sustenance from them; just as, a little later, he draws strength from Lerse's face and longs that he might see Georg once more: 'Ach dass ich . . . mich an seinem Blick wärmte!' (V, p. 292). The maturity and sublimity that we feel in Götz's last acts spring from the maturation and sublimation of a once physical experience which now has ripened into a spiritual dimension, and from the corresponding development within the image pattern denoting it.

It is the same with the other verbal structures. Georg, the 'brave Junge' of the early scenes, after his heroic death becomes 'Der **beste** Junge unter der Sonne und **tapfer**.' (V, p. 292). His physical prowess has matured into a valour of spirit which is expressed in the intensification to 'tapfer', an epithet hitherto reserved for his patron saint St George – his 'tapfern Patron' (I, p. 24). This transfiguration is completed through Georg's doubled association with the sun: here, when Götz calls him 'der beste Junge unter der Sonne', and earlier, when he had longed to *warm* himself 'an seinem Blick' (V, p. 292). Georg remains the life-giver to Götz that he has been all along, and Götz dies when this source of life is extinguished. More: at the end, this life-giving quality is surrounded with an aura of sanctity; for at the last, the sunny image of the boy – 'der goldne Junge' as Maria calls him (V, p. 291) – merges with the image of the saint in his 'goldene Rüstung' whose valour Georg had vowed to emulate (I, p. 24).

Such changes are reflected in the metamorphosis of the word 'Wohlsein'. This word which once denoted a vigorous sense of physical well-being, in the final version recurs at the beginning of the last scene; and now it is imbued with something of the unearthly serenity of a late Beethoven quartet. 'Allmächtiger Gott. **Wie wohl ist's** einem unter deinem Himmel. Wie frey! Die Bäume treiben Knospen und alle Welt hofft. **Lebt wohl** meine Lieben . . . ' (V, p. 291.) This is the well-being of an immaterial spirit no longer bound by gravity, privileged to partake of sun and sky and the purity of the air, without yet rejecting the sweetness of life and past experience. There is no longer any distinction between the physical enjoyment once denoted by 'Wohlsein' and the purposive activity encompassed by 'Wohlthun'. The two have utterly merged. As Götz uses the word 'Wohlsein' to express a sublimated, mental state, so the image of 'Wohlthun' is sounded at the last in a context so humbly physical that we might well miss it altogether, were it not for the lingering accent we are compelled to give to the word 'wohl': when Götz asks whether the prison keeper might permit him to enjoy the sun for a half hour, Elisabeth replies: 'Gleich! Und er wirds **wohl thun**.' (V, p. 289).

Thus, through the images associated with his figure and through their development, Götz is restored to some of that wholeness of experiencing and that reciprocity in the relation with his environment which was denied to him in the original conception of the play. Here is an organism that *is* in touch with its environment, capable of drawing sustenance from the world around it; here we witness a knitting together of the physical and mental spheres which had gaped apart, into that oneness of being of which, in the letter to Herder, the young poet had spoken; and here is a mellowing and a maturing all round, belying the symbol of dissociation which gives the play its name. The severed hand is still the governing symbol of *Götz von Berlichingen mit der eisernen Hand*. But its force is on the wane as a maturer creativity injects new life into the play on its deepest plane: the level of its verbal weave.

V

But the transformation of the total import which impresses itself on every reader of the second version is only in part due to the exfoliation of a *new kind* of verbal material: organic images capable of articulating psychosomatic wholeness of experience. On a deeper level yet, it is due to the *new way* in which such meaning-structures are poetically handled. The behaviour of the words themselves: the relation of a structure to its verbal surroundings, to other structures and to the whole of which it forms part is such as to warrant the assertion that the forms of language themselves have become an analogue of organic process.[31] Take for instance Götz's repeated reference to his 'Knechte' at the beginning of his monologue and at the end of the scene with Georg. In the *Urgötz,* such recurrence has the character of a mechanical repetition. The practical concern expressed at the beginning in the question 'Wo meine Knechte bleiben?' (I, p. 11) is echoed in the final statement 'Meine Knechte! Wenn sie gefangen wären und er hätte ihnen gethan, was wir ihm thun wollten.' (I, p. 15). The intervening material – the conversation with Georg, first lighthearted and then grave as Georg beseeches Götz to let him go to battle – has done nothing to change its quality. In the final version, the statement 'Wo meine Knechte bleiben' is repeated verbatim. Only the words 'Es ist unbegreiflich' are added. But it is no longer the same statement. Stripped of all practical context, it reverberates with the sense of destiny of Götz's prophetic words: 'Ich sage dir Knabe, es wird eine theure Zeit werden, Fürsten werden ihre Schätze bieten um einen Mann den sie jetzt hassen' (I, p. 15); and the simple addition 'Es ist unbegreiflich' serves to deepen that sense of foreboding. Indeed, the repeated statement carries the whole future in it. For at the end of the drama Götz will repeat the same question for Georg who has gone out as Götz's Knechte have done now and who will not return. The verbal pattern in the new version shows an accretion of meaning which we can only describe by saying that it has 'grown'. And indeed it exhibits the principle of all biological growth: the assimilation of elements from its verbal environment and their organisation according to its inherent pattern.

In the original version of Götz's conversation with Georg, Götz, hearing that Georg had tried on Hans's armour, calls him 'braver Junge' (I, p. 13). In the second version, the image recurs twice. As soon as he sets eyes on the boy in his grown-up armour, he says 'Du bist brav!' (I, p. 11). At the end of the scene the same statement recurs, slightly varied. 'Du bist ein braver Junge', says Götz (I, p. 14). And again the statement has 'grown'. For it has assimilated all that intervened between its first occurrence and its repetition: the revelation of the boy's resourcefulness. Every incident the boy has reported testifies to this quality: his wish to accompany Götz into battle to retrieve his master's bolts, his confession how he coaxes Götz's men into telling him what happened in battle by whistling to them and teaching them jolly tunes; and the fact of his having fed and saddled the horses in readiness for Götz's orders. This resourcefulness, this flair for retrieving spent energy becomes associated with Georg's character henceforth. It gives his valour its peculiar flavour. Later, in battle, when Götz has got into a tight spot, Georg gives him his own horse, kills a soldier who is about to attack Götz and helps himself to the dead man's horse: 'Ich half euch von einem Feind und mir zu einem Pferde.' (III, p. 156). When Götz's castle is beleaguered and Lerse finds himself short of ammunition, Georg comes along with a leaden drainpipe to cast into bullets, saying: 'Der Regen mag sich einen andern Weeg suchen, ich bin nicht bang davor, ein braver Reuter und ein rechter Regen kommen überall durch.' (III, p. 169). Then, as he climbs onto the roof to dismantle the drainpipe, an enemy, aiming at him, shoots a pigeon: 'sie stürzt in die Rinne', Georg recounts, 'ich dankt ihm für den Braten und stieg mit der doppelten Beute wieder herein.' (III, p. 170). This same life-retrieving vitality returns at the end, as has been seen, but now in a significant intensification. When Maria calls him 'ein goldner Junge', when Götz longs to warm his heart at the sight of him – the sight which had at the first elicited the words 'Du bist brav' – and continues, saying: 'Er war der beste Junge unter der Sonne und tapfer' – the final association with the all-giving sun rounds off the pattern of his valour and makes explicit his func-tion in the bigger life of Götz in which he shared. From the first 'Du bist brav' to the last 'Er war der beste Junge unter der Sonne und tapfer' the same law of life has been operative, announcing itself at first as predetermined tendency, then emerging as the law of his being and revealing itself, finally, as his destiny. Such stability of a basic pattern persisting throughout the divers parts and phases of a structure and reflected in them is the distin-guishing mark of organic form. It is indeed only when a conca-tenation of structures reflects one common life-quality that we describe it as an organism with an abiding identity. Thus, by imprinting on his unliving and unchanging verbal structure the stamp of vital form, the poet is able to project the illusion of being in organic process: of growth, development and maturation in time.

Georg, the retriever of life, is the most precious part in the larger life of Götz. He is, as Götz calls him, the apple of his eye (IV, p. 180). Yet he also surpasses the structure in which he shares. For he goes out into the world and returns enriched, whilst Götz returns from his encounters progressively depleted. It is Georg that is the replenisher of his life, the source of regeneration. Thus the boy both reflects and transcends Götz's unavailing courage. And again: such surpassing reflection of the larger structure in the smaller, more vital one is the hallmark of the relation between the generations, between procreator and progeny. It is because the configuration of their relation bears the stamp of genetic pattern that Georg is felt to be the true son of Götz, rather than Carl, his bodily progeny, and that we perceive in the extinction of the young a tragic biological reversal which the old cannot survive.

Such poetic materials, drawn from a deep organic level of experiencing, and themselves organically structured, turn out to possess an astonishing organising force and show themselves capable of transforming or else displacing a surprising amount of discursive matter. Even before the end of the first act, the associated image patterns of valour and vitality have gathered sufficient momentum to displace the whole theoretical discussion which in the first version had followed upon the story of the holy child, with its contradistinctions between holiness and goodness, contemplation and activity, weakness and strength. All these relations, and more, are formally realised by a single added **allusion** to the dominant image complex: 'Gebe nur Gott dass unser Junge mit der Zeit **braver** wird, und dem Weislingen nicht nachschlägt, der so treulos an meinem Mann handelt.' (I, p. 32).[32] Similarly, the extension of this discussion into the second act, with its references to Carl and Götz and Weislingen, is altogether obviated (*UG* II, pp. 101ff) and so is a large part of the conversation between Weislingen and Adelheid about his restless inactivity (II, pp. 110ff). The single juxtaposition, deftly interpolated between these scenes, of the 'seidene Buben' at the court of Bamberg and the 'braven Leute' around Götz – in the *Urgötz* it had been 'ehrliche' (II, p. 117) – with one stroke evokes these qualities and defines their reference in a fashion which is both more economical and potent and obviates their discursive explication. This is all the more interesting as the deleted passages happen to bear unmistakable traces of Goethe's own recent experience. In the first version, for example, Adelheid complains that 'statt des acktiven Manns' she had expected to find in Adelbert, she found a 'krancken Poeten' whose morose inwardness she had condoned too long. 'Ich dacht: er hat sich neue, noch unentwickelte Kräffte gefühlt da er sich an einem grosen Feind mas, es arbeitet ietzo in seiner Seele, die äussere Ruhe ist ein Zeichen der innern Würcksamkeit.' (II, p. 110). But she continues sardonically, 'die Fäulniss arbeitet auch. Aber zu welchem Zweck!' (II, p. 111). A letter to Salzmann, announcing that he is working on the *Urgötz*, reveals the roots of this rejection of inwardness in the poet's personal experience:

Ich dramatisire die Geschichte eines der edelsten Deutschen, rette das Andenken eines braven Mannes, und die viele Arbeit die mich's kostet, macht mir einen wahren Zeitvertreib, den ich hier so nöthig habe, denn es ist traurig an einem Ort zu leben wo unsre ganze **Wirksamkeit** in sich selbst summen muss.

He goes on to write:

In sich selbst gekehrt, ist's wahr, fühlt sich meine Seele Essorts die in dem zerstreuten Strassburger Leben verlappten. Aber eben das wäre eine traurige Gesellschaft, wenn ich nicht alle Stärke die ich in mir selbst fühle auf ein Object würfe, und das zu packen und zu tragen suchte, so viel mir möglich, und was nicht geht, schlepp ich.[33]

The Goethe that speaks here is clearly not a 'krancker Poet'. Years before he wrote *Werther* he had grasped the need for an active and vigorous intercourse between self and non-self, between what is inward and what is outward, between mind and medium; and he now uses this insight, and even his formulation of it, in the very work that had occasioned it: Elisabeth admonishes her pious sister-in-law, who in her fear for Weislingen seeks refuge in prayer, saying: 'Nur dann reflecktirt Gott auf ein Gebet wenn all unsre Kräffte gespannt sind, und wir doch, das weder zu tragen noch zu heben vermögen was uns aufgelegt ist.' (II, p. 103). Here as elsewhere the young poet draws on his own experience and formulations, transposing them into different contexts and employing them for different purposes. But for all the creative disposition attested by such a lively traffic between the person and his art, much of the material that had found its way into his work proved too directly personal and, thus, resistant to a full poetic organisation. The poet himself recognised this soon enough and wrote to Herder: 'Genug, es muss eingeschmolzen, von Schlacken gereinigt, mit neuem edlerem Stoff versetzt und umgegossen werden'; the *edlere Stoff* being, precisely, poetic structures more highly organised in themselves and thus potent to impart organisation to their surrounding matter. The same proved to be true of the great number of metaphors drawn from the biological and cosmological spheres. Many of these could be jettisoned in the final version, not by any means only because Goethe realised the truth of Herder's charge 'dass Euch Schäckessp. ganz verdorben' and saw that what was needed was a slow and more thorough assimilation of the Englishman's genius, but, more basically, because, dealing with natural process on the deepest level, such rhetorical ornamentations of his theme had lost their purpose.

Indeed we may go further and suggest that the organic

'behaviour' of the words that were patterning themselves under his hands taught the young poet a biological fact he had not appreciated in the first flush of delight about the 'Man with the Iron hand': the involvement of every living organism with its environment. As we know nowadays, an organism cannot be adequately defined in terms of what is 'inside the skin'. It reaches far out into what is outside it. The very air we breathe and the food we take in is environment incessantly incorporated, broken down, assimilated and returned again. From this, its nurturing soil, a living thing is isolated at its peril.

We have seen how, in the final version of the play, Goethe strengthened the food symbolism. In this version, too, it is that the dying Götz, during his brief moments in the prison garden, amongst the burgeoning trees, says: 'Meine Wurzeln sind abgehauen' (V, p. 291). By some poetic anticipation Goethe had, from the start, defined Götz's being out of touch with his social environment as a biological impairment. Now, at the end of his work on the play, he is ready to state the nature and extent of this impairment with relentless precision – in the metaphor of truncation. The mortal blow to Götz's life is dealt precisely to that part of him which extends into his environment. Is it possible that the young poet's understanding of the external world increased as he gained insight into the laws of art, into the 'growth' of poetic structures, i.e. their ability to seize upon elements from the 'outside' to enhance their own vitality?

Perhaps the most remarkable result of the poet's creative release and the consequent poetic organisation of his materials is the change effected in the overall conception of the play. The conciliatory tone at the end and the modulation from despair and tragedy into a more serene key, which are so striking from the latter half of the *Kerkerszene* onwards, have often been remarked; critics, of late, have tended to put these changes down to a deepening of the young poet's experience of Christianity.[34] Such arguments, however, tend to put the aesthetic cart before the horse. In the first place, the changed conception that has emerged is not Christian in character, but bears the stamp of an organic, unitary view of life.[35] More importantly, this organic conception has gradually seeped through to the surface of the drama from the deepest levels of its verbal structure. It is at this depth, in the artist's encounter with his verbal medium, in the flowering of an associative language, in the emergence of organic images and in their patterning along organic lines, that we must seek the source of the transformations that took place. The overt modulation of conception and feeling-tone is the *result* of these linguistic events, not their cause. We can in fact isolate the precise point where the transformation, which has been secretly going on throughout, reaches the surface of the drama and alters its outward course. This breakthrough occurs toward the end of the *Kerkerszene* when all seems lost and Götz, overwhelmed by adversity from all sides, accepts defeat. In the *Urgötz*, the hero's resignation, expressed in the words of the Gospel, 'Meine Stunde ist kommen', is underpinned by his desperate addition: 'Ich hoffte nicht dass es eine der Wintermitternächtlichsten seyn sollte.' (V, p. 263). From then on there is no letting up on the mood of bleakest despair. It envelops the drama to the end. In the final version, the acceptance of death ushers in a modulation into an altogether sweeter key, effected, significantly, by a series of free poetic associations. Goethe no longer insists on describing, with a stubborn pedantry of feeling, the precise colouring of Götz's despair. Instead, he lets himself be carried by his words, and they carry him to the healing awareness of the perennial processes of life. The words of Christ – 'Meine Stunde ist kommen' – modulate to that most perfect formulation of human acceptance, the words from the Lord's prayer, 'Dein Wille geschehe' (except that Götz says, more obliquely as yet, 'Sein Will geschehe' – V, p. 289); and these words, followed as they are by the plea for 'our daily bread', in turn give rise to the next association. Elisabeth asks Götz: 'Willt du nicht was essen?' *(ibid.)* It is in answer to this question that Götz asks to be allowed out into the prison garden, 'dass ich der lieben Sonne genösse, des heitern Himmels und der reinen Luft.'

Here, at the end, we witness the confluence of the poetic developments we have seen taking shape throughout the final version: the flowering of an associative idiom, the emergence in and through it of a primordial image drawn from the sphere of organic being, and its power to attract and transmute all else: for what follows after its recurrence, here, at the end, is the final scene, that unearthly coda on the themes of well-being, sustenance and valour in which life and death mingle and tragedy has no place. As Edward Bullough sums up the business of raising poetic pitch:

> You cannot write a play in prose and later turn it into verse without disturbing the whole relief of it, the interdependence of its parts, the colour of its sentiment and **in the last resort** the fundamental conception from which it sprang.[36]

Looking back upon the process of revision, Goethe tells us in *Dichtung und Wahrheit*: 'Ich hegte nun, anstatt der Lebens-

beschreibung Götzens und der deutschen Altertümer, mein eignes
Werk im Sinne . . . '[37]; and this remains by far the most accurate
description of the transformation we have witnessed and the
creative processes that went into its making. *Götz von Berlichingen
mit der eisernen Hand* ceased to be what, given its model – 'ein
Menschenkind mit viel Gebrechen' – it could only be imperfectly:
a portrait of a vital nature. In place of it, the poet created a
symbolic structure the very form of which reflects the rhythms of
organic life. He did so by letting the representational aspects of
his work recede,[38] and by allowing the composition itself to
become the frame of its internal references. And thus, nursed in
the shelter of a deep artistic seclusion, his work could ripen to
maturity.

Part Two

EROS OR APOLLO ?

Kunst! O in deine Arme wie gern entflöh ich dem Eros!
Doch, du Himmlische, hegst selbst den Verräter im Schoss.

(Eduard Mörike)

Ich wandre in Wüsten da kein Wasser ist, meine Haare sind mir
Schatten und mein Blut mein Brunnen. Und euer Schiff doch
mit bunten flaggen und Jauchzen zuerst im Hafen freut mich.

(Goethe to J. C. Kestner, 1773)

5

Goethe to Herder, July 1772, and the 'Künstlergedichte': An Artist learns about Loving

Art bids us touch and taste and hear and see the world, and shrinks
from what Blake calls mathematical form, from every abstract thing,
from all that is of the brain only, from all that is not a fountain jetting
from the entire hopes, memories, and sensations of the body.

(W. B. Yeats: *The Cutting of an Agate*)

I

The foregoing chapters will have made it clear that, beneath an
unruffled surface, a process of fermentation was going on in
Goethe during the year which separated his *Urgötz* from the final
version of the play. It will also have become apparent why the
revolution which was in fact taking place in the twenty-two-
year-old could only announce itself in an unobtrusive and, as it
were, subterranean fashion within the framework furnished by his
subject. 'Ich sprang in die freye Lufft, und fühlte erst dass ich
Hände und Füsse hatte': in these words the young poet, in his
address *zum Schäkespears Tag*, had recounted the sense of liberation he experienced when he shed the straitjacket of the French
classicists and instead adopted the free stance of the British giant
in his *Götz*.[1]

And yet, ironically, there he was, and remained, encumbered
with two heroes, Götz and Selbitz, the former one-handed and the
latter one-legged, and both truncated and doomed, for all their
massive vitality. Perhaps the very hopelessness of his subject-
matter forced this dogged young man to seek liberation at a
deeper level, indeed at the only level where emotional release
could issue in a true creative liberation. For, in his revision of the
Urgötz, he pursued the theme of his play – an organic mode of
being – by going 'quite under ground', into the very texture of the

language in which he was fashioning his vision, allowing organic images to infiltrate the verbal fabric, there to pattern themselves and their linguistic environment according to organic laws. 'Dead to the world', his poetic life kept 'house unknown' and thus 'recover'd greennesse'. And indeed, within a year of writing *Urgötz* this subterranean development enabled the poet to endow his hero with a new body and a living hand, a body and a hand made of language.

But in fact the forces that had been set in motion by his poetic exercise in dissociation were to rise to the surface only a few months after the completion of *Urgötz*. They are rumbling in the letters written at this period; they erupt in the letter to Herder of July 1772, written in response to his mentor's strictures of the first draft, finally to sweep everything before them in the group of poems known as 'Künstlergedichte' which Goethe threw off between 1773 and 1774. To these two documents, one discursive and one poetic, we must now turn our attention.

It is a strange letter, that of July 1772 to Herder. We seem to witness the actual event of a conception rather than to read about it. With the precision of a poetic statement, its very first words catch the dominant mood which informs the letter in its entirety: centrifugal, yet emanating from a centre of stillness.

> Noch immer auf der Wooge mit meinem kleinen Kahn, und wenn die Sterne sich verstecken, schweb' ich so in der Hand des Schicksals hin, und Muth und Hoffnung und Furcht und Ruh wechseln in meiner Brust.

A fluid state, made up of multifarious sensations and tensions suspended between conflict and resolution and accepted in their fluidity. For sure, there is lability in this succession of changing states, but also there is a sense of purpose, hidden as yet or only glimpsed. A measure of control there is in the image of the little craft, but also the knowledge that such control is limited and can never hope to match the power of the element which carries the poet and which may, at any moment, destroy him. And is there not an affinity between the element which cradles his craft and the destiny which cups him in its hand? Both are unfathomable forces and to both, nevertheless, he entrusts himself.

How many strings are touched here which Goethe will sound time and time again. The mind is sent forward to poems such as *Auf dem See* and *An den Mond*, vibrant with the recollection of 'froh – und trüber Zeit' and yet tranquil in such recollection; to *Seefahrt* and *Egmont* with their peculiar blend of mastery and humility, a mingling bred of the hero's confidence that he is at one with the elements and with his destiny. One thinks of Egmont himself as he is revealed in the central image of the play, nimbly holding the reins of a chariot drawn by no ordinary horses along an ordinary human path, but swept along a cosmic course by Apollo's sun steeds that daily arise from the sea and nightly return to the sea. One thinks of Tasso as he perceives the world reflected in the wave, only to be buffeted about by its anger; and indeed one's thoughts run forward to the last letter of the poet, a letter to Humboldt,[2] in which once again he will speak, as he had done in the wonderful poem *Dauer im Wechsel,* of permanence and flux, and in which he will once more touch on the mysterious interlacing of purposiveness and spontaneity, of conscious control and unconsciousness in the creative act. Statements, all of these, of creativity in life and art, and all of them couched in the imagery of water, the creative element Goethe was to extol in the *Klassische Walpurgisnacht* and symbol *par excellence* of creativity, as we shall see in the concluding chapter of this book. And here he is, a young man at the outset of his voyage into life and art, envisaging himself afloat 'auf der Wooge mit meinem kleinen Kahn,' cradled in the hand of destiny. A creative hand, after all?

What follows to a nicety reflects the mood that is ushered in by these opening words. Breathlessly, the poet darts here and there, stringing together snatches from Pindar's odes, quoting bits of Homer, of the Koran and a word or two of Herder's own *Fragmente*; alluding to the Greek and Roman poets and philosophers he has read, turning from them back to the plastic arts, to music and the craft of cutting quills, to his own relation to Herder (charmingly couched in a reference to Götz), and from there back to Herder's *Fragmente,* to a recent personal discord with his mentor, to the *Gemeinschaft der Heiligen* und to Merck, and back again from there to his own *Götz* and Lessing's *Emilia Galotti.* A tumultuous document, seemingly utterly centrifugal – 'Es geht bei mir noch **alles** entsetzlich durch einander', Goethe himself confesses – yet all the time gravitating towards *one* inner centre and strangely unified: 'Und doch muss das **alles eins** sein'. The contrast between the 'alles' in the first sentence and the demand that this manifold be one is real enough; yet it signifies, not a dichotomy, but a fruitful tension. With the urgency of one chasing the tail-end of an illumination, Goethe ranges over the whole gamut of his experiencing – his feelings, his sensations, his thinking and his doing – testing them out in the sudden discovery of what is missing in them all and what he has now found: 'Meisterschaft, *epikratein,* Virtuosität'. He has found 'the essence of all mastery', in life as well as in art. It lies in the oneness of mind and body, of head, heart and hand, of vision, medium and execution, in all manner of creative activity. The young poet has made the discovery which he will put into practice, not many months later, in the revision of his *Urgötz*: the discovery that language can, and must, body forth the mind's inspiration; and the underlying discovery that he himself is one and indivisible, a psychosomatic whole.

II

A great deal of research, some of it published since this book was first begun, has demonstrated the seminal importance of Pindar's poetry on the one hand and of Herder's teaching on the other for the formation of the insight that was to crystallise in this letter.[3] It has been shown to what extent this insight depended upon the theory of knowledge and art formulated in Herder's *Plastik* with its emphasis on kinaesthetic experience rather than the experience of sight – a theory itself indebted to Cheselden's successful operation on a blind boy and the philosophical interest aroused by this event: all these, no doubt, topics which were frequently discussed between Herder and Goethe during the poet's stay in Strassburg between 1770 and 1771. The importance, at this precise moment in the life of Goethe, of Herder's *Fragmente,* which propound a cognate theory of language and poetry, has also been shown in detail.[4] And indeed, such investigations seem to cover what appear to be the two burning centres of preoccupation in this letter. For although the young poet mentions his reading of Homer, Xenophon, Plato, Theokritus and Anacreon, these interests were superseded by the spell of Pindar, 'wo ich noch hänge'. And of the impression made on him by Herder's *Fragmente* his words leave no doubt.

In the circumstances, it is somewhat surprising to find that the seal with which Goethe secured this letter bore the head of Socrates. This is the first time that Goethe uses a seal bearing this imprint.[5] What is the significance of this gesture at this moment? True, in his previous letter to Herder, written a few months earlier, he had announced his intention of dramatising the life and death of Socrates. He had spoken of the philosopher in impassioned terms, calling him 'Mein Freund und mein Bruder!' 'den ich nur mit Lieb Entusiasmus an meine Brust drücke,' and he had exclaimed: 'Wär' ich einen Tag und eine Nacht Alzibiades, und dann wollt' ich sterben!'[6] Clearly, he had been reading the *Symposium*; and other allusions in this letter and earlier ones make it probable that he had also read the group of dialogues which have for their theme the trial and death of Socrates, the *Georgias* and the *Phaedrus*. However, by the time he came to write to Herder again, the young poet, rather dispiritedly, had drifted away from his plan to dramatise the story of Socrates. ' . . . um den Sokrates forscht' ich in Xenophon und Plato. Da gingen mir die Augen über meine Unwürdigkeit erst auf . . . . ' This is the last we hear of his project.

But did Herder's *Fragmente* really take Goethe's attention away from the figure of Socrates as presented by Plato, and from the *Phaedrus* and the *Symposium* in particular? The portion of the *Fragmente* which had excited him most, the sixth section of Chapter III, deals with the problem of the interrelation, in poetry, between feeling and thought on the one hand and expression on the other: 'Wie Gedanck und Empfindung den Ausdruck bildet'.[7] In his endeavour to drive home to the reader the indivisibleness of thought and expression in poetry, Herder had resorted to a number of analogies expressing such closeness, only to reject them again. Thought or feeling, he had urged, cleave to expression more closely than a garment, or even the skin, to the body; more closely than a girl clings to her betrothed or, even, than man and wife to each other, in the act of love; more closely than twins, born and bred together, as inseparable as Helena and Hermia in Shakespeare's *A Midsummer Night's Dream*. 'Für ihn [i.e. den Dichter] muss der Gedanke zum Ausdrucke sich verhalten . . . wie die Seele zum Körper, den sie bewohnet.'[8] This, Herder judges, is the only analogy that will do justice to the interpenetration of mental and material elements in the creative act; and to elucidate the mysterious nature of such interlacing, Herder, in a memorable passage, resorts to the Platonic myth of the incarnation of the soul:

> Es fällt mir ein Platonisches Mährchen ein, wie der schöne Körper ein Geschöpf, ein Bote, ein Spiegel, ein Werkzeug einer schönen Seele sey, wie in ihm die Gegenwart der Götter wohne, und die himmlische Schönheit einen Abdruck in ihn gesenkt, der uns an die obere Vollkommenheit erinnert: ich sezze diese schöne Sokratische Bilder zusammen und zeige meinen Lesern ein Bild, dass Gedanke und Wort, Empfindung und Ausdruck sich zu einander verhalten, wie Platons Seele zum Körper.[9]

This Platonic myth he then freely renders as follows:

> Aus dem seeligen Reich der Götter ward die Empfindung, wie die Seele des Plato, heruntergesandt in den Schoos der irrdischen einfältigen Natur. In dem Schoos dieser gesunden und starken und

fruchtbaren Mutter sollte die Bewohnerin des Himmels einen schönen
und blühenden Körper sich zum Wohnhause bereiten: daher nahm
sie das zarteste und feinste Geblüt ihrer Mutter zur sanften Hülle, und
ward die Schöpferin des Gebäudes rings um sich. Kein Sturm widriger
Wallungen und kein Blizstral von ungesunden Zuckungen hinderte
ihr Gewebe, in welches sie, ohne Gefühl gewaltsamer Störungen ihr
Bild voll ruhiger Stille eintrug: als das Bild einer Freundin der Götter
und Gespielin der Göttinnen. Sie vollendete ihre Schöpfung: sie
brachte die Frucht zur Reife: sie vollführte den Pallast ihrer Woh-
nung: ihr gelang das Bild ihrer selbst, das von ihr zeugen sollte. Kurz!
der himmlische Gedanke formte sich einen Ausdruck, der ein Sohn
der einfältigen Natur war, sie aber in den schönsten Jahren seiner
Mutter: er ward in ihrem Schoosse reif, ohne gewaltsame Gährungen,
und mit einer stillen Grösse vollendet. Er wand sich seiner Gebährerin
sanft vom Herzen, und bei seiner Geburt beglückten ihn die Grazien,
und Göttinnen lächelten ihn an.[10]

Perhaps the Platonic myth to which Herder here resorts to
elucidate his insight into the nature of poetic language deserves
some closer attention,[11] to help us understand Herder's own
meaning, as well as Goethe's reception of this message. For with
the incarnation of the immortal soul in an earthly frame none
other than Eros comes into being, that recollection of immortality
shot through with desire which inflames the human soul when a
beautiful object reminds it of its former state.

In the *Phaedrus* and even more candidly in the *Symposium*, Eros
is represented as a morally indeterminate, ubiquitous force which
holds sway over the spheres of nature and spirit alike, bridging the
gap between them and preventing the universe from falling into
two separate halves. Eros, according to the *Symposium*, governs the
relation of the natural elements to one another as much as that
between the different parts of the individual body; it rules the
sexual relations between male and female of any species, animal
or human, and it inspires the physical and spiritual relation
between the lover of the beautiful and the object of his love; it is
the force which animates any creation sprung from such intercourse, be it music or poetry or wisdom or the pursuit of virtue
and honour; finally, it permeates the mind of the philosopher who
has given himself over to the contemplation of universal beauty.

'Now the truth about every activity is that in itself it is neither
good nor bad,' Pausanias, in the *Symposium*, explains to his fellow
diners: 'So with the activity of love and Love himself.'[12] Socrates,
initiated into the mysteries of love by Diotima, agrees with
Pausanias and in his turn proceeds to define Eros as being neither
good nor bad, neither beautiful nor ugly, neither wise nor

ignorant, neither god nor man. He is an intermediate spirit, a cosmic Protean force assuming numberless shapes, driving all animate beings to procreate, so that they may retrieve a measure of the immortality which had been theirs before they became embodied.

'Procreation', Diotima had explained to Socrates,

> can either be physical or spiritual . . . All men, Socrates, are in a state of pregnancy, both spiritual and physical, and when they come to maturity they feel a natural desire to bring forth . . . [13] Those whose creative instinct is physical have recourse to women, and show their love in this way, believing that by begetting children they can secure for themselves an immortal and blessed memory hereafter for ever; but there are some whose creative desire is of the soul, and who conceive spiritually, not physically, the progeny which it is the nature of the soul to conceive and bring forth . . . When by divine inspiration a man finds himself from his youth up spiritually pregnant . . . as soon as he comes of due age he desires to bring forth and to be delivered, and goes in search of a beautiful environment for his children; for he can never bring forth in ugliness . . . Everyone would prefer children such as these to children after the flesh. Take Homer, for example, and Hesiod, and the other good poets; who would not envy them the children that they left behind them?[14]

Thus Diotima, through the mouth of Socrates. The interrelation between physical and spiritual begetting, between physical pregnancy and physical labour and the pregnancy of the spirit that is 'great with child', longing to be delivered from the 'pains of travail', can rarely have been more graphically presented.

The closeness of the correspondence between Plato's account of creativity and Herder's theory of poetic language is striking indeed and can hardly be sufficiently emphasised. Intent as Herder was on driving home the bodiliness of the verbal medium in which the poetic vision is conceived, he could not have found a more appropriate analogy than that furnished by the Platonic myth of incarnation, or indeed a more welcome notion than that of spiritual pregnancy held out to him, time and again, in Plato's *Symposium*. Indeed, in the passage from the *Fragmente* quoted above, Herder, to serve his own ends, modifies the notion of spiritual pregnancy, using it in a far more naturalistic sense than Plato had done. Diotima had told Socrates:

> When by divine inspiration a man finds himself from his youth up spiritually pregnant . . . as soon as he comes of due age he desires to bring forth and to be delivered, and goes in search of a beautiful environment for his children; for he can never bring forth in ugliness.

There is no question here but that the whole complex of pregnancy, fertilisation and delivery[15] is lifted out of its biological
context and transferred to the sphere of men: it is a man that is
pregnant in the first instance and the beautiful environment he
seeks in order to deliver himself of his progeny is the company,
physical and spiritual, of another man. Herder, in his turn, in
speaking of poetic procreation, reverts to the original, biological
context and accordingly changes his metaphor: in the creative act,
'Empfindung' descends and is conceived in the 'schönen und
blühenden Körper' of a 'starken und fruchtbaren Mutter'. Within
her maternal lap, the poetic vision creates for itself a womb: '[sie]
nahm . . . das zarteste und feinste Geblüt ihrer Mutter zur
sanften Hülle, und ward die Schöpferin des Gebäudes rings um
sich.' Within this womb, vision then creates its 'Gewebe, in
welches sie . . . ihr Bild voll ruhiger Stille eintrug': and the body
which forms itself from this tissue, inside the maternal womb, is,
precisely – the articulated body of language.

The organic twist which Herder here gives to Plato's notion is
not accidental. In an essay dating from 1766 entitled *Ist die
Schönheit des Körpers ein Bote von der Schönheit der Seele?* Herder
adduces Plato's *Phaedrus* in defence of a thesis which, as its title
indicates, is in many respects a forerunner of that expounded in
the *Fragmente*. This is how, in a free paraphrase, he recounts the
argument of Plato's dialogue:

Unsere Seelen, erzält er, sind aus dem Reiche der Götter herunter-
gesandt, entweder zum Lohn für ihre schon geübte Tugenden, oder
zur Strafe für ihre Laster. Hiernach richtet sich ihr Schicksal in dieser
Welt. Einer schönen Seele ward der Leib einer blühenden Mutter
angewiesen; wo sie sich selbst aus dem zartesten Geblüt einen Körper
bereitet, der durch seine Schönheit ihre Ehre, ihr angenehmes
Wohnhaus, das Werkzeug, mit dem sie voll seliger Ruhe würket, und
der Spiegel seyn soll, in dem sich ihre Schönheit offenbaret. Die
bösartigen Seelen wurden hingegen in den Schoos lasterhafter Mütter
gewiesen; ihr Leib sollte ein dunkler Kerker, und ihr Antlitz der
Spiegel seyn, in dem sich die schwarze Gemüthsart des Geistes
abspiegelte.[16]

This passage is a free rendering of the twenty-fifth chapter of
Phaedrus where indeed good souls are assigned 'to some celestial
spot', whilst bad souls 'go to the prison houses beneath the earth,
to suffer for their sins.' But nowhere in the *Phaedrus* or indeed
anywhere else, in treating of the incarnation of the soul, does
Plato resort to the metaphor of the mother and the womb in
which the soul creates its own likeness.[17] In both instances, in the

metaphysical argument of this earlier treatise as well as in the aesthetic context of the *Fragmente*, Herder has freely introduced the biological metaphors of mother and womb; partly, no doubt, in deference to an age which took less kindly than the age of Plato to overt homosexuality, but principally, I am inclined to think, in order to drive home, more emphatically even than Plato had done, the analogy between physical and mental creativity, to underpin the *organic* character of poetic creation and, finally, to demonstrate inescapably the bodiliness of poetic language.[18]

How 'pregnant' are these passages of the *Fragmente*, pregnant with Plato's experience of Eros as an all-pervasive principle informing physical and mental creativity alike and implicating the creator, in whichever sphere he may be productive, in the psychosomatic totality of his being. And indeed, Herder's more naturalistic handling of the biological metaphors and the way in which he exploited them served to enhance his account of creativity and to saturate it, even more than Plato had done, with organic and erotic overtones. No single word used in these paragraphs and in the earlier essay referred to above is perhaps as telling as the word 'Werkzeug'. The beautiful soul, we read in the essay of 1766, descends into the body of a mother in her bloom, 'wo sie sich selbst aus dem zartesten Geblüt einen Körper bereitet, der durch seine Schönheit . . . das Werkzeug, mit dem sie voll seliger Ruhe würket . . . seyn soll': 'Werkzeug' here means not only the tool *with* which the beautiful soul works and *through* which she organises her matter, but, quite literally, the living stuff *in* which she works, endowed with the same life-principle as its creator and organising itself spontaneously. This is the connotation with which the word is used in the aesthetic context of the *Fragmente*. The animating vision, its shaping tool and the living medium in which vision is conceived and grows to fruition, have become one in an account of creativity which takes organising nature for its model. What a revelation this word must have been to the young Goethe who, but a few months earlier, had fashioned an image of uncreativity in his Götz; a noble mind, dissociated from the corrupt medium of his environment and equipped with a hand which, although 'mehr werth als Reliquienhand, durch die das heiligste Blut geflossen ist', is nevertheless no more than a 'todtes Werkzeug'! [19]

III

It is difficult to fathom the excitement with which Goethe must have received Herder's account of the poetic act as a conception in the depths of bodily being, issuing in the bodiliness of poetic language; an account saturated with the Eros of Socrates, initiate into the mysteries of love, whom the young poet had embraced in love, exclaiming: 'Wär' ich einen Tag und eine Nacht Alzibiades, und dann wollt' ich sterben!' Last but not least, an account by one to whom he himself stood in a stressful relationship, to whom he had written, in words curiously reminiscent of those he had addressed to Socrates: 'Jetzt eine Stunde mit Ihnen zu sein, wollt ich mit – bezahlen.'[20, 21]

Our best guide to the manner in which the young poet received Herder's message is the imagery in which he speaks of it. It is the same imagery which Herder himself had used in the vital passages of the *Fragmente*: the imagery of conception. As, in Herder, the immortal soul descends into the beautiful body to inhabit it and there to engender its likeness, as divine inspiration is sent down into the lap of one pregnant with language, there to be conceived and brought into bodily being, so for the young Goethe Herder's vision of poetic incarnation 'ist . . . wie eine Göttererscheinung über mich herabgestiegen, hat mein Herz und Sinn mit warmer heiliger Gegenwart durch und durch belebt . . . '. Goethe has conceived the bodiliness of language in the depth of his own being, and 'Herz und Sinn' are through and through imbued with the fertilising force of what he has thus assimilated. 'So Innig hab' ich das genossen.'

As he has received Herder's message, so he receives the message of Pindar. 'Ich wohne jetzt in Pindar, und wenn die Herrlichkeit des Pallasts glücklich machte, müsst' ichs sein.' Again we must attend to the imagery Goethe is using here. For, time and again, Herder, in the section of the *Fragmente* which had so excited the young poet, had spoken of the beautiful body, and the body of language, as the dwelling-place, or indeed the 'Pallast' into which soul or thought descends, there to engender its creation. Goethe has now entered into the very body of Pindar's language. 'Ich wohne jetzt in Pindar'. Its forms, felt through from their burning centre, to him have become expressive forms: and fructified by this experience of another's body, he now conceives 'in mir selbst' what it is to make poetry. 'Seit ich die Kraft der Worte *stethos* und *prapides* fühle, ist mir in mir selbst eine neue Welt aufgegangen', he writes. Certainly Herder was not exhorting his pupil to think 'with the belly – or even with the blood!'[22] But at this moment the young poet is using the word 'belly', just as he is using its equivalent, Herder's own 'Pallast', to express that in his innermost being he has conceived a whole new world – the world of poetically articulated language. No wonder that he can now exclaim: 'Armer Mensch, an dem der Kopf alles ist!' with Götz's wounded words 'Mein Kopf was ist an dem?' still ringing in his head.

The importance of Plato's myth of incarnation as the background into which Herder's and Goethe's view of language and poetry is set can hardly be overestimated. For this myth enshrines, once and for all, the indivisible oneness of body and soul, and the knowledge that creativity of every kind, be it physical or mental, is a manifestation of the all-pervasive force of Eros, rooted in the psychosomatic depth of being. No wonder, then, that Goethe sealed a letter fraught with such illumination with the head of Socrates.

We need only envisage the ubiquity of the Socratic Eros, the creative principle *per se*, to understand the wide spectrum of Goethe's preoccupation in this letter, his equal concern with all manner of creative mastery, whether it be in life or in art, and the ease of his transition from one to the other.

Again, imbued as Goethe was with the Platonic myth of incarnation, creative process, like the commerce of the soul with its body, was bound to present itself to him as essentially unconscious process. He rejects his own *Urgötz* as he rejects Lessing's *Emilia Galotti*, because both are 'nur gedacht', thin products of the head that are transparent to the intellect; and to such brain-children he now opposes, in the concluding sentence of the letter to Herder, intimations of an unconscious kind of creativity, again both in life and in art: 'Wenn Schönheit und Grösse sich mehr in dein Gefühl webt, wirst du Gutes und Schönes thun, reden und schreiben, **ohne dass du's weisst, warum.**' Here, too, we must take note of the image to which the young poet resorts. For *weben* is used here with the same connotation with which Herder had employed it in the passage of the third *Fragment* quoted above: 'Kein Sturm widriger Wallungen und kein Blizstral von ungesunden Zuckungen', we read there, 'hinderte ihr Gewebe, in welches sie, ohne Gefühl gewaltsamer Störungen ihr Bild voll ruhiger Stille eintrug.' For the young Goethe, as for Herder, *weben* and *Gewebe* signify that unconscious, organic and, therefore, blind process by which *'Empfindung'*, in the body of language, creates its own womb, and inside that tegument brings to fruition a fully articulated verbal product. The Erdgeist, in the *Urfaust*, weaving 'am sausenden Webstuhl der Zeit' (HA III 1. 155), is speaking of unconscious creative process, and so is Mephistopheles, when he contrasts the apparatus of logic with a

> Weber – Meisterstück,
> Wo *ein* Tritt tausend Fäden regt,

> Die Schifflein herüber hinüber schiessen,
> Die Fäden **ungesehen** fliessen,
> *Ein* Schlag tausend Verbindungen schlägt   (ll.1923ff.)

a passage so important to Goethe that, slightly altered and entitled *Antepirrhema,* it was to become one of his major poetic
statements on cosmic creativity and as such came to conclude a
late essay in which, perplexed by the antinomies that lie at the
end of discursive thinking, he seeks refuge in the creative mode.[23]

Again, the insight into the bodiliness of language, nourished by
the Platonic myth of incarnation, was bound to lead to the poet's
emphasis on kinaesthetic ranges of experience in the poetic act:
'Dreingreifen, packen ist das Wesen jeder Meisterschaft', he writes
to Herder:

> Ihr habt das der Bildhauerei vindicirt, und ich finde, dass jeder
> Künstler, so lang seine Hände nicht plastisch arbeiten, nichts ist. Es
> ist alles so Blick bei Euch, sagtet Ihr mir oft. Jetzt versteh' ichs, tue die
> Augen zu und tappe. Es muss gehn oder brechen. Seht, was ist das für
> ein Musikus, der auf sein Instrument sieht!

And in a footnote:

> Ich kann schreiben, aber keine Federn schneiden, drum krieg' ich
> keine Hand, das Violoncell spielen, aber nicht stimmen pp.

These are perhaps the most crucial words of this letter. It has been
shown to what extent Goethe's comprehension of language as a
material medium, to be moulded and fashioned as the sculptor
moulds and fashions his clay, was fructified by the theory of
knowledge to be expounded in Herder's *Plastik,* which formulates
the discovery of the time that tactile sensations are essential to
visual perception and indeed form the basis of all our later
'Ge-fühle' and 'Be-griffe', in their most differentiated form.[24] It has
also been shown that Goethe's insight into the material character
of the verbal medium was inspired to an even greater degree by
Herder's description, at the beginning of the sixth section of the
third *Fragment,* of the task confronting the modern poet.[25] Out of
personal touch with his readers, the modern poet is denied the aid
of bodily expression through which the bard of old could communicate his feeling to his audience. The expression of his face,
the movement of his arms, the tears in his eyes, do not find their
way on to the printed page. In the place of his own body and its
natural eloquence, the modern poet is forced to create a living
body of words, artificial, it is true, but no less expressive:

Du musst den ganzen Ton deiner Empfindung in dem Perioden, in der Lenkung und Bindung der Wörter ausdrücken: du musst ein Gemälde hinzeichnen, dass dies selbst zur Einbildung des andern ohne deine Beihülfe spreche, sie erfülle, und durch sie sich zum Herzen grabe: du musst Einfalt und Reichthum, Stärke und Kolorit der Sprache in deiner Gewalt haben, um das durch sie zu bewürken, was du durch die Sprache des Tons und der Geberden erreichen willst – wie sehr klebt hier alles am Ausdrucke: nicht in einzelnen Worten, sondern in jedem Theile, im Fortgange derselben und im Ganzen.[26]

There can be no doubt but that these words made a powerful imprint on the young poet's mind; but we must not forget that the fountainhead of the whole conception of language as the physical body of inspiration is Plato's myth of the incarnation of the soul which lies at the back of Herder's theory of poetry and informed the very texture of Goethe's experiencing, steeped as he then was in his 'friend and brother', Socrates.

Besides, poet that he was, Goethe knew more about the power of his own verbal medium and, for that matter, any artistic medium than his teacher Herder. In the passage just quoted from, Herder argues with power and acumen that the poet can only communicate his personal feelings and affections by transmuting them into the expressive forms of which his medium is capable. When Goethe writes: 'ich finde, dass jeder Künstler, so lang seine Hände nicht plastisch arbeiten, nichts ist', he is telling us this and more. And once again, he is telling us more through the form of his statement. For he does not speak of the artist using his hands plastically. Rather does he speak of hands working plastically, by themselves as it were. It is not for nothing that the hands are the logical and grammatical subject of the clause: they have become the dominant agents in the commerce between 'inner' and 'outer'. How far the young poet has moved from the iron hand of his Götz! The artist's hands, 'those living hands which true hands should be', are more, even, than skilled executors of the mind's intention. They are possessed of their own wisdom, derived from the tactile exploration of their medium, a bodily communion which taps hidden veins of experience. The mind, it is true, guides the hand; the hand, in turn, informs the mind with its wisdom, modifying, magnifying and transforming the vision as it is being articulated.

And as the hands take over from the artist's mind, so with the feet of the charioteer's horses:

Wenn du kühn im Wagen stehst, und vier neue Pferde wild unordentlich sich an deinen Zügeln bäumen, du ihre Kraft lenkst, den

austretenden herbei, den aufbäumenden hinabpeitschest, und jagst
und lenkst, und wendest, peitschest, hältst, und wieder ausjagst, bis
alle sechzehn Füsse in einem Takt ans Ziel tragen . . .

Again we must attend to the form of this sentence, to its syntax
and rhythm. The 'du', logical and grammatical subject of the
whole period which dominates the earlier phases of the activity
Goethe is describing, eventually altogether disappears. It is not
even there as an object. The horses' feet, at the end, become the
grammatical subject, just as they emerge as the carrying force of
this multifarious activity. And it is only when their activity
becomes autonomous that the rhythm, syncopated and obstreperous at first, begins to flow and comes to express the oneness
of mental and physical drives moving in unison in the creative
act: 'in **einem** Takt'. This is 'Meisterschaft, *epikratein,* Virtuosität',
and through the rhythmic force of Goethe's language, through the
clash of stresses and their gradual resolution, we feel his growing
mastery as we follow his words.

It is such sure knowledge of the creative feedback from the
physical to the mental pole of experiencing, from medium to
mind, which distinguishes the poet from the critic. There is some
interesting evidence to show how, in the last analysis, Herder
missed this vital point. In *Fragmente* III, 6, just before he formulates his tenet that thought and expression cleave to one
another in the same fashion in which Plato's soul cleaves to the
body in which it is incarnated, Herder considers a number of
other analogies expressing inseparable closeness. In this connexion
he mentions 'Shakespears Freundinnen', that is, Helena and
Hermia in *A Midsummer Night's Dream*, of which he was translating
portions at that very time. There can be no question but that he
was acquainted with the speech of Theseus in Act V Scene 1:

> The lunatic, the lover, and the poet,
> Are of imagination all compact.
>   . . .
> The poet's eye, in a fine frenzy rolling,
> Doth glance from heaven to earth, from earth to heaven;
> And as imagination bodies forth
> The forms of things unknown, the poet's pen
> Turns them to shapes, and gives to airy nothing
> A local habitation and a name.

One would have thought that Herder either found, or recognised,
in this speech, his own theory of poetic language as in a nutshell:
here is his notion of the creative thought or feeling 'bodying itself

forth'; here is his notion that the poet's pen transmutes the nascent forms of feeling and vision into tangible shapes. But it appears that he was blind to the most exciting part of Shakespeare's message – the concretion born of the artist's contact with his medium which enables his pen to give 'to airy nothing/ A local habitation and a name'. This is the very insight Goethe formulates time and again in his letter, most graphically when he writes 'dass jeder Künstler, so lang **seine Hände nicht plastisch arbeiten,** nichts ist.' In *Aelteste Urkunde des Menschengeschlechts,* written in 1776, Herder discusses love and marriage as aspects of primaeval life. In this context he quotes part of Theseus's speech as follows:

> the lovers eye in a fine frenzy rolling
> doth glance from heav'n to earth, from earth to heav'n
> and as imagination bodies forth
> the forms of things unknown, the lover's eye
> turns them to shape and gives to aiery nothing
> a local habitation and a name.[27]

Edna Purdie thinks that this travesty was committed deliberately.[28] This is most likely since, in *Kalligone,* written at about 1800, he quotes the correct text in Schlegel's translation.[29]

Not only does Herder miss the most thrilling part of Shakespeare's message, that is to say, the disciplining and concretising feedback from the artist's medium to his vision. Both here as well as in his handling of Plato's myth of incarnation, he reduces the more differentiated, culturally conditioned phenomenon to its primitive form, reverting from the *poet's* imagination and the *poet's* pen to the lover's imagination and the lover's eye in the one case, and in the other, from Plato's sophisticated notion of a *man's* sublimated experience of pregnancy to a woman's physical experience of child-bearing. Both instances point up the limitations inherent in the very nature of Herder's brilliance: his heavy reliance on the power of analogy – 'Was wir wissen, wissen wir nur aus Analogie'[30] – and his habit of pressing, both here and elsewhere, towards the source – the *Ursprung* – of later cultural phenomena, here lead him to the blurring of distinctions which are significant. If we press analogies too far, Goethe knows, 'so fällt alles identisch zusammen.'[31]

Goethe, on the other hand, in his letter to his mentor discovers the fructifying force of medium, and he implements what he has discovered through the very form of his language. In the manner no less than in the matter of this letter, we witness a growing together, on the deepest level, of what but a few months earlier had been dissociated. We recall how, in September 1771, in his speech in honour of Shakespeare, he had written: 'Ich sprang in die freye Lufft, und fühlte erst dass ich Hände und Füsse hatte.' This statement turned out to be premature. For it to become true, he had to write his *Geschichte Gottfriedens von Berlichingen mit der eisernen Hand dramatisirt,* and to transcend dissociation by creating a relentless image of touch-impairment and progressive mutilation. Now he has done with it. He feels himself a torso no more. He has a body, hands and feet, and he knows them to be at one with the mind in all manner of creative mastery. It is only in such oneness of head, heart and hand, of body and mind, as he now experienced, that Goethe was able to conceive the force which was to become, and remain, the guiding power of his art and life – the force of creative Eros.

IV

Goethe's letter to Herder saw the conception of a new, creative mode of being; the 'Künstlergedichte' which began to pour out of Goethe in 1773 announce the birth of what was then conceived. For in these poems it is that the mutilated hand of Götz is finally born into life. And a jubilant birth it is. The human hand, a cypher of dissociation only a year earlier, has become the symbol of an ultimate oneness of the mental and physical aspects of the psyche and of the continuance of such oneness in the outer world. Gone is that negation of living touch, the iron hand, clumsy minister of a vision itself conceived in the isolation of inwardness. There is scarcely a poem belonging to this group, and not a single one that touches upon the central processes of art-making, which does not extol the living hand. It is the creative hand which Goethe now exalts or, rather, the most sensitive portion of the most creative of hands: the artist's fingertips, intelligent informers of his mind, alive to sensation from within and to touch from without, transmitting the mind's messages to its physical medium and in turn informing it with the insights derived from living contact with that source. And now the young poet exults in the slow circulation of artistic vision from the outward object that may have sparked it off, through the eye, through the heart and through the fingertips onto canvas or into clay and back from there to the fingertips, to heart and mind and eye. But now nothing is lost 'auf dem langen Wege, aus dem Auge durch den Arm in den Pinsel'.[32] On the contrary, everything is gained; body, felt-through form, and that uniqueness of experience and that concreteness in its articulation by which a work of art becomes singularly expressive of universal feeling imports.

The question has sometimes been asked why Goethe, in this group of poems, should so frequently have chosen to cast himself in the role of the sculptor or painter, rather than in that of the poet. It has been suggested that he did so because he found it easier to objectify and to communicate his insights into his own art in terms of a fellow art from which he had a modicum of distance and that, moreover, the would-be painter in him derived some clandestine gratification from such projection.[33] The previous section of this chapter, however, should have made it clear that these were not the true reasons. Goethe *had* to speak in terms of an art which uses a physical medium in order to give expression to his newly made discovery of the bodiliness of being: the bodiliness of his own, immaterial, medium of words on the one hand, and, on the other, the bodiliness of the poet's response to this, his medium in the creative act. More than forty years later, weary of the classicistic will towards plasticity of form and drawn towards new horizons, the poet could say:

Mag der Grieche seinen Ton
Zu Gestalten drücken,
An der eignen Hände Sohn
Steigern sein Entzücken;

Aber uns ist wonnereich
In den Euphrat greifen,
Und im flüssgen Element
Hin und wider schweifen.[34]

But these lines were written on the threshold of old age, and old age, according to Goethe, is 'stufenweises Zurücktreten aus der Erscheinung';[35] it is a time when words, for Goethe, had become 'eher Versteck als Leib seines Geistes'.[36] Now, thrilling to the discovery that language is body and, moreover, a kind of natural extension of his own bodiliness, to be fashioned and moulded as the sculptor fashions and moulds his clay, he has qualified to enter upon his long Greek apprenticeship. He delights in kneading the shape of his sentences, in feeling the tackiness of his words, as it were, and he delights in speaking of his very own, poetic experience under the image of the plastic arts. And the insight that 'dreingreifen, packen ist das Wesen jeder Meisterschaft' reverberates no less in a poem directly concerned with his language than in those extolling the tangible materials of the formative arts. How can the poet discover the poetic potential of his language, the short poem *Sprache* asks – by looking on, inactively? Or by theorising about it? 'Greif milde drein', 'fass' an zum Siege': let the poet seize his language and grapple with it and he will uncover its riches even as the sculptor, grappling with his block of stone, uncovers the forms that are hidden in its depth.

'If poetry comes not as naturally as leaves to a tree, it had better not come at all,' so Keats wrote to J. Taylor in 1818.[37] It would be difficult to capture the freshness and the utterly unpremeditated spontaneity of these poems more precisely than does this statement by a fellow poet, of much the same age as the young Goethe himself. They simply *had* to come, and they came as naturally and as artlessly (which is not to say formlessly) as young leaves in springtime. They are carried by such a surge of generalised vitality that it is hard to draw the line between physical and mental creativity on the one hand, and between the physical and the mental components in either of these: they run fluid into one another. Sensation and sensibility, feeling and formative impulse are galvanised into inner affinity; they seek, seize and transform one another. No power remains unawakened, none remains separate. Creativity informs every fibre of the poet's being.

This creative fusion and transmutation of what was dead while it was separate is accomplished before our eyes in the poem *An Kenner und Liebhaber*, as perfect an epigraph for *Werther* as any.

> Was frommt die glühende Natur
> An deinem Busen dir,
> Was hilft dich das Gebildete
> Der Kunst rings um dich her,
> Wenn liebevolle Schöpferkraft
> Nicht deine Seele füllt
> Und in den Fingerspitzen dir
> Nicht wieder bildend wird.

The whole splendour of creation, of nature and of art, remains unavailing and extraneous unless their lines converge in a glowing inner centre of creativeness. However possessively clutched to his bosom, 'die glühende Natur', *natura naturans*, remains inaccessible to a Werther (and how familiar from Werther's lips is the phrase 'an deinem Busen'!); however greedily appropriated, 'das Gebildete der Kunst', the highest products of nature working through man, in their formedness exclude a Werther from themselves (and again, how familiar the 'rings um dich her' is to the reader of Goethe's novel!). To this barren separateness the poet has given expression in the most telling manner. He has given over to each

of the twin forces, art and nature, a separate sentence, each
complete, each constructed and modulated in the identical
fashion with the other one, both running alongside one another
yet never touching, like two electrical wires that remain disconnected. Once the separate forces fuse, as they do in the words
'liebevolle Schöpferkraft', the creative current, like the line of the
sentence, streams irresistibly from soul to fingertips into the
nascent forms emerging from such a union.

In *Lied des physiognomischen Zeichners*, it is the threefold use of the
word 'Sinn' which drives home the completeness of the union
between the mental and the physical aspects of experiencing in a
state of heightened creative awareness.

> O dass die innre Schöpfungskraft
> Durch meinen Sinn erschölle,
> Dass eine Bildung voller Saft
> Aus meinen Fingern quölle!
> Ich zittre nur, ich stottre nur,
> Ich kann es doch nicht lassen,
> Ich fühl', ich kenne dich, Natur,
> Und so muss ich dich fassen.
> Wenn ich bedenk', wie manches Jahr
> Sich schon mein Sinn erschliesset,
> Wie er, wo dürre Heide war,
> Jetzt Freudenquell geniesset,
> Da ahnd' ich ganz, Natur, nach dir,
> Dich frei und lieb zu fühlen,
> Ein lust'ger Springbrunn wirst du mir
> Aus tausend Röhren spielen,
> Wirst alle deine Kräfte mir
> In meinem Sinn erheitern
> Und dieses eigne Dasein hier
> Zur Ewigkeit erweitern.

Sinn is the most comprehensive of terms, denoting not only the
organs of sensory perception, but the sense or meaning we perceive and even the mind, taken as a whole. Goethe's use of it here,
at three decisive points in the poem, signifies that in the creative
state the total psychophysical area is vitalised and, so to speak,
drawn into the magnetic orbit: there is no barren place. This
permeation of the entire person by creativeness gives rise to an
experience of inner space, of opening horizons. And indeed, a
sense of inner expansion, first evoked by the 'erschölle' at the end
of the second line, with its suggestion of echoing spaces, pervades
the poem in growing measure: the words 'erschliessen', 'erheitern'
and 'erweitern', all with the identical prefix signifying disclosure

and opening up, tell their own tale. The last four lines of the poem
show a Goethe at the end of one phase of his development and
glimpsing the beginning of another, longer phase. They call to
mind his slightly anguished demand in the letter to Herder, just
after his declaration that all his multifarious activities must
become one: 'Ich mögte beten, wie Moses im Koran: "Herr mache
mir Raum in meiner engen Brust." '38 The young man's prayer
has now been granted. Creativeness has brought with it the
experience of inner space. At the same time, the delighted discovery that creativeness unlocks the bounds of self and time is but
the first glimpse of a recognition which will form the cornerstone
of the mighty artifice of Goethe's life, of his scientific thinking and
practical activities as much as of his poetry: the recognition which
the eighty-year-old Goethe, in the poem Vermächtnis, was to com-
pact into the formula: 'Der Augenblick ist Ewigkeit.' Such eternity, however, as the poet was to experience in his maturity and
old age, was bought at the price of relentless discipline and
renunciation of immediacy. Here, at the first burgeoning of
genius, the word 'Ewigkeit' is devoid of any such associations. It
betokens a joyous sense of release and of a growing-space which,
as yet, know of no limits.

It is the utter simplicity and naturalness with which the
business of art-making is presented in these poems which sends the
mind back, time and time again, to Keats' dictum. And indeed,
as Keats likens poetry to the burgeoning of a tree, so, throughout
this group of poems, the making of art, the maker and his final
product are all associated with images drawn from plant and
animal life. In Der Adler und die Taube the poet speaks of himself
as an 'Adlerjüngling'; he feels failure physically as if he had had
'die Schwingkraft weggeschnitten', just as the young artist in
Künstlers Apotheose experiences his creative difficulties as a physical
impotence:

> Und wenn ich dann nicht weiter kann,
> Steh' ich wie ein genestelter Mann.

The work of art itself is envisaged as a dove, or alternatively as a
flower in the poet's garden. When, in Lied des physiognomischen
Zeichners, the poet prays

> Dass eine Bildung voller Saft
> Aus meinen Fingern quölle!

we think of such 'Bildung' as of some juicy plant with sap rising
in it. And some similar association suggests itself in the marvellous
upward thrust of the lines from Kenner und Künstler:

> Wo ist der Urquell der Natur,
> Daraus ich schöpfend
> Himmel fühl' und Leben
> In die Fingerspitzen empor . . .

But the physical aspect of artistic creation is borne in on us more forcefully than by its imagistic associations with bird and sap and plant. It is impossible to overlook the intertwining, throughout these poems, of the aesthetic and biological spheres of *human* experiencing, of art-making and love-making, of creation and procreation; using these words to encompass both, the sex act and the rearing and caring for what has been thus engendered. In *Kenner und Künstler* the identity of the two modes of creativity is apodeictically stated and confirmed through the single pronoun which serves to link both spheres:

> Dass ich mit Göttersinn
> Und Menschenhand
> Vermög' zu bilden,
> Was bei meinem Weib
> Ich animalisch kann und muss . . .

In *Des Künstlers Erdewallen*, too, art and love are inseparably interwoven, for all the realism with which the poet portrays the blessings of domesticity in an artist's life. The daily grind of the struggling young artist is real enough; nevertheless the Muse reminds him that he needs the chores of living, the 'hacken und graben' and 'Erde . . . Essen, Lieb' und Schlaf' just as much as he needs tranquillity and inspiration. And indeed, she only reminds the artist of what we have seen for ourselves. For it is the painter's thought of his loved ones, his 'Gutes Weib' and his 'Köstliche Kleinen', still peacefully asleep, that leads to the rejuvenating awareness of the sunrise and thence, by an effortless transition, to his own art. As he stands by the window and watches the break of day, the painter says: 'Und dieses Herz fühlt wieder jugendlich'; a few lines further on, the sight of his painting elicits an almost identical response. The presence of his goddess 'Überdrängt mich wie erstes Jugendglück'. In the very next line, such easy blending of the natural sphere and the domain of art leads to a crucial statement in which every verbal juxtaposition testifies to the fact that the creative and the erotic mode of experiencing have become one:

> Die ich in Seel' und Sinn, himmlische Gestalt,
> Dich umfasse mit Bräutigams Gewalt . . .

whilst the impassioned lines that follow –

> Wo mein Pinsel dich berührt, bist du mein,
> Du bist ich, bist mehr als ich, ich bin dein,
> Uranfängliche Schönheit, Königin der Welt!

arrest our attention, not only because of their obvious eroticism, but because of the theory of art they imply: the 'uranfängliche Schönheit', so far from being 'Platonic', a mental image of the painter's ideal *prior* to its execution as the 'ur' would imply, in fact is the *end*-result engendered by the incandescing contact with his medium! From such contact there ensues a vision the final perfection of which far transcends anything the artist might have conceived in the inwardness of his mind. The poet here touches upon the mystery of all creation, spiritual as well as biological, a mystery he was to sum up many years later in the words:

> Eine geistige Form wird aber keineswegs verkürzt, wenn sie in der Erscheinung hervortritt, vorausgesetzt, dass ihr Hervortreten eine wahre Zeugung, eine wahre Fortpflanzung sei. Das Gezeugte ist nicht geringer als das Zeugende, ja es ist der Vorteil lebendiger Zeugung, dass das Gezeugte vortrefflicher sein kann als das Zeugende.[39]

Again, passionate concern for both, his children and his picture, his physical as well as his artistic progeny is mingled in the young painter's words:

> Du wohnst bei mir, Urquell der Natur,
> Leben und Freude der Kreatur!

Already in *Kenner und Künstler*, it may have been noticed, the poet has used the words 'Urquell der Natur' with the same double signification – that is to say, as the *common* spring of biological and artistic creativity.

The interlacing of the biological, erotic sphere and the domain of art is even more marked in *Anekdote unsrer Tage*. It determines the very form of a poem which sets out side by side two seemingly disparate events, one erotic and the other one artistic, and relates them in a strictly parallel fashion. The speaker leads his friend first to his girl and then to a picture gallery. The identity of the feeling-structure exhibited in both these situations is never spelt out; but it is demonstrated by the identity of the speaker's response in both instances and, for that matter, by the unwavering negative reaction on the part of his friend. As he sees his 'Maidel jung', the speaker of the poem exclaims:

> Und um mich war's gar bald getan,
> Die Sinnen gingen mir über.

In the art gallery, 'Voll Menschenglut und Geistes', he experiences a similar if enhanced reaction:

> Mir wird's da gleich, ich weiss nicht wie,
> Mein ganzes Herz zerreisst es.

Finally, profoundly stirred as he is by the works of art before him – he calls them 'meine Göttersöhne' – he expresses the poignancy of their impact in the words:

> Mein Busen war so voll und bang,
> Von hundert Welten trächtig.

The speaker's reactions to two separate situations are not only the same in kind: together they constitute the progressive phases of one poignantly sensual response which is sparked off by the sight of the beloved and then fanned into full flame by the experience of art. It is surely significant that the youth prays that the painter of the pictures which have moved him thus be rewarded by 'die allerschönste Braut', and that his own excitement, the excitement of conception, presently issues in the physical act of throwing himself 'in süsse Liebesbanden'.

If the excitement vouchsafed by the perception of art evinces a predominantly feminine character – the words 'zerreissen' and 'trächtig' tell us so – the excitement aroused in the artist by the actual handling of his medium is predominantly male. Once we are alive to the depth and constancy of the overlap between the artistic and erotic spheres, our eyes become sharpened to this significance in a great many of Goethe's images. The *Hand*, the *Fingerspitzen* into which the artist feels 'Himmel und Leben . . . empor', from which new life *quillt, liebevoll*; the *Pinsel*, the *Griffel*, the *Kohle* which 'wird Gewehr': – all these are clearly phallic symbols, and their recurrence in an aesthetic context shows how charged with erotic energy the creative process has become in this phase of the poet's career. It is into such perspectives that the poem *Sprache* needs to be placed, with its complementary metaphors of 'der Urne Bauch' and 'das Schwert'. The body of language releases in the artist what is in effect a characteristically masculine excitement. His sword penetrates into the fertile depths of his linguistic medium. No better illustration could be found than this poem for S. Alexander's thesis that 'not parthenogenesis but bisexual creation is the true analogy for the creative process.'[40]

Naturally the temptation arises to ask whether this new dynamism in its entirety springs from the discovery of the bodiliness of language or whether, perhaps, it has roots in some decisive erotic experience on the part of the young poet. I shall not attempt to go over biographical facts which might conceivably throw some light on this question. On the contrary, the 'Künstlergedichte' of this very young man give us so complex an insight into the vagaries of the creative household as to make us wary of asking such a question at all. The most interesting glimpse into the interrelation between life-experience and an art itself so heavily charged with erotic energy is perhaps furnished by *Künstlers Morgenlied*, and to this poem we now turn.

V

From the beginning this poem shares with the others of its vintage the unselfconscious mingling of the mental and physical spheres, of art and nature, and the feeling that both represent *one* source of vivification. This parity is brought out beautifully in the second stanza:

> Wenn morgends mich die Sonne weckt,
> Warm froh ich schau umher,
> Steht rings ihr ewig Lebenden
> In heil'gem Morgenglanz.

In the same breath the speaker worships the rise of the young day and the statues of antiquity; and such sturdy balance between mental and physical experience is confirmed, time and again, by the coupling of words such as *warm* and *froh, ewig* and *Lebende, heilig* and *Morgenglanz*. The boundaries between the mental and the physical realms, and indeed between art and reality, become ever more blurred as the speaker, performing his sacred rites to the text of Homer, loses himself and all consciousness that he is in the presence of art, and rapturously merges his identity with that of his hero. He himself is one in the crowd of Patroclus's friends; he is swept into battle with them and with them he fights for the dead body of his idol: 'Ich dränge mich hinan, hinan'.

In view of such fluidity, the reader might well surmise that the second portion of the poem altogether relinquishes the realm of art to tell us something of the human side of life in a studio. For here a love relationship moves to the fore, and it seems to be the shift of consciousness to the sphere of personal experience which imbues the concluding stanzas of the poem with their incomparable note of tender, blissful and impudent triumph. Can such a triumph be explained by anything but the reality, actual or recollected, of a fulfilled love relationship? Let us see what the poem tells us.

The excitement of the battle has ebbed away and, calmed by the finality of Patroclus's death and the thought of his funeral rites, the speaker comes back to himself, to his own life and its familiar setting. Presently his gaze falls upon the picture of his beloved before him:

> Und find' ich mich zurück hierher,
> Empfängst du, Liebe, mich,
> Mein Mädchen! Ach, im Bilde nur,
> Und so im Bilde warm.

True, this is a reminiscence, but reminiscence with a touch of warm reality lingering about it still: for the girl's picture – a picture he himself has painted, as becomes clear from the following stanza – has captured the warmth of her response to him and made it available to him even now. The next lines, the most revealing of lines for the understanding of an artist's mentality, tell us how this picture came into being. The speaker recalls the occasion when his beloved lay next to him, he and she full of desire:

> Ach, wie du ruhtest neben mir,
> Mich schmachtetst liebend an,
> Und mir's vom Aug' durchs Herz hindurch
> In'n Griffel schmachtete —

With a magical immediacy these words illuminate a crucial event: the transmutation of a life response into an art response, of a physical passion into what Samuel Alexander calls a 'formal passion'. As the girl languishes for her companion, and no doubt he for her, a switch takes place in his consciousness, the switch which was to be matchlessly described some hundred and thirty years later by Edward Bullough.[41] It is a mental shift from being part of the immediate practical situation, from being driven by mounting desire to bring it to a head and thus to resolve its stresses, to perceiving the girl and her response to him with a new kind of awareness. The young artist has disengaged the force of his beloved's longing from his personal affections, redirecting it towards an altogether different context and making it available for his creative impulse. We are not told what occasioned the switch of attention which all of a sudden made the young man reach out for his 'Griffel'. Perhaps it was a fleeting perfection in the girl's pose or some accidental effect of light and colour which struck his eye and made his excitement jump a groove, as it were, from his beloved back to his preoccupation with the medium of his art and the technical problems presented by it. However that may be, suddenly the force of the girl's desire, instead of releasing an answering desire in him and thus issuing in the physical consummation of their love, becomes diverted on impact. It flows 'vom Aug' durchs Herz hindurch', not into his loins but into his draughtman's 'Griffel'. [42] This is not to say that his response has taken on the objective tinge of the outside observer, the voyeur. Nothing could be further from the truth. The directness of the phallic symbolism, the sensual passion of the following lines and the tremendous emotional release evinced by the concluding stanzas forbid such an interpretation, as indeed do the unity and sweep of the lines we are examining. The girl's longing continues to communicate itself to him in the urgency of an artistic excitement itself longing to overflow into expression in a bodily medium, and all the continuity and immediacy of this experience is compacted into the last two lines of the stanza:

> Und mir's vom Aug' durchs Herz hindurch
> In'n Griffel schmachtete —

The young artist is, and remains, engrossed in his beloved and in sensitive rapport with her mood. At the same time, his engrossment has undergone a change of direction and quality, a transmutation which we can virtually grasp in the metamorphosis the word 'schmachtete' has undergone. It is the feeling or idea of her passion which he now perceives and which imparts itself to his 'Griffel'. Her *Schmachten* has sparked off in him a graphic vision which is now in the process of being evolved, directing every touch and movement of his hand, and which in its turn is being modified and informed by the exploration, past and present, of the medium he is handling. This medium – style and slate in the case of the artist who is speaking here and words in the case of the poet who is telling us of his own creational processes through the symbolism of graphic art – this medium now has *become* the beloved and the languishing body of the beloved.[43] The excitement of the artist has been lifted bodily, as it were, out of one context to become operative in another. And it is in this context that it finds its consummation as is, I think, indicated by the eloquent dash that ends the stanza.

In its entirety, the longing of the young artist has become transferred from the person of his beloved next to him to the feel and touch of his material, and it is the impregnating excitement derived from this new contact which fructifies, feeds and formulates his nascent conception.

In this creative encounter, the artist is both male and female. We know it from the operative word 'Griffel'. For *Griffel* in German, like *style* in English, denotes not only the sharp, pointed, and obviously phallic tool with which the artist is impregnating his vision. It also has a botanical meaning no doubt familiar to the young Goethe, denoting the protruding part of the female organ of plants which receives the pollen in impregnation. *Griffel* signifies both the impregnating force of the material medium and the result of such an impregnation – the artistic conception.[44] Could the unity of the mental and the material aspects of creative process, and indeed its bisexual character be more compactly conveyed?

Unless this transference of passion to a new arena is noted, it is tempting to read the following stanza as a straightforward statement of physical consummation:

> Wie ich an Aug' und Wange mich
> Und Mund mich weidete,
> Und mir's im Busen jung und frisch
> Wie einer Gottheit war!

Placed, however, as these lines are in an unequivocally aesthetic context, we have no warrant to interpret them as signifying biological fulfilment. On the contrary, we should regard them as evidence of the completeness with which an initial biological drive, when transferred to another, non-biological sphere, may be satisfied in this, its sublimated activity. The completeness of the fulfilment that stems from the gratification of the formative impulse becomes apparent from the concluding stanzas of the poem. For here the speaker's mind returns from the recollection of the lovers' tryst that ended in a picture, back to that picture and to the promise it holds for the future. The voice that speaks is the jubilant voice of love triumphant. The release and the confidence reflected in these lines are total. The speaker ranges over the whole gamut of emotions, from the most exalted to the most earthy; his beloved will be his ideal, the virgin with the holy infant at her breast, then a nymph he chases, little tail up, and finally his Aphrodite with whom he will lie, defiant of the envy of the gods. This is the authentic voice of fulfilment. But if we interpret it as physical fulfilment within the context of an actual love relationship, we have missed the most exciting part of the message. The love situation, in this poem, has merely provided what Gottfried Benn calls 'einen dumpfen schöpferischen Keim, eine psychische Materie'[45] for the artist, nothing more. So far as the poet tells us, there is no clear evidence of a physical consummation; and certainly it is not any physical consummation which leads to the exuberant sense of fulfilment at the end of the poem. On the contrary. That fulfilment, described in a series of images which designate an ever more intimate fusion of the exaltedly spiritual and the earthy, reflects the *withdrawal* of energy from the love situation and the fusion of vision and medium in the artistic act.

Is *Künstlers Morgenlied*, then, correctly described as a love poem? The answer is, I believe, yes. In the first instance, it is a love poem in the simple sense that a considerable portion of it is inspired by, and addressed to, a young girl to whom the speaker stands in an erotically charged relationship. But to rest one's explanation here would not account for the fact that the poem is called *Künstlers Morgenlied*: it is also a dawn song by an artist, that is to say by one who is freshly in love with the pagan splendour of bodiliness and who experiences it first in the art of Greece and then, by a marvellously fluid transition, in relation to his own medium. The more powerful erotic overtones stem from the speaker's artistic excitement whence they overflow, attaching themselves to the overt subject-matter of the poem and endowing it with its resonance.

In fact, *Künstlers Morgenlied* is a love poem in much the same sense in which the culminating poem of the whole group, *Des Künstlers Erdewallen*, may be so called. Here, the overt object of the artist's passion and its underlying cause coincide. In the most rapturous lines, easily the finest lines of the whole cluster of poems, the painter addresses Venus Urania thus:

> Meine Göttin, deiner Gegenwart Blick
> Überdrängt mich wie erstes Jugendglück,
> Die ich in Seel' und Sinn, himmlische Gestalt,
> Dich umfasse mit Bräutigams Gewalt.
> Wo mein Pinsel dich berührt, bist du mein,
> Du bist ich, bist mehr als ich, ich bin dein,
> Uranfängliche Schönheit, Königin der Welt!

But then, who is Venus Urania, if not the principle of pure beauty in its mythological embodiment? Venus Urania, the 'Heavenly Aphrodite', figures in Plato's *Symposium* as well as in the *Symposium* of Xenophon. In both she is contradistinguished from the common Aphrodite, and in Plato's dialogue she is introduced at an all-important point of the argument, at the very place where Socrates begins to introduce the notion of love as a morally indeterminate force with a plurality of characters and referents.

'We all know,' Pausanias argues,

> that Aphrodite is inseparably linked with Love. If there were a single Aphrodite there would be a single Love, but as there are two Aphrodites, it follows that there must be two Loves as well. Now what are the two Aphrodites? One is the elder and is the daughter of Uranus and had no mother; her we call Heavenly Aphrodite. The other is younger, the child of Zeus and Dione, and is called Common Aphrodite. It follows that the Love which is the partner of the latter should be called Common Love and the other Heavenly Love.[46]

Translating the language of myth into a modern aesthetic idiom, we might say, with Samuel Alexander, that the heavenly Love inspired by Venus Urania is that 'formal passion' which arises in the process of evolving an artistic conception in a given artistic medium;[47] that is to say, a passion generated by the artistic process itself and directed towards it, to the exclusion of any external referent. Thus, in extolling Venus Urania, the speaker, in *Des Künstlers Erdewallen*, is extolling nothing outside the creative process of which, as we saw earlier on in this chapter, the 'uranfängliche Schönheit' is paradoxically the end-product. The genesis of the work of art has become its overt, and indeed its dominant theme. Accordingly, the words with which, at the end of the poem, the Muse comforts the harassed young artist suggest that his works, from now on, will be instinct with the rapture that went into their making and thus speak of themselves, whatever their ostensible subject:

> Hast Zeit genug, dich zu ergötzen
> An dir selbst und an jedem Bild,
> Das liebevoll aus deinem Pinsel quillt.

Could it be that again it was Socrates who opened the young poet's eyes to the ubiquity of creative Eros and helped him interpret the confusing experiences upon which he was happening as he went about exploring his inner situation in the 'Künstlergedichte'? The experience, for instance, that love, initially directed towards an external object, may metamorphose into the pure passion of the artist for the bodiliness of the medium which has begun to invade his imagination and his emotion, with the result

that the girl next to him is left high and dry?[48] Or the converse
experience that the erotic excitement engendered by the contact
with his artistic medium may attach itself to some outside
referent, such as the 'Maidel jung' in *Anekdote unsrer Tage*,
henceforth to be understood as originating from this vicarious if
respectable source? Certainly many of these poems give one the
impression that the young poet is breaking new ground. He does
not tell us in them what he knew before; it is the poems themselves which confront him with discoveries made, and understood,
in the act of writing:[49] and no single discovery is re-iterated as
urgently as that of the fluid boundaries between life-experience
and art-experience and of the mysterious sublimations and sub-
stitutions that take place in the creative act.

The theoretical writings of this period too are fraught with the
same preoccupation: already in the review of Sulzer's *Die Schönen
Künste*, published in December 1772, Goethe writes:

> Denn um den Künstler allein ist es zu tun, dass der keine Seligkeit des
> Lebens fühlt als in seiner Kunst, dass, in sein Instrument versunken,
> er mit allen seinen Empfindungen und Kräften da lebt. Am gaffenden
> Publikum, ob das, wenn's ausgegafft hat, sich Rechenschaft geben
> kann, warum es gaffte, oder nicht, was liegt an dem?[50]

These lines evince a lively awareness of the fact that the private
import a work of art has for the artist, an import that is
inseparable from the erotic engrossment experienced in the creative act, may be a very different thing indeed from the public
import it assumes in the eyes of the 'gaffenden Publikum',[51] and
at times barely discernible in it. The poet's imagination circles
even more insistently around this complex of problems in the
essays published under the title *Aus Goethes Brieftasche*, together
with some of the most erotically labile of the 'Künstlergedichte',
for example *Anekdote unsrer Tage*, *Künstlers Morgenlied* and *Kenner und
Künstler*. In *Nach Falconet und über Falconet* we read:

> Die Welt liegt vor ihm [dem Künstler], möcht ich sagen, wie vor
> ihrem Schöpfer, der in dem Augenblick, da er sich des Geschaffnen
> freut, **auch alle die Harmonien geniesst, durch die er sie her-
> vorbrachte und in denen sie besteht.**[52]

And, in a more earthy vein:

> Was der Künstler nicht geliebt hat, nicht liebt, soll er nicht schildern,
> kann er nicht schildern. Ihr findet Rubensens Weiber zu fleischig! ich

sage euch, es waren seine Weiber, und hätt er Himmel und Hölle, Luft, Erd und Meer mit Idealen bevölkert, so wäre er ein schlechter Ehmann gewesen, und es wäre nie kräftiges Fleisch von seinem Fleisch und Bein von seinem Bein geworden.[53]

What a splendidly outrageous reversal of all accepted aesthetic priorities! So far from making the vigour and vitality of Rubens's art contingent upon the quality of his life-experience, the young poet deduces the wholesomeness of the painter's fleshly progeny from the vigour and vitality of his artistic love affairs! The love which Goethe demands as the prerequisite of art is the pure love of the artist;[54] and the biblically flavoured 'ich sage euch, es waren seine Weiber' is not a reference to the pleasurable hours the painter may have spent with his models, but solely to the erotically saturated interpenetration of medium and vision in the creative act. And when he writes, earlier in the same essay:

Ein grosser Maler wie der andre lockt durch grosse und kleine empfundne Naturzüge den Zuschauer, dass er glauben soll, er sei in die Zeiten der vorgestellten Geschichte entrückt, und wird nur in die Vorstellungsart, in das Gefühl des Malers versetzt,

adding:

und was kann er im Grunde verlangen, als dass ihm Geschichte der Menschheit mit und zu wahrer menschlicher Teilnehmung hingezaubert werde?[55]

– what else is he saying but what he has been formulating all along, in the 'Künstlergedichte' as well as in these theoretical pronouncements: that what the recipient gets out of the work of art is congruent, but not identical with what the artist himself has put into it? That it is part of the complicated commerce of art that the onlooker or reader receives imports of the nature and origin of which he knows precious little and that none the less they are meaningful communications, '**mit und zu** wahrer menschlicher Teilnehmung'? That, so to speak, he receives these communications in a different currency from the one in which they were issued?

It is remarkable how little Goethe's notions on this tricky question were to change in the course of his long life; testimony, surely, of the finality with which his artistic character was crystallising, once and for all, during these crucial months and years. Leaving chronology aside for a moment, let us consider two more statements in evidence of this continuity of development, one from the middle period of Goethe's life and the other from his age. Looking back upon his readers' tiresome hunt for the 'real' story behind *Werther*, nearly forty years after the time with which we are concerned, Goethe laconically writes 'dass Autoren und Publikum durch eine ungeheure Kluft getrennt sind, wovon sie, zu ihrem Glück, beiderseits keinen Begriff haben.'[56] Years later still, a foolish bit of advice that he ought to show his 'real' affection for the young lady he had eulogised in *Trilogie der Leidenschaft* prompts the comment:

> Ich habe nun noch eine besondere Qual dass gute, wohlwollende, verständige Menschen meine Gedichte auslegen wollen und dazu die Spezialissima, wobei und woran sie entstanden seien, zu eigentlichster Einsicht unentbehrlich halten, anstatt dass sie zufrieden sein sollten dass ihnen irgend Einer das Speziale so ins Allgemeine empor-gehoben, damit sie es wieder in ihre eigene Spezialität ohne weiteres aufnehmen können.[57]

'Die Spezialissima, wobei und woran sie entstanden seien' – these, Goethe insists, are the poet's private affair. Not indeed in the Schillerian sense that they are too embarrassingly 'real' to be divulged in public; the irony of the subjunctive 'seien' tells us that such a reading would be beside the point. Rather, the careful and secretive 'wobei und woran' hints at less readily communicable ranges of experience. It hints, I would suggest, at the existence of an altogether private love affair between the poet and his words, *occasioned* by his initial love experience but not identical with it. This artistic 'affair' has intervened between him and his passion for Ulrike von Levetzow just as it had intervened, years earlier, between Charlotte Kestner and himself, placing a bar – not indeed between the public and his work – but between his readers and a sensibility which has emerged subtly changed. The reader, Goethe indicates, cannot directly *share* this experience; but he can *absorb* it 'ohne weiteres', more or less unconsciously, alongside the other, more public imports his poem articulates. Yet paradoxically it is this intimately personal erotic involvement of the artist with his medium which authenticates his poetic statement of passion and imbues it with those universal rhythms of sentience which are accessible to all.[58]

Let us return to our period. Only now are we in a position to appreciate how little the poet's attitude regarding this most intimate of creational problems changed during the half century which separates the 'Künstlergedichte' from the statement just discussed. For the cryptic 'wobei und woran', from the letter to Zelter, is matched by the words a very young man wrote, fifty-six years earlier, to the girl he loved. While he was busy composing *Werther*, Goethe apologised to Charlotte Kestner for not having answered a note of hers more promptly and explained his omission as follows:

> Das macht du bist diese ganze Zeit, vielleicht mehr als jemals in, cum et sub . . . mit mir gewesen. Ich lasse es dir ehstens drucken – Es wird gut meine Beste. Denn ist mirs nicht wohl wenn ich an euch dencke?[59]

The mysterious 'in, cum et sub' refers to the holy sacrament. The body of Christ is taken by the communicant *in*, *with* and *under* the form of the wafer and the wine. Translating the allusion, Lotte has been with him 'in, cum, and sub' the form of the creative communion with his own medium, a communion at once more primitive and more symbolical than the relation with Lotte was fated to be. The concluding question is wholly delightful in the generosity of its *non sequitur*. Does Goethe really mean that his novel *Werther* will be good because the cockles of his heart are warmed when he thinks of the Kestners who caused him so much pain, or is his meaning not rather that the activity of fashioning poetry from such suffering and frustration has filled him with an awareness of well-being which sheds an afterglow of pleasure on those he loved, even though he left them in pain?

The geniality of this passage is at least as significant as the devil-may-care attitude of which one might suspect the speaker in *Künstlers Morgenlied*, for showing us how the poet assimilated the complexities of being an artist into his fuller humanity. Of course he is aware of the fact that his life presents problems different from and more complicated than do those of his fellow-men – a poem like *Der Adler und die Taube* leaves no doubt of that. Yet nowhere does he adopt the uncommitted, self-consciously individualistic stance of *l'art pour l'art*. True, in the 'Künstlergedichte', the erotic excitement engendered by the process of creation frequently cuts across the erotic bonds that connect the young speaker with others; but of the existence of such human bonds there can be no doubt. In this group of poems, it is the professional author, the critic and the connoisseur who are characterised as unloving and socially uncommitted in addition to being uncreative. Creativeness, on the other hand, is allied with the capacity for strong and warm personal bonds as well as with the lively awareness that the individual is embedded in the sustaining community and, ultimately, depends upon being at rights with the world and its maker. Poems such as *Ein Gleichnis*, *Dilettant und Kritiker*, *Anekdote unsrer Tage*, *Kenner und Künstler*, *Rezensent*, and *Denk- und Trostsprüchlein* all carry the same message; and the charming little poem *Der Autor* makes it clear that the young poet, in the very midst of the 'Geniekult', already possessed that marked awareness of the interrelation between author and public which we tend to associate with the mature phase of Goethe's classicism:

> Was wär ich
> Ohne dich,
> Freund Publikum!
> All mein Empfinden Selbstgespräch,
> All meine Freude stumm.

As long as we bear in mind Goethe's marked trend towards personal and social integration, we may enjoy the subtle estimate of the author of *Werther* which Thomas Mann, in his novel *Lotte in Weimar*, puts onto the lips of the poet as he looks back:

> Gut gemacht, talentvoller Grasaff, der schon von Kunst so viel wusst wie von Liebe und heimlich jene meint, wenn er diese betrieb, – spatzenjung und schon ganz bereit, Liebe, Leben und Menschheit an die Kunst zu verraten.[60]

'Verraten'? May be, in the sense that the girl in *Künstlers Morgenlied* has been left high and dry while her young man was busily painting her picture. But surely not 'verraten' in any deeper sense. For although the poet has indeed tumbled to the awareness that often, when he seems to speak of love between the sexes, he in fact means the creative Eros of the artist, that artist is in fact committed to love, life and humanity. More than that, his art-making has itself become imbued with love, life, and the primordial drives of humanity. It is because, from this early point onwards, Goethe's creativity is itself natural process, in the sense that it stems from the transposition of a biological drive and rhythm to another, linguistic context, that we feel the emerging forms to be natural forms and judge that these poems speak to us with the authentic voice of love. And again, if Goethe's creativity has become natural process, it is because his encounter with his medium has itself become an erotic encounter – that is to say, an event which is patterned along the lines of a basic biological event.

As the first creative surge of youth was spent and the poet grew older, wiser, and – after his return from the Italian South – more disillusioned, the relation between nature and art was to present itself to him as less simple than here, at the outset of his poetic career. Not indeed that even at this early point he was blind to the 'unnaturalness' of art, which is inevitable if it is to be art. The early review of Sulzer as well as the introductory section to *Aus*

Goethes Brieftasche leave no doubt of that. But it is a far cry from a young artist's inborn knowledge that every form, even the most felt form, 'hat etwas Unwahres',[61] to the stark recognition dominating the 1790s, that, in the modern world at least, 'Die Natur . . . von der Kunst durch eine ungeheure Kluft getrennt [ist], welche das Genie selbst, ohne äussere Hülfsmittel, zu überschreiten nicht vermag.'[62] True, even at this time of estrangement between art and nature, Goethe held fast to the conviction that it is the artist's task to be true to nature and to produce something resembling her own phenomena. But for the mature man the achievement of this goal involved the almost superhuman efforts which Schiller so understandingly described in the letter which was to gain him Goethe's friendship:[63] it meant a rediscovery of the laws by which a once unalloyed nature and the ancient artists who were themselves nature, went about their business of organisation, and a reconstitution of the artist's psyche according to such an intellectual model of nature, enabling him, as Goethe has it,

> wetteifernd mit der Natur, etwas geistig Organisches hervorzubringen, und seinem Kunstwerk einen solchen Gehalt, eine solche Form zu geben, wodurch es natürlich zugleich und übernatürlich erscheint.[64]

Thus, even at that strained time of maximal artistic consciousness, Goethe's conviction that in the creative act natural process is at work in the artist remained unshaken; and indeed he, for his own part, was no more inclined in 1797 to divulge the 'ewig Geheimniss'[65] of creativity than he had been in the days of his youth; he fended off Schiller's attempts to probe into his creative development,

> . . . da diese regulierte Naturkraft so wie alle unregulierten durch nichts in der Welt geleitet werden kann, sondern wie sie sich selbst bilden muss, auch aus sich selbst und auf ihre eigne Weise wirkt.[66]

Besides, the 'Künstlergedichte' themselves bear witness to the unity and continuity of Goethe's later development. For it was not until 1789 that Goethe added the final portion of *Des Künstlers Erdewallen*, entitled *Künstlers Apotheose*. This poem, with its emphasis on the architectonic component of art-making, and its watchwords: 'Die Kunst bleibt Kunst!' and 'Die Kunst hat nie ein Mensch allein besessen' unashamedly expounds the credo of Goethe's classicistic period. But would Goethe have appended it to the early group of poems had he not felt that, for all its emphasis on the art-character of art and its premium on consciousness, the addition was fundamentally of a piece with the view which had inspired the earlier poems and had he not still felt committed to that view?

At some moment during the breakthrough to his own creative depths, which took place between the writing of the *Urgötz* and the final version of the play, written about a year later, a truth dawned on the young poet which he was never again going to relinquish: the recognition, deeply stirring although at times alarming, that art is a second nature and that artistic process is natural process, not just for the Ancients or for Shakespeare, but for him, Goethe, as well. 'Goethe is bedded down into nature like a huge thinking tree,' it has been said.[67] It is of this, the rooting, once and for all, of creative process in the unconscious depths of biological process, that the 'Künstlergedichte' tell us with disarming directness. In his letter to Herder of 1772, Goethe had discovered the bodiliness of his verbal medium. The poems that followed upon this discovery testify to the fact that his creativity itself had now become a kind of bodily loving.

6

Die Leiden des jungen Werther : A Requiem for Inwardness

Sing of human unsuccess
In a rapture of distress . . .
(W. H. Auden: *In Memory of W. B. Yeats*)

'No great work of art dare want its appropriate form,' Samuel
Taylor Coleridge once said. To which we might add that no artist
engaged upon the creation of a great work of art dare miss his
appropriate form. For, at some times, and for some artists, form,
like the net below the tightrope walker's feet, may be a matter of
life and death. The young author of *Die Leiden des jungen Werther*
was, if not a tightrope walker, at any rate a somnambulist. He
himself confesses, in the thirteenth book of *Dichtung und Wahrheit*,
that he wrote 'dieses Werklein ziemlich unbewusst, einem
Nachtwandler ähnlich'.[1] 'Unbewusst' – this word takes us back to
Goethe's letter to Herder written about two years before the
composition of *Werther*—and it means here what it had meant
before: the bodying forth of a highly wrought dynamic pattern,
conceived and articulated in the depth of organic being, 'ohne
dass du's weisst, warum'.[2] And the image of the sleepwalker,
about to come to the fore in *Egmont* soon after the completion of
Werther, emphasises both the skill and the abnormal dangers of a
performance which, seeing yet unseeing, controlled and yet uncontrollable, maintains itself this side of death by a giddy feat of
deftness and co-ordination.

A matter of life and death *Werther* was and remained for the
poet throughout the span of nearly sixty years by which he
survived his hero.

So etwas schreibt sich indess nicht mit heiler Haut . . .   [3]

Das war ein Stoff, bei dem man sich zusammenhalten oder zu
Grunde gehen musste . . . [4]

Ich weiss recht gut, was es mich für Entschlüsse und Anstrengun-
gen kostete, damals den Wellen des Todes zu entkommen . . . [5]

Es sind lauter Brandraketen! – Es wird mir unheimlich dabei und ich
fürchte, den pathologischen Zustand wieder durch zu empfinden aus
dem es hervorging . . . [6]

Utterances such as these, taken at random from almost any phase
of Goethe's career, leave no doubt of the fact that the poet
connected and continued to connect his novel with a life and
death struggle within himself.

> Zum Bleiben ich, zum Scheiden du erkoren,
> Gingst du voran – und hast nicht viel verloren.[7]

The late lines to the 'vielbeweinter Schatten' epitomise the
attitude the poet took up, time and again, towards the figment of
his youthful imagination. It was, or so it seemed to Goethe, a
choice between Werther and himself. One or the other had to go.
As it turned out, Werther was invented and brought to his tragic
end so that Goethe himself might live. This is the burden of the
passage in *Dichtung und Wahrheit* in which Goethe, at great length,
describes toying with the idea of suicide at the time immediately
before writing *Werther* and reports his eventual resolution to live:

Um dies aber mit Heiterkeit tun zu können, musste ich eine
dichterische Aufgabe zur Ausführung bringen, wo alles was ich über
diesen wichtigen Punkt empfunden, gedacht und gewähnt, zur
Sprache kommen sollte.[8]

The same insight, perceived from a different and, I believe, more
telling angle, is to be found in a statement of Goethe's reported to
us by Caroline Sartorius. Replying to the question of what is the
'truth' behind *Werther*, the relation between his 'real' and his
fictional self, Goethe answered

Dass es zwei Personen in einer gewesen, wovon die eine untergegan-
gen, die andere aber leben geblieben ist, **um** diese Geschichte der
ersteren zu schreiben, so wie es im „Hiob" heisst [I, 16]: Herr, alle
Deine Schafe und Knechte sind erschlagen worden und ich bin allein
entronnen, **Dir Kunde zu bringen.**[9]

The angle, as I have said, is different. Contrary to the statement
in *Dichtung und Wahrheit*, Goethe here does not say that he had to
write in order to live: on the contrary, he tells us that he had to

live in order to write – 'um diese Geschichte der ersteren zu schreiben'. We shall come to this difference presently. But what remains unchanging, from the verses composed as an epigraph to the second edition of the novel in 1775 to the introductory poem of *Trilogie der Leidenschaft* written nearly fifty years later, is the poet's relation to his hero. He speaks of him as if he were not a fictional character at all but a person: a friend, a companion, a double whose 'grässlich Scheiden' enabled him, the poet, to live. Or did it? In a late conversation with Eckermann, a couple of months before he composed the poem *An Werther* which was to preface *Trilogie der Leidenschaft*, Goethe makes a remark about his hero which seems eerier still than the figure of his double in the poem: 'Das ist auch so ein Geschöpf ', he said, 'das ich gleich dem Pelikan mit dem Blut meines eigenen Herzens gefüttert habe', adding that he gave so much of himself, 'so viel Innerliches aus meiner eigenen Brust', that it would have been sufficient to fill ten volumes of the size and kind of *Werther*.[10] The pelican is an ancient symbol for Christ who gave his life for those who fed of his flesh and drank of his blood. The pattern between creator and created has become reversed. It is not Werther who dies so that his creator might live. It is Goethe who dies so that his creation might live. The many veiled allusions in the novel itself to Werther's Passion[11] find a startling echo in the intimation here that, in giving life to the creature of his own imagination, the poet himself endured a Passion and that he himself died a sacrificial death.

Indeed, how dangerously interwoven his own fortunes at the time of writing *Werther* were with those of his hero, is proven by the many contemporaneous documents, both by Goethe and others, as well as by the poet's retrospective account of the period in *Dichtung und Wahrheit*. Is it accident that to describe his own labile state at the time immediately preceding the composition of *Werther*, Goethe, in his autobiography, should resort to the imagery of water which he had so tellingly used in the novel itself to symbolise the hero's unbridled impulses, an elemental force which will destroy Werther as it destroys every familiar landmark in his beloved valley? Goethe's account, in *Dichtung und Wahrheit*, of the conception and composition of *Werther* is similarly framed by images of water. The very first sentence devoted to the novel relates how his empathy with things natural 'trieb mich an das wunderliche Element, in welchem Werther ersonnen und geschrieben ist';[12] whilst the sentence concluding the section on the composition of the novel picks up the same image, in significant intensification:

. . . ich hatte mich durch diese Komposition mehr, als durch jede
andere, aus einem stürmischen Elemente gerettet, auf dem ich durch
eigene und fremde Schuld, durch zufällige und gewählte Lebensweise,
durch Vorsatz und Übereilung, durch Hartnäckigkeit und
Nachgeben, auf die gewaltsamste Art hin und wieder getrieben
worden.[13]

Nowhere is the intermingling of 'truth and fiction' brought
home more startlingly than in the following passage from the
twelfth book of *Dichtung und Wahrheit*:

Ruht nun, wie man sagt, in der Sehnsucht das grösste Glück, und
darf die wahre Sehnsucht nur auf ein Unerreichbares gerichtet sein, so
traf wohl alles zusammen, um den Jüngling, den wir gegenwärtig auf
seinen Irrgängen begleiten, zum glücklichsten Sterblichen zu
machen. Die Neigung zu einer versagten Braut, das Bestreben Meisterstücke fremder Literatur der unsrigen zu erwerben und anzueignen,
die Bemühung Naturgegenstände nicht nur mit Worten, sondern auch
mit Griffel und Pinsel, ohne eigentliche Technik, nachzuahmen: jedes
einzeln wäre schon hinreichend gewesen, das Herz zu schwellen und die
Brust zu beklemmen.[14]

Whose heart and whose chest? The young poet's or that of his
hero? Every word in Goethe's self-portrait would seem to fit his
Werther as well as himself: the attachment to a girl already
engaged (a circumstance which is here ironically avowed as the
condition of a young man's bliss), the derivative relation to the
literary genius of foreign nations – Homer, Ossian or Goldsmith
as the case may be – the dilettantish attempts at artistic
utterance in an alien medium – all these forms of uncreativity
which Goethe singles out his Werther too encounters, like so many
closed roads barring his way into the world. And, given the
romantic premiss that only the unattainable is worth having, that
is to say, the ideal hatched and harboured in the inwardness of
the mind, we inevitably arrive at the state of inner congestion and
intolerable outer constriction which in the end drives Werther to
put a bullet through his brain.

Indeed, it is our reading of this autobiographical passage pertaining to the young poet's own condition which has yielded up
the key concepts we need in order to outline the subject of *Die
Leiden des jungen Werther*. Goethe's novel is concerned with inwardness, with its tragic uncreativity as well as with the undying
glory of its impulse. It is almost a shock to realise that between
Götz von Berlichingen mit der eisernen Hand, revised and published in
1773, within a few months of Goethe's departure from Wetzlar,

and *Die Leiden des jungen Werther*, written within the year following, there runs, unmistakably and terribly, the thread of one continuous theme. True, vital, active and basically unintrospective as he is, Götz knows next to nothing of the disease with which he is stricken. Only his hand and the gulf that separates him from Adelheid tell us that his creativity is flawed, and the secret cause of his sickness only becomes apparent when, incarcerated, the dying hero cries 'Freyheit! Freyheit!' and Elisabeth, his wife, adds the epilogue: 'Nur droben droben bey dir. Die Welt ist ein Gefängniss.' Where the allegiance to an inner reality, an untested and unattainable ideal of the mind, rules supreme, the world, so wide and welcoming at first, in the end is bound to be experienced as a prison house.

The fact that, in speaking of *Götz*, I have inadvertently touched upon one of the principal poetic motifs of *Werther* – the world become a prison – goes to show how deeply the themes of these two works, worlds apart yet written within one year of one another, are intertwined. But in that span of time, what an astounding intensification! Gone is the bustle of Götz's world, crammed with colour and movement and instinct with the sense of history in the making, and gone, above all, is the burly figure of the hero himself, so unsuspecting in the simplicity of his relation to himself. Instead, we are made to gaze into an endless well of loneliness, to follow the movement of the consciousness of one person, dedicated to the exploration of his inner world and pledged to experience this universe of feeling with an intensity which is bound, in the end, to lead to its own exhaustion. The supremacy accorded to the inner life, the reliance placed upon it, and the demands made upon it – in fact, those 'übertriebene Forderungen an sich selbst'[15] which, in *Dichtung und Wahrheit*, Goethe diagnoses as the real killer that attacked the best among the German young – all these, in Werther, are absolute. And so, correspondingly, for all his power of empathy and the flashes of insight that are granted to him, is his obtuseness to the nature and the claims of reality. To gain an impression of this disregard and of the subjectivism that ensues from it, it is not necessary to follow the poet into the maze of detail through which, miraculously, he has built up his picture – to refer, for instance, to the oft quoted words: 'Auch halte ich mein Herzchen wie ein krankes Kind; jeder Wille wird ihm gestattet', or, indeed, to take a count of the number of references to this much abused organ – the word 'Herz' occurs no less than seven times in the first letter alone! We must discern that pattern as a whole and the direction in which it moves. To perceive this, we need only look at the opening words of the novel, words addressed by Werther to a cherished friend:

> Wie froh bin ich, dass ich weg bin! Bester Freund, was ist das Herz
> des Menschen! Dich zu verlassen, den ich so liebe, von dem ich
> unzertrennlich war, und froh zu sein!

From this opening statement let us turn to Werther's last
completed letter:

> Wie mich die Gestalt verfolgt! Wachend und träumend füllt sie meine
> ganze Seele! Hier, wenn ich die Augen schliesse, hier in meiner Stirne,
> wo die innere Sehkraft sich vereinigt, stehen ihre schwarzen Augen.
> Hier! Ich kann Dir es nicht ausdrücken. Mache ich meine Augen zu,
> so sind sie da; wie ein Meer, wie ein Abgrund ruhen sie vor mir, in
> mir, füllen die Sinne meiner Stirn.

Like two milestones, these two statements map out the beginning
and end of Werther's path; its beginning – an open-eyed
egocentricity which overrides all regard for the other; its end – a
trail losing itself in some landscape of the interior, where frag-
ments of a once lovely reality reappear, grotesquely dismembered,
magnified and amorphous.

This is the last and most horrifying instance of that
characteristic movement of Werther's mind from what lies in front
of him to a reality at the back of his eyes through which the poet,
from the beginning of the novel onwards, defines Werther's recoil
into inwardness and his ever more distorting subjectivity. For all
his longing to lose himself in the embrace of another – a union
Ganymed achieves by a few resolute thrusts[16] – Werther never goes
out towards the world, to meet it on its own terms and to be
renewed by such an encounter. Instead, he takes the world into
himself, more and more rapaciously and less and less availingly.
For what, at first, had seemed infinite pastureland, abounding
with sustenance and refreshment – ' . . . man möchte zum
Maienkäfer werden, um in dem Meer von Wohlgerüchen
herumschweben und alle seine Nahrung darin finden zu können',
Werther exclaims in the opening letter of the novel – becomes
progressively more impoverished as Werther's huge shadow falls
across it and engulfs it until, in the end, he has nothing to feed
upon but what has been touched and tainted by his own
devouring eyes and mind,[17] and he is in truth as nature appears
to him – 'ein ewig verschlingendes, ewig wiederkäuendes Un-
geheuer'. Werther, we may say, incorporates his environment and
starves to death in the midst of an unparalleled glut;[18] and

whatever resists being thus incorporated into his self – and it is more and more as time draws on – is rejected as alien.

Here, as in every other respect, Goethe's novel is the polar opposite of his earlier *Götz* where the attrition of an organism is caused by its progressive dissociation from the world in which it is placed and on which its life depends.[19] The problem has remained the same, only the signs are reversed. Subject and object, person and environment, placed poles apart in the earlier drama, in the experience of Werther coalesce. In passage upon passage, the poet drives home that Werther incorporates the world as, at the end, he introjects his beloved's eyes, straining to turn his gaze inward there to meet hers, and perceiving nothing except the pain of organs thus brutally abused.

> Mein Freund, wenn's dann um meine Augen dämmert und die Welt um mich her und der Himmel ganz in meiner Seele ruhn . . .
>
> Ich kehre in mich selbst zurück und finde eine Welt! . . .
>
> . . . wie fasste ich das alles in mein warmes Herz, fühlte mich· in der überfliessenden Fülle wie vergöttert, und die herrlichen Gestalten der unendlichen Welt bewegten sich allbelebend in meiner Seele . . .
>
> Genug, dass in mir die Quelle allen Elendes verborgen ist wie ehemals die Quelle aller Seligkeiten. Bin ich nicht noch eben derselbe, der ehemals in aller Fülle der Empfindung herumschwebte, dem auf jedem Tritte ein Paradies folgte, der ein Herz hatte, eine ganze Welt liebevoll zu umfassen?

These are but a few of the statements in which Werther himself articulates the characteristic inward movement of his sensibility. Their effect is powerful, and their cumulative effect overwhelming.

But no direct statement of a subject – and Werther's inwardness is the subject at the centre of this book – can rival the force that accrues to it if it is dramatically enacted. And this enactment of the hero's sensibility the poet has achieved through the form of his novel. The appropriateness of this form, its naturalness and its high art, its daring and its discipline, its spontaneity and its objectivity, will forever remain one of the marvels of literature. An epistolary novel, it is modelled, no doubt, on Rousseau and Richardson, but unlike them it dispenses with the give and take of a reciprocal correspondence embodying a variety of points of view capable of modifying one another. Instead, it confines itself to the letters of one character only, written in the intimacy of an unchallenged seclusion, in streams or snatches as the impulse takes him, and always, inevitably, transmitting to us a world that has been filtered through his sensibility, perceived and interpreted by him, with no verification or comment in his narrative as to the truth or distortion in his perception: and this, surely, is the form which uniquely fits its subject.[20] To say that it fits Werther's inwardness as a glove fits the hand or as a garment fits the body is not enough. One could go through the whole battery of analogies which Herder, in his *Fragmente*, had marshalled in his endeavour to formulate the relation between 'Empfindung' and 'Ausdruck' in poetry and, like him, one would dismiss them all again and resort to the Platonic myth of incarnation as the only analogy that will do justice to the relation between *this* subject and *this* form.[21] If ever there was an inner form – a form 'die alle Formen in sich begreift' as Goethe has it,[22] this is it; and it issues in a linguistic body which, organically and in its entirety, articulates the structure of a sensibility which would incorporate the world into its 'innig Innerstes'.

But to extol the naturalness of a form which, with the greatest flexibility and ease, adapts itself to the twists and torsions of one man's subjectivity, is not enough. The true marvel is that such responsiveness to disturbance as the poet evinced should have yielded any form at all, in the true sense of the word. We recall Coleridge's dictum that 'no great work of art dare want its appropriate form'. It might be more fitting here to say that few artists have dared to discover a form such as this one. It is an elemental form, like that of a whirlwind or a whirlpool, caused by extreme disturbance and made of it, arresting the shape of that disturbance and holding it up to our contemplation only to withdraw it again, almost as soon as it has been glimpsed. It would be hard to find a better illustration of Edward Bullough's principle of the 'Antinomy of Distance'[23] than this novel by a youngster as intrepid as he was distressed. It was a tightrope walk well and proper, this performance of Goethe's, with aesthetic distance at vanishing point, yet never wholly disappearing; subjecting himself and his readers to the full brunt of an almost unendurable tragedy, yet shielding himself and us from overexposure by the most translucent of veils – the texture of his language.

'Wo aber Gefahr ist, wächst das Rettende auch'; – just because he went out on a limb and, in a curious mixture of discipline and addiction, placed himself behind one pair of eyes only, the eyes of Werther whose single vision becomes ever more narrowed, ever more inward-turned and distorted as the novel draws to its close, the young poet forced himself into creating a highly wrought piece of poetic prose. For it is only in the structure of his language, in the deployment of poetic motifs which reflect, enact and symbolise Werther's drift towards disintegration, and in a verbal filigree which creates numberless ambiguities and formal links designed to aid our perception where that of Werther fails, that the poet was able to embody the vision his narrator so conspicuously lacks. The point of view of this novel, the pair of eyes through which we are supposed to perceive this world, is obviously not to be found in the person of its hero, nor, as has been suggested, in the recipient of Werther's letters, Wilhelm;[24] it resides within the fabric of the language, in its densely patterned articulacy. It is only with the eyes of the language that we see the full truth the poet is presenting to us; the truth of Werther and of a world which, by the logic of form and subject alike, is given to us as a content of Werther's distorting inwardness. To recreate that mangled truth, the poet had to resurrect it in the artificial body of his language. Always, he had to write a counterpoint into the melody, to create, by means of a verbal texture vibrant with internal resonances, a full score inaudible to Werther himself, but, for us, complementing and correcting his single voice. Surely he would have said of this astonishingly controlled work what, fifty-five years later, he was to say about *Die Wahlverwandtschaften*: 'dass darin kein Strich enthalten, der nicht erlebt, aber kein Strich so, *wie* er erlebt worden.'[25] And indeed, within a couple of months of finishing the manuscript of *Werther*, the young poet did make a statement foreshadowing the one just quoted; and although this statement occurs ostensibly in connection with *Clavigo*, we may take it that it gathers up insights into the nature of the artistic process gained during the much more passionate engrossment with his novel. The secret of writing poetry, he confides to Fritz Jacobi in the summer of 1774, 'ist die Reproducktion der Welt um mich, durch die innre Welt die alles packt, verbindet, neuschafft, knetet und in eigner Form, Manier, wieder hinstellt . . . '[26] The young author of *Werther* knew in 1774 what the aged poet verbalised in 1830 – that an artist cannot make use of a single element as it has offered itself to his experience in a non-artistic context, that he must assimilate it and create it anew in the body of his medium, and that the aesthetic 'Lebensorganisation'[27] he is thereby articulating, although in some ways a 'reproduction' of past experience, nevertheless cuts across the structure of such experience all along the line.

One of the devices by which this extraordinary young man succeeded in bodying forth characters that appear to be fullblooded, seen and felt in the round, whilst, in fact, they are presented to us through a single pair of eyes with a fixed and narrow field of vision, Goethe himself reveals in the thirteenth book of *Dichtung und Wahrheit.* Incorrigibly sociable as he was by nature, he would hold imaginary conversations with a number of partners summoned for the purpose. Like himself – and indeed like Lotte as she emerges from the poet's description in the previous book – these would be of a predominantly objective and receptive cast of mind. The poet would submit to them the proposed content of Werther's letters, and would politely defer to the wisdom of their judgment.[28] What a delightful and telling stratagem on the part of one who, decades later, was to acknowledge the *Gegenständlichkeit* of his thinking, his art-making and his scientific method as the mainspring of his genius![29] Proliferating his own objectivity as it were, the young poet stations observers, very much like himself, at different points, placing them all around his subject, thus ensuring a stereoscopic depth of vision such as Werther's single pair of eyes could never have achieved and embedding this vision in a language rich with the deposit of layers and layers of perception.

Such a careful assimilation of the objective world[30] cannot be too sharply contrasted with Werther's rapacious ingestion of it. Goethe submits his conception to other eyes than his own, he tests it against the touchstone of objective reality. And then again, he allows his medium to mould his vision and to body it forth – and an artist's medium is another representative of reality. As against this, Werther altogether denies the objective pole of experiencing. He incorporates as much of the world as he can, thus denying it a separate existence. Where this is not possible, he dismisses it as alien. But whether he experiences the world as part of his self or as incompatible with it in the end matters little. For in neither case does he experience it as a partner in the conversation of life, distinct from him and therefore able to enter into a creative relationship with him. For all his desperate attempts to get across the gulf of his selfhood and to reach Lotte, Nature or God, Werther is alone – inward, alienated and barren.

To articulate this barrenness was no easy matter for the poet. To demonstrate it through Werther's relation to the outside world, through his failure to come to terms with the claims of work or even with the people he most loves, was not sufficient. For always, except in the editorial report appended at the end of the novel, Goethe had to lend his narrator his own marvellous powers of expression to enable him to give voice to his sufferings – and where we suspect the gift of 'Melodie und Rede',[31] we think that there may yet be a road from inwardness out into the world. And so the poet had to disentangle himself from his creation, and let

Werther's inarticulateness bespeak itself, unequivocally and preferably in a medium not shared by his creator.

This is where the art motif, familiar to Goethe from *Emilia Galotti*, so happily modulated in his letter to Herder and throughout the 'Künstlergedichte', proved useful. Not that the young poet lacked other reasons for bringing in this motif here, a crowning discord in a statement of uncreativeness in which, quite obviously, he was painfully and personally involved. Had he not, in his account of that condition which was about to issue in the composition of *Werther*, singled out his own endeavours to express himself 'nicht nur mit Worten, sondern auch mit Griffel und Pinsel'? Indeed, a dozen years were to go by before this great poet, plagued all the while by hope alternating with self-doubt, persuaded himself that he was born, not to be a painter, but a writer.

But whatever the deeper motives which induced the poet to return to the symbolism of the visual artist in *Werther*, he certainly needed to do so for strictly technical reasons. To show Werther failing to express himself as an artist was to dramatise his inarticulateness, his verbal eloquence notwithstanding. Merely to have left his hero protesting this inarticulateness would have involved the poet in a dilemma: either he could have let Werther carry his point and lose his case; or Werther's increasing incoherence would by and by have invaded the linguistic texture of the novel which is not only its glory but its articulated body and, most of all, the guarantor of its vision. (And indeed, it is precisely at the point where Werther's incoherence threatens to issue in linguistic chaos that his voice is cut short and the voice of the editor takes over.) The poet had no choice then but to let Werther's inarticulateness enact itself. Thus alone could he hope to authenticate, on the deepest level, that inwardness which is not only the subject of the novel but the determinant of its form.

From the first, Werther's relation to art receives its distinctive slant from the fact that the poet has associated it with Lessing's *Emilia Galotti*. As we saw in the first chapter, Werther, at the very beginning of the novel, echoes the sentiments voiced by the painter Conti, and he dies with Lessing's tragedy lying open on his desk – the self-same tragedy which, two years earlier, Goethe had condemned as 'nur gedacht'.[32] Thus, in this novel, it is a symbol of uncreativeness. How could it be otherwise for a poet who, in the two years that separated the publication of *Emilia Galotti* from the composition of his own *Werther*, had never ceased to extol the creative power of the human hand and had learned that the miracle of poetry lies in the fact that it bodies forth inspiration in the immaterial medium of words, even as the sculptor bodies forth his vision in the tangible reality of stone or clay? *Emilia Galotti*, however, is an emblem of uncreativeness not only because in this tragedy hands are agents so destructive that even a painter will disown them as ministers of his vision; it functions as a symbol of uncreativeness in Goethe's novel in the same sense as do Homer, Ossian and even Klopstock. The increasing importance these literary figures assume argues the derivativeness of Werther's experience, because he lives with and through the art of others rather than being productive himself; and, one might add, because he identifies with the matter of these poets rather than showing any awareness of their form.

Thus the frame in which Goethe has placed Werther's relation to art from the beginning suggests that something may well be amiss with it. Six times in all in the novel does Werther contemplate expressing himself in an artistic medium, and on three of these occasions he produces results. This is not much for one who thinks himself a 'grosser Maler', nor indeed does it take long to dispose of his productions. On the first of these occasions (I, May 26) he draws the two little boys of the schoolmaster's daughter, sitting on a plough opposite him. 'Mich vergnügte der Anblick', Werther writes and goes on to report 'dass ich eine wohlgeordnete, sehr interessante Zeichnung verfertigt hatte.' On the second occasion (I, July 24), he writes that, having vainly tried three times to draw a portrait of his Lotte, he finally cut her silhouette, 'und damit soll mir gnügen.' On the last occasion (II, June 11) he writes from a visit to a prince undertaken to mark time between his failure at the embassy and his return to Lotte: 'Das Beste, was ich hier getan habe, ist mein Zeichnen.' This is all. Obviously he himself does not rate his efforts highly. The words he uses to describe his sketch of the children – *wohlgeordnet, interessant, verfertigen,* sound curiously unreal from Werther's lips. They do not express him and his intensity. Rather do they smack of the vocabulary of the Philistines whom he attacks in a biting persiflage, a few lines further on in the same letter. Lotte's silhouette is *faute de mieux* and Werther's 'damit soll mir gnügen' expresses resignation.[33] Of the last series of drawings we hear nothing.

In no case then does the objective quality of Werther's products, by his own tacit admission, amount to much; and this is connected with the fact that on all three of these occasions he evinces a marked – indeed a quite unusual – degree of psychical distance from what he is doing. On the last occasion, before his return to Lotte, he feels at a low ebb and there is nothing in the distant tone of the reference to his drawings to suggest any involvement in depth. The sight of the little boys gives him pleasure. But again, there is no deeper concern here, nor indeed is there any sign of a different kind of concern, kindled by the activity itself, by his engrossment with the medium in which he has chosen to work. Explicitly he says that he produced the picture 'ohne das mindeste von dem Meinen hinzuzutun' (May 26). In the third case, the obverse is true. His passionate involvement with his subject, Lotte, is obvious enough. But having failed to draw her, he now chooses a medium which by its own rigid inexpressiveness imposes the greatest possible distance upon him. The silhouette is pure out-side, a contoured blank. In cutting Lotte's silhouette, therefore, Werther is doing no more than to transfer his own inarticulateness on to paper. Hence his resignation. Thus, when Werther does resort to paper and pencil – or for that matter to scissors – the resultant products have the quality of images glimpsed through opera glasses held the wrong way to the eyes: they appear over-distanced and unreal. Not a tithe of Werther's intensity has gone into these pictures. It is all there, untransmuted and nakedly personal, surrounding the descriptions of his products with a fuzzy fringe of generalities and irritation.[34]

Far more interesting are those occasions – three in all – when, after a shortlived aesthetic excitement, Werther altogether abandons the idea of seeking utterance in any artistic medium. For here the characteristic inward movement of his sensibility is brought into full play, and we see the dominant side of his nature. The earlier excess of distance here gives way to a total loss of distance, alienation gives way to introjection, and expression altogether ceases.

Take the first of these occasions, the letter of May 10, when Werther, like Conti, claims to be a great painter without lifting a hand.

> Ich bin so glücklich, mein Bester, so ganz in dem Gefühle von ruhigem Dasein versunken, dass meine Kunst darunter leidet. Ich könnte jetzt nicht zeichnen, nicht einen Strich, und bin nie ein grösserer Maler gewesen als in diesen Augenblicken.

The first thing that strikes one is Werther's physical posture.[35] He does not sit, or stand, let alone step back from what he sees: he lies, his heart close to the objects that excite him, and his eyes unseeing. To this lack of spatial distance corresponds a steady decrease of psychical distance. It is as though we were watching a camera moving in upon its subject. A long shot first, then a gradual drawing near culminating in a series of close-ups

magnified in all their blinding detail, and then, finally, a blur as
the lens moves too near any longer to focus. Passing from the sun
on the surface of 'his' forest to the shady mysteries within, to the
microscopic life of insects, worms, mosses and grasses close to his
heart, Werther progresses towards an ever greater inwardness and
intensity of experience until, in the end, 'die Welt um mich her
und der Himmel ganz in meiner Seele ruhn'. There is no distance
and no object left. Werther has, as it were, incorporated the
outward scene within himself. There is no mention of any
medium, only the exhausted cry: 'Ach, könntest du das wieder
ausdrücken, könntest du dem Papiere das einhauchen, was so voll,
so warm in dir lebt, dass es würde der Spiegel deiner Seele . . .'
But art is never, as Werther seems to think, a mere mirroring or
mechanical reproduction of reality. It implies the breaking down
of the experiential context in which the object was first offered to
the artist's perception, and its recreation 'in eigner Form, Manier',
that is to say its articulation in the wholly artificial body of an
artistic medium. And, most of all, it means the transference of
whatever excitement attached to the initial experience to the
nascent art product itself, to the feel of the material in which it is
taking shape and to the interpenetration of vision and execution
in the creative act. Of such an encounter with the 'other', of the
emotional release and the renewal of energy it affords, Werther
knows nothing. With increasing intensity, he remains riveted on
his initial experience until, in the end, he cries out: ' . . . ich
erliege unter der Gewalt der Herrlichkeit dieser Erscheinungen.'
This threefold reiteration of the overpowering impact the outward
'phenomena' have made upon him demonstrates the unbalancing
effect of his subjectivism and warns us of the perils that lie in store
for an inwardness thus cruelly inflated.

   For the second time, on May 30, Werther's aesthetic impulse is
aroused and frustrated when he meets the peasant lad and is
swept off his feet by the boy's passion for his mistress. This time,
it occurs to him to paint a picture in words; but, from the very
outset of the letter, he rejects the idea of transmuting the emotional 'Szene' in which he has participated into the artificiality of
a 'scene' in a narrative. 'Muss es denn immer gebosselt sein, wenn
wir teil an einer Naturerscheinung nehmen sollen?' Once again we
witness the same pattern – a steady decrease of psychical distance
and the familiar introjection of what, to begin with, was separate
and outside. He begins by describing the 'heisse sehnliche
Verlangen' of the boy, and he ends up by borrowing the same
images to describe his own condition; confessing 'dass bei der
Erinnerung . . . mir die innerste Seele glüht, und . . . dass ich,

wie selbst davon entzündet, lechze und schmachte'. He *is* the boy, even now, as more palpably he will be the boy when he cries at the end: 'Du bist nicht zu retten, Unglücklicher! Ich sehe wohl, dass wir nicht zu retten sind'.[36] He has taken the other into himself and vicariously experiences the passion belonging to another in the inwardness of his own soul.

A dozen times, in ever swifter succession, Werther breaks in on his description of the boy with protestations of his concern and of his inability to express this concern. At first, his reactions to what he perceives take the form of interpolations which remain grammatically and logically subordinated to his central subject. But gradually these interpolations gain ground and spread until, like a cancerous growth, they have invaded his principal statements, and his original subject is blighted into insignificance. Before our eyes we see the death of an aesthetic experience. Not for one moment does Werther attempt to explore this experience for its own sake, disengaging it from his emotions until it stands out, free and complete, capable of exfoliating into a viable reality. On the contrary, the germinal image becomes ever more enveloped in the web of his personal affections, until eventually it is choked. The inevitable outcome of this strangulation of vision by the person is Werther's decision not to see the boy's beloved. 'Warum soll ich mir das schöne Bild verderben?' he asks, little suspecting that, unfructified by contact with reality, the image has died in his innermost self.

The third, and last, revelation of Werther's artistic impotence comes in the letter of July 24, at the end of which Werther confesses that three times he attempted to draw Lotte's portrait, only to 'prostitute' himself three times. Beset as he is by intensity and frustration, he realises more urgently than ever before that he must find a way of expressing what has so violently impressed itself on him, and that, in order to do so, he must come to grips with some material medium:

> Noch nie war ich glücklicher, noch nie war meine Empfindung an der Natur, bis aufs Steinchen, aufs Gräschen herunter, voller und inniger, und doch – Ich weiss nicht, wie ich mich ausdrücken soll, meine vorstellende Kraft ist so schwach, alles schwimmt und schwankt so vor meiner Seele,[37] dass ich keinen Umriss packen kann; aber ich bilde mir ein, wenn ich Ton hätte oder Wachs, so wollte ich's wohl herausbilden.

What irony and what ambiguity of phrasing! Even as he utters the desire that he may body forth in external form that inchoate something which oppresses him, his own words give him the lie:

' . . . ich bilde mir ein': here, in a nutshell, is that fatal recoil into inwardness, that involution of the germinal image which we have witnessed twice in succession, as well as the futility of his creative pretensions. And what does he imagine he will turn out? Pies. 'Ich werde auch Ton nehmen, wenn's länger währt, und kneten, und sollten's Kuchen werden!' Admittedly this is humorous. But it is also desperate and has the ring of truth. Even the imagined end-product of Werther's aesthetic activities reflects the characteristic of his sensibility in all contexts, in and out of art. In the same manner in which he has taken into himself and incorporated the image of the world and of the peasant boy's beloved, and in the same manner in which he will suck Lotte into the whirlpool of his inwardness, so too the ludicrous pies of which he speaks, here, signify, not a true giving out, but a taking back into himself, an act of incorporation.[38]

At the risk of sounding ridiculous, let me stay with Werther's pies for yet another moment. They are pure matter, caked together by an extraneous mould. This is significant. For it shows once again what we have noted on every one of the three occasions when Werther's aesthetic impulse seems to be aroused. His emotions remain riveted to the *matter* of his experiencing, whether this be the natural phenomena that so impressed themselves on him at the outset of the novel or the 'Naturerscheinung' of the peasant lad's red-hot passion. He never seems to be able to withdraw his emotions from their immediate practical context and to transfer them to the aesthetic arena, concerning himself with the 'how' rather than the 'what' of his experience. The thought of investing this intensity in a grapple with a material medium suggests itself to him only once – with pies as the imagined product!

The point deserves to be stressed, for it leads us into the heart of the difference between Goethe and his hero. The difference – it need hardly be said – is that between a creative mode of experiencing and an essentially uncreative one. A couple of illustrations may illuminate it further. When Werther, at the end of his description of the peasant lad, writes

> dass bei der Erinnerung dieser Unschuld und Wahrheit mir die innerste Seele glüht, und dass mich das Bild dieser Treue und Zärtlichkeit überall verfolgt, und dass ich, wie selbst davon entzündet, lechze und schmachte

our thoughts are transported back to the stanza in *Künstlers Morgenlied* discussed in the previous chapter:[39] there, a year before the composition of *Werther*, the poet had written:

Ach, wie du ruhtest neben mir,
Mich schmachtetst liebend an,
Und mir's vom Aug' durchs Herz hindurch
In'n Griffel schmachtete –

We had seen how in these lines, the complex of feelings denoted by the word *schmachten* is lifted out of its original environment, to become operative in a new, aesthetic context. This capacity to abstract from a given area of experiencing and to recognise, or actively to exhibit, the logical structure of that experience in another context, is the basis of our symbol-making faculty. And such manoeuvrability Werther does not possess. He is quite unable to transfer his *Schmachten* – a vicarious emotion in the first place – to a verbal or painterly context, there to fashion a virtual object symbolising his feelings. Again, on that lovely evening of May 10, when he is overpowered by the beauty of the setting sun, he cannot do what the young poet, two years before, had appeared to do so naturally: on seeing a similar scene, Goethe had run to friends, asked for a pencil and paper and – so he reports to Kestner – 'zeichnete zu meiner grossen Freude, das ganze Bild so dämmernd warm als es in meiner Seele stand.'[40] Goethe has distilled the essence of that feeling of dusky warmth with which his soul embraced the eveningscape, and re-created it 'in eigner Form, Manier', that is to say, in terms of light and shade. He has transferred the experience to a new context. Werther is capable of no such abstraction or indeed of the freedom of movement which depends on it. Obsessively, he clings to the raw material of the initial experience until it dims his eyes by its intensity. In Shakespeare's words, 'he's full of matter.'[41]

This inflexibility on the part of his hero Goethe has been at great pains to demonstrate, both inside the context of his art-making and out of it. And rightly so, for here lies the root of Werther's uncreativeness. He has a certain passionate passivity – the words are etymologically cognate – and this causes him to cling to first impressions in their first immediacy and not to let go of them. One thinks of Lotte's pale pink bow he so pathetically drags around with him, or of the blue frock coat with the yellow waistcoat he insists on having tailored so that it shall exactly match the one he wore when he first met Lotte, and in which he asks to be buried; or of the obduracy with which he kisses Lotte's notes, refusing to be weaned of this habit by the sand she uses to blot the ink; or of the annoyance with which, at the end of an outpouring of unparalleled bitterness, he complains: 'Ein unerträglicher Mensch hat mich unterbrochen. Meine Tränen

sind getrocknet. Ich bin zerstreut.' (II, July 29.) Even the fact that
he understands children and that they love him is not entirely to
be booked to the credit side of his nature, as has often been
supposed. He understands that not a tittle in the stories told to
them may be changed because he himself shares their fixation on
the first impression. But, as Goethe remarks in *Maximen und
Reflexionen*, 'der Irrtum ist recht gut, so lange wir jung sind; man
muss ihn nur nicht mit ins Alter schleppen'.[42] The immediacy and
realism which is appropriate to the young child, in Werther
becomes a fatal flaw. 'Ein zweijähriger Knabe', Goethe observes in
the same section of his maxims –

> hatte die Geburtstagsfeier begriffen, an der seinigen die bescherten
> Gaben mit Dank und Freude sich zugeeignet, nicht weniger dem
> Bruder die seinigen bei gleichem Feste gegönnt. Hiedurch veranlasst,
> fragte er am Weihnachtsabend, wo so viele Geschenke vorlagen,
> wann denn sein Weihnachten komme. Dies allgemeine Fest zu
> begreifen, war noch ein ganzes Jahr nötig.[43]

Is it quite accidental that the young Werther just cannot wait
until Christmas Eve to see his Lotte and to receive his presents,
alongside the other children? He simply cannot see the pattern in the
particular, nor recognise it again in a more generalised instance or in
a different context altogether.

This the young poet himself was able to do in supreme
measure. The whole symbolic structure of his novel depends on
this capacity. He could abstract psychological patterns pertaining
to the hero himself and re-create them, in controlled variations, in
the peasant lad, in the mad secretary, and even in the ghost-like
figures of Ossian. He could take the rhythms of Lotte's sensibility
and re-enact them in the deft sketch of the schoolmaster's
daughter, or in no figure at all, but in a pure idyll instinct with
Lotte's tranquillity, such as that of the peasant girls foregathering
by the well. And, most of all, he could take the characteristic
structure of Werther's sensibility – his inwardness – and from it
fashion the inwardness of the novel's form, down to the last detail.

In the previous chapter we saw how, in the 'Künstlergcdichte',
the young poet began to explore the Protean nature of creative
Eros, registering the transference of energy from the sleeping
beauty by his side to the picture of Venus Urania, and even
recognising that it is the excitement of creation itself which
furnishes the deepest import of a work of art, alongside its more
public ones. I believe that in *Die Leiden des jungen Werther* Goethe
for the first time experienced in dead earnest that mutability
around which his imagination had skirted in the almost contem-

poraneous group of poems. In the novel itself, this experience found only oblique expression – in Werther's inflexibility, so important an aspect of his uncreativeness, and in the poet's chameleon-like capacity to enter his subject in a thousand shapes. We know the consequences of Werther's inability to let go of the raw material of experience and, ultimately, to let go of his self. It means alienation, not only from what he cannot thus incorporate, but – paradoxically – from himself as well: more and more as he brings up the same dreary materials, conditioned always by him and his sensibility, he has a sense of *déjà vu*; and it is this monotonous repetition which, in the end, undermines his morale almost more than anything else.

Goethe himself knew only too well the dangers of becoming an outsider to oneself and of seeing life as a series of nauseating repetitions, as meaningless as the chatter of monkeys. In *Dichtung und Wahrheit*, he attributes his own *taedium vitae* and that of his contemporaries to this cause above all others.[44] And indeed, had he not himself, like his Werther, been an outsider, first in the household of Henrich Adam Buff and then in that of Sophie von La Roche? However cherished, had he not been the odd man out, first with Charlotte Kestner and then with Maximiliane Brentano? But what a difference between creator and creation! Where Werther will not let go of what he has once seized and becomes alienated from his own experience by its fixity, the young poet exposes himself to two successive experiences of the same kind, and from them abstracts their abiding pattern. And that emotional pattern, contemplated with a detachment forced upon him by the situation – a situation, however, which was ultimately of his own choosing – he was able to transmute into a characteristically aesthetic response, combining participation with psychical distance.

That this was no easy matter is proven, both by his account of the period in *Dichtung und Wahrheit* and by the thinly disguised note of awe and terror with which, as we have already seen, he was to refer to his novel as long as he lived. True, at times he would play down that reaction. 'Es ist eine sehr angenehme Empfindung,' he writes in Book thirteen of his autobiography,

> wenn sich eine neue Leidenschaft in uns zu regen anfängt, ehe die alte noch ganz verklungen ist. So sieht man bei untergehender Sonne gern auf der entgegengesetzten Seite den Mond aufgehn und erfreut sich an dem Doppelglanze der beiden Himmelslichter.[45]

Such 'Doppelglanz' may be pleasant enough to contemplate from the safe distance of age; experienced from nearby, however, such a flickering double vision in an uncertain light may hold perplexities of its own. Referring to the same constellation, his simultaneous love for Lotte and Maximiliane, Goethe adds, a little later in the book:

> Bei meiner Arbeit war mir nicht unbekannt, wie sehr begünstigt jener Künstler gewesen, dem man Gelegenheit gab, eine Venus aus mehrern Schönheiten herauszustudieren, und so nahm ich mir auch die Erlaubnis, an der Gestalt und den Eigenschaften mehrerer hübschen Kinder meine Lotte zu bilden, obgleich die Hauptzüge von der geliebtesten genommen waren.[46]

The distillation of such creative Eros as will eventually fashion a Venus, from diverse erotic encounters, on the written page sounds positively idyllic; and indeed, the young poet of *Künstlers Erdewallen* had not yet come up against the more disquieting aspects of such artistic transactions. But the poet of *Werther* did: there is not only passionate conviction, but anguish in the reply Goethe sent to Kestner in answer to the latter's critical reception of his novel:

> Ich wollt um meines eignen Lebens Gefahr willen Werthern nicht zurückrufen . . . Werther muss – muss seyn! – Ihr fühlt ihn nicht, ihr fühlt nur mich und euch, und was ihr angeklebt heisst – und truz euch – und andern – eingewoben ist – Wenn ich noch lebe, so bist dus dem ichs dancke – bist also nicht Albert – Und also – [47]

In effect this letter says what, twenty-five years later, Goethe was to say with incomparably greater assurance about his *Wahlverwandtschaften*: 'Das Gedichtete behauptet sein Recht, wie das Geschehene.'[48] But when poetry becomes as real as this, it also exacts its toll. Goethe himself was ready to pay the price, and he expected his friends to do the same. They must understand, he pleads, that 'das Gedichtete' is more real than the reality from which it sprang, and worth a sacrifice. The old Albert, Johann Christian Kestner, is still there, thank God: and to this circumstance Goethe knows that he owes his life and the life of the new Albert, the Albert of the book. But that new Albert, bodied forth from the poet's depths and woven into the living texture of his novel, is more real than reality itself, and his image overlays the familiar one. And so it is with Lotte who has overnight become a legend and so, indeed, it is with the young poet himself and the whole complex of relationships in which his sense of identity had been rooted. He and his feelings are no longer what they were before he composed his novel. The figments of his imagination, things made up of words, are flesh of his flesh and blood of his blood, and they stand between him and his assurance of being real. Yet not even for the sake of that assurance will he recall them, any more than Tasso will disband the shapes that crowd his imagination:

> Er scheint uns anzusehn, und Geister mögen
> An unsrer Stelle seltsam ihm erscheinen. (I, 1.)

No, the young author of *Werther* did not write in order to live. Writing complicated living, and the game would scarcely have been worth the candle. Fifty years later, the aged poet was to admit just that, in the poem addressed to the suicide. Rather he lived in order to write, like Job's servant escaping by the skin of his teeth from almost total disaster, 'dir Kunde zu bringen'. And in the process of doing so, and so that his creation might live, he himself died the death of the artist who loses himself and all the familiar landmarks of his identity as he 'bodies forth the forms of things unknown . . . and gives to airy nothing a local habitation and a name.'[49] He died the death any artist must expect to die who transfixes the living flux of feeling so that he may exhibit the permanent patterns of sentience. That Goethe himself remembered the 'composing' of his *Werther* as a kind of dying becomes clear from the image in which, in his autobiography, the moment of inception is described: it was the news of Jerusalem's death which, from one moment to the next, precipitated the plan of *Werther*. At that moment, the poet tells us, the structure of the novel, in its entirety,

> schoss von allen Seiten zusammen und ward eine solide Masse, wie das Wasser im Gefäss, das eben auf dem Punkte des Gefrierens steht, durch die geringste Erschütterung sogleich in ein festes Eis verwandelt wird.[50]

The poet, we remember, had used the image of water, both in *Dichtung und Wahrheit* and in his *Werther*, to characterise the lability and fluidity of feeling he shared with his hero. Now, at the moment of composition, this flux is arrested. Life and movement are frozen, time itself stands still, all is structure, pattern, permanence.

Ice, we well know, is a permutation of water. Whether it be liquid or solid, the physical properties of the element remain unchanged. Only its form is different. And yet, when the cascading drop hangs suspended in mid-air and the flow of life is frozen to a standstill, it is difficult to feel continuity. Did the young poet who, by his admission, had saved himself 'durch diese Komposition mehr, als durch jede andere, aus einem stürmischen Elemente . . . auf dem ich . . . auf die gewaltsamste Art hin und wieder getrieben worden'[51] recognise that throughout this metamorphosis he had remained one and the same? Did he know, as his Tasso was to do, that in his Protean nature alone lay his stability, his identity and, perhaps, his hope of redemption? Probably not. He knew it five years later, when, in the only letter addressed to Sophie von La Roche since the days of *Werther*, he summed himself up in the cryptic words: 'ich bin wie immer . . . die warme Kälte'.[52] At the time when his composition crystallised, however, and he awakened from his somnambulist state to find his feelings frozen into icy clarity, he did not yet know as Tasso and Faust will do, that such a *Stirb und Werde* was to be the pattern of his life. It was, I believe, the first artistic death he died and therefore, perhaps, the worst. Besides, unsure as he was of his poetic vocation, he did not yet accept its hazards for his destiny. That had to wait until, at the end of his Italian journey, after a veritable Passion lasting from Christmas 1787 to Easter 1788, he buried his hopes of being a visual artist, took up his cross of being a poet and at long last completed his *Tasso*.

> Der Mensch wird begraben in geweihter Erd, so soll man auch grosse und seltne Begebenheiten begraben in einen schönen Sarg der Erinnerung, an den ein jeder hintreten kann und dessen Andenken feiern. Das hat der Wolfgang gesagt, wie er den Werther geschrieben hat.[53]

Thus Goethe's mother. I believe that in the sarcophagus the young poet wrought for Werther, he buried more than his hero whose unproductive inwardness made him a stranger on this earth, a lonely 'Wanderer und Waller'. Beside him, he laid to rest his first experience of another loneliness – the alienation of the artist whose inner world has become the matrix of shapes more real than reality – a creative ordeal for which, later on, Tasso was to find imperishable utterance:

> Verbiete du dem Seidenwurm, zu spinnen,
> Wenn er sich schon dem Tode näher spinnt:
> Das köstliche Geweb entwickelt er
> Aus seinem Innersten, und lässt nicht ab,
> Bis er in seinen Sarg sich eingeschlossen.   (V, 2)

He laid to rest the recollection of a death endured so that his work might live, and be a memorial and a meeting place for the many who know not what the shrine contains.

7

Torquato Tasso : A Poet's No Man's Land

Nicht Zeit ist's mehr, zu brüten und zu sinnen,
Denn Jupiter, der glänzende, regiert
Und zieht das dunkel zubereitete Werk
Gewaltig in das Reich des Lichts – Jetzt muss
Gehandelt werden, schleunig, eh' die Glücks-
Gestalt mir wieder wegflieht überm Haupt,
Denn stets in Wandlung ist der Himmelsbogen.

(Schiller: *Wallensteins Tod*)

I

Insensibly, spring has come to Belriguardo. Even now the snow is
melting on the hilltops and dissolving in a trembling haze. The
springs are once again rustling. Freshly burgeoning branches sway
gently in the morning breeze beneath a silken sky. Already the
foliage of the evergreen trees promises to offer richer shade, and
mingled with it is the hue of young verdure. The flowers have
opened their eyes and the gardeners are busy. A world in which
everything had seemed to stand still has quietly renewed itself.

Such stirrings are reflected in the human scene. The quiet
gardens of Belriguardo are alive with movement, there is a coming
and a going. Alfons, Duke of Ferrara, has only just accompanied
his womenfolk to his country seat, so that they may enjoy these
lovely days in the perfection of such surroundings. He is expecting
Antonio Montecatino, his Secretary of State, to call in on his way
back from Rome 'auf einen Augenblick' (I, 2), and before the day
is out both men will travel back to town to attend to business of
state. Even Leonore Sanvitale who only this day has arrived with
her namesake, the Duke's sister, to enjoy the countryside with her,
is thinking of leaving this haven of peace in order to rejoin her
family in Florence.

All these comings and goings, however, are overshadowed by

the great event of this day. Torquato Tasso, poet at the court of
Alfons and its by far most wayward member, is seen slowly
approaching, and in his hand he carries a book. The Princess
watches him as he comes nearer:

> Schon lange seh ich Tasso kommen. Langsam
> Bewegt er seine Schritte, steht bisweilen
> Auf einmal still, wie unentschlossen, geht
> Dann wieder schneller auf uns los, und weilt
> Schon wieder.   (I, 2)

And, as Tasso joins the waiting party, his own words seem to echo
those of the Princess:

> Ich komme langsam, dir ein Werk zu bringen,
> Und zaudre noch, es dir zu überreichen.   (I, 3)

So saying he hands over his epic, *Gerusalemme Liberata,* to his
master and patron.

It is a moving moment indeed. A moment for which, more or
less patiently as the case may be, the princely couple have waited
for years. Always Tasso seemed to have postponed the end, just
when it had seemed in sight. Hesitantly, almost reluctantly, he
had moved towards the completion of his work, with the same
halting stance with which, now, he finally delivers it to the
waiting group.

> Er kann nicht enden, kann nicht fertig werden,
> Er ändert stets, ruckt langsam weiter vor,
> Steht wieder still, er hintergeht die Hoffnung:
> Unwillig sieht man den Genuss entfernt
> In späte Zeit, den man so nah geglaubt.   (I, 2)

So the Duke had been complaining a moment or two before the
poet arrived on the scene. But now that this distant man has
terminated his seclusion and is giving his work, and himself, to the
world he has so long shunned, he sheds his reticence like a cocoon
and responds to the warmth of his reception overwhelmed, with
the vulnerable intensity of a newborn. The praise showered upon
him seems to sear him, and it takes all the kindliness and tact of
the two Leonores and the Duke, his patron, to restore him to a
measure of equanimity.

The violence of Tasso's response momentarily troubles the
members of the court, even as his withdrawal had done before.
For the tone which prevails at the court of Ferrara, for all its

appearance of spontaneity, is sophisticated in the extreme. Restraint, so tactfully exercised as to seem perfectly natural, is the unspoken rule. The Princess and her brother are dedicated to the things of the mind as their distinguished mother had been before them, and as convinced that the cultivation of art and knowledge is one of the glories of true statesmanship; and Leonore Sanvitale characterises not only her friend, but something of the temper and tradition of the place when she says:

> . . . stets ist dein Anteil gross
> Am Grossen, das du wie dich selbst erkennst.   (I, 1)

Indeed, it is this unquestioning identification with suprapersonal values which has made Ferrara what it is – a centre of learning and a haven of civilisation in an age bursting with vitality and vigour and given to the ready use of force.

> Hier zündete sich froh das schöne Licht
> Der Wissenschaft, des freien Denkens an,
> Als noch die Barbarei mit schwerer Dämmrung
> Die Welt umher verbarg . . .   (I, 1)

Words like 'schwere Dämmrung' and 'Barbarei' momentarily recall the twilight world of Goethe's *Iphigenie*. But here, in this sanctuary, and at a later age, all is peace and light and violence is banished. Or perhaps 'banished' is not quite the proper word to use. It might be truer to say that force has been filtered into play and form, refined into the graceful strength of tournaments, into the brilliance of rhetoric and of learned conversation. Thus sublimated and seen as from a distance, the primitive drives of men are safe to contemplate and even welcome.

> Ich höre gern dem **Streit** der Klugen zu,
> Wenn um die **Kräfte**, die des Menschen Brust
> So freundlich und so **fürchterlich** bewegen,
> Mit Grazie die Rednerlippe spielt;
> Gern, wenn die fürstliche **Begier** des Ruhms,
> Des ausgebreiteten Besitzes, Stoff
> Dem Denker wird, und wenn die feine Klugheit,
> Von einem klugen Manne zart entwickelt,
> Statt uns zu **hintergehen**, uns belehrt.   (I, 1)

But what of the deeper drives, the undercurrents of love and hate, of jealousy and envy? The word *Kreis* – a crucial and recurrent word in this play – tells us something about that. It

signifies that the pattern of relations which obtains in the noble
circle of this court is governed by a changeless form. A form so
graceful and so aristocratic that surely it must insinuate itself into
the being of the temperamental poet. For how could the spectacle
of ordered freedom fail to impress itself upon one as sensitive to
form as he? Of all the news brought by Antonio, had it not been
the vision of a whole cosmos revolving around the single figure of
the Pope that had most vividly imprinted itself upon Tasso's
mind? Had he not confessed to the Princess, shortly after his
encounter with Antonio:

> Nein, was das Herz im tiefsten mir bewegte,
> Was mir noch jetzt die ganze Seele füllt,
> Es waren die Gestalten jener Welt,
> Die sich lebendig, rastlos, ungeheuer
> Um *einen* grossen, einzig klugen Mann
> Gemessen dreht und ihren Lauf vollendet,
> Den ihr der Halbgott vorzuschreiben wagt.   (II, 1)

Besides, the court to whose entourage he belongs is the reflection
in miniature of that of the Pope's empire. The members of this
circle, too, are, and remain, on its circumference, equidistant from
one another and from the centre to which they all relate: the
Princess and the Duke. For all the openness and ease of tone, one
senses from the beginning an invisible boundary line to which the
characters themselves are alive. Distance is in the air, shrouding
these figures as with a translucent veil. And not by any means
only so as to insulate them from the shock of passion. On the
contrary; in this play, and in this courtly circle, distance is the
very element of love, the space in which relationships can live and
breathe,[1] ensuring the freedom of each to share in those objective
values which grace existence with significance and form, and, in
so doing, fostering a marriage of true minds. It is as though, by
some common instinct, all conspired to guard this spirit of
inclusiveness. It is the most precious possession Ferrara boasts, the
very foundation of a philosophy of love which, miraculously,
flowers into a love of philosophy.

    For – it need hardly be said – this Renaissance court of Ferrara,
ruled as it is by an unmarried brother and sister, is through and
through imbued with the philosophy of Plato.[2] Oddly enough, it
is the vital and entirely unplatonic Leonore Sanvitale who introduces this subject of discourse. She is content to admit that
what passes between Tasso and the two Leonores is not really
love:

> Hier ist die Frage nicht von einer Liebe,
> Die sich des Gegenstands bemeistern will,
> Ausschliessend ihn besitzen . . .
> Uns liebt er nicht, – verzeih, dass ich es sage! –
> Aus allen Sphären trägt er, was er liebt,
> Auf einen Namen nieder, den wir führen,
> Und sein Gefühl teilt er uns mit; wir scheinen
> Den Mann zu lieben, und wir lieben nur
> Mit ihm das Höchste, was wir lieben können.   (I, 1)

No less surprisingly, it is the intellectual Princess who will not hear of such high flown notions. With an unexpected touch of malice, she replies:

> Du hast dich sehr in diese Wissenschaft
> Vertieft, Eleonore, sagst mir Dinge,
> Die mir beinahe nur das Ohr berühren
> Und in die Seele kaum noch übergehn.   *(Ibid.)*

In fact the Princess understands very well what Leonore is driving at, even though she refuses to admit it. For it is she and not her friend who is the 'Schülerin des Plato', as Leonore reminds her, and the exalted conception of love which her friend has just expounded is in fact her own, engrained by temperament and breeding, the very air she breathes and indeed the only hope for Tasso and herself. It is to Eros, divine husband of Psyche and companion of the gods, that Leonore Sanvitale refers when she expatiates on the poet's love:

> . . . Er tobt nicht frevelhaft
> Von einer Brust zur andern hin und her;
> Er heftet sich an Schönheit und Gestalt
> Nicht gleich mit süssem Irrtum fest, und büsset
> Nicht schnellen Rausch mit Ekel und Verdruss.   *(Ibid.)*

And it is of the same immortal spirit, and in the same vein, that the Princess will speak to Tasso later in the play, when she invokes her vision of the Golden Age:

> Die Schönheit ist vergänglich, die ihr doch
> Allein zu ehren scheint . . .

she admonishes him, and continues, with urgency and passion:

> Wenn's Männer gäbe, die ein weiblich Herz
> Zu schätzen wüssten, die erkennen möchten,

Welch einen holden Schatz von Treu und Liebe
Der Busen einer Frau bewahren kann;
. . .
Wenn euer Blick, der sonst durchdringend ist,
Auch durch den Schleier dringen könnte, den
Uns Alter oder Krankheit überwirft;
Wenn der Besitz, der ruhig machen soll,
Nach fremden Gütern euch nicht lüstern machte:
Dann wär uns wohl ein schöner Tag erschienen,
Wir feierten dann unsre goldne Zeit.   (II, 1)

The Princess urges a love which penetrates beneath physical
appearances as Leonore had done – and done, or so it seems, for
the same reason. For as we have seen, in Plato's view, love at its
highest is a communion of spirits rather than of flesh and blood;[3]
in the *Phaedrus* it is a sharing by kindred souls of the highest
goods, of which they once partook before they were embodied in
an earthly frame. This sharing of a universal good is the crux of
Leonore's assessment of the relationship between Tasso and
themselves I have quoted. And precisely this is the crux of the
Princess's reply to Tasso's words about the Golden Age:

Mein Freund, die goldne Zeit ist wohl vorbei;
Allein die Guten bringen sie zurück.
. . .
Noch treffen sich verwandte Herzen an
Und teilen den Genuss der schönen Welt;   (II, 1)

The operative word, in the accounts of both Leonores, is 'teilen'.
In the universe of discourse of this tragedy, love is not an
appropriation of one person by another. It is a joint participation
in values which are suprapersonal. Hence Leonore's assumption:

Hier ist die Frage nicht von einer Liebe,
Die sich des Gegenstands bemeistern will,
Ausschliessend ihn besitzen . . .   (I, 1)

and hence the admonition with which the Princess, at the
beginning of the second act, closes the conversation which has
fairly swept Tasso off his feet:

. . . Viele Dinge sind's,
Die wir mit Heftigkeit ergreifen sollen:
Doch andre können nur durch Mässigung
Und durch Entbehren unser eigen werden.
So, sagt man, sei die Tugend, sei die Liebe,
Die ihr verwandt ist. Das bedenke wohl!   (II, 1)

Love as a 'holde Schule'; 'hold', but a discipline none the less; love linked with virtue and, like virtue, based on temperance and moderation; indeed, the whole paradoxical notion of love appropriating its object by renouncing its physical possession – all this is the purest Plato, though it is not the Plato of the *Symposium*; and if Leonore, in claiming that she is a novice to his teachings, is perhaps guilty of an understatement – a forgivable one, since by the law of her nature she is bound to stay on the fringe of such an esoteric creed – the Princess at any rate has studied her *Phaedrus* and let her mind and soul be soaked in its philosophy of love.

In the *Phaedrus*, love appears at the gateway from the earthly to the divine, as the winged power of the soul through which it is reborn to eternal truth and beauty. As Eros himself is conceived as a winged god, so Plato conceives of the human soul as winged: in its primordial condition the soul, covered with feathers, travels with a band of immortals high in the vault of heaven, rising beyond it even to glimpse the beauty on the other side. It is a spectacle bathed in brightness. Then, impeded by its mortal part, the soul sinks down to earth and is embodied in a human frame. As it is severed from the sight of the beauty on which it had feasted, the feathers which bore it aloft begin to shed. It is then that the sight of beauty in this world may cause it to recollect the heavenly splendours of which it once partook, and it is then that, drawn by love and desire towards the object which recalls its divine origins, its wings once again put forth feathery plumage. Thus lovers in this world love each other for the immortal glory they reflect. Restraining their physical appetites which hold them down to earth, they walk through life together and together aspire to be reborn to their pristine estate, pledged to beauty and truth.[4]

Thus love in the *Phaedrus*. It seems likewise between the Princess and the poet. Their love for one another is the break of day, the gateway to a new and higher life:

> Ihn musst ich ehren, darum liebt ich ihn;
> Ich musst ihn lieben, weil mit ihm mein Leben
> Zum Leben ward, wie ich es nie gekannt . . .   (III, 2)

the Princess confesses to her friend. Twice in the course of the tragedy, she relives the moment when she first set eyes on him,[5] first as she recounts it to Tasso himself and then to her namesake; and

> Der Augenblick, da ich zuerst ihn sah,
> War vielbedeutend.   (III, 2)

He came at her sister's hand at the moment when she took her
first faltering steps out of the darkness of her sickroom into the
brightness of an unaccustomed day. We do not know much of
Leonore's illness except that it was a time of deprivation and deep
withdrawal from the world:

> Mit breiten Flügeln schwebte mir das Bild
> Des Todes vor den Augen, deckte mir
> Die Aussicht in die immer neue Welt.
> Nur nach und nach entfernt' es sich und liess
> Mich, wie durch einen Flor, die bunten Farben
> Des Lebens, blass, doch angenehm, erblicken.
> Ich sah lebendge Formen wieder sanft sich regen.   (II, 1)

Then Tasso came and with him came

> Der Sonne Pracht, das fröhliche Gefühl
> Des hohen Tags, der tausendfachen Welt
> Glanzreiche Gegenwart . . .   (III, 2)

The Princess does not tire of reiterating the Platonic association of
her love with the radiance of the day, and when she thinks that
Leonore will take him from her, that the day will come when

> Die Sonne hebt von meinen Augenlidern
> Nicht mehr sein schön verklärtes Traumbild auf . . . *(Ibid.)*

life, in her imagination, is at once plunged in deepest gloom:

> Welch eine Dämmrung fällt nun vor mir ein!   *(Ibid.)*

If Tasso is the light of her day, it is not simply because she loves
him; rather because his coming has endowed her existence with
some ultimate and unquestioned significance. The ingredients of
her past life – her thinking, her learning, her discipline and her
self-denial, in short, the elements of her *Bildung* – all these,
through her love for Tasso, have fused into one vibrant whole. In
the radiance of her love the meaning of life stands revealed, and
the moderation she asks Tasso to exercise in the name of such love
seems but a small price to pay for its beauty.

It seems the same with Tasso. For him, too, love means the
dawning of 'der neue Tag', and he does not tire of reiterating the
image in ever new variations. He only needs to see her, to hear her
speak, 'So wird ein neuer Tag um mich herum' (II, 1).

He speaks thus extravagantly even at the outset of their encounter at the beginning of the second act. His concluding words

are uttered in a transport which frightens the Princess by its
violence:

> Welch einen Himmel öffnest du vor mir,
> O Fürstin! Macht mich dieser Glanz nicht blind,
> So seh ich unverhofft ein ewig Glück
> Auf goldnen Strahlen herrlich niedersteigen.   *(Ibid.)*

He too experiences love as a renewal, as a birth into a higher state
of being; and this experience is unforgettably rendered by the
lines of the monologue which follows upon their conversation:

> Der Blindgeborne denke sich das Licht,
> Die Farben, wie er will; erscheinet ihm
> Der neue Tag, ist's ihm ein neuer Sinn.   (II, 2)

In terms which are unequivocally Platonic, he declares:

> Mit meinen Augen hab ich es gesehn,
> Das Urbild jeder Tugend, jeder Schöne;   (II, 1)

and:

> Das Göttlichste erfuhr ich nur in dir.   *(Ibid.)*

Indeed, the exfoliating of a new spiritual organ which he has
here conveyed in terms of sight, has also found expression in a
reiterated image that is yet closer to the Platonic myth. Love has
unfolded the wings of Tasso's soul. Three times he uses the image
before tragedy ensues. First, when he dedicates his poem to the
princely couple:

> Du warst allein, der aus dem engen Leben
> Zu einer schönen Freiheit mich erhob;
> Der jede Sorge mir vom Haupte nahm,
> Mir Freiheit gab, dass meine Seele sich
> Zu mutigem Gesang entfalten konnte;   (I, 3)

Then, more intimately, when he dedicates himself and his life to
the Princess:

> O lehre mich, das mögliche zu tun!
> Gewidmet sind dir alle meine Tage.
> Wenn, dich zu preisen, dir zu danken, sich
> Mein Herz entfaltet, dann empfind ich erst
> Das reinste Glück, das Menschen fühlen können;
> Das Göttlichste erfuhr ich nur in dir.   (II, 1)

Love has unsealed his lips and given him 'Melodie und Rede';
and both times this liberation of creative power is experienced as
a metamorphosis to a higher state, nearer to the divine, and as a
partaking of it in freedom of the spirit. On the third occasion
Tasso uses the image of exfoliation in an earthier vein already
familiar to us from the 'Künstlergedichte'.[6] The poet's soul is a
plant and his poems are the fruit thereof; both, he and they,
organic beings, are subject to organic laws. This is how Tasso puts
it, at the end of his monologue, in a kind of prayer:

> – Schwelle, Brust! – O Witterung des Glücks,
> Begünstge diese Pflanze doch einmal!
> Sie strebt gen Himmel, tausend Zweige dringen
> Aus ihr hervor, entfalten sich zu Blüten,
> O dass sie Frucht, o dass sie Freuden bringe!
> Dass eine liebe Hand den goldnen Schmuck
> Aus ihren frischen, reichen Ästen breche!   (II, 2)

For all the difference between this metaphor and the earlier,
visual one – and we shall have to consider this difference presently
– the idea of a metamorphosis from one stage to another, from
blindness to sight and from branch to blossom and fruit, remains
constant, and so does the upward movement 'gen Himmel'. In
these lines Tasso expresses his complete trust in the fructifying
force of love. It is here for him as it was in the 'Künstlergedichte'
for his creator: the spheres of mental and physical creativity have
fused, to the point where they are no longer distinguishable. In
the 'Künstlergedichte' the young poet had prayed

> Dass ich mit Göttersinn
> Und Menschenhand
> Vermög' zu bilden,
> Was bei meinem Weib
> Ich animalisch kann und muss . . .[7]

Here, too, in this tragedy of Goethe's manhood, Tasso, in one
all-embracing metaphor of growth and flowering and fruitbearing,
encompasses the hopes both of the poet and the man. The longing
for happiness which swells his breast precipitates a surge of
creative energy in him, and of both alike he speaks in terms of
bodily experience and of unconscious organic process.

For all its richer vitality, this fusion of creativity and love seems
to reflect the experience of the Princess. For her as for Tasso, love
is the passage to a more creative life. Both believe in the all-pervasive, fertilising and refining force of love and it is because of this

faith – the faith of Plato, enshrined in the poetry of the *Symposium* and the *Phaedrus* – that both experience their love as a rebirth and speak of it in images which are fraught with mystical allusions. And indeed, who would blame the lovers for thinking that the realms disclosed by kindred manifestations of Eros are themselves kindred regions of the human soul? That his making of art, and her love of the arts, are twin shoots stemming from one root, sprung from the common soil of one humanity? If love has vivified the cultural values to which the Princess feels committed, love, for Tasso, has quickened the creative force which is productive of such values; formative experiences, both, and both designated by the same word – *bilden*. Tasso *bildet*, and the kind of values he creates are productive of the *Bildung* which flowers at Ferrara. The very ambiguity of the word – perhaps the verbal pivot of the tragedy as a whole – the fact that, throughout the drama, it is used to signify, now the creative activity itself, now its products and now the enjoyment of what is being created, would seem to confirm the lovers in their faith that his *bilden* is germane to her *Bildung*, that the creative mode which produces the values by which humanity exists is itself a stable and civilised mode of existence. Everything in the drama conspires to prove this sup-position of the lovers and we are made to share a conviction which is steadily supported by the verbal filigree of the play. Moreover, are not his *bilden* and her *Bildung* doubly and triply linked in that, throughout the play, they are associated with identical expecta-tions? Both hold the promise of a higher life; both are the source of a brighter light; and both engender nearness. As Tasso hopes for 'Frucht' *and* 'Freuden', as he prays

> Dass eine liebe Hand den goldnen Schmuck
> Aus ihren frischen, reichen Ästen breche!   (II, 2)

and thinks of the Princess possessing him as he creates for her – 'bildend' – so she in turn confesses that it is his song which draws her closer and will win her over in the end:

> Es lockt uns nach, und nach, wir hören zu,
> Wir hören, und wir glauben zu verstehn,
> Was wir verstehn, das können wir nicht tadeln,
> Und so gewinnt uns dieses Lied zuletzt.   (II, 1)

Finally and most importantly; both, Tasso's *bilden* and the *Bildung* of the Princess, are quickened by the hope that through such growth they may achieve the liberation and the full development of all their powers. This is the force of the Princess's *streben*. And what else could conceivably be the force of his *entfalten*? *Bilden*, for both, seems rich with humanistic overtones; and for both it means a metamorphosis – the growing and the spreading of their spirits' wings.

II

These expectations, and the foundations on which they rest, are shattered in the final scenes of the tragedy. Admittedly, we had had warnings before. But the signals had been confused, pointing in opposite directions and, seemingly, cancelling each other out.

We had been alerted with the Princess when Tasso, at the mere mention of the 'goldne Zeit', had lost himself in a poetic dream of man as part of the natural order, unconsciously sharing in the gratifications granted to animals, 'wie frohe Herden im Genuss . . . ' (II, 1), a pastoral, it is true, but not without its dionysiac undertones; nourished, not by the restrained and sublimated account of human existence in Plato's *Phaedrus*, but by the orgiastic vision of Eros as a cosmic principle which we know from the *Symposium*. Despite the Princess's reminder that in a human context loving means the mastery of our animal drives and is tantamount to deprivation, moderation and sublimation all along the line, Tasso, in the monologue following upon their encounter, had reiterated his own sense of life as being rooted in unconscious nature. He had dedicated himself and his creativity to the Princess in words so sensuous that they would have frightened the Princess, had she heard them, although to us such unselfconscious acceptance of the instincts is familiar from the Goethe of the 'Künstlergedichte':

> Ihr bin ich, bildend soll sie mich besitzen,
> Mein Herz bewahrte jeden Schatz für sie.
> O hätt ein tausendfaches Werkzeug mir
> Ein Gott gegönnt, kaum drückt ich dann genug
> Die unaussprechliche Verehrung aus.
> Des Malers Pinsel und des Dichters Lippe,
> Die süsseste, die je von frühem Honig
> Genährt war, wünscht ich mir . . .   (II, 2)

And as Tasso here likens his creativity to the unconscious ardour of the bee so too, in the concluding words of this monologue to which we have already referred, he likens the creative urge which has seized his whole being to the unconscious flourishing of a plant.

Such unconscious organic process the poet, towards the end of the play, reveals as the mainspring of his creativity. The Duke has just appealed to Tasso to stop working for a while and to restore 'die schöne Harmonie der . . . Sinne' which stress and tension have all but destroyed, as the foregoing events have proven. He begs him not to lose himself in fruitless introspection and appeals to the human being in him to take the artist in hand: 'Der Mensch gewinnt, was der Poet verliert' (V, 2).

To this appeal Tasso replies as follows:

> Ich halte diesen Drang vergebens auf,
> Der Tag und Nacht in meinem Busen wechselt.
> Wenn ich nicht sinnen oder dichten soll,
> So ist das Leben mir kein Leben mehr.
> Verbiete du dem Seidenwurm, zu spinnen,
> Wenn er sich schon dem Tode näher spinnt:
> Das köstliche Geweb entwickelt er
> Aus seinem Innersten, und lässt nicht ab,
> Bis er in seinen Sarg sich eingeschlossen.
> O geb ein guter Gott uns auch dereinst
> Das Schicksal des beneidenswerten Wurms,
> Im neuen Sonnental die Flügel rasch
> Und freudig zu entfalten![8]   (Ibid.)

'Just try and tell a silkworm not to spin . . .' Words do not offer themselves that could readily convey the enormity of this statement, addressed by a courtier to his Prince, in the refinement and urbanity of this setting. To render the shock of their impact, let us borrow the words Antonio will use after the final cataclysm:

> Wenn ganz was Unerwartetes begegnet,
> Wenn unser Blick was Ungeheures sieht,
> Steht unser Geist auf eine Weile still:
> Wir haben nichts, womit wir das vergleichen.   (V, 5)

Even here, before Tasso's fatal embrace of the Princess, *terra firma* has begun to quake. Before our eyes, before our very feet, the poet's words have opened up a chasm, the chasm of inwardness of which, a moment earlier, the Duke had warned him; and in its depths all that had seemed incontestable and beautiful and human is swallowed up—the whole fair world of learning that is encompassed in the name Ferrara, the fragile fabric of its relationships and the humanity of its manners and its morals. The shy young poet who walks about dreamily posting songs on trees, who charms the women by his helplessness, in his heart of hearts knows that he is an outcast from the circle in which he moves. More than that: he knows that, in the sense in which the word is valid here, he is bereft of humanity. He is an elemental being, a worm, most rudimentary of creatures, fitted and kept to serve a single end: to spin the yarn of poetry.

Mercilessly, one by one, Tasso's words recall the hopes he had cherished together with the Princess – that his genius might lift him to a sphere of light, and life, and love, in which he and she might dwell together – only to repudiate and dash them. One by one, he gathers up the threads that have steadily if unobtrusively run through the play, to entwine them in a tissue of despair:

> Ich halte diesen Drang vergebens auf,
> Der Tag und Nacht in meinem Busen wechselt.   (V, 2)

Yet what does this drive alternate with, other than itself? The poet does not say. But before, he had already told the Duke, in a number of curiously tautologous statements, that to him a varied life such as might be conducive to the 'schöne Harmonie der hergestellten Sinne' is repellent. His *Fleiss,* for him, is all. *Fleiss* is his illness and his health, his work and his recuperation.

> . . . Mir lässt die Ruh
> Am mindsten Ruhe . . .   *(Ibid.)*

he had argued when pressed to take a holiday and:

> . . . ich bin gesund
> Wenn ich mich meinem Fleiss ergeben kann,
> Und so macht wieder mich der Fleiss gesund.   *(Ibid.)*

For him to be with his work, and only that, is to be at rest:

> . . . ganz
> Ruht mein Gemüt auf diesem Werke nun.   *(Ibid.)*

From the beginning the Princess had understood him when she had said:

> Und seine Seele hegt nur diesen Trieb,
> Es soll sich sein Gedicht zum Ganzen ründen.   (I, 2)

This 'Trieb' dominates him to the exclusion of any other. It does not alternate by day and night; rather does it reverse day and night. What is day to others, to his creative self is night, even the day of love which was to shine upon the Princess and himself. The only day, for him, is the night in which the worm entombs

itself as it emits its precious thread – 'Bis er in seinen Sarg sich
eingeschlossen.'

Again, and similarly:

> Wenn ich nicht sinnen oder dichten soll,
> So ist das Leben mir kein Leben mehr.   (V, 2)

Life becomes death and death becomes life. What is life for
others, even the radiant life held out to him by the Princess, for
Tasso's creative self is death. The only life, for him, is that of the
assiduous worm, 'Wenn er sich schon dem Tode näher spinnt'.

Finally: creativeness had promised nearness – 'Frucht' *and*
'Freuden'. What it brings instead is the inexorable isolation of one
whose engrossment has been too long and too deep: 'Bis er in seinen
Sarg sich eingeschlossen.'

In the face of this reality, all the hopes are blighted which had
been centred on the poet's education, not only by the Princess but
by every character in the play; all the efforts collapse that had
been expended in the endeavour to make him a social asset as well
as his art, to teach him to enjoy himself as others enjoy his poems.
How patiently they had tried to attune him to their world! How
carefully they had sought to shape him to their mould and to
instil into him their values!

> O dass er sein Gemüt wie seine Kunst
> An deinen Lehren bilde! . . .   (I, 2)

> Wir wünschen ihn zu bilden, dass er mehr
> Sich selbst geniesse, mehr sich zu geniessen
> Den andern geben könne . . .   (III, 4)

> Wir wollen nichts von dir, was du nicht bist,
> Wenn du nur erst dir mit dir selbst gefällst.   (V, 4)

All this is null and void in view of the poet's 'otherness'. Tasso
himself *bildet*, it is true. Indeed, his creations are instrumental in
making the culture around him what it is. His poems adorn his
time as the raiments of silk he so loves to wear – 'ein seiden Kleid
mit etwas Stickerei' – adorn their wearer, marking him out as a
being possessed of leisure and the luxuries of human life. But the
poet learns that he himself is not part of the culture he creates and
serves. When eventually he leaves Ferrara, he will shed his silks
and don the worker's garb, 'den schwarzen Kittel'. The refinement
of an aesthetic culture – 'die schöne Harmonie der hergestellten
Sinne' – is not for him. He is the slave of the one skill with which

nature has equipped him; and it is not for nothing that towards
the end of the play, as he gains insight into the law that governs
him, savage images of slavery begin to crowd into his mind. True,
his *Fleiss,* his *Trieb,* his *Drang,* bear a human name – it is his
Bildungstrieb; and its products are eminently human. But the
appearance of any kinship barring that of name between the drive
that operates in Tasso and the *Bildungstrieb* that animates the
members of the court, in this drama is tragically misleading.

In a review dating from 1772, the young Goethe, imbued with
the dread of the disintegrating force of nature, yet drawn to view
man and animal as part of a creative continuum, had written:

> Was wir von Natur sehen, ist Kraft, die Kraft verschlingt, nichts
> gegenwärtig, alles vorübergehend, tausend Keime zertreten, jeden
> Augenblick tausend geboren . . . Und die Kunst ist gerade das
> Widerspiel; sie entspringt aus den Bemühungen des Individuums sich
> gegen die zerstörende Kraft des Ganzen zu erhalten. Schon das Tier
> durch seine Kunsttriebe scheidet, verwahrt sich; der Mensch durch
> alle Zustände befestigt sich gegen die Natur . . . [9]

In this classical tragedy, the poet's impulse to fashion coherent
rhythmic structures out of words, an impulse so primitive and so
specialised, has been excised from the human world,[10] and is
viewed as an extension of that blind constructional instinct that
operates in the animal world: in spider, bird and bee and – in the
silkworm:

> Das köstliche Geweb entwickelt er
> Aus seinem Innersten, und lässt nicht ab,
> Bis er in seinen Sarg sich eingeschlossen.   (V, 2)

Entwicklung, Bildung – sacred watchwords in the age of German
classicism and sacred watchwords in the world of Renaissance
Ferrara: what have they come to on this poet's lips? The word
entwickeln, as Tasso uses it, is stripped of all its richer human
associations. No longer does it signify the untrammelled
development of the person in the fullness of his gifts – physical,
mental and emotional. 'Ent-wickeln', as Tasso uses it, denotes the
operation of a single physiological function, the unravelling of the
precious thread; and this elemental activity, ironically, goes hand
in hand with the destruction and entombment of the person as a
whole.

III

For all its being couched in cadences of mellifluous beauty, this

account of the creative state has a fiercely tragic quality about it.
Never perhaps has the incompatibility of the artistic mode with
the demands of human existence – 'Die Disproportion des Talents
mit dem Leben' as Goethe himself termed it[11] – been expressed
with a passion more quietly definite. The only other statement
known to me that is resonant with a force of such finality
was made more than a hundred years later, by one possessed of
Goethe's own fastidious tact and as wary as the author of *Tasso* of
poetic self-exposure. Listen to the account of creativity which
Hugo von Hofmannsthal, in an imaginary conversation, ascribes
to the novelist Balzac.

> Haben Sie eine grössere Reise auf einem Dampfschiffe gemacht?

the Frenchman asks his companion;

> Entsinnen Sie sich da einer sonderbaren, beinahe Mitleid erregenden
> Gestalt, die gegen Abend aus einer Lücke des Maschinenraumes
> auftauchte und sich für eine Viertelstunde oben aufhielt, um Luft zu
> schöpfen? Der Mann war halbnackt, er hatte ein geschwärztes Gesicht
> **und rote, entzündete Augen.** Man hat Ihnen gesagt, dass es der
> Heizer der Maschine ist. Sooft er heraufkam, taumelte er; er trank
> **gierig einen grossen Krug Wasser** leer, er legte sich auf einen Haufen
> Werg und spielte mit dem Schiffshund, er warf ein paar scheue, fast
> schwachsinnige Blicke auf die schönen und fröhlichen Passagiere der
> ersten Kajüte, die auf Deck waren, sich an den Sternen des südlichen
> Himmels zu entzücken; er atmete, dieser Mensch, mit Gier, so wie er
> getrunken hatte, die Luft, welche durchfeuchtet war von einer in Tau
> vergehenden Nachtwolke und dem Duft von unberührten Palmenin-
> seln, der über das Meer heranschwebte; und er verschwand wieder im
> Bauch des Schiffes, ohne die Sterne und den Duft der geheimnisvollen
> Inseln auch nür bemerkt zu haben. Das sind die Aufenthalte des
> Künstlers unter den Menschen, wenn er taumelnd und mit blöden
> Augen aus dem feurigen Bauch seiner Arbeit hervorkriecht.[12]

'Dieser Mensch' is Tasso, entombed in his art; but he is also the
creator of *Tasso* – who conceived his tragedy in its final form,
'Abgeschlossen von der äussern Welt',[13] lying seasick and absolutely motionless in the 'Walfischbauch' of the ship which carried
him to Sicily.[14] Only then, fifteen years after writing *Die Leiden des
jungen Werther*, did Goethe feel sufficiently secure to enact the
creative trauma he had endured as a young man and finally to
fashion it into poetry. As the poet-hero of his tragedy spins himself
into the coffin of isolation and death, he experiences before our
eyes that terrifying alienation which is the condition of creativity;
an experience shared by all whose inner world is productive of

forms which are themselves prescriptive for reality.

Leonore Sanvitale – of all the characters in this tragedy the most realistic interpreter of Tasso's sensibility – is the first to recognise the 'otherness' of the poet. Had she not warned the Princess, saying:

> Er scheint sich uns zu nahn, und bleibt uns fern;
> Er scheint uns anzusehn, und Geister mögen
> An unsrer Stelle seltsam ihm erscheinen.   (I, 1)

Had she not recognised that from the outset the artist experiences life in a manner which is subtly yet decisively different from that of other mortals? That he is ultimately pledged, not to this Leonore or that, but to the quest for his ideal which he distils from his semi-real earthly encounters, much as the young Goethe himself, in his *Werther*, had distilled fiction from the composite reality of Charlotte Buff and Maximiliane von La Roche? And had she not realised that the mobile spirit of the artist needs such a 'Doppelsinn' behind which he pursues the invincible passion for his art, even as his creator had confessed, almost, to depending upon the 'Doppelglanz' of the two luminaries from which he had drawn his own inspiration? And do we not discern the poet's intention behind this clever woman's explanation? For what could have induced Goethe to give the name Leonore to the two female characters out of a total cast of five,[15] if not the wish to draw attention to such an indeterminacy and even impersonality in the feeling life of an artist whose fiercest passions are committed to Venus Urania, who presides over his secret addiction – the bodying forth of art forms? However sincerely the poet protests that the Princess is 'Das Urbild jeder Tugend, jeder Schöne', however much he declares:

> Es schwebt kein geistig unbestimmtes Bild
> Vor meiner Stirne, das der Seele bald
> Sich überglänzend nahte, bald entzöge   (II, 1)

her image, to him, is as elusive as the shadow cast by a cloud which any fleeting movement may disturb, and the only enduring reality is that of the poetic figures he has culled from this model. As the young Goethe had cried: 'Werther muss – muss seyn',[16] so Tasso proclaims of his figments:

> Es sind nicht Schatten, die der Wahn erzeugte,
> Ich weiss es, sie sind ewig, denn sie sind.   (*Ibid.*)

And indeed, at the end, the reality of the Princess herself will be no more than a veil or disguise, which is dispelled by the superior truth for him of his poetic vision:

> Wie lang verdeckte mir dein heilig Bild
> Die Buhlerin, die kleine Künste treibt.
> Die Maske fällt: Armiden seh ich nun
> Entblösst von allen Reizen – ja, du bist's!
> Von dir hat ahnungsvoll mein Lied gesungen! (V, 5)

In this drama, the classical Goethe who had lived in the light of the South and disciplined his eye and his hand to see and feel things as they are, mercilessly exposes the dangers of that inwardness to which the poet is subject, however different such inwardness may be from the unproductive introversion of a Werther. And what could attest the severity of his judgment more eloquently than the use to which he now puts the once archetypal images of the creative activity, the images of *weben* and *spinnen*?[17] As Tasso compares himself to the silkworm, his words forge a most sinister bond between his productive *Sinnen* and *Dichten* and *Spinnen*, and those *Gewebe* in which time and again he feels himself entrapped; and in the course of the action the threads of the creative and the pathological become inextricably entwined. It is the projection of his own disordered mind he glimpses when, beside himself with anger at Antonio's reserve, he sees '[der] Spinne schmutziges Gewebe' clinging to the walls of Belriguardo (II, 3). He will see many another phantom web, woven by conspiracy and cunning, and by and by such webs will cloud his vision and envelop him in darkness. Alfons had seen it all at the beginning, saying:

> . . . und so wird nach und nach
> Ein frei Gemüt verworren und gefesselt. (I, 2)

Leonore had begged Tasso to understand

> Dass niemand dich im ganzen Vaterlande
> Verfolgt und hasst und heimlich drückt und neckt! (IV, 2)

'Du irrst gewiss', she had assured him and had added, with a significant *double-entendre* of the word 'dichten':

> . . . und wie du sonst zur Freude
> Von andern dichtest, leider dichtest du
> In diesem Fall ein seltenes Gewebe,
> Dich selbst zu kränken. (*Ibid.*)

But Tasso is unwilling to believe

> . . . dass alle List
> Und alles heimliche Gewebe sich
> Allein in meinem Kopfe spinnt und webt!   (IV, 3)

More and more he persuades himself that his delusions are reality, exclaiming:

> . . . Deutlich seh ich nun
> Die ganze Kunst des höfischen Gewebes!   (IV, 5)

until, in the end, he is entangled in a fictitious web woven of his own 'Hirngespinste':

> Abscheulich dacht ich die Verschwörung mir,
> Die unsichtbar und rastlos mich umspann,
> Allein abscheulicher ist es geworden.   (V, 5)

IV

But the banishment of the poet *into* the world of universal forms and private phantoms he is busy weaving is, perhaps, the lesser part of Tasso's tragedy. More tragic is the reverse – his banishment, at a given moment of time, *from* the inner world of his art. This predicament appears to be familiar to one of Goethe's later heroines, Ottilie; and it is to her – a creature, like Tasso, both elemental and initiated into the secrets of creativity – that we may turn for an understanding account of it.

'Wie am Handwerker so am bildenden Künstler,' Ottilie writes in her diary,

> kann man auf das deutlichste gewahr werden, dass der Mensch sich das am wenigsten zuzueignen vermag, was ihm ganz eigens angehört. Seine Werke verlassen ihn, so wie die Vögel das Nest, worin sie ausgebrütet worden.
> . . . In den Tempeln zieht er eine Grenze zwischen sich und dem Allerheiligsten; er darf die Stufen nicht mehr betreten, die er zur herzerhebenden Feierlichkeit gründete, so wie der Goldschmied die Monstranz nur von fern anbetet, deren Schmelz und Edelsteine er zusammengeordnet hat. Dem Reichen übergibt der Baumeister mit dem Schlüssel des Palastes alle Bequemlichkeit und Behäbigkeit, ohne irgend etwas davon mitzugeniessen. Muss nicht allgemach auf diese Weise die Kunst von dem Künstler entfernen, wenn das Werk, wie ein ausgestattetes Kind, nicht mehr auf den Vater zurückwirkt?[18]

The poet, it is true, is less abruptly severed from his work than the sculptor or the architect. The insubstantial shapes he has created linger on in his mind, and in this, we have seen, lies the source of a disorientation the depth of which the visual artist, confronted by the forms which he has bodied forth in space, does not know. Such a blurring of what is past and what is present, of what is his and no longer his, represents the poet's especial danger.

Tasso – and in saying this we are touching upon the structural core of the tragedy – has finished his epic, or so he thought. He has surrendered it into the hands of his patron, and in doing so has stepped out of his creative seclusion. This is the *prägnante Moment* in which the poet has divined the *Lebenspunkt* of his tragedy. From this angle, what has been seen as the tragedy of one man, Tasso, is suddenly clarified as a highly differentiated poetic structure in which each of the protagonists – the Princess and Antonio as well as Tasso – is subjected to the same dynamic law, outward, from containment to non-containment. The pattern is identical for all, as if they were all in one gravitational field and subject to the same gravitational pull. For the Princess, too – 'So lieblich angelockt, so hart bestraft!' – has been drawn by the events of the day to relinquish the reserve imposed upon her by temperament and illness, and it is upon this flowering of her relationship with Tasso, compressed into these poignant moments, that the poet bids us focus our attention. And so, too, Antonio has uneasily emerged from the armour of purposiveness in which his duties had so long ensconced him.[19] All are precipitated into a state of transition and uncertainty and, as we have seen, such inner stirrings are reflected in the movements of the characters upon the scene. The Duke and Antonio have come for some short moments of relaxation, only to leave again. Eleonore Sanvitale is about to head for Florence, into a future beset by tremors, suddenly, of transience; and the Princess, we know, will flee from Belriguardo before the day is out.

Amidst all these comings and goings, it is Tasso's hesitant steps out of his engrossment into the world of relationship which act as the catalyst of the changes we witness in every direction. His faltering entry into the world it is which precipitates each and all into a passing configuration in which, through the interplay of excited sensibilities, a floodlight is turned upon every facet of the group before it breaks up.

This Platonic circle, in fact, so quiet seemingly and so securely founded by mature minds committed to enduring values, turns out to be a dynamic form, glimpsed in the very first scenes of the tragedy only to dissolve before our very eyes. Indeed, the poet in this drama has chosen that moment of transition which offers him the greatest compositional values, a moment which, a decade later, he was to analyse in his essay on the Laokoon-group;[20] and the *Hochgestalt* at the heart of this changing constellation in whom Goethe has captured the essence of transition, is the figure of the poet himself.

In letting go of his poem, Tasso has surrendered his 'einzig Eigentum', his 'einzig Gut'; not, as he imagines it to be, a material asset to keep need and hunger at bay, but an armour against inner chaos and disintegration. His whole economy had been geared to the needs of his poem; his deepest drives had been engaged in it and contained in this engrossment. Now he has stripped himself of his cocoon, perhaps too soon,[21] and has emerged from it like a butterfly drawn to take wing: 'rasch und freudig', 'im neuen Sonnental', yet faltering at the light of the day. But perhaps this simile – Tasso's own, we remember – is misleading after all. For the metamorphosis of the silkworm, endowed with a single skill, into the moth gifted for flight and flight alone, is a sweeter and simpler process than the metamorphosis of the creative artist back into a being fitted to respond to the varied demands of human life. Tasso's inner *Gestalt*, the organisation of his whole being to a creational end, has broken down: his poem has left him as the bird relinquishes the nest; and the elemental energies that had nourished his creation are released from their engagement. He is swept 'Upon Time's toppling wave';[22] and what was creative Eros has turned into naked libidinal drives.

Thus the tragedy the poet endures is not only the generic tragedy of the creative artist – his alienation from reality in the creative act.[23] *This* creative artist is a poet; and at the precise moment in the creative cycle which his creator has chosen to single out, Tasso endures the even bitterer alienation from his own creative self and the dread – so well known even to the Goethe of 1772 – of disintegration. In the review to which reference was made earlier,[24] the young Goethe had acclaimed the preservative power of art against the destructive forces of nature. In 1823 – the year of the *Marienbader Elegie*, in which Goethe was vainly to invoke the shade of Tasso and all the creative powers of mind and soul to defend him against the onslaught of yet another annihilating passion – the poet wrote words which echo this early insight as from a great distance:

> Die Idee der Metamorphose ist eine höchst ehrwürdige, aber zugleich höchst gefährliche Gabe von oben. Sie führt ins Formlose, zerstört das Wissen, löst es auf. Sie ist gleich der vis centrifuga und würde sich ins

Unendliche verlieren, wäre ihr nicht ein Gegengewicht zugegeben: ich meine den Spezifikationstrieb, das zähe Beharrlichkeitsvermögen dessen was einmal zur Wirklichkeit gekommen. Eine vis centripeta, welcher in ihrem tiefsten Grunde keine Äusserlichkeit etwas anhaben kann.[25]

But it was only by enduring the repeated collapse of a personality the structure of which he had come to regard as constant, as well as by his phenomenal *vis superba formae,* that Goethe, time and again, found the inner strength to renew this belief. And even his Faust has to learn that to resist the dread venture of change is in truth to die; he has to suffer extinction before, in the greatest metamorphosis of all, he becomes a nursling of immortality.[26] Contrary to his hero, the poet and the scientist never went back on his knowledge that living form is patterned flux of elements which incessantly form, break down and form anew. 'Der Deutsche', Goethe wrote,

hat für den Komplex des Daseins eines wirklichen Wesens das Wort Gestalt. Er abstrahiert bei diesem Ausdruck von dem Beweglichen, er nimmt an, dass ein Zusammengehöriges festgestellt, abgeschlossen und in seinem Character fixiert sei.

Betrachten wir aber alle Gestalten, besonders die organischen, so finden wir, dass nirgends ein Bestehendes, nirgends ein Ruhendes, ein Abgeschlossenes vorkommt, sondern dass vielmehr alles in einer steten Bewegung schwanke. Daher unsere Sprache das Wort Bildung sowohl von dem Hervorgebrachten, als von dem Hervorgebrachtwerdenden gehörig genug zu brauchen pflegt.[27]

But however closely intertwined a man's life and thought may be – and in what figure of the modern world are these two as united as they were in Goethe? – to know transience is one thing, to live with such knowledge is another. *Torquato Tasso* is the first of a series of works of art – *Die Natürliche Tochter, Pandora* and *Faust II* belong here – in which the poet, at the height of his creative powers, yet face to face with mortality, gave utterance to his deep dread of disintegration: and not only to the terror of the breaking up of form in death, but to the dread, above all, of that inexorable disintegration of the creative configuration which every artist is time and again forced to endure. Tasso himself experiences such a waning of his inner *Gestalt* when he surrenders his poem and instead receives the scorching gift of a laurel wreath; and it is this inner loss he mourns when, after his collision with Antonio, he returns the imperishable token, saying:

Wer weinte nicht, wenn das Unsterbliche
Vor der Zerstörung selbst nicht sicher ist?   (II, 4)

this inner transience he means when he asks with horror and incredulity:

> Hat nicht die Ankunft dieses Manns allein
> Mein ganz Geschick zerstört, in einer Stunde?
> Nicht dieser das Gebäude meines Glücks
> Von seinem tiefsten Grund aus umgestürzt?   (IV, 5)

this inner annihilation he sees completed when he cries:

> . . . Hat der Schmerz,
> Als schütterte der Boden, das Gebäude
> In einen grausen Haufen Schutt verwandelt?   (V, 5)

– an image which will eventually give way to the final metaphor of the disintegrating ship.

Faced with this collapse of a creative configuration he had thought stable and on which he had come to rely, Tasso strains, ever more feverishly, to seek refuge in the safety of his art. And ever more painfully he misses the mark.[28] True, his *Kunsttrieb* is still functioning. But its organising power is failing before our eyes. It is no longer the heart of a sound body; rather it is a nerve twitching still in a limb that has been severed, or a cancerous tissue invading a healthy system. We have seen how Werther's practical and personal responses from the outset invade any aesthetic experience he might have and blight its structure at its core. In exactly the opposite fashion, Tasso's *Kunsttrieb*, strong still and summoned to keep chaos at bay, invades and destroys the living tissue of the relationship between him and the Princess. In increasing measure, his poetic conceptions become divorced from the reality of which they are born, and destructive of it. Visions such as those of himself as a pilgrim returning to Sorrento, or as a caretaker minding the Duke's remotest estates are fatal to the relation between the Princess and himself because of their obsessional quality and their unrelatedness to the reality-situation. Worse still, they are divorced from his own centre and doomed to remain artistically sterile in that they no longer command and engage his deepest vital drives.

> Beschränkt der Rand des Bechers einen Wein,
> Der schäumend wallt und brausend überschwillt?   (V, 4)

the young poet asks just before he embraces the Princess. The erotic significance of this image has been noted;[29] and indeed, it is plain enough. But its importance for the inner movement of the tragedy lies in the fact that it marks the catastrophic transition from containment to non-containment, from the disciplined passion of the artist who is content to remain engrossed in his 'eigenen Zauberkreise' and to respect the sphere of others, to the rampant passions of the man whose creative energies have been set free, cruelly to overwhelm him and to invade the privacy of the woman who had so delicately loved him.

It is Antonio who diagnoses this tragic swing from containment to chaos, from that brooding distance which the Princess, veiled and withdrawn herself, understands and yet wishes to dispel, to an all-demanding, all-engulfing explosion into the world of relationship:

> . . . Bald
> Versinkt er in sich selbst, als wäre ganz
> Die Welt in seinem Busen, er sich ganz
> In seiner Welt genug, und alles rings
> Umher verschwindet ihm. Er lässt es gehn,
> Lässt's fallen, stösst's hinweg und ruht in sich –
> Auf einmal, wie ein unbemerkter Funke
> Die Mine zündet, sei es Freude, Leid,
> Zorn oder Grille, heftig bricht er aus:
> Dann will er alles fassen, alles halten,
> Dann soll geschehn, was er sich denken mag;
> In einem Augenblicke soll entstehn,
> Was jahrelang bereitet werden sollte,
> In einem Augenblick gehoben sein,
> Was Mühe kaum in Jahren lösen könnte.
> Er fordert das Unmögliche von sich,
> Damit er es von andern fordern dürfe,
> Die letzten Enden aller Dinge will
> Sein Geist zusammenfassen; das gelingt
> Kaum einem unter Millionen Menschen,
> Und er ist nicht der Mann: er fällt zuletzt,
> Um nichts gebessert, in sich selbst zurück.   (III, 4)

What else is this but the bi-sexual pulse of creativity which we have already noted in the discussion of the 'Künstlergedichte' and which we shall have occasion to note again in the final chapter of this book, in Faust?[30] Here as there, sharply defined, we perceive the feminine pole of conception and, juxtaposed to it, the masculine pole of penetration; only that the latter impulse, bereft of its insulating aesthetic context, is here shown as exploding with shattering directness into the sphere of human relationship, there to create the void which finds expression in the Princess's horrified 'Hinweg!'

At the close of the drama, in Torquato Tasso's final speech, this tragic transition from creative containment to chaos is once more taken up. With infinite nostalgia the poet recalls the tranquillity and the distance which were his while, creating, he experienced permanence in the midst of flux, 'Dauer im Wechsel':

> In dieser Woge spiegelte so schön
> Die Sonne sich, es ruhten die Gestirne
> An dieser Brust, die zärtlich sich bewegte.   (V, 5)

Even now, after the cataclysm, Tasso, with the pride of one who has understood himself and his fate, acknowledges that the strength which nature has granted to him is founded in his lability:

> O edler Mann! Du stehest fest und still,
> Ich scheine nur die sturmbewegte Welle.
> Allein bedenk und überhebe nicht
> Dich deiner Kraft! Die mächtige Natur,
> Die diesen Felsen gründete, hat auch
> Der Welle die Beweglichkeit gegeben.
> Sie sendet ihren Sturm, die Welle flieht
> Und schwankt und schwillt und beugt sich schäumend über.
> *(Ibid.)*

But the knowledge that his creative power lies in such infinite capacity for change fails to illuminate the present:

> Ich kenne mich in der Gefahr nicht mehr,
> Und schäme mich nicht mehr, es zu bekennen.
> Zerbrochen ist das Steuer, und es kracht
> Das Schiff an allen Seiten. Berstend reisst
> Der Boden unter meinen Füssen auf!   *(Ibid.)*

There is no hope in these words, no glimmering of immortality or even of redemption through development. For now, at the nadir of his existence, the poet no longer envisages his creativity in terms of organic images germane to human growth, as the metamorphosing of bough into blossom and of blossom into fruit. To speak of his gift, he turns to elemental nature, changeless, intractable and inhuman. The Platonic dream is dreamt to an end. Unsublimated, elemental being has the final say. There is nothing left in these closing words except a sense of devastation, of fragmentation and disintegration – an endless chaos in which every human form is broken up.

In the desolation of such images – the final images not only of the poet but also, virtually, of the play – all that was there before seems blotted out: the sunlit scene, the peaceful park, the stillness and the sadness and the grace that was Ferrara. Could it be that Goethe wrote these closing lines in the peaceful gardens of Florence on his way back from eternal Rome to the 'Kimmerische Norden', between one banishment and another? Could it be that there, in the loveliness of Belvedere, he found utterance for the sense of desolation that beset him as he turned his back on the radiant configuration of living and creating, of drawing and sculpting and loving under Southern skies, and finally took up the cross of being a poet, that is to say of one banished into the 'Symbol-, Ideen- und Nebelwelt'[31] of an inexorable inwardness and of an incorporeal medium? The words which originally concluded the *Italienische Reise* make this seem likely. 'Bei meinem Abschied aus Rom', Goethe writes,

> empfand ich Schmerzen einer eignen Art . . . Den grössten Teil meines Aufenthalts in Florenz verbrachte ich in den dortigen Lust- und Prachtgärten. Dort schrieb ich die Stellen die mir noch jetzt jene Zeit, jene Gefühle unmittelbar zurückrufen . . . Wie mit Ovid dem Lokal nach, so konnte ich mich mit Tasso dem Schicksale nach vergleichen. Der schmerzliche Zug einer leidenschaftlichen Seele, die unwiderstehlich zu einer unwiderruflichen Verbannung hingezogen wird,[32] geht durch das ganze Stück.[33]

Perhaps there, in the midst of agony and inner death, remembering the exiled initiate into the secrets of metamorphosis, Goethe himself experienced a metamorphosis when he least expected it, as, in cadences of poignant perfection, he fashioned the tragedy of being a poet. A note written to the Duke Carl August of Weimar, shortly before the end of his work on *Torquato Tasso*, suggests that such a rebirth had in fact taken place: 'Tasso wächst wie ein Orangebaum sehr langsam,' Goethe wrote to his master. 'Dass er nur auch wohlschmeckende Früchte trage.'[34] Moving words, these, and movingly reminiscent of Tasso's prayer that the tree of his creativeness may yet be heavy with a crop of golden fruit. It seems that, drawn though he be into the exile of his inwardness, a poet will retrieve his inner South.

Part Three

THE BENIGN
CIRCLE

It is a false notion that more is gained by receiving than giving
– no the receiver and the giver are equal in their benefits . . .

(Keats to J. H. Reynolds, 18 February 1818)

Nathans Lächeln ist eine der Linien, wo sich Gott und Menschen berühren.

(H. Laube)

And all must love the human form,
   In heathen, turk or jew.
Where Mercy, Love & Pity dwell,
   There God is dwelling too.

(Blake: *The Divine Image*)

8

Minna von Barnhelm : The Currency of Love

I dare not say I take you; but I give
Me and my service, ever whilst I live
Into your guiding power.
> (Shakespeare: *All's Well That Ends Well*)

In the first scene of Act II of *Minna von Barnhelm* Franziska, during a conversation with her mistress over breakfast, finds occasion to make one of those general observations on human behaviour which so readily spring to the lips of Lessing's characters. 'Man spricht selten von der Tugend, die man hat; aber desto öfter von der, die uns fehlt.' Minna seizes the opportunity afforded by this maxim to speak about her inarticulate lover. He is full of virtues and he speaks of none. Neither of his valour, nor of his uprightness nor of his nobility. 'Er spricht von keiner; denn ihm fehlt keine.' This sounds altogether too good, and, needled by Franziska's irony, she admits that there might conceivably be one exception: 'Ich besinne mich. Er spricht sehr oft von Oekonomie. Im Vertrauen, Franciska; ich glaube, der Mann ist ein Verschwender.' Thus she saves her idol from ridicule by allowing him the one redeeming weakness that saves him for humanity. And whether or not she is correct in her psychological assumption that he must possess the opposite quality from the one he protests, she has put her finger on something of importance here, more important than she herself can know: for the poet has chosen to deal with, as the major theme of his comedy, the giving and taking that form the reciprocity of love, and to speak of these exchanges in terms of monetary symbols.[1]

Minna herself only knows of the magnanimous deed which made her love Tellheim before she ever set eyes on him: of his payment, out of his own pocket, of the sum levied on the Saxon estates at the end of the war. What she does not know is the train of misfortunes his kindheartedness has brought upon him: his dishonourable discharge from the army, his impecuniousness and his humiliation. Nor indeed can she know of the more recent events with which we have become acquainted in the preceding scenes: of Tellheim's removal from his room – which is now her room – because of his inability to pay the rent; of his resolve nevertheless to pay the innkeeper with the contempt he deserves; of his decision to dismiss his remaining man servant Just rather than get into his debt; of his refusal to touch the money that Paul **Werner**, his old comrade-in-arms, had left for his use; of his refusal to take money owed to him by a brother officer and returned by his widow: all of which events are underwritten and sealed, as it were, by Just's highhanded rejection of Werner's money at the end of the first act.[2]

This is generosity indeed. In fact, the first act seems to have done little else beside bearing in upon us, scene by scene, in a variety of situations and with a number of widely different characters, the deep unwillingness of the hero to take anything from anybody; a refusal which, for all his rectitude, leaves us just a trifle uneasy. Suspicions are strengthened when, in the second act, Tellheim presents himself again to the young woman he intended to marry and who innocently supposes him to be the man with whom she fell in love, saying 'Dieser Tellheim bin ich eben so wenig, – als ich mein Vater bin. Beide sind gewesen. – Ich bin Tellheim, der verabschiedete, der an seiner Ehre gekränkte, der Krüppel, der Bettler.' (II, 9.)[3] 'Der Bettler'? A beggar is one whose hand is outstretched only to take, who himself has nothing to give. How can it be that Tellheim has come to think of himself as, of all things, a beggar? As we see him, the one thing he seems quite unable to learn is this – that he too must take and not always be the giver, learn that he may not be able to maintain this perpetual stance of dispensing, giving out, without accepting any return. Our suspicion deepens as we reflect that he would have spared the widow of his brother officer Marloff a pang of humiliation, had he admitted a little more of his own state of need. She indicates some such feeling when she says: 'Edelmüthiger Mann! Aber denken Sie auch von mir nicht zu klein. Nehmen Sie das Geld, Herr Major . . . ' and a little later, when she accepts his lie and his money resignedly, saying: 'Ich verstehe Sie; verzeihen Sie nur, wenn ich noch nicht recht weiss, wie man Wohlthaten annehmen muss' (I, 6). Again, his fear of being the taker seemed to make him more than a little gruff to Just:

Just: Ich bin Ihnen nichts schuldig, und doch wollen Sie mich
          verstossen?
Tellheim: Weil ich dir nichts schuldig werden will. (I, 8)

This is not a gracious thing to say; and Just has to go to very great lengths of abrogating his pride, comparing himself to the ugly poodle who follows him against his will, in order to get the better of his master's pride. So the oversimple picture of a man of shining generosity is eroded, stroke by stroke, as our suspicions mount, and we are not surprised when Minna's happy expectations of giving help to the man she loves so deeply are rebuffed. She has now grasped that he is in a bad way and has confidently told herself that this, too, has its good side: 'Unglück ist auch gut. Vielleicht, dass ihm der Himmel alles nahm, um ihm in mir alles wieder zu geben!' (II, 7.) But she had not reckoned with her lover's inability to take anything – not even from her, and not even his happiness. It is a gallant but disappointed Minna who, having been brought up short by his incomprehensible withdrawnness, exclaims: 'Sie . . . haben Ihre Minna noch, und sind unglücklich? Hören Sie doch, was Ihre Minna für ein ein-gebildetes, albernes Ding war, – ist. Sie liess, sie lässt sich träumen, Ihr ganzes Glück sey sie.' (II, 9.) Why can Tellheim not take the offering of her love? Could it be that the inability to take is also an inability to give? An inability to love which is nothing if not a give and take? 'Unglücklicher Mann', Minna surmises, 'wenn Sie gar nichts lieben!' (II, 9.)

On this unspoken question in Minna's mind Act II ends. In the third act, suspicions have become certainty, and the problem before the lovers has become plain to all eyes. This act is Paul Werner's.[4] Werner is shown as a real master in the art of giving, and Lessing uses him to bring out how far Tellheim really does fall short, set against the measure of this simple but goodhearted man. He does this by having Werner pretend to bring Tellheim, as if from his widow, the money owing from Marloff. In fact he lies about it, as Tellheim had lied about it; but the difference in the manner of their lying is all-revealing. Werner is superior to Tellheim in the art of disguising his generosity so as to spare his friend humiliation. For whereas Tellheim had merely pretended that Marloff's debt had already been paid (so that to accept the money would be tantamount to stealing it), Werner is happy to let Tellheim believe that he is serving his own interest in looking after his friend. The widow has sent him a lesser sum than she owes him, he reports, because she also had to pay back some money to Werner. First things first. 'Sie können auch schon eher Ihre hundert Thaler ein Acht Tage noch missen, als ich meine Paar Groschen' (III, 7). In thus hinting that he is not only able to give but ready to take as well – just as later on in this scene when he reminds Tellheim of his former hope that Tellheim would repay him when he was old and in need – he sanctions the act of acceptance. This is the way, too, in which Minna had given to the rake Riccaut de la Marliniere, easing him into taking her gift of money as if he were doing her a favour. But even so Tellheim cannot accept. 'Ich erkenne dein Herz und deine Liebe zu mir', he says. 'Aber ich brauche dein Geld nicht.' *(Ibid.)* He is poor. 'Man muss nicht reicher scheinen wollen, als man ist.' Werner's protestations that we are not poor 'so lange unser Freund hat' fall on deaf ears. Tellheim cannot take anything from him. Primly he retorts: 'Es ziemt sich nicht, dass ich dein Schuldner bin' *(ibid.)*.

At this point, in the exact centre of the play, we witness the sharpest and ugliest verbal duel in the drama. Werner reminds Tellheim, as neither Just nor Minna had done, that his superior is in fact hopelessly indebted to him:

> Sie wollen mein Schuldner nicht seyn? Wenn Sie es denn aber schon wären, Herr Major? Oder sind Sie dem Manne nichts schuldig, der einmal den Hieb auffieng, der Ihnen den Kopf spalten sollte, und ein andermal den Arm vom Rumpfe hieb, der eben losdrücken und Ihnen die Kugel durch die Brust jagen wollte? – Was können Sie diesem Manne mehr schuldig werden? Oder hat es mit meinem Halse weniger zu sagen, als mit meinem Beutel? – Wenn das vornehm gedacht ist, bey meiner armen Seele, so ist es auch sehr abgeschmackt gedacht!

Werner is not putting himself above his friend. He is simply reminding him of the reciprocity of giving and taking in any relationship worthy of the name, a reciprocity which makes it idle to sort out the credits and the debits on either side. Idle not only to count up how much the one has given to the other, and whether that sum exceeds the amount which he received in turn. But idle because, as a human relation develops, it becomes ever more impossible to distinguish between what is giving and what is taking. For in a relationship based on love the very act of giving springs from the need to give and thus is also a taking, just as the very act of taking, because it fulfils the other's need to love, by that token is itself also a giving. This is what Minna – herself an avid giver and taker – had painfully experienced when Tellheim, in their first encounter in the play, had refused to let his need be hers. When he had wrenched himself from her arms and run off, denying his need of her and unable to take the love she wanted to give him, she had felt deprived, as deprived as a mother feels when her child refuses to take her milk. 'Franciska', she had cried, 'bin ich nun glücklich?' (III, 3.) She had felt as pitiable and poor as Tellheim with whom Franziska had so readily sympathised. And she had been right to feel so lost, for in refusing to sanction his own need to take, he had also refused to sanction her need to give – a need so strong and honest that she had not shunned the appearance of running after her man in the first place, and later on positively invites the impression of being 'ein Sächsisches verlaufenes Fräulein, das sich ihm an den Kopf geworfen' (V, 9).

We are now clearer about the reasons why Tellheim's dealings with the officer's widow, and with Just, and with Minna, had made us so uneasy. Lessing is showing us what lies behind the rigidity of such an attitude of refusal to take from others: in Tellheim it covers up his refusal to give of himself. It is this ultimate identity of giving and taking in a living relationship which Werner now pinpoints, when he recalls how much he had relied on the prospect of Tellheim supporting him in his penurious old age. Werner makes these points in a bluff exaggerated way like an old soldier, it is true; but fundamentally he is serious and addressing himself to Tellheim in the language of relatedness. He ends by regretting that he can no longer count on his old friend: 'Nein, das denk ich nicht mehr. – Wer von mir nichts annehmen will, wenn ers bedarf, und ichs habe; der will mir auch nichts geben, wenn ers hat, und ichs bedarf. – Schon gut!' (III, 7.)

Clearly, Tellheim is in a bad way. What has happened to the man whose overflowing generosity had won Minna's heart before she had ever seen him? It is in the consequences of that deed of magnanimity that we find the roots of his trouble. Significantly it is in the scenes following the tell-tale encounter with Werner that we, and Minna, first learn of the true nature and extent of Tellheim's ill fortune. Tellheim had responded fullheartedly to the troubles of the defeated enemy. He had given to them of his money and of himself, freely. But what he had given had been ill received. His deed had been interpreted by his own King as part of a shady deal with the enemy, and instead of having the money he had given away refunded to him, all he had received was a slap in the face: to be the object of sordid suspicions and the ruin of his career. The world had not honoured the IOU it owed him. This is why he now feels that both he and the world are sullied, why he refuses his comrade's widow the real gift of his tears, making the excuse to her that 'Sie finden mich in einer Stunde, wo ich leicht zu verleiten wäre, wider die Vorsicht zu murren' (I, 6). This is why he counters Werner's assurance 'Einem Manne, wie Sie, kann es nicht immer fehlen' with the acid retort 'Du kennst die Welt!' (III, 7), and why now, as he tells Minna of the reward he received for his trust, he laughs in a manner that makes her flesh creep.[5] 'O, ersticken Sie dieses Lachen, Tellheim!' – she beseeches him, 'Es ist das schreckliche Lachen des

Menschenhasses!' And again, a moment later: 'Ihr Lachen tödtet mich, Tellheim! Wenn Sie an Tugend und Vorsicht glauben, Tellheim, so lachen Sie so nicht! Ich habe nie fürchterlicher fluchen hören, als Sie lachen.' (IV, 6.) She quite correctly divines what this laughter betokens. Tellheim no longer believes in any meaningful connection between virtue and reward. The return he received when he gave of his best has shattered his faith in Providence, the same faith to which the poet testifies in a celebrated passage in the *Hamburgische Dramaturgie*,[6] and the faith to which Minna herself, a moment later, will declare her passionate allegiance: 'Die Vorsicht, glauben Sie mir, hält den ehrlichen Mann immer schadlos; und öfters schon im voraus.' And on top of this the knock he has taken has shattered his belief in his own worth. He and the world are unworthy partners in a dishonourable partnership.

Thus here already, in this comedy, the barrenness of the relation between the self and the world is symbolised by the self-same bungling hand which, in *Emilia Galotti*, five years later, was to become the principal poetic metaphor of the play.[7] The hand, here as there, is the negotiator between what is within and what is without, between the realm of ideals and the realm of action, between the mind in its inwardness and the 'other', the material medium of the world. Executor of the mind, it yet belongs to the world of objects, actions and desires; and its allegiance being thus divided, it tends tragically to forget or to betray the vision with which it is entrusted. Tellheim has lost his fortune and his reputation in the unhappy 'Handel' which made the King fear for his honour (V, 9). Even the IOU, the only palpable proof of his integrity, 'kam' – as he puts it – 'aus meinen Händen' (IV, 6). And in the pursuit of his rough soldierly calling, in a world rent by war, he has, in fact, lost the use of his right hand. His arm is paralysed. This signifies more than the small physical blemish which Minna thinks it is. It is the visible token of a deeper damage wrought within himself and in his relation to the world when his country disinherited him and blackened his name. 'Aber sagen Sie mir doch, mein Fräulein,' he exclaims in distraction, 'wie kam der Mohr in Venetianische Dienste? Hatte der Mohr kein Vaterland? Warum vermiethete er seinen Arm und sein Blut einem fremden Staate?' (IV, 6.)

Tellheim is a cripple as truly as he is a beggar, and by the same token. For the relation of give and take with the world has broken down. He is no longer capable of taking – of taking anything, or from anyone. And although he continues to give, his giving is without love and tinged with contempt, for the hand that gives as

well as for the recipient; and that is why his gifts enrich no one.
His contempt is perceptible when he refers to the IOU he has
from Marloff as 'den Bettel' as he holds it in his hand and tears
it up (I, 7). It is brought out expressly when he tells Just how he
ought to pay the innkeeper on his behalf: 'Er hätte mich nicht
wieder mit Augen sehen, und seine Bezahlung aus deinen Händen
empfangen sollen. Ich weiss, dass du eine Hand voll Geld mit
einer ziemlich verächtlichen Miene hinwerfen kannst.' (I, 4.) The
living currency of love, the give and take of relatedness which in
this play is symbolised by money, for Tellheim has become
devalued. He will not take because he has learnt to expect a bad
return from a corrupt world. And he gives without making his
giving acceptable and so mutes the response. He suppresses the
need to give which alone sanctions the giving and the taking and
fuses both in an experience that is enriching to the giver as well
as to the recipient. He has withdrawn himself from the circulation
of love in which want answers want, in which giving, by fulfilling
its need, becomes a taking, and receiving, by fulfilling the need of
the giver, becomes a giving, and both, the giving and the taking,
yield unending dividends.

Of this unfailing source of fulfilment in the reciprocity of love
Tellheim knows nothing; and, cut off from this knowledge, he is
bankrupt in body and mind. He assesses what he is and what he
has by reference to himself alone, and, worse still, by deference to
extraneous standards. Judged thus, and only thus, outside the
context of his relationship with Minna and what it makes of him,
he is the cripple, the beggar. He cannot be her equal. And equal
he must be. In his own as yet uncomprehending mind, Tellheim
has no right to be still accepted as Minna's future husband unless,
by the extraneous standards which are all he knows, he can be
seen again to be her equal; and yet this is just what is not within
his power. His dilemma is absolute. What happens when Minna,
by a stroke of genius, pretends to be as poor as he is, is revealing.
He for his part immediately feels himself her equal once more,
just as he was when they first met. 'Unser beider Umstände', he
now pleads, ' . . . sind nicht mehr glücklich, aber wiederum
einander gleich. Gleichheit ist immer das festeste Band der Liebe!'
(V, 5.) But she, for her part, at once rejects this outward conception of equality. Her unfailing feminine intuition will have
nothing of this assessment of 'equality', measured separately and
by the standards of convention; and to it she opposes the conception of an inward equality in the face of each other's growing
needs in the living reciprocity of love.[8]

Her last words before she finally decides to teach her lover a lesson mockingly and sadly expose the sterility of such separateness: 'Nein, keines muss das andere, weder glücklicher noch unglücklicher machen. So will es die wahre Liebe!' (IV, 6.) Upon this idiotic declaration follows her announcement that, poor and disinherited as she is herself, she can no longer be his.[9]

But the scales have been tipped and in the twinkling of an eye Tellheim is transformed. Minna needs him; he is once again wanted; and in an instant the need to give all of himself which had received such a rude check when he had given all he had to the defeated enemy is revived. Now he positively flows out, irrepressibly. And his giving, in love, at once becomes a taking. Virtually his first words, as he hears of Minna's predicament, are: 'Nun brauch ich dich, ehrlicher Werner!' (IV, 8), and his first action on conveniently finding Werner who has meanwhile been looking for him—'so gehts mit dem Suchen' – is to ask him for all he has, stormily and impetuously: 'Ah, ich brauche ietzt nicht deine Nachrichten: ich brauche dein Geld. Geschwind, Werner, gieb mir so viel du hast; und denn suche so viel aufzubringen, als du kannst' (V, 1). Werner knows that in thus avidly taking his money, Tellheim is at long last truly giving. For he responds by grumbling happily: 'Damit ich ihm nichts vorzuwerfen habe, so nimmt er mirs mit der Rechten, und giebt mirs mit der Linken wieder'; and the remainder of the scene is given over to Tellheim asking for more, and yet more, and Werner rejoicing in the gift of such a taking. It is interesting that already in this scene we are informed that Tellheim is to be reimbursed by the Treasury, although the excited hero himself takes no notice of the news. Does he need to be told? Does he not in every deeper sense already know that there is a return in the very act of giving? He knows it from the joyfulness with which Werner lets himself be ransacked, from the ludicrous 'O Jammer!' and 'O Freude!' with which his friend accompanies his every changing mood, intoxicated with the joy of loving and of being asked to give; above all, he knows it from the rush of strength and power that has returned to him the instant that Minna has once again made him feel wanted. It is the passionate need to give, his 'Mitleid', which has opened up the blocked channels of his soul to the circulation of love and over-powers him with the fulfilment of giving before ever his squandered riches have been restored to him. When the return does come – 'da mir das Glück soviel zurückgiebt, als genug ist, die Wünsche eines vernünftigen Mannes zu befriedigen' (V, 9) – it only comes to confirm a knowledge that he has already, by learning to allow the free circulation of love within his soul, won for himself at last.

Thus the arrival of the King's letter of pardon is not the *deus ex machina* it is usually taken to be.[10] It would never avail if Tellheim had not already learnt his lesson. But still Minna has not quite done with her beloved. He has as yet to understand the true meaning of reciprocity. And here the pretended equality which had so promptly resuscitated her lover's affections turns out to be a fresh obstacle. For how will he learn not to be sidetracked from the inner reciprocity (which is her concern) by that outward equality which so obsesses him, an equality which she herself has been instrumental in creating? So, after all, we can see that the King's letter is a godsend: it allows Minna to tip the scales again, because it again and finally destroys the economic equality – false and sterile to her – between her lover and herself. Tellheim is restored now to his honour and his fortune, whilst Minna herself continues in self-inflicted destitution. Her lover must now find a more cogent ground for their solidarity than their common bankruptcy had been. He must learn that love establishes a reciprocity of its own which is altogether independent of the changing configurations of the lovers' outward circumstances and incommensurable with them.

Thus his taskmaster, propelled by the relentless logic of love (or is it perhaps the relentless love of logic? In a character from Lessing's pen it is difficult to be sure), puts poor Tellheim through his paces once again. It is not enough that he experiences that white-hot desire to give, at which point giving becomes indistinguishable from an elemental need; that he is ready to compare himself to Minna's shadow and threatens to follow her as humbly and as doggedly as Just had followed him and the poodle had followed Just. He must learn to take, actually and literally, for all the woman's physical dependence on the strength and protection of the male. And what he still has to learn to take is – his ring. The precious ring given to him 'von lieben Händen' (III, 5) and pawned by him: the ring of betrothal given to him by Minna, and returned to him now, its rightful owner, without his knowledge. It is the token of her giving love, and he had parted with it because he would not take: not only because he would not accept Werner's money which could have been used to pay his bill, but more deeply, because he would not 'take any more' from life itself. True, he does not know that the ring that Minna has returned to him is in fact his own – his ring from her. Nevertheless, his insistence on bestowing upon her what it is his office to receive, his blind unquestioning belief that she has returned to him the ring which he had given to her, and thus rejected him, and his own violent repudiation of Werner and the money he has brought – all this shows that Minna was right in not calling off the game before. Taking is still a thorny problem for Tellheim which he must learn to face. For all his compelling need to give, the fear is still alive, deep within him, that the return from the world will be that his own gift will again be thrown back in his face.

Does he take back his own ring in the end? He does nothing of the sort. Listen to Minna: 'Soll ich ihn nun wieder nehmen?' she asks with that irrepressible impetuousness which is her most endearing trait, as he begins to realise that the ring he is holding in his hand is his own ring, the ring she had given to him – 'soll ich? – Geben Sie her, geben Sie her!' (And the stage direction reads: 'Reisst ihn ihm aus der Hand, und steckt ihn ihm selbst an den Finger.') 'Nun? ist alles richtig?' (V, 12). Yes, everything is as it should be. For giving, in this play, is taking and taking is giving. Tellheim must give his beloved her own gift in order that he may receive it from her hand and Minna must take from his hands what she so passionately wants to give. In the reciprocity of love giving and taking are fused beyond all possibility of separation. For to give, in love, is a need, and to take, in love, is a gift, and in each and in both there is return without end.

Return without end – these words evoke the image of the two rings themselves, the tokens of love which the lovers have exchanged. [11]'The circle of the ring eternally goes out eternally to return upon itself. And as it is with the symbol of love, so it is with love itself: so the riches that flow out to the other ever return to the self, in the circulation of the currency of love.

9

Nathan der Weise : The Spoils of Peace

The quality of mercy is not strain'd;
It droppeth as the gentle rain from heaven
Upon the place beneath. It is twice blest;
It blesseth him that gives and him that takes . . .

(Shakespeare: *The Merchant of Venice*)

I

Undoubtedly, Mammon is the presiding divinity of Lessing's last play. Money is endlessly displayed, exchanged and talked about. And curiously enough, it is a benign deity; it is the patron of communication. It is there on the stage, as momentous encounters take place and strangers are drawn into the circle of loving which in the end binds all to all: Nathan's money fills the stage as the Knight Templar and Saladin confirm the bond which each had sensed when the Muslim spared the Christian's life. His treasures are spread about when he reveals to the Lay Brother the circumstances in which the little Christian girl Recha was given to him and when the true connections between her and the Knight Templar, between both and Saladin and between all and the Jew are for the first time glimpsed. And Saladin's own treasures preside over the fifth act in which his and everyone's longings are fulfilled and surpassed; the act which ends 'unter stummer Wiederholung allerseitiger Umarmungen'.

Money and treasures are offered or actually change hands in the manifold relations of this play, as a token of good will, initiating or cementing contacts. Precious gifts are offered by Nathan as a home-coming present to Daja, Recha's nurse. By Daja as a thank-you to the Knight Templar. By Nathan to the same. Saladin gives money to every beggar; to his sister, for winning her game of chess with him (though even more, we are told, for losing!); money is given by Sittah to her brother Saladin as a thank-you for such generosity; by Saladin to the Mameluks for the good news they bring; by Nathan to the Lay Brother. And lastly and most importantly, money is given by Nathan to Saladin in confirmation of their friendship and returned to him in the same spirit at the end.

And of course, money is talked about endlessly, not only in those scenes in which it is offered and accepted. Daja talks about Nathan's generosity to the Jew himself and to the Knight Templar. Al-Hafi, Saladin's new treasurer, tells Nathan about his master's passion for giving and his consequent bankruptcy. Saladin and Sittah are taken to task by the Dervish for giving what they have not got and emerge from this debate poor, yet feeling rich in their generosity. They talk about the prodigious wealth of the Jew and, later on, about their plan to bleed him. Nathan and Al-Hafi talk about the surpassing freedom of being penniless, a conversation which ends on the famous words

> Der wahre Bettler ist
> Doch einzig und allein der wahre König!   (II, 9)

Nathan, asked about truth, soliloquises about money, and money forms the concluding topic of the decisive encounter with the Sultan. Saladin talks about money with Sittah as Nathan's riches are being carried in. Nathan and the Lay Brother speak of money as they feel their way towards one another. Saladin argues himself out of giving a reward to his Mameluks as they bring the news that he is once again affluent, and then into doing so after all. And his welcome to Nathan in the final scene consists in offering him money in his turn:

> Die Karavan' ist da. Ich bin so reich
> Nun wieder, als ich lange nicht gewesen. –
> Komm, sag' mir, was du brauchst, so recht was Grosses
> Zu unternehmen! Denn auch ihr, auch ihr,
> Ihr Handelsleute, könnt des baaren Geldes
> Zu viel nie haben!   (V, *Letzter Auftritt*)

In fact, to cite the occasions on which money figures in this play is tantamount, almost, to enumerating the scenes of the drama in their entirety. Money there is in all. It pervades its texture, now as prop, now as literal reference, turn by turn as image and as overt theme of discourse. But everywhere it seems the vehicle of human communication.[1]

And Nathan himself: our first association with a Jew in medieval times is with money. For in those days Jews were debarred virtually from every profession except that of the money-lender. From the first moment of the play we are never allowed to forget Nathan's association with money and the desirable goods that money can buy. Nathan has come home from a journey to the Orient, laden with cash and treasures. His first words tell us so. The riches he has brought back home are fabulous. The whole city of Jerusalem is astir with the news, Sittah tells Saladin (II, 2). Daja tells the Knight Templar that he has returned

> Mit zwanzig hochbeladenen Kameelen,
> Und allem, was an edeln Specereyen,
> An Steinen und an Stoffen, Indien
> Und Persien und Syrien, gar Sina,
> Kostbares nur gewähren. (I, 6)

And Nathan himself confirms the truth of these reports at the end of his audience with the Sultan:

> Ich komm' von einer weiten Reis', auf welcher
> Ich Schulden eingetrieben. – Fast hab' ich
> Des baaren Gelds zu viel. – (III, 7)

His riches are so much in evidence that we may well wonder, as does Daja, why he is not called 'Nathan der Reiche':

> Sein Volk verehret ihn als einen Fürsten.
> Doch dass es ihn den Weisen Nathan nennt,
> Und nicht vielmehr den Reichen, hat mich oft
> Gewundert. (I, 6)

Indeed, the title of the play, in hinting at yet other expectations than those which are so abundantly fulfilled, makes one wonder: why is the man that is so patently 'der Reiche' called 'der Weise'?[2] What is the connection between his wisdom and his wealth? The Knight Templar sardonically suggests:

> Seinem Volk ist reich und weise
> Vielleicht das nehmliche. (Ibid.)

But clearly this is not it. Nathan is not the 'Stockjude' who is shrewd enough to be rich. Daja replies:

> Vor allen aber
> Hätt's ihn den Guten nennen müssen. Denn
> Ihr stellt Euch gar nicht vor, wie gut er ist.
> Als er erfuhr, wie viel Euch Recha schuldig:
> Was hätt', in diesem Augenblicke, nicht
> Er alles Euch gethan, gegeben! (Ibid.)

We are not allowed to stop puzzling. Once again, in the second act, the connection between Nathan's wealth and wisdom becomes the subject of discussion. Sittah reminds Al-Hafi of his pecunious friend

>   – dem
> Sein Gott von allen Gütern dieser Welt
> Das Kleinst' und Grösste so in vollem Maas
> Ertheilet habe.—
> . . . Das Kleinste: Reichthum. Und
> Das Grösste: Weisheit.   (II, 2)

Al-Hafi pretends to have forgotten his own praises and rejoins:

>   Wahrhaftig? Der
> Ist endlich, wieder heim gekommen? Ey!
> So mags doch gar so schlecht mit ihm nicht stehn. –
> Ganz recht: den nannt' einmal das Volk den Weisen!
> Den Reichen auch.   (Ibid.)

Nathan's riches seem almost an adjunct to his wisdom, and this impression is confirmed when Al-Hafi concludes the embarrassing topic, remarking:

>   Nun, ists der Reiche wieder:
> So wirds auch wohl der Weise wieder seyn.   (Ibid.)

Casually, almost reluctantly, Al-Hafi concedes the identity between the reality of the man and his name. The truth is out. We had suspected it all along and it is finally confirmed in the encounter with the Lay Brother in which the sombre background of Nathan's serenity is disclosed. For when 'Herr Nathan' expresses his surprise at the fact that the Lay Brother knows and evidently respects him, the latter explains:

>   Je nu; wer kennt Euch nicht? Ihr habt so manchem
>   Ja Euern Nahmen in die Hand gedrückt.
>   Er steht in meiner auch, seit vielen Jahren.   (IV, 7)

This is a very strange image, and that it is not accidental is proven by the fact that both speakers continue to draw on it. It is equivalent, roughly, to saying 'You have imprinted your personality on many people's minds and memories by your giving'; but the difference to the paraphrase is vital. For in the Lay Brother's formulation it emerges that Nathan's name is nothing apart from his doing, his giving. Nathan der Weise is what he does. His title to wisdom lies in his 'impressive' giving.

But still we do not know where such riches come from. Sittah tells Saladin of a strange rumour:

> Er habe Salomons und Davids Gräber
> Erforscht, und wisse deren Siegel durch
> Ein mächtiges geheimes Wort zu lösen?
> Aus ihnen bring' er dann von Zeit zu Zeit
> Die unermesslichen Reichthümer an
> Den Tag, die keinen mindern Quell verriethen.   (II, 3)[3]

But, brother and sister decide, no grave can be the source of Nathan's wealth. For one thing, 'Narren lagen da begraben!' Moreover this is not a living source. But Nathan's riches seem to replenish themselves. They argue some inexhaustible spring:

>   Auch
> Ist seines Reichthums Quelle weit ergiebiger
> Weit unerschöpflicher, als so ein Grab
> Voll Mammon.   (Ibid.)

And indeed, the action bears out what Daja had said at the beginning: he is 'die Grossmuth selber' (I, 1). He will refuse even to lend money

> Damit er stets zu geben habe –   (II, 3)

and Daja, disarmed and exasperated by such magnanimity, exclaims

> So seyd Ihr nun!
> Wenn Ihr nur schenken könnt! nur schenken könnt!'   (I, 1)

Indeed throughout the play we see him giving – to her, to Recha, to the Knight Templar, to the Lay Brother, to Saladin: to all and sundry, endlessly and ever; and such wealth is juxtaposed to the beggarliness of the Templar and the Dervish and to the bankruptcy of Al-Hafi's master, Saladin. Thus the question persists: from what secret source does Nathan replenish the riches he so recklessly depletes? What is the 'mächtiges geheimes Wort' which unseals the fount of his unfailing wealth?

Only once in the play do we hear of Nathan being the recipient rather than the giver; and he receives, not indeed money, nor a precious ring, but a human life.[4] As he is about to refresh the Lay Brother's memory of him by pressing a mite into his hand, the latter interrupts him, saying:

> Wenn Ihr mir nur erlauben wollt, ein wenig
> Euch *meinen* Nahmen aufzufrischen. Denn
> Ich kann mich rühmen, auch in *Eure* Hand
> Etwas gelegt zu haben, was nicht zu
> Verachten war.   (IV, 7)

The gift he refers to is Recha, the little Christian girl he had
brought to Nathan eighteen years before, within a day or two of
the pogrom in which his wife and seven sons were burnt to death.
At that time, after storming and raging against destiny, Nathan
had surrendered himself to the will of God.

> Ich stand! und rief zu Gott: ich will!
> Willst du nur, dass ich will!   *(Ibid.)*

and, in the instant he had given himself up, he had received the
strange child.

>   Indem stiegt Ihr
> Vom Pferd', und überreichtet mir das Kind,
> In Euern Mantel eingehüllt. – . . .
>   . . . ich nahm
> Das Kind, trugs auf mein Lager, küsst' es, warf
> Mich auf die Knie' und schluchzte: Gott! auf Sieben
> Doch nun schon Eines wieder!   *(Ibid.)*

What is the nature of the connection between Nathan's offering
and his receiving? It is not enough to say that this modern Job, by
the grace of God, is granted a recompense for his losses – 'auf
Sieben . . . Eines' – the instant he accepts them. The connection
between giving and receiving, between virtue and reward at
which Lessing hints in this, the poetic testament of his humanism,
is subtler and more compelling. When the voice of reason once
again prevails, Nathan makes a choice in which he is aided by the
love of God:

>   . . . ich will!
> Willst du nur, dass ich will!

It is a choice to abide by what he has known all along: the
goodness of Providence, a renewed choice to continue to love and
revere the Divine – even now. This choice to love, at this moment
of tribulation, is the surpassing deed of his life. He recalls it as
such when he relates it to the 'fromme Einfalt' of the Lay Brother.

> Noch hat mich nie die Eitelkeit versucht,
> Sie jemand andern zu erzählen. Euch
> Allein erzähl' ich sie. Der frommen Einfalt
> Allein erzähl' ich sie. Weil die allein
> Versteht, was sich der gottergebne Mensch
> Für Thaten abgewinnen kann.   (IV, 7)

In this choice to love and revere lies the inexhaustible fund from which Nathan replenishes his riches. For, as he gives himself over to God – 'gott-ergeben' is what he calls himself – and commits his hope, his reason, his will, in short, his entire life into the hands of his Maker, life is returned to him anew, as a gift. He is released into the circulation of love. From this moment onward, he accepts whatever comes to him in gratitude for what he has received; for whatever it be, it answers to his deepest need to offer thanks for the gift of life, and thus it contains its own fulfilment. As the Knight Templar has it in a similar situation:

> Alles, was
> Von dir mir kömmt, – sey was es will – das lag
> Als Wunsch in meiner Seele.   (IV, 4)

which means: everything you ask of me – be it a demand or a denial – is answering my deepest need. In giving I receive.

This surely is the meaning and the miracle of Recha. For let there be no mistake about it: the Christian child which Nathan receives from Providence, as his own children lie murdered at the hands of Christians, is a bitter-sweet blessing. A lesser man might have proved unequal to the challenge of such a gift. Nathan accepts it in the fullness of his gratitude and in doing so, is requited.

Thus it is the power of love to draw sustenance from the world – 'sey was es will' – and to fulfil itself even in the act of loving, which is the source of Nathan's riches. It is indeed an inexhaustible source. For loving generates its own enrichment. It creates its own internal rhythm, setting up a self-sufficient circle of strength flowing out from the self and coming back to it which is prior to all external gratifications and independent of them. But also love actively transforms the world. At the high noon of classical Idealism, in his last play, Lessing has embodied the unanswerable faith which inspires Kant's *Critiques*, Goethe's *Iphigenie, The Magic Flute, Fidelio* and Beethoven's *Choral Symphony*. The world is amenable to human striving because the human mind, in the creative encounter with the world we call experience, is itself instrumental in shaping it; because human reason and human

goodness have the casting vote in determining what the face of
this world shall be in the first instance. The gods are bound to
answer Iphigenie's prayer and Thoas cannot but hear the voice of
humanity and truth. The prison gates are bound to yield before
the ardent loyalty of Leonore, releasing the captives from their
man-made hell. The forces of night are bound to retreat before
Sarastro's wisdom and the earnest striving of the lovers. And
likewise, Recha and the Templar and Saladin are bound to
respond to Nathan's love and to return like for like. For his
devotion adopts the demand of the hour as his deepest need and,
in so accepting it, transforms it.[5]

II

In unsers Busens Reine wogt ein Streben,
Sich einem Höhern, Reinern, Unbekannten
Aus Dankbarkeit freiwillig hinzugeben,
Enträtselnd sich den ewig Ungenannten:
Wir heissens: fromm sein![6]

'Fromm sein,' the surge of desire to offer up the self in an act of
thanksgiving, is the source of the golden harmonies which temper
the angular prose of *Minna von Barnhelm* and the broken cadences[7]
of *Nathan der Weise* and transfigure them into poetry. Minna is a
'fröhliches Geschöpf' who offers such devotion to her Maker and
to the man destined for her by Heaven, confident 'dass ihm der
Himmel alles nahm, um ihm in mir alles wieder zu geben!' (II, 7.)
It is with her as with Nathan: her riches, like his, lie in the
self-sufficiency of a love which replenishes itself as it spends itself,
not in her outward wealth. Indeed it is no accident that Lessing's
two most life-accepting plays should abound in human relationships which are so patently modelled on the configuration of
the religious consciousness: the relation between the Giver of life
and His creature, between Saviour and saved. The number of
rescues, actual or virtual, which occur in these two plays is
nothing short of astounding, equalled only by the number of
'Rettungen' the poet himself undertook throughout his life. As
Werner has twice saved Tellheim's life in battle, so Tellheim has
saved Just in illness and so Just has saved his poodle from
drowning; so Tellheim has saved the Saxon estates in times of
distress and so, in every deeper sense of the word, Minna comes to
the rescue of her shipwrecked lover. Again, as Saladin has spared
the Templar's life, so the latter has, in his turn, risked this

'Geschenk' (II, 7) to rescue Recha from being burnt to death: Recha who had already once been saved by Nathan, who had himself been saved in battle by Assad, the Sultan's younger brother. What is more, the situation between rescuer and rescued is reversible. Werner knows that Tellheim *might* have saved him as he in fact saved Tellheim, and the devotion inspired by this knowledge is absolute. So too, Minna feels inextricably indebted to the man she loves and Saladin and Nathan feel no less dependent on those they saved than the Knight Templar and Recha depend on them, their actual saviours.

What function can we assign to this series of identical situations other than that they parallel in the human sphere the experience of gratitude which, in the solitary instance of Nathan, is disclosed at its religious source, and that they serve to release, in that sphere, a fund of unconditional love which increases in the spending and elicits corresponding riches in the recipient? The religious impulse of surrendering the grateful self to the giver of life reverberates in every one of these situations, in varying degrees of consciousness, and in every instance something of the same release of love is experienced and communicated. Minna and Nathan know of the religious overtones of their devotion, and Tellheim and the Templar, those two doubting Thomases, learn to give praise to Providence as they are taught to love their fellows. But, however unconscious some of Lessing's characters remain of the source of their feeling, its quality remains unchanged. However little care Just's poodle has received from its owner – 'Noch hat er keinen Bissen Brod aus meiner Hand bekommen' (I, 8) – the dog performs his finest tricks unasked and is rewarded by his own display of gratitude. However gruffly Tellheim tries to rid himself of Just, Just continues to be his devoted servant and argues, and by no means untruthfully, that for all his services he still is in his master's debt. And so, on a conscious level, it is between Minna and her lover. At least from her end of the affair. Minna knows that she is coming to Tellheim's rescue because from the moment she first saw him, he gave her life as she has known it since – her happiness, her beauty and her riches; and it is because she herself is aware of the religious mainspring of her love – her first impulse on finding him is to send a grateful thought to Heaven – that for all her givingness she is happy to own that she is hopelessly indebted to him, and expects him to be humble enough to do likewise. 'Denn auch seiner Geliebten sein Glück nicht wollen zu danken haben, ist Stolz, unverzeihlicher Stolz!' (III, 12.) The lesson by which she teaches her beloved to eat humble pie is Tellheim's religious education. She teaches him to feel not only human love, but also that trust in Providence which he had lost when he had permitted his soul to become clogged by 'Aergerniss und verbissene Wuth' (V, 5).[8]

It is the same in Lessing's last play. In sparing the young Christian's life, the Sultan has tapped an inexhaustible source of gratitude. The lovely words the Knight Templar addresses to his saviour testify to the enrichment he experiences as soon as he permits his feeling to flow out to him:

> Alles, was
> Von dir mir kömmt, – sey was es will – das lag
> Als Wunsch in meiner Seele.

This experience will stand him in good stead in another situation, more taxing than the present one. For at the end, when Recha is taken from him as a bride and returned to him as a sister, he is able to address the no less lovely words to the Jew who – like the God of his Fathers – has taken life and given it back to him[9] in a way that has surpassed the young man's understanding:

> Ihr nehmt und gebt mir, Nathan!
> Mit vollen Händen beydes! – Nein! Ihr gebt
> Mir mehr, als Ihr mir nehmt! unendlich mehr!
>
> (V, *Letzter Auftritt*)

But yet another thing emerges from the final pledge which the Templar offers to his saviour. It is not the saved alone who is the gainer in this relationship. The returns of love are reciprocal:

> Hiermit empfange mehr,
> Als du mir nehmen konntest. Ganz der Deine!   (IV, 4)

the youth says to the Sultan. Saladin could take no more than his life. But in sparing that life he is receiving more: he gains the youth's undying devotion.

And Recha? The mainspring of her love for the young Templar is gratitude, that almost religious reverence which finds its first confused expression in her 'Engelschwärmerei' (I, 1). Her very 'Leben' is his 'Wohlthat' (I, 4). He gave it back to her. That is why she wants to kneel before him to adore her saviour and, through him, the Maker of them both. Daja is saying more than she herself can possibly realise when she calls Recha 'die fromme

Kreatur' (I, 1). She is defining nothing less than the appropriate response of creature to Creator. And who would gainsay that in this relation, too, the saviour gains as well as the saved? In risking his life for the unknown Jewish girl the Templar has saved his nearest and dearest, be she his bride or his sister.

And lastly, Nathan: his response to the Knight Templar who saved his daughter, and to the Sultan, the saviour of her saviour, is tinged with religious awe. 'Auf ewig' he declares himself bound both to the Knight Templar (II, 5) and to Saladin (II, 7); and in words recalling the young man's pledge of loyalty to the Sultan, he says:

> Kaum,
> Und kaum, kann ich es nun erwarten, was
> Er mir zuerst befehlen wird. Ich bin
> Bereit zu allem . . .   (II, 7)

He is prepared to give, and to give his all, because gratitude is the centre of his being; a sense of indebtedness which clamours to be expressed even as it is felt. That is why he can word his offer of financial help to the Sultan with a felicity which sanctions his gift and its recipient and teaches him, in the most palpable of fashions, that Nathan lives the truths he has propounded.

> Ich hätte noch Gelegenheit gewünscht,
> Dir eine **Bitte** vorzutragen   (III, 7)

the wealthy Jew says to the bankrupt emperor. But this closing incident of the parable scene does more than prove to the Muslim the Jew's disarming moral grace.[10] It also drives home to him, and indeed to us, the inseparableness of giving and receiving, for himself as well as for the beneficiaries of his generosity. He gains from his own good deed no less than they. Liberally and unsolicited, the returns of his impulsive act flow in; and as Nathan has known all along that

> . . . Gott lohne Gutes, hier
> Gethan, auch hier noch . . .   (I, 2)

so now the Muslim marvels at the goodness of Providence as it is revealed in the reciprocity of human love:

> Wie aus **Einer** guten That,
> Gebahr sie auch schon blosse Leidenschaft,
> Doch so viel andre gute Thaten fliessen![11]   (III, 7)

Nowhere has the poet portrayed this oneness of giving and receiving more charmingly than in the relation between Saladin and his sister; and here as everywhere else in the play, he has communicated his meaning in terms of monetary symbols. One of the conventions governing this idyll is that Saladin pays Sittah a double amount of money, not indeed when she has won at chess, but when she has lost a game to her brother. As she puts it when Saladin is about to concede victory to her:

>   . . . dabey find'
> Ich meine Rechnung nicht . . .
>   . . . gewann ich immer nicht am meisten
> Mit dir, wenn ich verlor? Wenn hast du mir
> Den Satz, mich des verlornen Spieles wegen
> Zu trösten, doppelt nicht hernach geschenkt?   (II, 1)

True, on this occasion Saladin gives her the special bonus which Sittah ordinarily receives for losing, even though she has won the game. But lest we expect a return to reason on the part of this fond and foolish couple, we are promptly informed that all the money which Saladin has been giving to his sister has in fact been secretly supplied by her. Her receiving has been a giving, in point of fact as well as feeling, just as his giving has been a receiving. Yet, she argues, even if she *has* given to him what she seemed to be receiving, this has only been possible because of what her brother had given her in the first place:

> Wer hatte, diess zu können, mich so reich
> Gemacht, als du, mein Bruder?   (II, 2)

she asks. To which he replies that if his giving is a receiving, is he not rich in being indebted to such a sister? 'Ich arm? der **Bruder** arm?'

It is as impossible to sort out the credits and the debits in this topsy-turvy account as it is to sort out who has which ring in *Minna von Barnhelm*. And as irrelevant. For the poet does not seriously intend us to find our way through these labyrinthine circularities: the regress is infinite and at the end of the exercise we know only what we have known throughout the plays, what every episode and every relationship goes to proclaim: that to give, in love, is a need and to take, in love, is a gift, and that in each and in both there is unending gain.

Thus everywhere the salutary circulation of a love which is replenished as it is expended, is confirmed in the reciprocity of enrichment experienced in relationship. It is finally reflected in the circular movement of the plot which traces the chain of repercussions set up by a single good deed and the transformations it accomplishes on this, its course back to its author. Saladin saves the life of the Knight Templar who used this 'Geschenk' to save the life of Recha, and therewith the faith of her father, who in turn uses his riches to come to Saladin's help who makes good his gift to the Templar, etc. etc. Already the first time the spiral comes back to him full circle, Saladin divines the pattern of events which will become fully revealed at the end of the play: he marvels

> Wie aus Einer guten That
> . . .
> Doch so viel andre gute Thaten fliessen!   (III, 7)

For, finally, Saladin experiences an overwhelming return for his goodness when, in full view of his riches which have come back to him, he embraces his brother's son and his new daughter, and Nathan, his friend and the father of his children. But this eventual return to the giver which, on the level of the outer action, appears to be a separate event in time, in fact is the reflection of an inner return which is experienced constantly and by every person who is in the living circulation of love: the return to the self of the love that, even in the act of loving, flows out to the 'other'. This secret circulation will sustain not only Saladin, but each and every one, at all times. This, surely, is betokened by the 'stumme Wiederholung allerseitiger Umarmungen' on which the curtain is rung down.

And yet, how fragile is this final harmony! For the magic circle of relatedness which closes as the curtain falls is sustained by the sufficiency of inner wealth in each: by the capacity of each to go out in love and to be fulfilled in doing so. But in a world rent by suspicion, strife and insecurity, who has the inner riches for such giving? Nathan, yes: his resources are as unfailing as is his humility. But the others? Saladin and the Knight Templar and even Recha, not to speak of such characters as Daja or the Patriarch? They all betray, or very nearly betray, relatedness: the Muslim all but murders his own blood in the Christian, the Christian all but throws the Jew to the mob whose chant 'Thut nichts! der Jude wird verbrannt' the Patriarch so busily recites, and even Recha is in danger of betraying the reality of relatedness to the insubstantiality of her 'Engelschwärmerei'; and that this too is a form of murder Nathan brings home to her, playfully, it is true, but not without the gravest undertones. When her saviour rebuffs her gratitude, she withdraws into the safety of her inwardness. By elevating her ungallant hero into an angel, she protects herself against any further insult she might suffer in return for her love, and, indeed, ultimately, from reciprocating his gift. It is the sterility of such an inner cult which Nathan identifies with characteristic intellectual ruthlessness:

> Nicht wahr? dem Wesen, das
> Dich rettete, – es sey ein Engel oder
> Ein Mensch, – dem möchtet ihr, und du besonders,
> Gern wieder viele grosse Dienste thun? –
> Nicht wahr? – Nun, einem Engel, was für Dienste,
> Für grosse Dienste könnt ihr dem wohl thun?
> Ihr könnt ihm danken; zu ihm seufzen, beten;
> Könnt in Entzückung über ihn zerschmelzen;
> Könnt an dem Tage seiner Feyer fasten,
> Almosen spenden. – Alles nichts. – Denn mich
> Deucht immer, dass ihr selbst und euer Nächster
> Hierbey weit mehr gewinnt, als er. Er wird
> Nicht fett durch euer Fasten; wird nicht reich
> Durch eure Spenden; wird nicht herrlicher
> Durch eur Entzücken; wird nicht mächtiger
> Durch eur Vertraun. Nicht war? Allein ein Mensch!   (I, 2)

It is significant that of all the array of arguments borrowed from the philosophical armoury of Wolff which Nathan advances against Recha's *Schwärmerei*,[12] this alone, the practical one, is already there in the prose draft of the play. It is the central argument, the one that is closest to the heart of the drama. Religious devotion finds its only adequate expression in an active intercourse between self and world. For the immanence of the human sphere alone permits of true reciprocity, of that two-way flow of love in which both, the lover and the loved, experience a miraculous enrichment. Recha is denying her saviour this potent source of life from hurt pride when she denies his humanity; and Nathan forces her, and us, into the realisation of what it means to betray the reality of human relatedness, when he harasses her with stories of the Templar's poverty, sickness and death:

> Nun liegt er da! hat weder Freund, noch Geld
> Sich Freunde zu besolden . . .
>   . . .
> Und du hast ihn getödtet!
> Hättst so ihn tödten können. –   (I, 2)

The theme of betrayal which is so persistently sounded in this play still reverberates at the very end. A tremor of shock runs through the Sultan's closing words, for all the lightness and the humour with which they are spoken: shock at the ever-present possibility that human beings may murder the love that might have grown between them: together, almost with mutual intent:

> Seht den Bösewicht!

Saladin scolds his nephew when the youth admits that he has had intimations of their kinship:

> Er wusste was davon, und konnte mich
> Zu seinem Mörder machen wollen! Wart! (V, *Letzter Auftritt*)

Such outgoing and active love as increases the life of giver and recipient, Lessing has embodied in the figure of the Jew. More precisely, he has embodied it in the central symbol of the play: the monetary symbol of Nathan's trading. The crucial words are spoken as Saladin hears of Nathan's wealth and is told that it derives from some mysterious, inexhaustible and living source. Saladin replies:

> Denn er handelt; wie ich hörte.

a statement which Sittah amplifies as follows:

> Sein Saumthier treibt auf allen Strassen, zieht
> Durch alle Wüsten; seine Schiffe liegen
> In allen Häfen. Das hat mir wohl eh
> Al-Hafi selbst gesagt; und voll Entzücken
> Hinzugefügt, wie gross, wie edel dieser
> Sein Freund anwende, was so klug und emsig
> Er zu erwerben für zu klein nicht achte:
> Hinzugefügt, wie frey von Vorurtheilen
> Sein Geist; sein Herz wie offen jeder Tugend,
> Wie eingestimmt mit jeder Schönheit sey.   (II, 3)

These are beautiful and very impressive lines. They evoke an image of a self perfectly attuned to the world, of a mind living in a vigorous intercourse with what is outside it. And because this mind accepts the 'other', the non-self, the material world so utterly and goes out to it in perfect trust, with its every power and sensibility, by every channel of communication, the encounter is creative and yields immeasurable dividends. In fact, the principal *donnée* of the play, Nathan's homecoming from a journey laden with the treasures he has garnered on his voyage, turns out to be the all-embracing metaphor of its meaning. For this play *is* about the returns the world yields to one who encounters it creatively, in outgoing and active love; and we must not miss the resonances of what is surely one of its most crucial statements: 'Denn er handelt'.[13] In these words which offer the key to Nathan's wealth and wisdom, under the image of commerce – *Handel* – the poet speaks to us of the necessity to realise the truths of religion practically, through our actions – our *Handeln* – a conviction which is writ large across every theological treatise that bears Lessing's name from the *Gedanken über die Herrenhuter* to the 'Kinderchen liebt Euch' which is the Alpha and the Omega of the *Testament Johannis*; perhaps indeed he speaks even of the necessity to body forth the truths of art through the enriching contact of the *Hand* with its medium, a possibility of which the author of *Philotas* and of *Emilia Galotti* seems to have despaired.

But then the hand, in Lessing's Virginia tragedy as well as in the earlier *Philotas,* had been a hapless tool. Here, in *Nathan,* Lessing's final testament, as well as in *Minna von Barnhelm,* the human hand is hallowed – by love. For Tellheim's hand, unfortunate, lamed in war, in the end is graced by the ring he had once received 'von lieben Händen' and had let go; the ring which Minna insists on returning to him, token of a love that returns to the self as it flows out to the beloved, in ever growing enrichment.

In the parable which Nathan tells Saladin, the precious ring, too, has been received 'aus lieber Hand'. That is all we know of its origin and indeed it is all we need to know. For its magic is the magic of love; of being loved and loving, accepted and acceptable. The ring which has its origin in a primordial act of love is passed on, we are told, by an act of love and as a token of love through the generations:

> Er liess den Ring
> Von seinen Söhnen dem Geliebtesten;
> Und setzte fest, dass dieser wiederum
> Den Ring von seinen Söhnen dem vermache,
> Der ihm der liebste sey; und stets der Liebste,
> Ohn' Ansehn der Geburt, in Kraft allein
> Des Rings, das Haupt, der Fürst des Hauses werde. –   (III, 7)

There is no set law of succession here to settle the question of inheritance. Emphatically, the ring does not go to the eldest son. It goes to the best beloved, by a choice of love. And the making of this choice is a reciprocal act involving both, the chooser and the chosen. For the magic powers of the ring can only become effective if and because the chosen son wears it 'in dieser Zuversicht'. To be 'angenehm' before God and men, he must know that his devotion is received, in the way in which Nathan knows that his surrender to God – Lessing, in *Die Erziehung des Menschengeschlechts*, called it 'heroische Gehorsam'[14] – has been accepted, that God chose him as he chose God. For only when love feels thus sanctioned can it flower into a vital need. Only then can it fulfil itself even as it flows out to the 'other'. Recha is secure in the knowledge that she is 'adopted' by a choice of love on the part of Nathan – in this play adoption, like journeying or trading, is a symbolic act[15] – but even so, the rejection she experiences at the hands of her second saviour at once makes her retreat into *Schwärmerei* as though she were unworthy of real affection. And what of the rejector himself, the obstreperous knight errant? Until the end, his past remains nebulous, no doubt on purpose. He has belonged to no one. His Muslim father left him to be brought up under rough northern skies by his Christian uncle; and he, Nathan speculates,

> Mag an Kindesstatt
> Vielleicht Euch angenommen haben! –   (V, *Letzter Auftritt*)

That is why it is not enough, now, for Saladin to give him back his life. That is why he risks the life he has been given without love, and passes it on without love, as the bucket he had used to put out the fire had passed on the water that had been poured into it:

> Der liess sich füllen, liess sich leeren, mir
> Nichts, dir nichts: also auch der Mann.   (III, 2)

It is not until Saladin accepts him in all his fierceness and with all his failings and adopts him, 'mit Seel und Leib', that he is released into the circulation of living love.

It is likewise with the chosen son of the parable. By being received in love, he is empowered to give in love and to feel fulfilled through such a giving. He is acceptable – 'angenehm' – and the most beloved of his brothers, not because of what he has, but because of what he does: because he flows out in love. To 'have', for Lessing, signifies a quality of being. To 'have' God in this play means to be—loving and beloved. To 'have' the true ring is to be—outgoing as is the ring.[16] As the circle of the ring goes out for ever, for ever to return upon itself, so the love of him that has the ring flows out to others to be returned to him. This is what the words of the judge betoken, with their emphasis on the outgoingness of the rightful claimant to the ring, of him who, paradoxically, concedes it to his brother:

>   . . . der rechte Ring
>   Besitzt die Wunderkraft beliebt zu machen;
>   Vor Gott und Menschen angenehm. Das muss
>   Entscheiden! Denn die falschen Ringe werden
>   Doch das nicht können! – Nun; wen lieben zwey
>   Von euch am meisten? – Macht, sagt an! Ihr schweigt?
>   Die Ringe wirken nur **zurück?** und nicht
>   Nach **aussen?** Jeder liebt sich selber nur
>   Am meisten? – O so seyd ihr alle drey
>   Betrogene Betrieger! Eure Ringe
>   Sind alle drey nicht echt. Der echte Ring
>   Vermuthlich ging verloren.   (III, 7)

This *out*going effect it is which is stressed in the judge's challenge to the rival brothers:

>   Es strebe von euch jeder um die Wette,
>   Die Kraft des Steins in seinem Ring' **an Tag**
>   Zu legen!

whilst the final judgment as to who has the true ring will be made

>   . . . wenn sich dann der Steine Kräfte
>   Bey euern Kindes-Kindeskindern **äussern**:   *(Ibid.)*

At every point plot and parable meet and interweave to form a homogeneous fabric of imagery and meaning.[17] It is with the precious ring as it is with Nathan's riches. The magic of both is the magic of outgoing, active love. Both Nathan and the true heir to the ring are rich, not through the introversion of self-love, but, paradoxically, by letting their riches go out into the world and be returned to them from the world with thousandfold increase. And are not both chosen, Nathan as well as the legendary son? The humble trader,

>   dem
>   Sein Gott von allen Gütern dieser Welt
>   Das Kleinst' und Grösste so in vollem Maas
>   Ertheilet habe.—
>   . . .
>   Das Kleinste: Reichthum. Und
>   Das Grösste: Weisheit . . .

who utilises nobly

>   was so klug und emsig
>   Er zu erwerben für zu klein nicht achte: (II, 3)

the meanest of realities – money: is he not a member of the
chosen race of whose place in the spiritual development of man
Lessing assures us in his *Erziehung des Menschengeschlechts*? Did the
poet choose a Jew to be the bearer of his message only because the
hero of Boccaccio's story which suggested the parable to him
happened to be a Jew, or perhaps also, and more fundamentally,
because he divined the life-acceptingness of this essentially
monistic faith? However that may be, Nathan, like Job, is sustained by the knowledge that there is a 'wunderbare Vergeltung in
diesem Leben', a knowledge latent in the Jewish ethos of going
out into this world actively to hallow and transform it, an ethos
which will come to fruition in the longed-for third age of
humanity.

The link between parable and plot is very appropriately furnished by the allusions to money in which Nathan's story is
embedded. At the conclusion of the audience Nathan offers
Saladin a loan of money, in confirmation of their new friendship
and of the shared values in which this friendship is rooted. But
money is already in Nathan's mind in the monologue preceding
the audience, as the Jew ponders the Muslim's request to let him
have the truth. The Sultan, Nathan doubtfully reflects, wants to
be given the truth as if it were hard cash. More precisely, as if it
were the newfangled currency

> Die nur der Stempel macht, die man aufs Bret
> Nur zählen darf . . .   (III, 6)

But, he asks himself, is truth of this order of reality? Can it be
known by counting digits, and be pocketed

> Wie Geld in Sack?   (*Ibid.*)

The analogy is a bad one, he decides. For such modern currency
is counterfeit. Its value is nominal. The figures imprinted on its
face bear no relation to its actual value. It is different, he reflects,
with the currency of old,

> Uralte Münze, die gewogen ward! –   (*Ibid.*)

for its value lies not in what it says but in what it is, and we know
it, not by taking cognisance of the letters inscribed on it, but by
experiencing its solid worth in the palm of our hand. It is such
currency that is commensurate with truth. Like the precious ore
of olden days, truth is nothing if not concrete lived experience.

Here, at the meeting point of parable and plot, in Nathan's reflections on the currency of truth, the nominalistic trend which pervades this play[18] is fully articulated in terms of the commanding poetic symbolism. It is here that the poet defines the perspectives for our understanding of Nathan's plea for religious tolerance and indeed of the repudiation, made time and time again in this drama, of any claim – be it made on behalf of Christianity or Fatherland or Truth – which is content to base itself upon the spurious right of name rather than on the weighty reality of experience and action.

Nathan knows what his creator knew and never tired of repeating in the idiom of his own time: God, the truth, even the ring have no thing-character, and to speak of them as if they belonged to the order of objects is to misuse language. We do not 'have' them as we 'have' even objects of knowledge, by an act of intellectual appropriation. Who may say that he 'has' the truth? or the true ring? or God?

> Wem eignet Gott? was ist das für ein Gott,
> Der einem Menschen eignet?   (III, 1)

Like Kant's Ideas of Reason, the truth about God is not such as to be intellectually apprehended, by an act of cognition. We do not 'have' him. We realise him in our doing, and we attest to his being through the quality of our relatedness. In this play money is indeed the presiding divinity. For in its universe of discourse, God is nothing if not the currency that passes from hand to human hand in the enriching reciprocity of love.

Nathan confirms this knowledge in a twofold fashion. Firstly in that he does what he has said. He does not 'have' the truth: he lives it. He offers good currency to his new-won friend. And what he does is in turn confirmed by the manner of his saying. Nathan declares his credo in the only way open to one who knows that the truth about God eludes the knowing mind. He shuns all theological abstractions and, instead, communicates the concreteness of his experience in the directness and concretion of the tale.

Even so, the snag shows in the telling. We cannot overlook the logical circle which returns, at different points of the spiral, throughout the parable of the ring. The legendary son possesses the ring in virtue of being the most beloved; and he is the most beloved in virtue of possessing the ring. The Father's love is invoked as proof of the genuineness of the ring; and the genuineness of the ring is, in turn, invoked as proof of the Father's love. Faith is based on historical tradition but historical tradition, in turn, is based on faith – the faith in the sincerity of the ancestors who have handed it down. Such logical circularity is unavoidable where the religious consciousness is forced to relinquish its native ground of feeling and action in order to explain itself to reason. For faith is intractable to reason and remains incapable of logical verification. And faith – the faith in the reality which is disclosed by feeling – is the beginning, the middle and the end of the experience of devotion.

However, the circularity at the heart of this play is more than a blemish inevitable within a thematic structure which insists that God is to be found, not in abstract theoretical thought, but in practical love. For does it not directly reflect that structure? The parable of the ring, itself circular, is the centrepiece of a play concerned with the circulation of riches, both within the confines of the single personality and in the reciprocity of love; and this circulation, in turn, is reflected in the very movement of an action which traces a recurrent round of enrichment until it comes to rest in the final circle of relatedness, in the embrace of all with all. Thus the circle, emblem of eternity, is not only very fittingly the commanding symbol of a play which is concerned with the eternal return of riches in the reciprocity of self and world. It is its total form. Such germaneness of theme and structure betokens the fact that Lessing's last poem is all of a piece. What is more, it testifies to the density and depth of the creative act from which it sprang, the poet's own doubts on this score notwithstanding. But that is another matter, with which we shall be extensively concerned in the next chapter.[19]

Part Four

OPEN CHANNELS

Der Künstler ist nicht ärmer als irgend einer unter den Leben-
den . . . Aber sein Schicksal ist nirgends als in seiner Arbeit . . .
In seiner Arbeit hat er alles: er hat die namenlose Wollust der
Empfängnis, den entzückenden Ätherrausch des Einfalls, und er
hat die unerschöpfliche Qual der Ausführung.

(Hugo von Hofmannsthal: *Über Charaktere im Roman und im Drama*)

How can we know the dancer from the dance?

(W. B. Yeats: *Among School Children*)

10

The Prose of Passion and the Poetry of Reason : Lessing's Creativity

Denn Recht hat jeder eigene Charakter,
Der übereinstimmt mit sich selbst, es gibt
Kein andres Unrecht als den Widerspruch.

(Schiller: *Wallensteins Tod*)

I

Whatever our estimate of Lessing's Virginia tragedy as a whole, the figure of Emilia, for most of us, fails to carry conviction. Old and more recent opinions to the contrary, we may take it that Emilia dies because she fears that the Prince would seduce her in the end.[1] We know it because on every level Lessing's *bürgerliches Trauerspiel* is concerned with the spoiling of intentions on the way to reality. This, we have seen, is the overall theme of the tragedy and it is pursued with the utmost singlemindedness on the level of action, character, imagery and, last but not least, on the level of intellectual discourse.[2] Odoardo's desire to preserve Emilia's pristine loveliness – a desire shared by Appiani and even by the Prince – comes to nought in a corrupt world. Emilia is abducted and Appiani murdered on the way to their wedding. 'Noch einen Schritt vom Ziele oder noch gar nicht ausgelaufen seyn, ist im Grunde eines und dasselbe.' Odoardo's determination to keep his hands clear of his daughter's blood is overtaken by the entry of the Prince. And as for the Prince himself: the passage from delight in Emilia's perfection to horror at the sight of her mutilated body is but a homiletic example of the curse which besets his life: the spoiling of any vision, however passionately conceived, as it nears reality. Vision in this play perishes by the wayside, and this theme is time and again sounded by the reiterated image of the *langer Weg* and of the hand which destroys even where it would create. Whether it is Appiani's and Emilia's vision of moral beauty or the painter's vision of physical beauty, the melancholy message is the

same: however small the distance between vision and reality,
however short the way, it is longer than the way from the mind
to the hand, and infinitely less protected.

In such a thematic context, it would seem clear how the poet
would have us envisage the character of Emilia herself. Her
virginal integrity perishes as she enters the world, even as Nature's
vision of her became corrupted as it took material form. Emilia
too is embodied and 'auf dem langen Wege' from the eye through
the heart and back to reality her vision is spoilt. 'Auch meine
Sinne, sind Sinne.' Her body betrays her mind.

Even taken by themselves, without the aid of the context in
which the poet has embedded them, Emilia's character and
psychological development seem clearly defined, and by no means
only from the retrospect of the final act, as Lessing's brother Karl
presumed.[3] Her deference to a high-principled and puritanical
father together with her dispassion towards a man who himself
puts her father before his bride-to-be,[4] suggest that her erotic
springs have not yet been tapped and that she may well wake up
when it is too late. This awakening had in fact begun to take place
when Emilia met the Prince at the house of Grimaldi, and we
witness the after-effects of the encounter with him at church.
We cannot argue away the force of the 'Er' and 'ihn selbst' –
intimate references to the Prince who occupies *her* mind but no
one else's – as she rushes back home to tell her mother of the
events in church; and in interpreting the significance of her lapse,
had we not better rely on the psychological instinct of the young
Schiller who in *Kabale und Liebe* 'borrowed' Emilia's slip of tongue
to tell us about Luise's engrossment with the President's son[5] than
on scholars who maintain that poets could not have known about
unconscious mechanisms before Freud systematised their intuitive
insights? The human soul in its depths has always been the
province of the poets, and the Oedipus complex derives its name
and connotation from Sophocles's play written some two thousand
years earlier, not vice versa. Modern psychology has 'invented'
nothing whatever. It merely formulates phenomena and
configurations that have been constants of the human psyche and
of human experience since human beings began to experience and
which have been available to the divinatory powers of poets since
poets began to write poetry.

Besides, the 'ihn selbst' in this scene is not an isolated bit of
evidence. It comes at the end of a long speech which, if anything,
is more revealing. For the mysterious 'es' which assails Emilia
from behind her back as her eyes and her conscious mind are
lifted heavenward, towards the altar, that 'es' which, try as she

may, she cannot shut out or silence, describes, fundamentally, not the impingement on her consciousness of an outsider: to wit, 'ihn selbst', the Prince. It describes, rather, an event inside her: the disturbing recognition of the existence of nameless forces deep within herself; those forces precisely which Freud, some hundred and fifty years later, was to name the 'Id'. And who knows whether, here too, the psychologists' nomenclature was not fed by the intuitive knowledge of the poets?

We have varied grounds then for assuming that Emilia's tragedy was to have been the impossibility of preserving her unravished beauty vis-à-vis the reality of life. We have her own word for it when she tells her father in the final scene: 'Verführung ist die wahre Gewalt.' Thus we must imagine Lessing seeking to picture Emilia not only as possessed of formal perfection but as Italianate and sensuous, inflammatory and yielding, seductive to others and herself open to seduction.[6] This is indeed what she herself tells us when she reminds her father:

> Ich habe Blut, mein Vater; so jugendliches, so warmes Blut, als eine. Auch meine Sinne, sind Sinne. Ich stehe für nichts. . . . (V, 7)

and when she confesses that after one hour in Grimaldi's house '. . . erhob sich so mancher Tumult in meiner Seele, den die strengsten Uebungen der Religion kaum in Wochen besänftigen konnten' *(ibid.)*. The unnamable forces that arose then, for fear of which she now dies, are the very forces which in the second act she had evoked by the eloquent 'es'.

How is it that, knowing as much about her as we do, we nevertheless fail to be persuaded of the necessity of her tragic fate? In order to see how the poet has implemented – or failed to implement — a character both alluring and open to seduction, the examination of three passages would suggest itself: first the painter's verbal portrait of a beauty which is at that very moment inflaming the Prince with the desire to possess her, then Emilia's reaction to his advances in church and, finally, her summing up of the situation vis-à-vis her father in the penultimate scene.

Conti's eulogy begins promisingly enough, when Conti dismisses the Prince's attempts to draw him on the subject of Emilia's beauty, saying:

> Und eines jeden Empfindung sollte erst auf den Ausspruch eines Malers warten? – Ins Kloster mit dem, der es von uns lernen will, was schön ist! (I, 4)

Such beauty as that of Emilia, he says in effect, is not an academic issue. It is 'hot stuff' and any man with his five senses

and his instincts intact can appreciate it unaided. So far so good.
But now listen to the *verbal* evocation of her charms. This is how
Conti continues:

> Dieser Kopf, dieses Antlitz, diese Stirn, diese Augen, diese Nase, dieser
> Mund, dieses Kinn, dieser Hals, diese Brust, dieser Wuchs, dieser
> ganze Bau, sind, von der Zeit an, mein einziges Studium der
> weiblichen Schönheit. –

We had expected the artist to evoke, in words themselves inflamed
with sensuous excitement, that blend of innocence and seductiveness which has turned the Prince's head. Instead of this, we get
a catalogue of anatomical items, systematically listed one by one,
piece by piece, from the top downward. What image can the bare
demonstrative repeated elevenfold evoke, by its very auditory
baldness, if not that of a stereotype, an unruffled perfection with
no *soupçon* of wayward charm? What indeed can the imperious
gesture which we must imagine as accompanying the painter's
words suggest if not a beauty itself majestically controlled?

It is true, Conti's eulogy is not meant to provide more than a
frame in which we may exercise our imagination. The device
chosen by the poet here to convey visual beauty is precisely the
one which he commends in *Laokoon*.[7] There, in Chapter XX, we
read:

> Der Dichter der die Elemente der Schönheit nur nach einander zeigen
> könnte, enthält sich daher der Schilderung körperlicher Schönheit, als
> Schönheit, gänzlich. Er fühlt es, dass diese Elemente nach einander
> geordnet, unmöglich die Wirkung haben können, die sie, neben
> einander geordnet, haben; dass der concentrirende Blick, den wir
> nach ihrer Enumeration auf sie zugleich zurück senden wollen, uns
> doch kein übereinstimmendes Bild gewähret; dass es über die
> menschliche Einbildung gehet, sich vorzustellen, was dieser Mund,
> und diese Nase, und diese Augen zusammen für einen Effect haben,
> wenn man sich nicht aus der Natur oder Kunst einer ähnlichen
> Composition solcher Theile erinnern kann.[8]

Hence, a little further on in the same chapter, Lessing commends
Anakreon for the device he employs to mediate physical beauty.
Anakreon lets the poet instruct a painter standing by his side as
to how he is to paint his subject:

> 'So', sagt er 'mache mir das Haar, so die Stirne, so die Augen, so den
> Mund, so Hals und Busen, so Hüft und Hände!' . . . Seine Absicht
> ist nicht,

Lessing continues,

> dass wir in dieser mündlichen Direction des Mahlers, die ganze
> Schönheit der geliebten Gegenstände erkennen und fühlen sollen; er
> selbst empfindet die Unfähigkeit des wörtlichen Ausdrucks, und nimt
> eben daher den Ausdruck der Kunst zu Hülfe, deren Täuschung er so
> sehr erhebet, dass das ganze Lied mehr ein Lobgedicht auf die Kunst,
> als auf sein Mädchen zu seyn scheinet.[9]

Lessing is here giving us the kind of reason which prevailed
upon him, later, to place his eulogy of Emilia's beauty on the
painter's lips, in view of a portrait representing that beauty. Our
imagination is to be aided in its task of realising a visual beauty
which language must despair of being able to evoke. But is
language as impotent as Lessing here makes out, and does the
descriptive poet serve his purpose by relinquishing his province
and addressing himself to our vagrant visual imagination? Or is
it not rather his business to create *verbal* equivalents of such
objects, or sensations, as may have stimulated his poetic
imagination, a world of words that is sufficient unto itself?[10] In
adopting the device of Anakreon, Lessing has failed to project
Emilia's beauty adequately, that is to say linguistically. He has
failed to infuse into his very language a sensuous excitement
analogous to that experienced by the painter and the Prince, and
it is this bankruptcy of his own poetic power which he pinpoints
in the melancholy admission on which his theoretical discussion of
the problem concludes:

> Was heisst aber dieses sonst, als bekennen, dass die Sprache vor sich
> selbst hier ohne Kraft ist; dass die Poesie stammelt und die Bered-
> samkeit verstummet, wenn ihnen nicht die Kunst noch einigermassen
> zur Dollmetscherin dienet?[11]

Thus Emilia's allurement fails to communicate itself to us when
it would have been most necessary, both from the point of view of
the external plot and of its inner motivation. What about her own
seduceability, i.e. the strength of those erotic promptings on which
the motivation of the tragedy hinges? The heroine does give away
the intensity of her preoccupation with the Prince as, 'in einer
ängstlichen Verwirrung', she bursts into her mother's room. We
have seen it and have given due weight to the significance of her
bewilderment. But we must also take note of the timing and the
context of her emotional outburst. It comes late, long after the
first haunted 'ihn selbst'. What follows her turbulent entry is not,
as one might expect, an agitated account of a meeting which has

frightened the life out of her: it is a series of reflections on the moral issues the encounter has raised, reflections which time and again relinquish the plane of the particular instance, the concrete situation, and assume the form and force of general philosophical pronouncements (II, 6):

> Was ist dem Laster Kirch' und Altar?
>
> . . . sündigen wollen, [ist] auch sündigen.
>
> . . . dass fremdes Laster uns, wider unsern Willen, zu Mitschuldigen machen kann!

A little tidying up and we have fully-fledged maxims on the moral condition of man. Emilia's transition from the personal 'I' to the 'we' appropriate to the generalising reflection and from the illicit advances of this man here and now to the abstraction of *das Laster* is of course significant; but nothing is more telling than the prevalence of modal auxiliaries in her ruminations. *Sein* and *sollen, können, wollen* and *müssen*—these words reverberate through her speeches; and what are they if not the alphabet of the human will, the modality of the moral consciousness? Emilia registers the forces of unreason, yes; she feels assailed by their very existence. But these forces do not stand a chance of prevailing. She meets them head-on, with her conscious mind alerted and in unbending control. They may alarm her, but they cannot overpower her.

Indeed it is only because her conscious mind is so rigidly bent on control that so little can upset her so much. Under its scrutiny, the smallest deviation from the norm becomes magnified and distorted:

> . . . was er sprach, was ich ihm geantwortet; – fällt mir es noch bey, so ist es gut, so will ich es Ihnen sagen, meine Mutter. Jetzt weiss ich von dem allen nichts. (II, 6)

The fact of the matter is that she had said nothing whatever to the Prince. He himself tells us so twice over:

> Mit allen Schmeicheleyen und Betheuerungen konnt' ich ihr auch nicht ein Wort auspressen. Stumm und niedergeschlagen und zitternd stand sie da; wie eine Verbrecherinn, die ihr Todesurtheil höret. (III, 3)

he tells Marinelli; and again, to Emilia herself, to whom there would surely be no point in lying:

> Auch ward ich durch die sprachlose Bestürzung, mit der Sie es anhörten, oder vielmehr nicht anhörten, genugsam bestraft. (III, 5)

So tight is Emilia's conscious hold on herself that she
hallucinates sensations and perceptions which have no basis in
reality. For surely she is deluded in thinking that she heard the
footsteps of the Prince follow her along the street, right into her
house and up the stairs. This is the burden of Claudia's comment
– originally Emilia's own: 'Die Furcht hat ihren besondern Sinn,
meine Tochter!' (II, 6). ' . . . sie soll bloss damit sagen wollen,'
Lessing writes to his brother Karl, 'dass sie nun wohl sehe, die
Furcht habe sie getäuscht.'[12] Emilia's hallucinations are not a
measure of her sensuality on the level of reality, the level of overt
action and behaviour. On the contrary, they testify to the rigidity
with which she represses her erotic drives and to the unrelenting
vigilance exercised by her consciousness.[13]

It is the same in the penultimate scene of the drama where
Emilia openly avows her motive for seeking death at her father's
hand:

> Ich kenne das Haus der Grimaldi. Es ist das Haus der Freude. Eine
> Stunde da, unter den Augen meiner Mutter; – und es erhob sich so
> mancher Tumult in meiner Seele, den die strengsten Uebungen der
> Religion kaum in Wochen besänftigen konnten! – (V, 7)

This is not the reality-fear of a hot-blooded young woman who
senses that she may at any moment be overpowered by her passions. It is the anxiety of an excessively controlled person at the
inkling of drives that may not be within the jurisdiction of the
controlling consciousness. And how prohibitive this censor is! The
arguments Emilia produces at the height of the battle against
temptation are syllogisms barely disguised:

> Gewalt! Gewalt! wer kann der Gewalt nicht trotzen? Was Gewalt
> heisst, ist nichts: Verführung ist die wahre Gewalt. (V, 7)

Supply the suppressed major premiss and the syllogistic skeleton
of the argument is laid bare:

> All real force is irresistible.
> Seduction is a real force.
> Ergo: Seduction is irresistible.

Emilia's argument runs on thus:

> Ich habe Blut, mein Vater; so jugendliches, so warmes Blut, als eine.
> Auch meine Sinne, sind Sinne.   (V, 7)

Here the logical form of the argument is even more obvious:

> Everyone with senses is open to seduction.
> I have senses.
> Ergo: I am open to seduction.[14]

No – the lady protests too much and argues too stringently to convince us of the reality of the dangers she foresees. This mind, this powerful reason, is not likely to be engulfed by passion. And here again we must note the emphatic reiteration of *müssen, können, sollen* and, above all, of *wollen* – the *wollen* of a mind which is bent upon its choice – words which testify to the fact that the moral consciousness is on the alert and in full charge of the situation. 'All is under control': this is the message which her words carry, despite themselves as it were, and this message is underlined by the paltriness of their sound. 'Gewalt! Gewalt! Verführung ist die wahre Gewalt' and 'Auch meine Sinne, sind Sinne': the cacophony of these repetitions belies the state of sensuous arousal they are designed to convey.[15] Emilia's two action-portraits reinforce the verbal sketch of the painter: the portrait of a woman neither seductive nor seduceable, but chiselled in majestic marble, virginal and cool, a true daughter of a tough Roman lineage.

II

As we turn from *Emilia Galotti* to the earlier *Philotas* – and having adopted this order in the first place I propose to keep to it here – it seems as though we shall have to abandon the line of argument we have so far pursued and switch to an altogether new track. For in the previous section of this chapter it has been argued that Lessing, paradoxically, was unable to banish an element of intellectual contrivance when he turned to the theme of human passion, and that he failed to create the depth-dimension of life. If, then, *Philotas* is a failure as a piece of dramatic poetry – and this would seem the general consensus – the reason for its deficiency must be a different one. For how could passion figure in a play in which there is no representative of the opposite sex and in which women, insofar as they are mentioned at all, are referred to with unconcealed contempt? Indeed, what place could passion conceivably occupy in a drama centred in a character whose outstanding quality is unrelatedness?

In answer to such questions which my own reading of *Philotas* may well have prompted, I would reply that this early tragedy is indeed a tragedy of passion, using the word 'passion' by no means only, or even primarily, to indicate that its young hero passionately cares for things of the mind – this Nathan does too, and in much greater measure: I would use the word in the quite specific sense that Philotas stands in a passionate relation to himself. He is enamoured of his own spirit.

Indeed, in this unseasoned but devastating play the young poet has penetrated to the very core of the Idealist experience of life and exposed its dangers in a cathartic act of an intensity which the author of *Emilia Galotti*, eleven years later, no longer felt; for in *Emilia Galotti*, written when the poet was himself entering upon the central relationship of his life, there is a constant reaching out for relatedness and a constant expectation of a return from the 'other', the world, which is only just defeated by the treacherousness of a life no one ever quite trusts. The road from vision to reality is long, too long as it turns out: but at least the characters set out on their journey in the first place, and their eagerness for life and their 'doom-eagerness', for the greater part of the time, are poised in a precarious balance. In this earlier tragedy the spirit, rearing up in all its arrogance, from the beginning casts a shadow over the world, so sinister and so huge that the self is bound to shrink back into its inwardness and, of its own free choice, to terminate its journey into a life scarcely begun.

No literary document of the second half of the Eighteenth Century reveals with such remorselessness the canker at the heart of the Neoplatonic experience of life: the self-adoration of the spirit which dooms it to the solipsism of *Schwärmerei* and to a contempt of life so absolute as to make the tragedy of an Emilia or a Werther appear like a mild variant of the true killer. To be sure, Werther, from the beginning of the novel, chafes against the imprisonment of his soaring spirit in the fetters of finitude. Yet it soars outward as well as upward, seeking to merge with the world and to imbibe sweetness from it as the bee sucks sweetness from flower after flower; and it is only gradually that he realises that his spirit can find neither shelter nor sustenance outside itself, and withdraws 'from the contagion of the world's slow stain'. Philotas's rejection of the world is instantaneous, and as soon as he awakens from the dream of childhood to the fact that his spirit is his body's captive and, hence, beholden to the world, he prises open his cell and escapes from it. The setting in which the youth wakes up to the reality of his condition and terminates it – the luxurious tent in which he finds himself – in fact is a poetic metaphor: it is an extension of his own body; and as soon as he becomes aware of his bodily existence and its lures, he perceives it as an intolerable captivity and breaks out from it. Like the King's 'Beischlaeferinnen' whom he suspects of owning the tent in which he has awakened to consciousness, the body is a loathsome bedfellow for the spirit that loves itself and itself alone. Philotas's end not only lies dormant in his beginning: his beginning *is* his end.

This short-circuiting of life is not only the destiny of the 'frühzeitige Held' of the drama, Philotas. It determines the structure of the tragedy in every detail and seals its fate as a living dramatic work of art. We have remarked the decussate arrangement of the figures in the play which results from the fact that each Prince is a prisoner in the antagonist's camp.[16] Of this total configuration we see only one half, that is to say, Prince Philotas at the court of King Aridäus. We have noted the blurring of perspectives resulting from this arrangement. The tenderer bonds that obtain in this play are only seen in reflection, through the vicarious affections offered to Philotas at the enemy's court. We do not see Philotas in relation to his own father any more than we see King Aridäus in relation to his own son, Polytimet.

The consequences of this poetic stratagem are far-reaching: on the one hand, we see all emotions at one remove, that is to say, in a form in which they are bound to appear weakened. At the same time, the love held out to Philotas shows that his ostensible enemies in truth are friends, and that his sally into the unknown is but the mirror image of a home-coming, in that he is accorded a reception precisely as friendly as that which his *alter ego,* Prince Polytimet, is receiving at the hands of Philotas's own father. But Philotas rejects this reception, refusing to reciprocate it and insisting that his friends are his adversaries. This, together with the vicarious character of all the feelings enacted on stage, makes for an effect which is very curious indeed: the relationships we see and the emotions engendered by them, at least on one side, are emptied of substance as it were and take on an air of unreality and even ghostliness. The casting of friends as enemies, occasioned by the plot and the crosswise deployment of figures this necessitates, and confirmed by Philotas who obdurately clings to his delusion—all this serves to reveal an enmity within the youth which is absolute. The apparent disguise serves to point the truth beneath the truth: Philotas's unrelatedness is not caused by the accidents of the situation in which he finds himself: it is as essential and incurable as is his unrelatedness to his own embodied self.

Thus the relationships in which the central figure seems involved are illusory in the same fashion in which Philotas's overt reactions to others are illusory: they are the responses of a 'false-self-system', to use a recently coined term,[17] a system designed to protect and hide his true self – his spirit – from any significant contact whatsoever. Any semblance of action and reaction between Philotas, the dissociated spirit *par excellence*, and the figures that surround him turns out to be deceptive. There is no meeting-point between them and, hence, no genuine interaction; and where this is so, can there be any dramatic action in the true sense of the word?

The only exception to the rule seems to be Philotas's response to his countryman and fellow prisoner, Parmenio. To him, the young Prince, who is otherwise exclusively related to his hidden spiritual self, does seem to go out with a measure of spontaneity. Indeed, his impetuousness fairly sweeps the old warrior off his feet. The old man is seduced by his Prince's charm, ready not only to lie for him as he is asked to do, but to commit any folly or crime on his behalf: 'Ich will alles, was du willst', he replies in answer to Philotas's flattery that he considers the older man not as his subject, but as his friend (and this is by no means the first piece of flattery Philotas uses in this conversation). And, slightly tipsily, as if he had tasted a potion too strong for his frame, Parmenio continues:

> Willst du sonst nichts? Soll ich sonst nichts thun? Soll ich für dich durchs Feuer rennen? Mich für dich vom Felsen herab stürzen? Befiehl nur, mein lieber kleiner Freund, befiehl! Itzt thu ich dir alles! So gar – sage ein Wort, und ich will für dich ein Verbrechen, ein Bubenstück begehen! Die Haut schaudert mir zwar; aber doch Prinz, wenn du willst, ich will, ich will –. (V)

Not without considerable manipulating, Philotas has got Parmenio where he wants him to be. He has got him to act as the tool of his self-destruction. Parmenio is ready to delay his ransom until it is too late. In the same way, by using his charms – 'Still! Wenn ich das Kind spielte? – Dieser Gedanke verspricht etwas' (VI), he murmurs as he hears the King approach his tent – he will obtain the second tool he requires: the sword he needs in order to kill himself. Thus Parmenio, like the sword, for Philotas is a means to an end. And that end is death which Philotas pursues with the determination of a hunter pursuing his quarry. Thus, even on the one occasion when relatedness seems to flower into being, it is only a guise of the radical dissociation which is the Prince's choice.

When the sword he desires is brought to him, he apostrophises it twice as 'liebes Schwerd'. First, still play-acting the child: 'liebes Schwerd! Welch eine schöne Sache ist ein Schwerd, zum Spiele und zum Gebrauche! Ich habe nie mit etwas andern gespielt' (VIII); then, in a serious aside: 'Liebes Schwerd! Wer doch bald mit dir allein wäre! – ' This is erotically charged language, as much so as Parmenio's response to him had been. But Philotas reserves such language for the tool that will set his spirit free from contact with his material self, before it 'rot inwardly and foul contagion spread'.

Only in one other context does the death-struck youth resort to language resonant with such tenderness: and this is when he speaks of his idea to wreck the balance of fortunes which might be his saving, by withdrawing his spirit from the bargain. He speaks of this idea to Parmenio, in words that veil more than they reveal. And how could it be otherwise, since communication of the spirit with any 'other' corrupts the vision from the start, and since to use the instrument of communication – speech – means entrusting the purity of the idea to a sensory medium, that is, to certain contamination? The thought which has come to him, he explains to Parmenio, ' . . . verschwindet, wenn ich ihn mittheile'. There is no indirect object here, no mention of a recipient. 'So zärtlich, so fein ist er, ich getraue mir ihn nicht in Worte zu kleiden' (V). We remember the vehemence with which, only eight years later, Herder was to reject the image of the body clothed in its raiments as a fitting analogy for the nature of the relation between thought and expression: in the speech of everyday life as much as in poetry, thought and expression cleave to one another as the soul cleaves to its body.[18] In 1759, Lessing's young hero dismisses language, most human and ethereal of all media, as a tool unequal to the mind that created it and endows the incorporeal vision with a tenderness which is, in truth, directed towards the spirit which harbours such treasures. Who would gainsay the narcissism inherent in this pathetic fallacy?

Continuing to speak of his 'grosser, schimmernder Entschluss' as he will call it in the following scene (VI), Philotas explains to Parmenio:

> Ich denke ihn nur, wie mich der Philosoph Gott zu denken gelehrt hat, und aufs höchste könnte ich dir . . . sagen, was er nicht ist. (V)

Neither the mystical elevation of the idea, nor the corresponding denigration of language which can only express what the idea is not, could be more sharply underscored than by Philotas here, resorting to the comparison with the godhead: for the transcen-

dent by definition eludes the categories at the disposal of embodied beings implicated in the phenomenal world, and thus is
truly inexpressible and un-speakable. Finally Philotas assures his
companion that his idea is, in truth, 'der unschädlichste Einfall
von der Welt; so unschädlich', he adds, 'als – als ein Gebet. Wirst
du deswegen zu beten unterlassen, weil du nicht ganz gewiss
weisst, ob dir das Gebet helfen wird?' *(Ibid.)* There is a great deal
of cynicism in this simile. Philotas has turned God into an 'unknown
God': 'Vater, den ich nicht kenne,' as Werther has it; and now he
likens his plan – the plan to destroy himself – to a prayer which may or
may not reach an unknown recipient. Both alike, the prayer into the
void, and the leap into the void of death, are acts of non-com-
munication; and the word *unschädlich*, in both contexts, jars on the
ear.

Philotas's intimations of his vision are vitally important because
they contain *in nuce* the complete aesthetics, metaphysics and
theory of communication that inform the universe of discourse of
this play. The place they occupy in its thematic structure corresponds exactly to that taken up by the utterances of Conti the
painter in *Emilia Galotti*. And it is here as it was there: both
Philotas and Conti have the last say: their words are borne out by
the meaning and movement of the two tragedies as a whole.

By the time that Philotas communicates – or, rather, fails to
communicate – his vision to his countryman, it is fully formed.
Before our eyes, however, we see this vision being 'born' – in the
monologue of the preceding scene. King Aridäus has left the
Prince's tent, having revealed to him that 'das wunderliche
Kriegesglück' (III) has not only delivered Philotas into his hands,
but, in return, given his own Polytimet into the hands of Philotas's father. In a surge of relief, Philotas exclaims:

> Götter! Näher konnte der Blitz, ohne mich ganz zu zerschmettern,
> nicht vor mir niederschlagen. Wunderbare Götter! Die Flamme kehrt
> zurück; der Dampf verfliegt, und ich war nur betäubt. – So war das
> mein ganzes Elend, zu sehen, wie elend ich hätte werden können?
> Wie elend mein Vater durch mich? – Nun darf ich wieder vor dir
> erscheinen, mein Vater! (IV)

For a moment, the young Prince welcomes the equipoise of the
scales of fortune and the thought of an honourable exchange, and
the tribulations which fate might have had in store for him –
captivity and ransom – to him seem deadly. As deadly, in fact, as
the stroke of lightning to which he very aptly compares the blow
which might have fallen upon him. For lightning is absolute in its
destructiveness: swift, cold, and—unlike other forms of light—-

never a harbinger of life, only of extinction. But his relief at the
thought that the deadly flash has missed him is shortlived. As the
idea crosses his mind that he might tilt the scales of fortune at the
price of his own life, he returns to the image once again. 'Und nun
– welcher Gedanke war es, den ich itzt dachte?' he muses;

> nein; den ein Gott in mir dachte – Ich muss ihm nachhängen! Lass
> dich fesseln, flüchtiger Gedanke! – Itzt denke ich ihn wieder! Wie weit
> er sich verbreitet, und immer weiter; und nun durchstrahlt er meine
> ganze Seele! – *(Ibid.)*

Philotas has caught the fleeting flash, and what but a moment ago
seemed deadly now becomes the source of his illumination: the
vision of death is spreading its light throughout his soul.[19]

From that moment onward, and before our eyes, through an
unbroken chain of syllogistic reasoning conducted, stroke by
stroke, with the remorselessness of a school logician, vision turns
into resolution. It is a contrapuntal debate between Philotas and
his absent father, designed to refute his father's imagined objections to his son's death and to justify his own resolve. This,
roughly, is how the argument would run if it were set out in full,
point counter point. And at the risk of seeming pedantic to some
of my readers (who are advised to skip the following pages), I shall
so set it out in full. For only when we exhibit the merciless
consistency of Philotas's mode of response – a rigorously intellectual response – to an existential situation, are we in a position to
get the measure of this character and the theme embodied in him,
and to assess the poetic status of this strangest of tragedies.

Philotas: Every seed or bud carries its end within itself.
        I am such a seed or bud.
        Ergo: I carry my end within myself.[20]

The organic images Philotas employs here would seem to indicate
that he uses the word *end* in the Aristotelian sense of *telos*, signifying the end or purpose which is inherent in the very structure
of a living thing or being: florescence and procreation in the
instances above. That this is not so, however, becomes clear from
the argument which follows hard on the heels of this one:

Philotas: Every being that has lived a given time has had
        time in which to learn to die.
        I have lived more than that given time.
        Ergo: I have had time in which to learn to die.

Philotas, it will be seen, has substituted another meaning of the
word *end* for the Aristotelian one. The end or purpose of life is to
learn to end it. The biological life and timespan, implied in the
Aristotelian concept of *end* and suggested by the organic imagery
Philotas had used in his first instance, is altogether suppressed.

There follows his father's – imagined – set of objections, based,
in their entirety, on the factor ignored by his son. This is how the
father's argument would run, if it were set out in its logical form:

Father: All those able to dedicate themselves to the welfare
            of the state know ends higher than life.
        All those who know ends higher than life are men.
        Ergo: All those able to dedicate themselves to the
            welfare of the state are men.
        You, Philotas, are not a man.
        Ergo: You are not able to dedicate yourself to the
            welfare of the state.

By a similar string of propositions the father then could be shown
to prove that his son is not a hero. Set out in full, his argument
would run, roughly, thus:

Father: All heroes are able to dedicate themselves to the
            service of the state.
        All capable of dedicating themselves to the service
            of the state must know ends higher than life.
        All who know ends higher than life are men.
        Ergo: All non-men are non-heroes.
        You, Philotas, are not a man.
        Ergo: You are not a hero.

It will be seen that, in every instance, the father operates with a
proposition embodying the assumption that Philotas is not – yet
– a man. From this, the two further conclusions that he is not yet
able to regard other ends as being higher than life, and that
therefore he cannot yet be a hero, follow with necessity.

Philotas, in his turn, proceeds to refute his father's assumption
and, thence, progressively defines what it means to be a hero.
Again he begins with an instance drawn from the botanical sphere
and reminiscent of the one with which his argument had started:

Philotas: Every conifer that can serve its end has reached
            maturity.
        This conifer can serve its end.
        Ergo: This conifer has reached maturity.

Here again, the use of the word end ('Zweck') must be noted. As
before it is not the inherent end which Aristotle has in mind when
he speaks of the acorn containing its own *telos* – the oak tree –
within itself: 'geprägte Form, die lebend sich entwickelt'.[21] The
end Philotas means is one that is extraneous to its life and, indeed,
terminates it.

Philotas's equivocal employment of the concept *end*, used now
in its Aristotelian sense and now as signifying death, would be
logically expressed as follows:

Philotas: Anything that can reach its end can fulfil its end.
             Anything that can die can reach its end.
             Ergo: Anything that can die can fulfil its end.

In the case of the conifer, the 'end' of this tree – in Philotas's own
meaning of the word – is to serve as a ship's mast. This instance
is then reformulated in general terms, thus:

             Every being that can fulfil its end has reached
                maturity.
             I can fulfil my end.
             Ergo: I have reached maturity.

This general principle – based, as we have seen, on an equivoca-
tion within the term *end* – is then applied to the human sphere
and to Philotas's own situation in particular; and as a result he is
able to refute his father's position:

Philotas: All that are able to dedicate their lives to the
                welfare of the state know ends higher than life.
             All who know ends higher than life are able to
                fulfil their end.
             All who can fulfil their end are men.
             Ergo: All that are able to dedicate their lives to
                the welfare of the state are men.
             I am able to dedicate my life to the welfare of the
                state.
             Ergo: I am a man; 'Ich bin ein Mann . . . ob ich
                gleich vor wenig Tagen ein Knabe war.'

Philotas's final argument runs thus:

             All men who know how to sacrifice their life to
                ends higher than life and are able to dedicate
                themselves to the welfare of the state are
                heroes.
             I am such a man.
             Ergo: I am a hero.

Content and form of Philotas's chain of reasoning are alike, and alike revealing. His imagined father, it will be seen, considers moral maturity to be logically and chronologically contingent on biological maturity. Philotas reverses the procedure. He deems biological maturity to be logically and chronologically contingent on moral maturity. He refutes the argument that he is *not* morally mature because he is not old enough. Instead, he argues that he *is* old enough because he has reached moral maturity. The difference between the conclusions reached by father and son in their imaginary conversation arises from the fact that each uses the word 'end' with a different connotation. By using a number of different, though ostensibly synonymous terms, such as *vollendet, vollkommen,* or *Zweck*, Philotas veils an underlying ambiguity of meaning. In the arguments put upon his father's lips, the word 'end' is used in a primarily biological sense. Philotas himself uses it in a 'moral' sense and, given his situation and the resolve he has made, the two meanings of the concept coalesce: for him, to fulfil his life's purpose is to terminate his life. By a series of logical short-circuits, he has argued time and life into non-existence.

This disregard of lived time is precisely what Philotas expresses by the form of his reasoning. The syllogism is a formal mode of reasoning designed to set out the applicability of a general rule or principle to a particular case or cases, demonstrating either that it is an instance of that principle, or that it is not an instance of that principle, or, finally, that the principle has only a limited application to the given instance. In the case of the syllogisms Philotas uses here, he subsumes his individual case and his particular characteristics under an abstract principle pertaining to all men. Thus he identifies himself with the properties predicated of the class to which he belongs, defining himself as a mere instance of that class. In its 'all or none' attitude this may betoken the sweepingness of youth. But where is the concrete encounter between a particular situation and a unique individual which is the stuff of living drama? Where is the 'Liebes-Dumpfheit und Kraft'[22] which is the prerogative of youth, that immediacy of experiencing in which thought, feeling and sensation run fluid in one indivisible continuum? Philotas only experiences himself generically, as a representative of humanity, as the denizen of an abstract Elysium 'wo alle Tugendhafte Freunde, und alle Tapfere Glieder **Eines** seligen Staates sind' (VIII).

Furthermore, the relations obtaining in a formal syllogism between class, individual and their respective properties are set out in such a manner that they are self-evident in the same fashion in which the properties of a geometrical configuration or algebraic equation are self-evident. Our use of the pure present in all of these is expressive of the fact, not that three plus three equals six here and now, but that this is the relation that obtains between these terms everywhere and at all times. Of course we intuit the relation between the terms of the syllogism in time, more or less swiftly according to our power to perceive formal relations; but of its essence intuition is instant, and equally of its essence every syllogism enunciates relations of timeless validity, a fact we express by the form in which we set it out verbally; *given that* p equals q and *given that* r equals p, *then* r *must at all times* equal q. We may say that we inspect the form of the argument *in* time, but that what we thus inspect in itself is not *of* time. Is this not tantamount to saying that the form of Philotas's reasoning is exactly congruent with the content of his argument? Neither his resolve to die nor the manner in which he reasons himself into this resolve is dependent on experienced time, time lived through. They are intellectual events as instant and discontinuous as the stroke of lightning which flashes past Philotas's inner eye at the beginning of his monologue; time, the matrix and the medium of life, has shrunk into insignificance.

It is hardly surprising that, in the ecstasy of the realisation that he is now a man, Philotas should apostrophise his excited heart thus:

> Die Brust wird dem Herzen zu eng! – Geduld, mein Herz! Bald will ich dir Luft machen! Bald will ich dich deines einförmigen lang-weiligen Dienstes erlassen! Bald sollst du ruhen, und lange ruhen – . . . (IV)

How reminiscent of Werther is the image of the imprisoned heart, and yet, what a world of difference there is between the two poets' use of it: for in Lessing's play it is not the heart which is the seat of feeling or of passion. It is no more than the master-spring and time-keeper of the body, and to the impatient spirit, contracted into a pinpoint of abstraction, its beating seems wearisome. Philotas has borne with time and arrested the deadly flash as long as it took his intellect to grasp that the 'end' of his life is to terminate his life: this done, he dismisses the pointless pulsing of his heart and, with it, life itself.[23]

Nowhere has the poet expressed the Prince's denial of time on his race to death more tellingly than by the employment of an image pattern which bespeaks the benign cycle of sequential organic existence: the imagery of seed, bud, blossom and fruit. The very words *seed, bud* or *blossom* call forth associations of pollen and fruit-bearing, of death and renewal. They bring to mind the cycle of the seasons, the life span of an individual, or the repetition of this cycle in the cycle of the generations. And all this is tantamount to saying that such images are pregnant with time and future. This is the association evoked by King Aridäus, when, on first meeting the Prince, he embraces him, saying:

> O welcher glücklichen Tage erinnert mich deine blühende Jugend! So blühte die Jugend deines Vaters! . . . ich umarme deinen jüngern Vater in dir. (III)

There is future in these words: the Prince's bloom will come to fruition, and a future seemingly forfeited by the fathers' hatred will be renewed in and through the offices of youth. But Philotas blights the expectations which his appearance had kindled in the King. He replies:

> Was kann es mir itzt helfen, dass du und mein Vater einst Freunde waren? Waren: so sagst du selbst. Der Hass, den man auf verloschne Freundschaft pfropfet, muss, unter allen, die tödtlichsten Früchte bringen. *(Ibid.)*

There is no future in the relentless past of this 'waren', no future even in the present. The Prince's blossom promises the deadliest of fruits. Such suspicions are nourished when Strato scolds the Prince for the rashness he had shown in battle and tells him not to repeat his mistake: 'Sonst möchte der werdende Held im ersten Keime ersticken' (III); or when Parmenio admonishes him: 'Du bist noch Kind! Gieb nicht zu, dass der rauhe Soldat das zärtliche Kind so bald in dir ersticke.' (V.) They are momentarily allayed when, in the central monologue, Philotas asks himself: 'Ich, der Keim, die Knospe eines Menschen, weiss ich zu sterben?' (IV.) They are confirmed in the very next sentence, when his hatred of life grafts a cruelly twisted meaning onto the words he has just used: the 'end' of life, the *telos* which is implanted in the seedling or the bud, is not fruition: it is death. There is more than a hint of cynicism when Philotas resorts to the image once again, shortly before he dies. He has rejected all the King's overtures for peace and Aridäus, sensing his implacability, exclaims:

> Du wirst dein Volk mit Lorbeern und mit Elend überhäufen . . .
> Wohl mir, dass meine Tage in die deinigen nicht reichen werden!
> Aber wehe meinem Sohne . . . (VII)

The King is beginning to understand the nature of the youth before him, as timeless and as barren as the laurels he will reap;

and his hopes for the future grow dim. It is at this point that, seemingly to reassure the King, the Prince replies:

> Die Frucht ist oft ganz anders, als die Blüthe sie verspricht. Ein weibischer Prinz . . . ward oft ein kriegerischer König. Könnte mit mir sich nicht das Gegentheil zutragen? *(Ibid.)*

These are the words of a little demon; not only promising a season of mellow fruitfulness when his death is about to unleash bloodshed and war, but invoking the archetypal association between bud and fruit when he has declared war on the order of nature and, indeed, on life itself. No wonder that, in the coda of the play, when the Prince has thrust his sword into his heart, the motif should once again be sounded, and sounded, this time, in the malignant meaning that has accrued to it. 'Ich habe dir einen tödtlichern · Streich versetzt, als mir', the Prince says to the bewildered King: '– Ich sterbe; und bald werden beruhigte Länder die **Frucht** meines Todes geniessen.' And, a little later on, with passion and finality: 'Sollte die Freyheit zu sterben . . . ein Mensch dem andern **verkümmern** können?' (VIII.) As Philotas sheds his mask together with his body, the imagery too that had spoken of organic process is stripped of its guise and now announces its real meaning: for this imperious mind bud and fruit had never betokened the living, growing self. From the beginning they had signified his spirit, a spirit whose sole task it was to apprehend death as the 'end' of life and which comes to fruition only as it avails itself of its 'Freyheit zu sterben'.

As Philotas destroys his own life, so also he destroys the illusion of life which it is the central business of dramatic art to create. Drama lives in that, through the rhythm of its action, through its very form, it enacts the organic process of life: growth, development, fruition and death.[24] True, it may do this by a tremendous foreshortening of perspectives. In *King Oedipus* the illusion of a life fraught with its own destiny is created in the short space of time that it takes the hero to hurtle to disaster, and Juliet grows from child to woman and even to the understanding of motherhood in the short space of a few days. But such short time is lived time. We feel it as such as we perceive speech and action flowering from the depth of beings who are rooted in their bodily selves; and, however brief it may be in itself, the hero's final farewell from life—as long as it is felt in his every aching fibre, and such pain is transmuted into 'Melodie und Rede'—to us becomes a long-drawn agony.[25] For Philotas, the little demon, the pulsing of the heart is tedious; and as time shrinks to vanishing point in the flash of illumination that comes to him, so the time of the drama he stamps with his being is not merely scant: it is not lived time, time 'proved upon our pulses'.[26] The time which Philotas creates about him is knowing time, not growing time. And a drama which is not instinct with the rhythms of organic process is stillborn.

Does this mean, then, that this extraordinary tragedy must be condemned as being 'nur gedacht' in the same sense in which the young Goethe condemns *Emilia Galotti* as 'nur gedacht'? The answer is, yes and no. For one thing, the poetic tools Lessing brings to bear on this youthful tragedy are far more appropriate to it than they are to a play that is overtly concerned with feeling relationships. The icy clarity with which the youthful poet handles the theme of unrelatedness is well matched to the icy clarity of his subject. But to base a defence of the play on such grounds comes dangerously near to falling into the naturalistic trap. Whatever its subject matter, poetry must be embedded in an idiom that is 'simple, sensuous, impassioned'. No: the fascination of *Philotas* has another, and a deeper source. In this early play, pledged though it be to a more untenable ideal of purity than the later tragedy, the poet has scored by capturing, with an authenticity altogether absent from his portrait of Emilia, the unconscious seductiveness that is the price of purity. 'Lilies that fester, smell far worse than weeds.' Fiercely virginal, repudiating all contact with reality and his own existential condition, the young Prince is possessed of a contagious seductiveness such as will surround, decades later, the demoniacal figures of Schiller's Jungfrau von Orleans and Kleist's Jupiter.

Could it be that the author of *Philotas*, a young man just thirty years old, was himself allured by the abyss into which he was gazing? That, in the act of giving utterance to the perils which lurk within the Neoplatonic view of life – the self-love of the spirit – he was stirred by what he had as yet to overcome in himself, and that the intensity of his vision overflowed into his tragedy, and charged it with erotic overtones? And could it be that, eleven years later, when he was on the way from the spiritual narcissism of youth to object-relatedness and maturity, the old theme proved no longer to have the old grip on him and its milder version lost the ring of passion? The answer is, I believe, yes. *Emilia Galotti* is dead. *Philotas* is formidable even in its failure. Death-bound though its central figure be, it spreads an icy light about it and gleams with the life of a demon.

III

The cards are stacked altogether differently in the case of *Minna von Barnhelm*. There is no question here of passion undermining the

strongholds of reason, apart perhaps from the intensity of
Tellheim's involvement with himself and the integrity of his spirit
which is the deeper cause of his resistance to Minna and marks
him as a not so distant descendant of Philotas. The lovers have
exchanged rings and, before the play begins, are sure of themselves and of one another. Nevertheless it is rewarding to recall the
circumstances preceding their betrothal. Minna has heard of the
generous loan which Tellheim had extended to the Saxonian
estates. 'Ich liebte Sie um dieser That willen, ohne Sie noch
gesehen zu haben', she tells him, and then continues a little later
in the same conversation:

> Die That, die Sie einmal um zweytausend Pistolen bringen sollte,
> erwarb mich Ihnen. Ohne diese That, würde ich nie begierig gewesen
> seyn, Sie kennen zu lernen. Sie wissen, ich kam uneingeladen in die
> erste Gesellschaft, wo ich Sie zu finden glaubte. Ich kam blos
> Ihrentwegen. Ich kam in dem festen Vorsatze, Sie zu lieben, – ich
> liebte Sie schon! – in dem festen Vorsatze, Sie zu besitzen, wenn ich
> Sie auch so schwarz und hässlich finden sollte, als den Mohr von
> Venedig. (IV, 6)

Rarely if ever can the ghost of Shakespeare's Othello have been
invoked for so incongruous a purpose as here, in this play. The
mere mention of his name brings to mind the image of a passion
so total and so defenceless in its totality that it is laid wide open to
destruction from within and without. And here this symbol is
evoked to help characterise an eminently reasonable attachment,[27]
perhaps even subtly to underscore this sobriety by the contrast it
implies. For Minna tells us, and tells us twice over, that she fell in
love with Tellheim for his goodness;[28] she confesses that she had
loved him before ever she had set eyes on him[29] and that,
moreover, she would have loved him just as much even had he
been as physically repugnant to her as no doubt the Moor of
Venice would have been in her eyes. More than that: she tells us
– and this too she tells us twice over – that she *resolved* to love the
man of whose goodness she had heard and to marry him. 'Ich kam
in dem festen Vorsatze, Sie zu lieben, – . . . in dem festen
Vorsatze, Sie zu besitzen.'

This is not the language of passion which unaccountably draws
together opposites, impervious to ary logic but its own. It is the
clear ringing voice of reason and volition familiar to us from the
lips of Emilia Galotti; and indeed, reason, and will geared to the
command of reason, are the dominant drives in Minna's character
and behaviour throughout the play.[30] Determined to salvage her
shipwrecked relations with the man of her choice, she travels

alone, accompanied only by her maid, across a country stricken
and rent by war, deep into the enemy's territory, there to seek him
out; and having found him, proceeds to reason him back to sanity
with a cheerful logic which remains unshaken by all the rebuffs
her lover deals her *en route*. In other times and in another setting,
such a character might be felt to be lacking in femininity. One
might well detect a strident note in the retort she gives to Franziska when the latter suggests that they had better put on their
fineries for the first round against poor Tellheim. 'Was redest Du
von Stürmen', Minna replies, 'da ich bloss herkomme, die Hal-
tung der Kapitulation zu fordern?' (II, 1). Again, however right
she is in substance, one might discern a touch of sophistry, even
of vindictiveness in her rejoinder to Tellheim's announcement that
reason and necessity compel him to forget her: 'Eine Vernunft,'
she replies,

> eine Nothwendigkeit, die Ihnen mich zu vergessen befiehlt? – Ich bin
> eine grosse Liebhaberinn von Vernunft, ich habe sehr viel Ehrerbie-
> tung für die Nothwendigkeit. – Aber lassen Sie doch hören, wie
> vernünftig diese Vernunft, wie nothwendig diese Nothwendigkeit ist.
> (II, 9)

These are but a few random illustrations of a disposition which is
established throughout the play; and the question arises how
Lessing succeeded in making a character as rational as Minna *come
to life as a woman*, when he failed in what would appear to be the
much more straightforward task presented by his tragic heroine.
For Emilia Galotti, by his own admission to his brother Karl, is
a girl pure and simple, untroubled by an intellectuality which
might complicate her overall picture and lend her an air of being
'brainy' or contrived.[31]

That he did succeed we cannot doubt. He succeeded brilliantly
and indeed twice over. His portrait of Minna as well as that of
Franziska are amongst the most felicitous delineations of female
characters on the German stage. Critical works on Lessing do not
offer a clue to the solution of this apparent paradox. Even that
most sensitive interpreter of Lessing's comedy, Emil Staiger, does
not ask how Lessing succeeds in projecting a successful image of
Minna's femininity.[32] He simply takes it for granted that he does.
We may infer it when he writes: 'Minna . . . tritt als Frau dem
starren Mann gegenüber wie das holde unwillkürliche Leben in
Menschengestalt der abstrakten Vernunft,'[33] or again when he
interprets her quibble about the 'Vernünftigkeit der Vernunft' as
'eine . . . Mahnung, elastisch zu bleiben wie das Leben selber.'[34]

But do coinages such as these, with the suggestion they carry of a plant-like unconscious vitality, really describe this purposeful young woman, and does the merciless dialectic she wages against Tellheim's conception of reason and necessity betoken the resilience of life and not rather the steeliness of a superior intellect? In this play we hear and see too little of life in its bounteous disorder and too much of purposive thought and behaviour to feel convinced by E. Staiger's affective epithets. Such emotive language may charm us into submission; it does nothing to explain how Lessing succeeds in making a woman who evinces the male drive of a Minna and who handles concepts the way she does, *come to life as a woman in the first place*. The critic who shirks this question also robs himself of the possibility of identifying the specific achievement of this play and of defining the conditions in which Lessing's genius prospered.

If Tellheim is no Othello, Minna is certainly no Desdemona; indeed, it would seem truer—if, on the face of it, preposterous—to suggest that she has something of the villain of the piece; an irresistible villain, it is true, but a villain none the less. She has Iago's sparkle and his intuition into the way that people tick – witness the confidence with which she predicts Tellheim's reaction to her prank. But, above all, she shares with Iago the artist's glee in conspiratorial designs for their own sakes, a delight which on one occasion at least threatens to run away with her.[35] The trick she plays on her beloved is as it were a play within the play, written, produced and acted by Minna. She evolves the scheme:

> Ein Streich ist mir beygefallen, ihn wegen dieses Stolzes mit ähnlichem Stolze ein wenig zu martern—(III, 12);

she deftly outlines motivation and plot:

> Der Mann, der mich ietzt mit allen Reichthümern verweigert, wird mich der ganzen Welt streitig machen, sobald er hört, dass ich unglücklich und verlassen bin (IV, 1);

she distributes the parts:

> Du wirst deine Rolle dabey zu spielen haben (III, 12)

and she gives the cue for the curtain to rise:

> Itzt wäre es Zeit! (IV, 6)

Zestfully she plunges into the role of the hapless maiden who is in

honour bound to renounce her beloved. When Franziska shows
signs of letting spontaneity get the better of art she tells her,
'*gebieterisch*': 'Ohne dich in unser Spiel zu mengen, Franciska,
wenn ich bitten darf! – ' (V, 5). Superbly, she turns the news of
her lover's reinstatement to her own account, exploiting the neat
reversal of their roles the better to drive home her lesson. She
herself admits at the end that her flight, her uncle's curse, her
disinheritance, were all 'erdichtet' and, accepting Tellheim's
charge that both she and Franziska were 'Komödiantinnen',
concedes with a sigh of relief: 'Leicht ist mir meine Rolle auch
nicht geworden' (V, 12).

In fact, this gifted young actress-producer shows every sign of
having gone to school with the author of the *Literaturbriefe*. For the
drama she enacts succeeds superbly both in arousing Tellheim's
pity and in catharising it. To reawaken his living compassion – that
wellspring of emotion of which everyone in Lessing's comedy so
liberally partakes, Werner and Just as well as Franziska and
Minna – is the end to which she assumes her role.[36] Not that
Tellheim is devoid of compassion; but unhappiness and nagging
doubt in the goodness of Providence have begun to dry up the
springs of sympathy within him. He is wounded and brittle. He
will take nothing, not from anyone, and not even from Minna. In
this circumstance, it is an inspired act of compassion – born of the
most delicate empathy – which prompts Minna to don the cloak
of poverty. For in doing so, she rekindles Tellheim's capacity to
love and allows it to gather momentum in a situation which is less
repugnant to him than that of being the beggar; whilst she casts
herself into a role which is within the range of his own experience
and into which his imagination can readily feel its way.

By thus experiencing himself outside himself, as it were,
Tellheim relives his earlier response and transcends its
inadequacy. Through his own need to give all of himself to Minna
he learns that the giver is the taker and that for Minna to receive
what he thus offers is a precious gift to him. By this act of
identification with Minna's 'suffering' from a vantage point
which is not crippling from the start, his sensibilities are enlarged
and the quality of his sympathy is immeasurably enhanced. He
literally transcends himself and he tells Minna so: 'Sie konnten
nicht vermuthen, wie sehr mich Ihr Unglück über das meinige
hinaus setzen würde' (V, 5). Minna's 'drama' has brought about
a true poetic catharsis. Tellheim himself marvels at the transformation that has taken place in him and repeatedly tries to find
words for what has happened to him: 'Wie ist mir?' he asks
himself, as soon as he has heard of Minna's plight;

Meine ganze Seele hat neue Triebfedern bekommen. Mein eignes
Unglück schlug mich nieder; machte mich ärgerlich, kurzsichtig,
schüchtern, lässig: ihr Unglück hebt mich empor, ich sehe wieder frey
um mich, und fühle mich willig und stark, alles für sie zu unterneh-
men – . (V, 2)

And, later in the same act, significantly just *before* the arrival of
the King's letter which restores his fortunes, he tells Minna how
compassion swept through the passages of his soul and cleansed it:

Aergerniss und verbissene Wuth hatten meine ganze Seele umnebelt;
die Liebe selbst, in dem vollesten Glanze des Glücks, konnte sich
darinn nicht Tag schaffen. Aber sie sendet ihre Tochter, das Mitleid,
die, mit dem finstern Schmerze vertrauter, die Nebel zerstreuet, und
alle Zugänge meiner Seele den Eindrücken der Zärtlichkeit wiederum
öfnet. (V, 5)

It is a brilliant act, Minna's comedy within the comedy of her
creator. One hardly knows who is holding the threads in his
hands, whose creative intelligence is at work and whose artistic
design is being executed – Lessing's or Minna's. It is *her* verbal
memory, *her* logic and, above all, *her* architectonic sense which
utilise the reversal of Tellheim's fortunes to construe an end to the
affair which matches its beginning with the perfect symmetry of
a mirror image. *Her* prank it is which, through its very form,
enacts the essence of the play: *quid pro quo*. What you give you
receive.

Dieses zur Probe, mein lieber Gemahl, dass Sie mir nie einen Streich
spielen sollen, ohne dass ich Ihnen nicht gleich darauf wieder einen
spiele. – Denken Sie, dass Sie mich nicht auch gequälet hatten? (V,
12)

And when, at the *peripeteia*, just before the renewed crisis she
herself is about to precipitate, she admonishes Franziska: 'O, über
die Vorbitterinn! Als ob der Knoten sich nicht von selbst bald
lösen müsste' (V, 9): do not her words adumbrate the poet's own
aesthetic credo, *his* confidence that the artist's plan should be 'ein
Schattenriss' of the grand plan of the universe and indeed should
accustom us to the thought that 'wie sich in ihm alles zum Besten
auflöse, werde es auch in jenem geschehen . . . '?[37]
Minna, the executor of the poet's design and designer herself,
the lovable little Demiurge within the comedy of her creator –
this is a far cry from the epithet with which we started: 'das holde
unwillkürliche Leben in Menschengestalt'. There seems little that
is 'unwillkürlich' about her, in any accepted sense of the word;

and if we insist, as indeed we must, that in Minna Lessing has projected an authentic image of life and has succeeded in capturing that spontaneity and charm which are the guarantors of life, we are ill-advised to discount that consciousness which is the hall-mark of her character or to argue that he succeeded in spite of it. Once we do so and subtract her consciousness from her personality, there is little left of it and nothing which is peculiarly Minna-ish. It would be truer to the facts to recognise in her very consciousness the key to the impression she creates and to argue that, if we are willing to accept Minna as being true to life, it is *not* because the ingredients of her character are predominantly instinctual – she is rational and argumentative to a degree – but because this character is embedded in a context and articulated by tools which are consonant with it. It is because all the characters in this play are compounded of the same stuff – [38] the same rationality, the same faith in human goodness and in the amenableness of feeling to reason, the same capacity for compassion and the same verbal retentiveness and intelligence – that we are predisposed to accept the portrayal of the heroine as being 'true to life' and convincing.

Convincingness is a matter of context and consistency. In this comedy all the characters are cast in the same mould: the uneducated speak the same language as the educated, the servants speak the same language as their masters. As Minna loves her Tellheim for his goodness, so Werner loves his Franziska for running off to help the Major rather than having a good time with him, and so Franziska endears herself to Minna by asking her to grieve at her beloved's plight rather than to rejoice at having found him again. And she concurs with Just in rating his honest devotion to his master higher than the airs and graces of the other servants who no doubt cut a more impressive figure with the girls. Werner shows as much acumen as Minna will do when he takes *ad absurdum* Tellheim's inability to be at the receiving end of a relationship. Franziska is as full of moral and psychological maxims as her mistress. And even Just, poor, simple Just, convinces Franziska of his worth by an account of his predecessors' failings in which he displays a sense for the niceties of suspense and timing, a verbal memory and wit and, above all, an architectonic sense that would do honour to the heroine herself. It is in such a universe of discourse that we adjudge the portrait of Minna to be 'true to life'. If in truth there were an Othello in this drama, if the poet's palette encompassed the deeper shades of instinctuality and passion, the self-same Minna would appear 'schoolmarmish'. In a different context, the identical ingredients would take on a different flavour. 'Truth', Oscar Wilde has said, 'is entirely and absolutely a matter of style.'[39] And probability, Edward Bullough has argued, is a matter of consistency of distance.[40] It is because all the characters are made of the same verbal stuff and are consistently viewed from the same aesthetic distance, because all and sundry speak the rationalistic language of the Enlightenment, that we are willing to accept Lessing's image of life as authentic, i.e. as consistent and contextually true.

But there is yet another reason for our acceptance, and one that is perhaps more basic still. It is because the poet's theme and the characters in which this theme is embedded are germane to his linguistic tools that we perceive outflowing spontaneity and abundance of life in *Minna von Barnhelm* where, in *Emilia Galotti*, we detect contrivance; and contrivance, precisely, because once again the poet allowed himself to become embroiled with the theme of passion. How is it that Lessing let himself be sidetracked from the path of sweet reasonableness he had so successfully pursued in *Minna von Barnhelm*, once more to try his hand at a genre so patently alien to him? In part, perhaps, we may explain this poetic relapse by reflecting on the concatenation of historical and personal events at the time of the final composition. Lessing wrote *Emilia Galotti* between 1771 and 1772, that is at a time when the *Sturm und Drang* movement with its premium on the irrational forces of feeling and impulse was taking the country by storm. However foreign the temper of this movement was to a man of Lessing's mould and age – he was forty-three years old – at this moment in his inner history its message may have spoken to him. For at this moment a no longer quite young man was reaching out for the central relationship of his life, the relationship with Eva König, his wife-to-be. He must have felt in closer rapport with the spirit of youth and the life of feeling than he had been since the days of his emotion-charged friendship with Ewald von Kleist, to whose melancholy heroism he had set a monument, more than ten years earlier, in his *Philotas*.[41] Besides, might it be that now, on the brink of final commitment – he began to write *Emilia Galotti* in Wolfenbüttel almost immediately after his engagement to Eva König in September 1771 – those deep-seated fears and suspicions of the 'other', the world, which had found their precipitate in *Philotas*, became revitalised, once again rose to the surface and found poetic utterance in *Emilia Galotti*, tragedy of half-hearted passion? For a tragedy of half-hearted passion it is. Its central theme is the clash between the forces of consciousness and the forces of impulse and instinct; and the outcome of this encounter remains in the balance. On the moral plane, the forces of consciousness and reason score a narrow victory. On the plane of physical reality, they are defeated; and defeated, in every instance, from the inside. In every character of that play the tragic flaw which leads to his or her undoing springs from a surge of instinctual drives which are neither sufficiently trusted nor sufficiently controlled to tilt the balance: timid sensuous promptings in the case of Emilia, a seductiveness beset by scruples on the part of the Prince, rage for ever quarrelling with reason on that of Odoardo. Orsina is tossed hither and thither by a tug of war between her intelligence and a passion she knows to be hopeless; Claudia, for the longest time the prototype of the prudent mother, at the end lets maternal instinct get the better of worldly wisdom and aids the deterioration of a situation already on the brink of disaster. Appiani, that strange and divided character, hovers between hopes of happiness and hallucinations of doom; and who would say where, in this melancholy man, reason ends and irrationality begins? His loving is staid enough; but perhaps one so deeply mistrusting of the world should not have loved at all. Perhaps it is in this pitifully shortlived aberration from the mould in which he is cast that we must seek his 'tragic flaw'.

Lessing, the creator of Appiani, was himself much too restrained to exploit the extravagant opportunities afforded to the dramatist by the Aristotelian requirement of the tragic flaw, and to create a tragedy on the grand and cosmic scale in which the bastions of reason are overrun by irrational forces attacking from within and without.[42] Nor indeed – but this is probably saying the same thing – did his ratiocinative idiom permit him to render such irrational forces in a manner that carries poetic conviction. The only passionate character he successfully portrayed is that of Orsina, and he succeeded in this precisely because he could use her powerful intelligence as a medium in which to exhibit her capriciousness.

Thus we are faced with a seeming paradox. In *Emilia Galotti* Lessing attempted to seize life at its unconscious source with the result that the semblance of life eluded him. Intent strains against idiom and the ensuing account of passion seems lifeless and contrived. In *Minna von Barnhelm*, on the other hand, Lessing is exclusively concerned with reason and the conscious top strata of experience. Yet the resultant harmony of inspiration and language engenders a poetic playfulness and spontaneity which informs the mood and movement of the whole and invests the character of the heroine – as rationalistic a character as any – with a 'rightness', an aura of poetic charm, in short with that ineffable semblance of life which, by a variant of the pathetic fallacy, we

incline to term 'das holde unwillkürliche Leben in Menschengestalt' or 'die unverwüstliche Güte des Lebens'.

IV

The flames of passion in *Nathan der Weise* subside as naturally as
the conflagration of Nathan's house in which that passion was kindled, and by the end of the play both, brother and sister, recognise
that it is better so. The family reunion on which the curtain falls
has been criticised.[43] Lessing, it is said, strains our credulity
beyond its limits by expecting us to believe that a young man,
freshly in love, could quite so gamely accept the discovery that his
beloved is his sister. The *idea* of the universal brotherhood of man,
it is felt, has got the better of the author with the result that
poetic truth has gone out and allegory has come in.

   And yet the poet has amply prepared us for the ending. Indeed,
he has done so throughout the course of the action and in a
variety of ways. For in this play as in *Minna von Barnhelm* consciousness reigns supreme and with it, the values of human consciousness: faith in the rationality of human beings and of the
world they inhabit; that is to say, faith in goodness, in our will to
abide by what we know to be good and in the amenableness of
feeling and instinct to what will and reason prescribe. The
Muslim Saladin and the Christian Templar share this faith with
the Jew. Each is willing to recognise error and each trusts that to
see it is tantamount to remedying it: Saladin, when he realises
that his affluence is beginning to make him parsimonious and
instantly resolves to let no such change occur; Recha in the first
scenes in which Nathan cures her of her 'Engelschwärmerei', when
she responds to her father's arguments with the touching
rejoinder:

> Mein Vater, wenn ich irr', Ihr wisst, ich irre
> Nicht gern   (I, 2)

the Templar, when he realises that the news of his consultation
with the Patriarch has leaked out and confesses to Nathan with
that candour which is so endearing a feature of his character:

> Was sollt' ich eines Fehls mich schämen? Hab'
> Ich nicht den festen Vorsatz ihn zu bessern?   (V, 5)

and Nathan himself, of course, when Christians had burnt his wife and seven sons and he had raged against Providence and the world for three whole days and nights:

> Doch nun kam die Vernunft allmählig wieder.
> Sie sprach mit sanfter Stimm': „und doch ist Gott!
> Doch war auch Gottes Rathschluss das! Wohlan!
> Komm! übe, was du längst begriffen hast;
> Was sicherlich zu üben schwerer nicht,
> Als zu begreifen ist, wenn du nur willst.
> Steh auf!" – Ich stand! und rief zu Gott: ich will!   (IV, 7)

Even in matters of love, does not the Templar from the beginning respond to the appeal of reason? Does he not seek out Recha, all ready to fall in love with her, because he has fallen in love with the goodness of her father? And, later on in the play, when he feels rebuffed by Nathan and sulks, is it not the thought of her 'höhern Wert' – the very worth Nathan has instilled in his adopted child – which he recognises to be the basis of his love and is not this thought enough to reconcile him to the Jew?

Here again it is as in *Minna von Barnhelm*: if we are willing to credit the Templar's love for Recha and hers for him, it is because their feeling is consonant with the climate of love as it is experienced throughout this play. Here, as in Lessing's comedy, love is tantamount to love of goodness: that between Recha and Nathan, Nathan and the Templar, between Nathan and the Sultan, between Saladin and the Templar and even the willy-nilly love that Daja bears the Jew. In such a powerful and homogeneous context we are willing to concede that what passes between Recha and her saviour is love; and in such a climate, in turn, we are willing to allow for the possibility that their love may shed its erotic overtones and yet remain love.

But the steadiest intimation of the *dénouement* comes from the poet's handling of his linguistic materials. The words themselves tell us that, placed though these characters be under the scorching skies of the Holy Land, passion is not their element. We know it from the recurrent association of passion with fire. For from the outset of this play fire figures as a cruel element. At the beginning of it looms the conflagration in which Recha all but lost her life, a near-disaster which haunts her mind throughout the opening scenes; and behind this accident there looms an even greater calamity: the death in flames, lit by misguided passion, of Nathan's entire family; a past catastrophe, it is true, but one which casts a giant shadow over the world of the play and which still reaches into the present in the Patriarch's 'Thut nichts, der

Jude wird verbrannt'. When, in such a context, the lovers, pondering the turmoil of their hearts, time and again resort to images of fire, we know that passion to them is perilous. It consumes their peace of mind. It obscures its object and obstructs the world. Recha realises this early on in the play, as soon as she has been allowed to see her saviour and to thank him face to face. True, at the beginning of this encounter, she had taunted the young man for his coldness in the midst of the flames through which he had carried her to safety:

> . . . der
> Ward nun so in die Glut hineingestossen;
> Da fiel ich ungefähr ihm in den Arm;
> Da blieb ich ungefähr, so wie ein Funken
> Auf seinem Mantel, ihm in seinen Armen;
> Bis wiederum, ich weiss nicht was, uns beyde
> Herausschmiss aus der Glut. –   (III, 2)

At the end she herself is amazed at her own calm, and, repudiating Daja's innuendoes that such cooling off will lead to a renewed attack of her 'heisse Hunger', to a 'neues Fieber', she retorts:

> Was Kält'? Ich bin nicht kalt. Ich sehe wahrlich
> Nicht minder gern, was ich mit Ruhe sehe.   (III, 3)

The Templar, on the other hand, finds it more difficult to pacify the turmoil his impulsive deed has unleashed in him. True, at first Recha had seemed to him as negligible as 'ein Funken auf seinem Mantel'. He had tried to shake it off, had tried, even, to rid himself of the only visible mark of the event – the burn upon his Templar's cloak which he asks Nathan to replace. And yet he is on fire. 'Ich brenne vor Verlangen', he replies to Nathan's 'Kennt sie nur erst' (II, 5). Later, when Recha breaks in on his rapture, asking where he had been all this time and where his mind is now, he replies 'Auf Sinai', to wit, the mountain upon which the Divine revealed itself to Moses amidst flames and smoke. He refuses to return to Nathan's house; for 'da brennt's'. To be exposed to the pangs of passion to him appears like being thrown into the fire once again. As he has it:

> Ich Tropf! ich sprang zum zweytenmal ins Feuer. –
> Denn nun warb *ich,* und nun ward *ich* verschmäht.   (IV, 4)

Eventually, as he argues himself back into a reasoned attitude towards the Jew, he begins to marvel

Dass
Ein einz'ger Funken dieser Leidenschaft
Doch unsers Hirns so viel verbrennen kann! –   (V, 3)

It is only because passion in this play is felt to be a soul-destroying force – how soul-destroying, we, no less than the Templar,
learn from the slightly sinister if sub-comical figures of Daja and
the Patriarch on the periphery of the action – that the Templar
is able to welcome the *dénouement* at the end and to praise
Providence for what he has gained in exchanging the searing
exclusiveness of passion for the tranquil affection between a
brother and a sister:

Ihr nehmt und gebt mir, Nathan!
Mit vollen Händen beydes! – Nein! Ihr gebt
Mir mehr, als Ihr mir nehmt! unendlich mehr!
(Recha um den Hals fallend)
Ah meine Schwester! meine Schwester!
(V, *Letzter Auftritt*)

The Templar addresses these words to the Jew. They might
equally well be addressed to the God of the Jews of whom Job
says: 'The Lord gave and the Lord hath taken away; blessed be
the name of the Lord.'[44] For it is here in *Nathan der Weise* as it was
in the earlier comedy: Nathan is the demiurge of the world he
dominates. He is the executor of the poet's intelligence who in
turn is the plenipotentiary of the Creator.[45] With flawless pers-
picacity Nathan foresees the course of the action and guides it. Its
tangled threads rest in his hand. He perceives the characters in
their quintessential humanity and he fashions them in this image
– not only Recha, but the Templar and Saladin as well. The
Templar himself realises that Nathan is more, not less, than
Recha's physical begetter. He is the Pygmalion to her

Die jedes Hauses, jedes Glaubens Zierde
Zu seyn erschaffen und erzogen ward. –   (IV, 7)

Whose creation is Recha in truth, he asks himself:

Geschöpf?
Und wessen? – Doch des Sklaven nicht, der auf
Des Lebens öden Strand den Block geflösst,
Und sich davon gemacht? Des Künstlers doch
Wohl mehr, der in dem hingeworfnen Blocke
Die göttliche Gestalt sich dachte, die
Er dargestellt? – Ach! Rechas wahrer Vater
Bleibt, Trotz dem Christen, der sie zeugte – bleibt
In Ewigkeit der Jude. –   (V, 3)

'Die göttliche Gestalt', in fact, is Recha's humanity. It lies midway between the spheres of angel and beast, between the material and the transcendant, between the scorching blaze of passion and the cold light of the intellect. The human mean which Nathan woos into reality, in himself as well as in others, is light which warms, passion illuminated – enlightened we may say – by consciousness and reason. In his theory as well as in his play, Lessing tells us that this is what it takes to be human, and there, as here, he tells us so through images of fire. 'Vielleicht', he writes in *Eine Duplik*,

> soll, nach Gesetzen einer höhern Haushaltung, das Feuer noch lange so fortdampfen, mit Rauch noch lange gesunde Augen beissen, ehe wir **seines Lichts und seiner Wärme zugleich** geniessen können.[46]

The same image returns in *Ernst und Falk*. Ernst has joined the order of the Freemasons and is disappointed with what he has found there: 'Der Rauch wird mich ersticken', he complains,

> ehe mir die Flamme leuchtet, und wärmen, sehe ich wohl, werden sich Andere an ihr, die den Rauch besser vertragen können.

But Falk holds out hope:

> So warte, bis der Rauch sich verzieht, und die Flamme wird **leuchten und wärmen.**[47]

Like the lovers of Mozart's last opera, the lovers of Lessing's last play must walk 'durch Flamm und Rauch'. And, like them, they must emerge from the fog of passion into the realm of 'Licht und Ordnung', into those more temperate zones where love is lit up with the light of consciousness and reason.

It is Nathan who, from the beginning of the play, divines the true nature of the bond between the lovers, even as he divines their true humanity. Indeed he recognises the bond between each and all; between brother and sister, between both and Saladin and between them all and himself. Beneath the welter of confused passions he perceives the archetypal bonds of filial and fraternal affection, and he teaches the others to recognise these bonds even as he teaches them to recognise themselves. The word *erkennen* fairly echoes through the closing pages of this play which is in every deeper sense a comedy of errors and of recognition. 'So eine Schwester nicht erkennen wollen!' the Sultan scolds the Templar; to which the latter replies: 'Verkenn' . . . nicht . . . mich!' 'Ah! seine Hand! Auch die erkenn' ich wieder!' Saladin cries as he sees his brother's writing, and he exclaims:

> Ich meines Bruders Kinder nicht erkennen?
> Ich meine Neffen – meine Kinder nicht?
> Sie nicht erkennen?

These recognitions, long foreseen by Nathan, take place as each discovers in himself 'die göttliche Gestalt' which the *Künstler*'s mind had presaged from the start: love lit up and tempered by awareness, like a flame which illumines as it warms.

It is vital for our understanding of this drama to see that in its universe of discourse the enlightenment of the intellect, so far from being a threat to feeling, goes hand in hand with it and indeed enhances it.[48] Nathan and Recha and the young Templar and Saladin and Sittah, all of them characters tinged with loneliness, experience a sense of enrichment as they 'recognise' the bonds that bind all to all. And so do the characters in *Minna von Barnhelm*. However, to concede the compatibility of intellect and feeling is not enough; for our present theme it is important to emphasise how intimately entwined these two spheres of human experiencing really are. Knowledge and feeling, clarity and depth, light and warmth in both these plays are inseparably interwoven. Together they make up the fabric of mature experiencing. Each is the condition of the other. It is only when feeling is released in depth that illumination comes, and it is only through an act of intellectual illumination that the capacity to feel is finally released. Such a simultaneous breakthrough Nathan achieves before our eyes and to this inner turning point we must now give our attention.

Nathan has at long last revealed to the Lay Brother the secret of Recha's origin which has been exercising our minds. He has received from the latter the breviary which will, he hopes, shed light on the riddle of the Templar's parentage and on the nature of his connection with Recha. The Lay Brother departs and Nathan stands, the unopened book in his hand; and now a kind of prayer rises to his lips:

> Gott!
> Dass ich nicht gleich hier unter freyem Himmel
> Auf meine Kniee sinken kann! Wie sich
> Der Knoten, der so oft mir bange machte,
> Nun von sich selber löset! –   (V,4)

Once again the poet uses the image of the knot which Minna had used at the corresponding point in the comedy, as Tellheim stood perusing the letter from the King which will restore his fortunes. 'O, über die Vorbitterinn!' So she had cut short Franziska's intervention: 'Als ob der Knoten sich nicht von selbst bald lösen müsste' (V, 9). And no doubt, Nathan's words, like Minna's, betoken the relief of the virtuoso in human relations that the *dénouement* of his daring play with human destinies is in sight, that the tangled skeins he holds in his hands are about to weave themselves into a design which is a mirrored likeness, not a mockery, of the pattern woven by Providence. But his words signify more. For Nathan here does not primarily speak as a creator in his own right, but as a creature *vis-à-vis* his Maker, not as one doing something but rather as one enduring an experience that has come to him unbidden. 'Wie sich der Knoten . . . nun **von sich selber** löset.' The experience he has just endured is the surrender of the last and most precious thing in his possession – Recha. For even in Nathan there had been a trace of possess-iveness. At the very beginning of the play he had proclaimed her as his 'Eigenthum', and understandably so; for it is he who has made Recha what she is. She is his handiwork. He knows her every thought, even her unconscious motives. She is his and no one is going to take her away from him lightly, certainly not 'der erste, beste'. Only a few moments earlier, as the Lay Brother approached and again as he departed, he had confessed how gladly he would keep the girl; and as the Lay Brother's intentions begin to dawn on him, Nathan too begins to resort to images of fire:

> Ich steh auf Kohlen, guter Bruder. Macht
> Es kurz. Das Pfand! das mir vertraute Pfand!   (IV, 7)

To lose Recha is once again to go through the ordeal of fire in which he lost his seven sons. This ordeal is precisely what he does endure; and he formulates the experience which is taking shape in him thus:

> Und ob mich siebenfache Liebe schon
> Bald an diss einz'ge fremde Mädchen band;
> Ob der Gedanke mich schon tödtet, dass
> Ich meine sieben Söhn' in ihr aufs neue
> Verlieren soll: – wenn sie von meinen Händen
> Die Vorsicht wieder fodert, – ich gehorche!   (IV, 7)

This is what, in *Die Erziehung des Menschengeschlechts*, Lessing calls the 'heroische Gehorsam' of the Jews. It is the obedience of Job who is forcibly reminded that he 'has' nothing, neither cattle, nor wife, nor sons, nor daughters, nor even his own skin and flesh, and that he depends utterly and totally on the Creator who made him a naked beggar. As Nathan resolves the sevenfold bond that ties him to Recha and surrenders to his Maker what he holds dearest, he is born anew, cleansed.[49] The knot is being untied. He loves Recha, knowing—as he knew once before—that she is not his but is being given to him; and even as he obeys the grateful need to love, it is being stilled. This is why he can counter the Lay Brother's

> —Gott gebe nur,
> Dass Ihr es nie bereuen dürft, so viel
> Für sie gethan zu haben!   (V, 4)

replying with perfect confidence:

> Kann ich das?
> Das kann ich nie. Seyd unbesorgt!

The man who says these words does not know what the future is about to bring. He has not opened the breviary. Recha may be taken from him, and she may be taken, not by the Templar but by the Patriarch whose hatred is pursuing him. The future is as yet impenetrable. If none the less Nathan's words breathe the serenest trust, it is because nothing can touch him any longer. Recha is safe within him. He has 'liquidated' his last property and it has become a flow of inner harmonies. He is pure and unimpeded passage. The world lies spread out flawless before him in the divinity of its design. Presently the forces of evil vanish and the good forgather round him. Recha remains his daughter, her brother becomes his son and Saladin his friend. It is so and it must be so. In the light of the inner harmonies the Theodicy stands revealed.[50]

It is no different in *Minna von Barnhelm*. Tellheim's realisation how hopelessly he depends on Minna releases a surge of loving which is fulfilled even as it is expressed. The concern for external status and possessions which had clogged his soul with 'Aergerniss und verbissene Wuth' ceases to be meaningful. And here, too, inner harmony transforms the world. It does not only appear so to Tellheim, when he asks in a spurt of confidence: 'Geht hier allein die Sonne auf?', when he coaxes Minna, saying: 'Folgen Sie mir nur getrost, liebste Minna; es soll uns an nichts fehlen.' The world is in fact transformed. Even as Minna predicts: 'Als ob der Knoten sich nicht von selbst bald lösen müsste', Tellheim reads the King's letter and the question of merit and reward which had tormented him so is resolved. The Theodicy is assured.

In the poetic world of these two dramas depth of feeling generates an unparalleled illumination of the understanding. The

fire that truly warms sheds light. Both are inseparable and both
in their unison – token of creative wholeness of experiencing –
conquer and transform the world. *This* is Enlightenment. And who
will say that such a reading of human experience is shallow? To
condemn Lessing's *Nathan der Weise* is to condemn Goethe's
Iphigenie and the faith Kant expressed in his three Critiques. It is
to condemn all the cherished manifestations of a humane age that
had the courage to believe in the creative primacy of the human
mind. It is also to reject one of the profoundest assessments of the
human condition that has been penned by human hand – the
Book of Job. For Job too receives back what he has lost, like
Nathan, the moment he surrenders all his claims. In that merciless
account of life, too, acceptance transforms the world. 'Und Hiob
starb alt und lebenssatt.' And who would gainsay that this is a
mystery of Grace?

We are at the heart of Lessing's religious thinking, and it is
worth pursuing our trend a little further into his theological
writings, to see whether they support our reading. And in fact
they do, in the most surprising fashion. In *Die Erziehung des
Menschengeschlechts* the poet traces the gradual development of the
conception of virtue from the Old Testament to the New, from the
naïve expectation of the Israelites to be rewarded for a virtuous
life here and now to the Christian acceptance of misfortune in this
world and the deferment of hope to the hereafter. This development, Lessing argues, was bound to take place in a world in which
virtue and reward are so blatantly at odds. Indeed, this incongruity turned out to be a blessing in disguise. 'Denn,' we read
in Paragraph 28,

> wenn schon aus der ungleichen Austheilung der Güter dieses Lebens,
> bey der auf Tugend und Laster so wenig Rücksicht genommen zu
> seyn scheinet, eben nicht der strengste Beweis für die Unsterblichkeit
> der Seele und für ein anders Leben, in welchem jener Knoten sich
> auflöse, zu führen: so ist doch wohl gewiss, dass, der menschliche
> Verstand ohne jenem Knoten noch lange nicht – und vielleicht auch
> nie – auf bessere und strengere Beweise gekommen wäre. Denn was
> sollte ihn antreiben können, diese bessern Beweise zu suchen? Die
> blosse Neugierde?[51]

Once again we encounter the image of the *Knoten*. It signifies
the ostensible incongruity between merit and reward, between
what is given out and what is received in return. And in the end
how is this knot resolved? By the Christian belief in a future life
in which justice will be meted out? Lessing believes, no. True,
such a belief constitutes an important advance in that it entails

the conception of the immortality of the soul. Human beings were bound sooner or later to tumble to this notion to help them bear the injustice of their lot on earth. But the belief in an immortal life in which justice will prevail is no more than a stepping stone in the development of mankind towards moral maturity, towards

> die Zeit der Vollendung, da der Mensch . . . das Gute thun wird, weil es das Gute ist, nicht weil willkührliche Belohnungen darauf gesetzt sind, die seinen flatterhaften Blick ehedem blos heften und stärken sollten, die innern bessern Belohnungen desselben zu erkennen. (Paragraph 85)

Once in a while, Lessing tells us, outstanding individuals of earlier ages have risen to the belief

> dass wer fromm sey auch glücklich seyn müsse, und wer unglücklich sey, oder werde, die Strafe seiner Missethat trage, welche sich sofort wieder in Segen verkehre, sobald er von seiner Missethat ablasse.

'Ein solcher', Lessing concludes,

> scheinet den Hiob geschrieben zu haben; denn der Plan desselben ist ganz in diesem Geiste. – (Paragraph 29)[52]

It is not difficult to translate the abstract moral concepts of virtue and vice and of reward and punishment back into the fuller statement of experience familiar to us from Lessing's dramas. Here as there, under the image of the knot, Lessing is speaking of the seeming incongruity between what is given out by a person in his wholeness and entirety – emotionally *and* morally *and* intellectually – and what he is receiving in return: the incongruity, to wit, which tortures Tellheim while he still looks to a return for his magnanimity in terms of outward status and recognition and feels cheated by the loss thereof; the sense of incongruity which casts its shadow over Nathan as long as he looks to the possession of Recha as the reward – one might almost say the retroactive condition – of the 'gottergebne Tat' he wrested from himself. The precariousness of Nathan's position *vis-à-vis* Recha is not altogether undeserved: it reflects an inner attitude which is not quite free of confusion. Both, Nathan as well as Tellheim, fail – emotionally as well as morally and intellectually – as long as they look for any vindication of their doing outside the doing itself, and continue to harbour any provisos whatever. As long as they give conditionally, their 'flatterhaften Blick' riveted upon external rewards, they deny themselves that inner return which lies in the

act of giving. Thus their ledger shows a deficit and the world to
them looks tarnished. As soon as the deepest springs of their
devotion are tapped – through a religious experience in the case
of Nathan and a mediate human relationship in the case of
Tellheim – their loving comes full circle: it pours forth with the
strength of an elemental need which is gratified even as it is
obeyed. Loving is output and intake, investment and return,
virtue and reward, question and answer all in one. It sets up its
own reciprocal rhythm and creates its own internal harmonies. In
the light of such abundance the 'knotty' question – intellectual,
moral, metaphysical – of the Theodicy literally resolves itself.
'Und Hiob starb, alt und lebenssatt.'

This unimpeded two-way flow of strength going out and returning to its source Lessing has expressed through a variety of
symbols. He speaks of it in terms of monetary currency and
Nathan's trading; in terms of his journeying into the world and
returning home, and of the ring. Last but not least, he speaks of
it through a symbol which we shall meet again in the discussion
of Goethe's *Faust*—the symbol of water.

Water is a central symbol in Lessing's last play. It plays a part
as large or larger than fire, and a more benign one. As Recha has
it at the very outset of the play:

> Denn seit das Feuer mir
> So nahe kam: dünkt mich im Wasser sterben
> Erquickung, Labsal, Rettung.   (I, 2)

And indeed, in this drama the experience of *Erquickung, Labsal,
Rettung* and its obverse is time and again articulated through the
imagery of water. Much play is made of its inexhaustible flow:
whether it be rain or tide or a fountain or spring, water returns to
its source and eternally replenishes itself. Nathan, Saladin, the
Templar and the Dervish – they are all associated with such
imagery. It characterises them both in their affluence and their
dearth; and, as behoves a play whose invisible and ubiquitous
protagonist is God, the Divinity is associated with water in its
purest and most life-giving form – rain. 'Des Höchsten Milde' and
'des Höchsten immer volle Hand' sends rain down over all the
world, falling and rising back to its undepleted source: symbol of
its Maker's bounty.

Such munificence is the foil against which the characters upon
the human stage are set. Take the Knight Templar, for instance:
an angry young man, unaware as yet of the living springs within
his self. He accepts and risks a life which is not truly his own; and
he passes it on as mechanically as the water bucket

>   . . . der bey
> Dem Löschen so geschäftig sich erwiesen.
> Der liess sich füllen, liess sich leeren, mir
> Nichts, dir nichts: also auch der Mann.   (III, 2)

Or take Sittah's brother Saladin, whose strength – for all the splendour of his manhood – mysteriously drains away, as though by some hidden leak or wound. Of him the Dervish says:

>   . . . sein Schatz
> Ist jeden Tag mit Sonnenuntergang
> Viel leerer noch, als leer. Die Fluth, so hoch
> Sie morgens eintritt, ist des Mittags längst
> Verlaufen –   (I, 3)

to which Nathan adds:

>   Weil Kanäle sie zum Theil
> Verschlingen, die zu füllen oder zu
> Verstopfen, gleich unmöglich ist.

Or take that princely beggar Al-Hafi, detached, free of worldly goods (*fakir* is the Arabic for poor) and self-sufficient in his humanity. Of him Saladin says:

> Al-Hafi gleicht verstopften Röhren nicht,
> Die ihre klar und still empfangnen Wasser
> So unrein und so sprudelnd wieder geben.   (I, 3)

And finally, of course, there is Nathan, resting within himself and attuned to his inner harmonies, yet outgoing, like God himself giving and taking 'mit vollen Händen'; whose riches are said to spring from a

>   Quelle weit ergiebiger
> Weit unerschöpflicher, als so ein Grab
> Voll Mammon,

which indeed it is, being the source of love.

Rain, tide, fountain and spring: through each and all of these symbols the poet speaks to us of the cyclic rhythm of human creativeness, of that self-sufficiency which paradoxically rests on the capacity to go out and expend life to the full – a gift which rests on an ultimate act of faith.

As we have seen, here and in the previous chapter, this return of what has been given out is an inner and instantaneous event. It is a mental phenomenon which is rooted in the cyclic nature of

all organic life. But it is also an event in time, and this aspect of
his theme too the poet has articulated in terms of the symbolism
of water. As Saladin discovers that his impulsive reprieve of the
young Templar has led to the rescue of Recha whose father is now
coming to his aid, he marvels

> Wie aus **Einer** guten That,
> Gebahr sie auch schon blosse Leidenschaft,
> Doch so viel andre gute Thaten **fliessen!**   (III, 7)

whilst Nathan, more aware and more tuned in to the eternal
harmonies which flow through him, asks his new friend:

> So weisst du nicht, wie viel von deiner Gnade
> Für ihn, durch ihn auf mich **geflossen?**

But the symbolism which is so consistently employed to articulate the theme of Lessing's last play calls up another echo
somewhat further afield. The mind is transported to that moving
autobiographical passage at the end of the *Hamburgische Dramaturgie* where Lessing the critic assesses his own status as a poet:

> Ich fühle die lebendige Quelle nicht in mir, die durch eigene Kraft
> sich empor arbeitet, durch eigene Kraft in so reichen, so frischen, so
> reinen Strahlen aufschiesst: ich muss alles durch Druckwerk und
> Röhren aus mir herauf pressen.[53]

Thus Lessing about himself. Could it be that in *Nathan der Weise*
too, the poet is speaking of himself, under the same image, but in
a different key? In the water images of that play we may, I
believe, discern the reflection of a poet who is engrossed in making
poetry and who, in such an engrossment, feels self-sufficient and not
wanting. Through the symbol of water and the associated symbols of
rings and riches, of journeying and home-coming, of hands and
Handeln, the poet affirms what his tragedy had denied: that what is
given out in trust is not lost, but returns to the giver in a cycle which is
infinitely enriching. He also tells us, I believe, in a muted voice, that
twice in his life at least he could, and did, give all of himself to the
most important 'other' in an artist's life – his artistic medium – and of
the rich returns and the inalienable fulfilment which this experience
brought to him.

It is not really surprising that the poet should be telling us so
much; that he should speak of his art experience – an experience
which is private and unshareable – in the same terms in which he
is communicating a poetic import which is public and accessible

to all. Not surprising because, looked at closely, the experience of being creative in life as it is formulated in *Nathan der Weise,* and the experience óf being creative in art, however divergent in some respects, evince a logical structure which is identical; and it is this consonance which makes it possible for one type of experience to become a symbol of the other.[54] Nathan's withdrawal from outward dependencies, the flow of inner harmonies, the unimpeded radiation outward that results from such a containment and in turn enhances its quality – all this reflects the artist's withdrawal in the creative act from the world of things and people, the loving communion between mind and medium which ensues, and the projection of such inner harmonies through a symbolic structure capable of communicating this experience *and* congruent ones. *Nathan der Weise* is 'about' the riches of creative living; but the innermost rhythm which informs this statement and makes it resonant is that experienced by its maker in the creative act itself.

V

The question remains how we can account for this release of creative energy in Lessing's two non-tragic dramas and how, conversely, we can explain the miscarriage of *Philotas* and the sense of failure which stamps the pages of *Emilia Galotti*; a failure brought home to us by the catastrophic reversal, in both tragedies, of the connotation of the poetic symbols which in *Minna* and *Nathan* signify fulfilment. For in *Philotas* as well as in Lessing's domestic tragedy, the hand destroys where it should or would create, *Handeln* issues in murder, the way is perilously long and the journey into life, if it is attempted at all, ends in disaster. The refrain of both tragedies is, in the words of Emilia, 'dass alles verloren ist'.

An answer to this question cannot be given in simple biographical terms. The Lessing who wrote *Nathan der Weise* was very much less happy than the author of *Emilia Galotti*. While he was writing his tragedy he was freshly engaged to Eva König, widow of a well-to-do merchant. When he came to write *Nathan der Weise* he was embittered by the attacks of Protestant Orthodoxy in the shape of Goeze; worse still, he had buried his wife of one year's standing and his son. Thus it is not any easily ascertainable outward happiness which set its seal on the pages of *Nathan der Weise*: indeed, we may detect more than a fleeting likeness between the Job-like tribulations of its hero and the bitternesses the poet himself had endured.

Such incongruity places the critic in something of a quandary. He may resign himself and accept the conflicting evidence of fact and fiction. Or he may seek to harmonise at a deeper level data which seem irreconcilable and endeavour to reconstruct, however tentatively, the poet's inner biography. This is the course I have chosen.

However much the play was in advance of the actual *Sturm und Drang* movement, we may read *Philotas* as the culminating testimony of Lessing's own brand of storm and stress: it has all the signs and symptoms of that idealistic passion we associate with youthfulness. Only this passion is turned inward upon itself, and its object is the spiritual part of the self. The fierceness of this passion led, as we have seen, to the creation of the remarkable figure at the centre of the drama, Philotas himself. The danger of unrelatedness which is inseparable from such introversion led – and this too we have seen – to the blighting of the drama as a living work of art. Given his hero's dissociation from his surroundings, the poet could not create the context of full-bodied relationships which it is the business of drama to project, nor indeed that depth-dimension of experienced life and time which is its primary illusion. Erich Schmidt neatly pinpoints this deficiency of the play when he writes: 'Lessing füllt in seinem kürzesten Stück drei Auftritte durch die längsten Selbstgespräche, die er je geschrieben hat.'[55]

The development that lies between *Philotas* and *Minna von Barnhelm*, written half a decade later, is that from the subject-orientated idealism of adolescence to the object-orientated idealism of manhood. The young man's involvement with his own spiritual self had given way to a passionate commitment to the things of the mind, to human reason and the moral, intellectual and social values to which it is pledged. Lessing had found himself; and it is in this frame that he had conceived of, and created, *Minna von Barnhelm*, a play in which love is tantamount to love of goodness and feeling is grounded in a structure of suprapersonal values which are binding on all.

It seems that this felicitous balance received a jolt when, relatively late in life, the poet dared to reach out for total relatedness. For anyone capable of writing a *Philotas* in the first instance, relationship must present a fundamental problem. The old inwardness, coupled with fear and suspicion of 'the other', the world, which had early on found expression in the philosophical framework of Neoplatonism, once again reared their head and found their poetic precipitate in *Emilia Galotti*, tragedy of half-hearted passion. We have seen that in this tragedy the conflict between the need to withdraw from the world and the impulse to reach out for contact with the world remained in the balance. This indecision, I am sure, reflects an unresolved conflict within Lessing himself. To say this is not to belittle the frustrations and disappointments and, most of all, the crushing sense of loneliness which beset him soon after taking up his appointment as librarian at Wolfenbüttel. But such trials as beset him, especially at the beginning of his residence there, can only in part account for the severity of the depressions to which he fell a prey.[56] As the relationship between him and Eva became closer and the time of their formal engagement – in September 1771 – drew nearer, Lessing, for no wholly convincing external reason, became the victim of an acute anxiety state. After lapsing into total silence for two months, he writes to Eva as follows:

> Ich bin in allem Ernste seit sechs Wochen so krank gewesen, als nur immer ein Mensch seyn kann, der nicht im Bette und nicht auf den Tod liegt. . . . Bey jeder Zeile, die ich anfing, trat mir der **Angstschweiss vor die Stirne**, und ich verlor alle Gedanken. Ich könnte Ihnen mehr, wie einen Brief an Sie, mit beylegen, die ich alle auf der ersten halben Seite wieder abbrechen müssen. Nach dem Pyrmonter Brunnen, den ich gestern beschlossen, nachdem ich ihn 18 Tage getrunken, scheinet mir ein wenig besser zu werden. Aber doch nur ein wenig.[57]

Depression deepens in the following years, and three months in 1772, nine months in 1774 and eight months in 1775 go by without as much as a single letter to his betrothed. Such deep withdrawals from the woman he truly loved cannot be glossed over as a consequence of his extraneous misfortunes, not even of the misfortune that their marriage had to be postponed from one year to the next. Nor is it enough to say that these withdrawals aggravated his unhappiness. They were, in fact, its underlying cause.

The reticence that characterises the correspondence between this man and this woman—they never dropped the formal 'Sie' during the long time of their engagement—has often been remarked and admired as a proof of the maturity of their relationship. And indeed their letters are deeply moving in their very sobriety and restraint. But this should not blind us to the fact that here were two people who found it exceedingly hard to cast their bread upon the waters. Indeed, Lessing, in Eva König, had found more than a match for his own vulnerable pride. Towards

the end of 1771, the business of Eva's late husband was threatened
by bankruptcy and Lessing makes her the offer to share, together
with her children, his pitiful existence at Wolfenbüttel. 'Wenn
Sie', he writes,

> lieber in dem elendsten Winkel, lieber bey Wasser und Brod leben
> wollten, als länger in Ihrer gegenwärtigen Verwirrung: so ist Wol-
> fenbüttel Winkels genug, und an Wasser und Brod, auch noch an
> etwas mehr, soll es uns gewiss nicht fehlen.—

to which he adds, in a humorous but significant rider:

> und alsdenn, meine Liebe, können Sie weiter keine Ausflucht haben,
> mir Ihr Wort zu halten.[58]

To this letter Eva replies as follows:

> Die ganze verflossene Zeit meines Lebens kann ich ruhig zurücke
> denken, bis auf den Augenblick, worinn ich schwach genug war, eine
> Neigung zu gestehen, die ich zu verbergen so fest beschlossen hatte;
> wenigstens so lange, bis meine Umstände eine glückliche Wendung
> nähmen . . . Denn der Vorsatz bleibt unumstösslich: bin ich
> unglücklich, so bleibe ich es allein, und Ihr Schicksal wird nicht mit
> dem meinigen verflochten. Meine Gründe hierüber wissen Sie, noch
> mehr, Ihre Aufrichtigkeit erlaubte Ihnen nicht, sie zu missbilligen;
> nennen Sie sie also nicht *Ausflüchte* – das Wort *Ausflucht* hat mich
> gekränket—Fragen Sie Ihr Herz, ob es in dem nehmlichen Fall nicht
> so handeln würde, und antwortet es Ihnen Nein, so glauben Sie nur,
> dass Sie mich nicht halb so sehr lieben, als ich Sie liebe.[59]

We think we hear Major Tellheim,[60] the all-giving 'Bettler' who
cannot take, saying to Minna:

> Der Unglückliche . . . verdient sein Unglück, wenn er . . . es sich
> gefallen lassen kann, dass die, welche er liebt, an seinem Unglück
> Antheil nehmen dürffen – (II, 9)

Surely, this is one of the most extraordinary instances of that
cross-fertilisation between life and art for which Goethe was to
coin the term 'wiederholte Spiegelungen'! And perhaps we may
discern, in the tragic course Lessing's personal life was soon
destined to take, yet another 'wiederholte Spiegelung'; for that life
seems to reflect back a pattern to which his art had long since
given utterance. Such consonance between art and life is only
granted to the great who imprint their stamp on all they do and
even on all that comes to them, leaving no room for accident or
chance. Is it accident, or is it the working out of a law long since

divined in a tragedy written in depression when the stars seemed
to shine favourably upon him, that Lessing's courtship with love
was to be as cruelly cut short as that of his melancholy hero, Appiani? Is it accident that the lease of happiness granted to him in
his marriage was too short for the old misgivings of reality finally
to be dispelled, for vision to be bodied forth in reality? Appiani
reflects: 'Noch Einen Schritt vom Ziele, oder noch gar nicht
ausgelaufen seyn, ist im Grunde eines' (II, 8). His creator, on the
day of his wife's burial, writes: ' . . . Ich muss . . . wieder
anfangen, meinen Weg allein so fort zu duseln.' For both alike the
road to fulfilment seemed barred, and barred by an inner destiny.

After not hearing from Lessing for many months during his
Italian trip – through the neglect of her friends her letters had not
reached him and he had lapsed into one of his inexplicable
silences – Eva writes to him: 'Warum vernachlässigen Sie mich
denn so ganz und gar? Vielleicht denken Sie jetzt wieder so, wie Sie
schon einmal gedacht haben. – Wollte Gott ich könnte dann auch so
denken!'[61] Seven months after Eva's death nearly three years later
Lessing writes to Elise Reimarus: 'Wie oft wünsche ich, mit eins in
meinen alten isolirten Zustand zurückzutreten; nichts zu seyn,
nichts zu wollen, nichts zu thun, als was der gegenwärtige
Augenblick mit sich bringt!'[62] Early on in his relation with Eva,
together with whom he was in the habit of entering stakes for public
lotteries, Lessing had jokingly called her a woman 'mit der man
schlechterdings nichts **verlieren** könne.' After her death, in the same
letter to Elise Reimarus just quoted, he writes: 'Ich muss ein einziges
Jahr, das ich mit einer vernünftigen Frau gelebt habe, **theuer
bezahlen.**' We know this imagery. It is the imagery of Tellheim who
knows the world and nevertheless looks for a return from it, deeply
fearful that he may in the end be the loser; it is the imagery of Emilia
who, at the close of the tragedy, concludes: 'Dass alles verloren
ist'.

A circle of experience has closed; and what lies within that
circle served to bring him happiness and bitterest unhappiness,
but not to change him. How little, indeed, the short-lived
matrimonial security he had experienced with Eva had done to
reconcile this proud and lonely spirit with a world he had always
distrusted, a letter written after his first-born son had died, on
Christmas Day 1777, may show:

> Meine Freude war nur kurz: Und ich verlor ihn so ungern, diesen
> Sohn! denn er hatte so viel Verstand! so viel Verstand! . . . War es
> nicht Verstand, dass man ihn mit eisern Zangen auf die Welt ziehen
> musste? dass er sobald Unrath merkte?—War es nicht Verstand, dass
> er die erste Gelegenheit ergriff, sich wieder davon zu machen?[63]

These are ferocious words, and once again they enunciate the
familiar dichotomy between spirit and world; an experience which,
nearly twenty years earlier, had induced Philotas to declare war
on life, as soon as he had entered it; which had made Conti brush
aside the miscarriage of his vision in reality, as though such
miscarriage were of no consequence, extolling, instead, the mind
that comprehends once and for all that it can have no truck with
matter:

> Aber . . . dass ich es weiss, was hier verloren gegangen . . . und
> warum es verloren gehen müssen: darauf bin ich eben so stolz, und
> stolzer, als ich auf alles das bin, was ich nicht verloren gehen lassen.
> (I, 4)

'Traugott' was the name Lessing had given to his first-born son:
an act of faith, surely, on the part of one who had written, just a
year earlier, that his wife was the only woman in the whole world
'mit welcher ich mich zu leben **getraute.**'[64] Now that the child lies
dead, he praises, in an outburst of unparalleled bitterness, the
precociousness little Traugott had shown in quitting a world he
had at once recognised as being an altogether unsavoury place.

By the time Lessing came to write *Nathan der Weise*, he had
finally cut his losses. The intimate chapter of his life was closed,
and he consolidated his resources on another level, opting for
temperate relationship within the framework of universal values
enjoined by human consciousness and reason. Like Nathan, he has
'liquidated' his personal assets; and like him, he has struck the
deepest vein of his creativeness, achieving a blend of outgoingness
and containment which is shot through with resignation. The
author of *Minna von Barnhelm* had already been well on the way
towards such an equilibrium. Now, by being true to himself and
accepting his fated pattern, he achieved final maturity as man
and poet.

Lessing's two non-tragic dramas, *Minna von Barnhelm* and *Nathan
der Weise*, are living works of art because here, and here alone, the
poet steered a middle course, avoiding the perilous extremes of his
nature: the excessive elevation of the inward, spiritual self, and
the denigration of what is physical and outward. He had exorcised
his demons, and with incomparable freedom and grace he now
moved within the gravitational field he had chosen to inhabit,
creating a world in which love, vigorous yet temperate, went hand
in hand with a passionate concern for the moral, intellectual and
social values enjoined by reason, reinforcing these values and
being reinforced by them in turn. This enlightened form of love,
we may say, became the cornerstone of a henceforth unshakable

belief in the goodness – that is to say the innate rationality – of the world.

The old abyss had closed. The old dichotomy had healed. And not only a psychological and metaphysical dichotomy but that artistic dichotomy which had bedevilled the author of *Philotas* and *Emilia Galotti*. For how can a poet who shrinks from the material world entrust his mind's vision to the material medium of his craft, confident that his language will carry his inspiration and, indeed, enhance it? It was only when Lessing learned to regard the world as a worthy and equal partner of the mind that he could trust language to be the worthy and equal partner of the mind's vision. Nothing convinces us of the creative liberation engendered by this poet's hard-won monism as much as the marriage, in his two non-tragic dramas, between poetic experience and poetic tools, between inspiration and language. Theme and idiom alike bespeak a warmth spiced by wit, a keen intelligence tempered by geniality, good humour and compassion. In these two plays alone – plays in which hands are graced by rings offered and received in love – the poet trusted his own hands to mould the material in which they worked until it bodied forth his mind's desired vision.

VI

Some of my readers who may have followed me so far, agreeing perhaps with the evaluations I have put forward and the reasons I have adduced for success or failure where I have perceived it, may yet be left with misgivings. How can it be, they may ask, that conceptions such as *Philotas* and *Emilia Galotti*, which stem from the unconscious levels of the author's psyche, should nevertheless result in poetic miscarriages? And how, conversely, is it that works such as *Minna von Barnhelm* and *Nathan der Weise,* sprung from the conscious strata of the poet's mind and proclaiming the message of sweet reason, should nonetheless be viable as works of art? Such questions deserve to be taken seriously, because of the bearing they have upon a vexed problem of aesthetics, the problem of the *Urerlebnis* versus the *Bildungserlebnis*.

An evaluative distinction between *Urerlebnisse* and *Bildungs-erlebnisse* such as was drawn by Friedrich Gundolf, or Emil Staiger's polarisation of 'genuine', 'original' poetry – that is poetry stemming from the poet's unconscious depths – and *Kunstpoesie* – that is poetry sprung from his conscious mind[65] – is untenable *per se* and spectacularly fails to do justice to a phenomenon such as

Lessing. The results of our investigations force us to question the validity of such concepts and to attempt their redefinition. They have shown that *Urerlebnisse* resulting in 'genuine' or 'original' poetry cannot be adequately defined in terms of the nature and point of origin of the stimuli that excite an artist into creativity. If we must use such terms at all, we should define them, rather, in terms of the quality of the formative processes to which an experience gives rise, whatever that was in the first place. Different artists are sparked off into creativity by different kinds of experience. What is one man's *Bildungserlebnis* may become another man's *Urerlebnis*. The young Goethe and lyric poets of the Romantic movement such as Novalis, Eichendorff and Brentano, to mention only some, responded creatively to what Gundolf calls *Urerlebnisse*: the experience of love, nature or death. Others, like Schiller – and not only in his *Gedankenlyrik* – were released into creativity by what, in the terminology of Gundolf, would certainly be classified as *Bildungserlebnisse*: that is to say, by moral sentiments and abstract ideas; whilst yet others respond creatively to literary forms and traditions, and to the sheer excitement of artistic experimentation: witness Horace, C. F. Meyer, Hofmannsthal or, indeed, the later Goethe. Wherever such *Bildungserlebnisse* give rise to a creative liberation in depth, wherever they permeate the poet's mind and emotion and imagination, setting off a profound linguistic excitement which is neither stilled nor stemmed until the poet 'discovers' his own vision in the work that has issued from his hands, I would be inclined to accord them the title of an *Urerlebnis*. To argue thus is to shift the attention from the periphery of the artist's personal response to the central sphere where the artist responds *qua* artist: to the creative encounter between his vision and his medium. It is this facet of the artist's experiencing which is the proper concern of the aesthetician.

We have seen that Lessing permitted himself to be ignited by the experience of reason rather than by that of passion. Passion, to him, was a threat from which part of his being involuntarily shrank. Thus, it inhibited his creativeness. As against this, the experience of reason, however culturally conditioned, derivative and 'sicklied o'er with the pale cast of thought' it may seem to some of us, to Lessing became an artistic *Urerlebnis*, as genuine in its own right as the love of Friederike was for the young Goethe. It had the sanction of his whole being and thus it liberated, and activated, his poetic potential in depth, sparking off that enchanted traffic between mind and medium, between inspiration and technique, which resulted in the bodying forth of two fully articulated works of art.

Minna von Barnhelm and *Nathan der Weise* are artistic *Urerlebnisse*, then, not because they are 'about' passion, but because they spring from a passionate encounter between mind and medium, from that interpenetration of the two in the creative act which Schiller so eloquently termed 'eine wirkliche Vereinigung und Auswechslung der Materie mit der Form'.[66] The assimilation of ideas into images and the congruence between theme and structure tell us so, and so do the symbols of rings and riches, of trading and homecoming, and of water coursing back to its origin. For such operational symbols speak, above all, of the fulfilment that is born of the interaction between self and world, between mind and 'other', between the mental and the material poles of human existence. What is more, the felicitousness of these works as a whole testifies to the quality of the experience from which they sprang. They have an authenticity about them, a density of life; and this endows them with a reality as incontestable as that of any natural object, by comparison with which *Philotas* and *Emilia Galotti*, for all the passion 'behind' them, appear unsubstantial and thin. This irradiation of life from a work of art has nothing to do with its representational virtues. *Nathan der Weise*, with its iambic metres, its chequered setting and its improbable plot, is much less true to 'life' than *Emilia Galotti* with its naturalistic prose and its meticulous anatomy of feelings. Nonetheless Lessing, here and in *Minna von Barnhelm*, has created a fiction, a pure semblance of life which we accept without reference to anything outside the work itself. This is the paradox: *Nathan der Weise* and *Minna von Barnhelm*, which are through and through imbued with consciousness and reason, *live*, and live with a life of their own, whilst *Emilia Galotti*, for all its being a tragedy of passion, leads a shadow existence which is anxiously borrowed from reality, and *Philotas*, for all its compacted power, is blighted as a work of dramatic art.

VII

'Start with the truth that a work of art is a particular material structure,' Samuel Alexander writes, 'and the concrete insight of the artist into his subject matter becomes intelligible.'[67] Because *Nathan der Weise* is born of a cross-fertilisation between mind and verbal medium, it succeeds in being surprisingly articulate about the inner life of feeling, of the body, and even about that borderland of consciousness where feeling and sensation run fluid into one another, blending in an ineffable continuum of experiencing. Nothing could be more unjustified than the reproach, so often levelled at *Nathan der Weise*, that its truths are generalised and abstract. To be sure, it does culminate in universal truths. But these are at all points rooted in concrete insights which are often foreign to Lessing's own temper and sometimes in advance of the conscious knowledge of his time. Take, for example, his insistence on the importance of impressions of sight and especially of touch for the development of the mind. We would expect such insight from a Herder or Goethe rather than from a Lessing. But here, in *Nathan der Weise*, sense experience is judged to be all-important. It is the basis for the growth of knowledge, of human relationships and even of suprapersonal loyalties. What Recha has learned from Nathan she has learned by word of mouth, in the here and now of direct experience; for

> Mein Vater liebt
> Die kalte Buchgelehrsamkeit, die sich
> Mit todten Zeichen ins Gehirn nur drückt,
> Zu wenig.   (V, 6)

Saladin loses at chess because 'die glatten Steine, die an nichts erinnern, nichts bezeichnen' do not imprint themselves on his mind any more than they impress themselves on his sense of touch (II, 1). The Templar is more deeply pledged to the Mohammedan Sultan, to whom his face had spoken, than to the Patriarch with whom he shares the length and breadth of the Christian dogma:

> Wie? die Natur hätt' auch nur **Einen Zug**
> Von mir in deines Bruders Form gebildet:
> Und dem entspräche nichts in meiner Seele?
> Was dem entspräche, könnt ich unterdrücken,
> Um einem Patriarchen zu gefallen? –
> Natur, so leugst du nicht! So widerspricht
> Sich Gott in seinen Werken nicht! –   (I, 5)

There is a whole monistic philosophy in these words; and it is rooted, as indeed it should be, in the Templar's faith in his own instincts and body, in the psychosomatic oneness of his being. This faith is shared by Saladin and Nathan and Recha. All four inch their way through a confused situation, as it were by scent, across the frontiers of race, convention and religion, guided by nothing but the imprint left by a human face, a gesture or a voice: and lo, their instinct leads them to the truth.

Such reliance on direct sensation gives Recha the knowledge

where she belongs, Daja's stories of Europe notwithstanding. It gives her the courage to ask:

> Und wie weiss
> Man denn, *für* welchen Erdklos man geboren,
> Wenn mans für den nicht ist, *auf* welchem man
> Geboren? –   (III, 1)

and to argue:

> Ein Bild der Deinen, das in deiner Seele
> Noch nicht verloschen, sollte mehr vermögen,
> Als die ich sehn, und greifen kann, und hören,
> Die Meinen?   (*Ibid.*)

This truth of instinct, sensation and feeling it is which, to Nathan, seems the miracle of miracles; and rightly so, since it betokens the ultimate meaningfulness of existence:

> Sieh! eine Stirn, so oder so gewölbt;
> Der Rücken einer Nase, so vielmehr
> Als so geführet; Augenbraunen, die
> Auf einem scharfen oder stumpfen Knochen
> So oder so sich schlängeln; eine Linie,
> Ein Bug, ein Winkel, eine Falt', ein Mahl,
> Ein Nichts, auf eines wilden Europäers
> Gesicht: – und du entkömmst dem Feur, in Asien!
> Das wär' kein Wunder, wundersücht'ges Volk?
> Warum bemüht ihr denn noch einen Engel?   (I, 2)

Even of the connection between the life of feeling and our digestive habits, and of that between both and money which we might regard as a discovery of our own psychoanalytical age, Lessing tells something in this play. The Templar, lonesome youth that he is, *likes* to eat dates notwithstanding the fact that this fruit 'verstopft die Milz, macht melancholisches Gemüt.' Indigestion suits him while he holds himself back from relationship, and we may surmise that, at the end of the play, this symptom will be cured! And what are we to say when Saladin, the man with the leak in his pocket, confesses that his father, the hoarder, is the cause of his deepest discomfiture; when he hints, mysteriously,

> Er kann nicht durch; **es klemmt sich** aller Orten;
> Es fehlt bald da, bald dort —   (II, 1)

or when, in answer to Sittah's question 'Was klemmt? was fehlt?'
he replies:

> Was sonst, als was ich kaum zu nennen würd'ge
> Was, wenn ichs habe, mir so **überflüssig,**
> Und hab' ichs nicht, so unentbehrlich scheint. –
> . . . Das leidige, verwünschte Geld!   (II, 1)

Such awareness of the significance of experience rooted in the
depths of bodily being permeates the play. It is this which informs
the distrust, voiced time and time again, against all manner of
abstraction. There is a crisp nominalistic breeze blowing through
its pages and war is waged against the tyranny of phrases and
clichés, of name and title and of all universal slogans – in short,
against every kind of semantic glibness which rests on an
abstraction from immediacy of experience. It is this conviction
which imparts their punch and bite to Nathan's repartees.

> . . . Und so fiel mir ein,
> Euch kurz und gut das Messer an die Kehle
> Zu setzen . . .

the young Templar confesses to the Jew; whereupon the latter
replies:

> Kurz und gut? und gut? – Wo steckt
> Das Gute?   (V, 5)

It is from this platform that irony is poured over the Patriarch
for those smooth generalisations which harbour all manner of
moral ambiguities, and for the preposterously smug impersonality
of his slogan 'Thut nichts! der Jude wird verbrannt'; from this
platform that war is declared against any name or title, be it the
name of father or brother or of Templar or of God, which remains
meaningless unless it has its roots deep in the reality of living. And
it is not in the name of some abstract idea of humanity, but of
living experience that war is carried right into the Christian camp.
Saladin wants to see his brother and sister marry two Christians,
also a brother and a sister. This dream Sittah shatters thus:

> Du kennst die Christen nicht, willst sie nicht kennen.
> Ihr Stolz ist: Christen seyn; nicht Menschen. Denn
> Selbst das, was, noch von ihrem Stifter her,
> Mit Menschlichkeit den Aberglauben wirzt,
> Das lieben sie, nicht weil es menschlich ist:

> Weils Christus lehrt; weils Christus hat gethan. –
> Wohl ihnen, dass er ein so guter Mensch
> Noch war! Wohl ihnen, dass sie seine Tugend
> Auf Treu und Glaube nehmen können! – Doch
> Was Tugend? – Seine Tugend nicht; sein Name
> Soll überall verbreitet werden; soll
> Die Namen aller guten Menschen schänden,
> Verschlingen. Um den Namen, um den Namen
> Ist ihnen nur zu thun.   (II, 1)

Sittah's words castigate the perilous centrifugal drift inherent in abstraction which is in turn inseparable from discursive language itself: the drift from the direct experience of the individual, from *my* experience here and now, first to the humanity of Christ, then to his teaching and finally to his name, a semantic entity which is made to cover a multitude of sins in that it is unrelated to the lived reality of those that use it. Saladin underscores the absurdity of this dissociation in thus continuing Sittah's argument:

> Du meynst: warum
> Sie sonst verlangen würden, dass auch ihr
> Auch du und Melek, Christen hiesset, eh
> Als Ehgemahl ihr Christen lieben wolltet?

to which Sittah replies:

> Ja wohl! Als wär' von Christen nur, als Christen,
> Die Liebe zu gewärtigen, womit
> Der Schöpfer Mann und Männinn ausgestattet!   (*Ibid.*)

The argument between brother and sister has come full circle, back to the sphere of direct experience from which it started. This alone is the native soil in which truth and goodness flourish. Cut off from their living roots, they become dried-up husks, empty words, counterfeits as worthless as 'neue Münze, die nur der Stempel macht'.

It is moving that Lessing, in this his last drama, should have swung around to a philosophy of language so far removed from the conceptualism with which we tend to associate him. It seems a far cry from the subordinate role assigned to language in *Laokoon* to the sovereign use the poet makes of language here, in *Nathan der Weise*, as a poetic instrument capable even of chastising the perils of discursive thought and speech; as far a cry as it is from the nervous imitation of life in *Emilia Galotti* to the serene semblance of it he wrought in *Nathan der Weise*. Lessing was entitled to speak of discursive language as he did, from the vantage point of the poet. For in his last poem, in praise of mature humanity, he had gained a new relation to words, more full-bodied and sensuous than ever before. Yielding to the power of a passion purged of all material references, words had themselves become 'a passion and a power'.

The poet had buried his dearest possession: he had been forced, even, to call off the battle against the forces of hypocrisy. And now, in this seclusion, a new freedom came to him. Like his Nathan, he learned to live and give, looking for no outward return. When Nathan knows that he must surrender his adopted child, he cries: 'Gott! Wie leicht/Mir wird . . . ' (V, 4). On the day of his wife's death, Lessing writes: 'Meine Frau ist todt: und . . . [ich] bin ganz leicht.'[68] There is liberation as well as renunciation in these words. Such lightness of touch is the salt of mature creativeness. Sprung from sorrow, it transcends sorrow and transfigures what it has renounced in the serenity of the poetic symbol.

> Was ich besitze, seh' ich wie im Weiten,
> Und was verschwand, wird mir zu Wirklichkeiten.[69]

At the last, disengaged from all external objects of his passion, the old fighter was free to experience the disinterested passion of the artist. It was then, in the finality of this seclusion, that he let the experience of creativeness flow out into words and that his medium returned his vision faithfully, and rich with a wisdom of its own.

11

Faust's Conquest of the Sea

Except a corn of wheat fall into the ground and die, it abideth alone:
but if it die, it bringeth forth much fruit.

(The Gospel according to St John, XII, 24)

I

Emboldened no doubt by Hugo von Hofmannsthal's manifesto on
art[1] which in turn derived its impetus from the French Symbolist
movement, artists and aestheticians have come to appreciate the
fact that, whatever its overt theme, art, on another plane, is also
about itself. And in their wake critics have begun to realise that,
as Goethe's poetry in its entirety reflects the phases and permutations of his creativity, so does the work which was his life-long
companion. *Faust*, it is being asserted with increasing frequency, is
a poem about creativeness. Ernst Cassirer has led later research,
both as aesthetician and critic. The abiding characteristic of
Goethe's theory of art, he argues, lies in the fact 'dass die Werke
nur als Ausdruck der bildenden Energien genommen werden, die
hinter ihnen stehen.' And he continues: 'Aber wenn diese Energien von dem jungen Goethe in die Subjektivität des Künstlers, in
seine leidenschaftliche innere Bewegtheit verlegt wurden, so
erscheinen sie jetzt' – he is speaking now of the Goethe of the
classical period – 'als eine Form des objektiven Werdens, in der der
Gegenstand selbst sich darstellt. Man erinnert sich des Wortes
Plotins,' he adds, 'dass Phidias, um den Zeus darzustellen, ihn so
gebildet habe, wie er selbst in die Erscheinung treten würde, wenn
er den Entschluss fasste, sich uns sichtbar zu machen.'[2] Of *Faust* he
writes: 'Nicht der Inhalt des Goetheschen Lebens, sondern sein
Formgesetz ist es, dessen Werden und Wandel die Faustdichtung,
ungewollt und notwendig, darstellt.'[3] More recent works on *Faust*
have tended to confirm the fruitfulness of this approach. Erich
Trunz treads in Cassirer's footsteps when he describes the theme
of Part II, Act II as being '. . . das ewige Gestalten und Umge-
stalten der Natur und ihr höchstes Geschöpf, der schöne Mensch,

geschaffen aus göttlichem Eros', and thence goes on to ask: 'Was ist dies alles? Ist es ein Sinnbild dessen, was in dem Menschen, der höchste Schönheit schafft, vorgeht?'[4] Or when, speaking of Act III, he writes: 'Arkadien ist die Seligkeit, die Goethe empfand, als ihm das *Faust*-Drama gelang, und Mozart, als er *Don Giovanni* vollendete.'[5] A more succinct formulation of the process whereby the erotically charged experience of making art may invade the work itself, there to emerge as its overt theme, cannot be readily imagined. Such insight is borne out in Trunz's assessment, for instance, of the *Klassische Walpurgisnacht*: 'Der 2. Akt gestaltet in wiederholten Variationen die Beziehung von Geist und Leben, das Schöpferische als Bewusstes und Unbewusstes, als Denken und Natur, wobei kosmisches Werden und künstlerisches Werden eine geheime Gemeinsamkeit des Gesetzes haben.'[6] Wilhelm Emrich, in his study of the symbolic structure of *Faust II*, starts from comparable premisses and thence is led to similar conclusions. At the beginning of his study he emphasises that ' . . . solche wachstumsartige Entstehung von Dichtung ist selbst vielfach Thema seiner Dichtung geworden';[7] and again: 'Die Entstehung von Natur- und Kunstwerken dringt bei Goethe immer wieder thematisch mit in die Kunst ein . . . '[8] The finding derived from such aesthetic premisses is summed up on the last page of Emrich's work: 'Das Werden und Wachsen der *Faust II*-Dichtung' – he writes – 'die Fülle ihrer Bild- und Symbolwelt war nur die unendliche Ausformung eines einzigen Themas, das hartnäckig in jedem Vers und Vorgang sich durchhielt, des Themas der Schöpfung.'[9]

It would be easy to show the growing consensus concerning the thematic unity of *Faust II* by quoting the views of authors such as H. Herrmann,[10] P. Stöcklein,[11] D. Lohmeyer[12] or M. Kommerell.[13] On the whole, however, such views are confined to the second part of the tragedy. By contrast, the thematic homogeneity of *Faust I* and, indeed, of the *Urfaust*, has frequently been denied. L. A. Willoughby declares: 'The *Urfaust* makes no attempt to fuse the theme of the despairing scholar with that of love's betrayal. The first meeting between Faust and Gretchen reads like the beginning of a new play, and its libertine hero bears but little resemblance to the earnest young professor in his study.'[14] Similarly, E. Trunz operates with the construct of four thematic units comprising both parts of the drama in its final form: the tragedy of the scholar, the lover, the artist and the ruler. Of these, the first two dominate the *Urfaust*. It falls into 'zwei grosse Szenengruppen, die Gelehrtentragödie und die Gretchentragödie.'[15] Trunz, it is true, concedes that 'schon im *Urfaust* kommt der Geist der Gelehrtentragödie voll zum Ausdruck, und die Gretchentragödie läuft lückenlos ab in strenger, straffer Folge.'[16] Yet he concludes: 'Aber ein Drama als ausgearbeiteter Handlungszusammenhang ist es noch nicht.'[17]

On the level of the plot this is no doubt true. Yet we feel unity, and unity not merely between the sequences of the *Urfaust*, however starkly they seem to be juxtaposed, but also between those breathtaking improvisations of Goethe's youth and the labyrinthine complexities of *Faust II*; and unity, above all, between the work which accompanied Goethe through life and the body of his thought and poetry as a whole. Such congruence is endangered on every level if we accept a reading of the *Urfaust* – and, by implication, of *Faust I* – which argues that the drama falls into two parts because its hero is at no point motivated as a whole person. For *Faust II*, we are being told – and rightly so – is a drama about creativity; and creativity in its turn – so we have seen for ourselves – for Goethe springs from an ultimate psycho-physical wholeness of being and responding. Götz's maimed hand, we saw, betokens a denial of such wholeness and thus becomes a symbol of uncreativeness. Likewise, Werther's sterility springs from his rejection of the material world and, ultimately, of his own physical self. He neither prizes nor practises the realisation of his dreams (surely Lotte is right in saying that he has sought her out, not despite the fact that he cannot possess her but because of it!); and this is true in matters of work and art no less than in the sphere of love. And that this inward youth is the spiritual descendant of Götz von Berlichingen mit der eisernen Hand and, indeed, of Emilia Galotti, may be seen from the fact that the first snatch of the novel Goethe jotted down is the passage in which Werther, rapturously and perversely, revels in the knowledge that the gun which will destroy him has passed through Lotte's hand.[18] For in this novel, too, whose hero walks side by side with his rival, aimlessly picking flowers and throwing them away again, the destructive hand, almost as much as in Goethe's earlier drama and Lessing's two tragedies, has become the symbol of an incurable rift between body and mind. The restoration of the hand is celebrated in Goethe's letter to Herder and in the ensuing 'Künstlergedichte', and in both it becomes, as we have seen, the symbol of the poet's new-won wholeness and creativity. Only where the person is one, where experience may course from head and heart to the tips of the fingers and back again, is creative Eros released. And even in his *Tasso*, Goethe concedes, once and for all, that creativeness is rooted in the depth of physical being.

Are we really to deny such wholeness of motivation to the figure who, later on in the drama, inflamed with creative Eros, will body forth beauty personified, with her to engender the genius of poetry? Such a step would be a grave one to take indeed, countenancing discontinuity and incoherence not only within the *Faust*-drama itself, but within the poet's most cherished and characteristic convictions. For, surely, Goethe's instinctive monism is the hallmark of his genius, setting him apart as a solitary figure in the modern Western world.

Fortunately, it is not necessary to accept such dichotomous readings of the *Urfaust* and, by implication, of *Faust I* as have been put forward. To show this, I propose to take under the magnifying glass an image complex of great extensiveness and power which furnishes a continuous link between the tragedy of the scholar and the tragedy of the lover in the first part of the drama, and between both and the second part of the tragedy. This is the imagery associated with the forms of water, most Protean of elements, ever constant, ever changing and ever replenishing itself at its origins, which became Goethe's foremost symbol of creativity from *Mahomets-Gesang* and *Wonne der Wehmut* onwards to *Trilogie der Leidenschaft*, and to the panegyric which concludes the *Klassische Walpurgisnacht*:

> Alles ist aus dem Wasser entsprungen!!
> Alles wird durch das Wasser erhalten!   (1. 8435f.)

True, in the *Faust*-drama itself it is only late that this symbol matures from its chrysalis-like stage of image and metaphor into the cosmic power as which it emerges at the end, as Faust's final antagonist.[19] But in one of its many guises, as mist or cloud, or rain, or stream, or lake, or tear, or rainbow, it is present all the time, helping to shape the poem, to give coherence to its diverse universes of discourse, and to articulate its deepest preoccupation – the preoccupation with the nature of creativity.

I would suggest, then, that from the young scholar's craving to escape from the desiccation of his study into the dew-bathed night there runs a straight line to the centenarian's resolve to give battle to the sea; and conversely – and taking into consideration Goethe's increasing awareness of his own intentions – that the hero's dying aspiration 'den faulen Pfuhl auch abzuziehn' is already adumbrated in the Lord's challenge to the Devil: 'Zieh diesen Geist von seinem Urquell ab . . .'. Thus, in tracing this complex in some of its ramifications throughout the drama, we may hope to shed light upon the hero's final quest, a venture which is puzzling in itself and the prelude to his dying; we may also hope to dispel apparent incongruence and demonstrate unity where we sense it: finally, we may expect to discover something of those creational imports which endow this work with its depth of resonance.

Before proceeding to a scrutiny of the tragedy in the light of our chosen symbolism, it will be advisable to take a look at the three prologues, chronology notwithstanding. For in every one of them the poet has introduced the imagery of water and has introduced it, at that, in positions of undoubted prominence.

Indeed, we must begin at the beginning. For the opening stanza of the first prologue – *Zueignung* – articulates the labile state which may herald artistic productivity and articulates it in terms of the permutations and properties of water. It is a fluid state wreathed in 'Dunst und Nebel' from which 'schwankende Gestalten' gradually materialise. And even here, at the inception of the creative act, we may discern that conflict between the need to be labile and the desire for permanence which – we have seen it in *Tasso* – characterises the closing stages of creation.[20] The poet, in *Zueignung*, endeavours to fix the forms which run liquid before his inner eye as, in Acts I and III of *Faust II*, the hero will endeavour to retain the form he has summoned out of mist and cloud, only to learn that he must let go of it again. However, before – even for the duration of the creative moment – the poet can fix the 'schwankende Gestalten' he must risk exposing himself to the force of their impact. For however much art is man's bulwark against elemental forces within and without, it can only come into being through an uncalculating exposure to those very forces, symbolised for Goethe, throughout his life, by water and its associated forms. This double pull – towards fluidity and towards rigidity – has found moving expression in the words 'Mein Busen fühlt sich **jugendlich erschüttert** . . . '. And indeed, the later stanzas confirm what the poet's timorousness in the face of his visitation has suggested: art demands a courageous immersion in inner chaos and flux. It presupposes the melting of all that has become hard, if need be in a veritable downpour of tears (and tears, need we be reminded, are water):

> Ein Schauer fasst mich, Träne folgt den Tränen,
> Das strenge Herz, es fühlt sich mild und weich;   (1. 29f.)

and these tears here are not merely the solvent that they are for the early Goethe of *Wonne der Wehmut*, *Sehnsucht*, *Werther* and, indeed, for the young Faust in his study;[21] in this prologue as in later poems such as *Hochbild*, *Äolsharfen* and *Aussöhnung* tears of sorrow usher in a creative mode of experiencing, in which the near and the distant, the particular and the universal, reality claimed and reality renounced merge in a symbolic vision which transcends both:[22]

> Was ich besitze, seh' ich wie im Weiten,
> Und was verschwand, wird mir zu Wirklichkeiten.   (1. 31f.)

The *Vorspiel auf dem Theater* culminates in the poet rejecting the cynical recipe for the making of a play, suggested alike by Stage manager and Fool. He will not hear of the 'Ragout' recommended by the former (any more than Faust, later on, will hear of Wagner's rhetoric which he calls 'ein Ragout von andrer Schmaus'), nor will he concoct a brew to please the multitudes as the Fool would have him do:

> In bunten Bildern wenig Klarheit,
> Viel Irrtum und ein Fünkchen Wahrheit,
> So wird der beste Trank gebraut,
> Der alle Welt erquickt und auferbaut.   (ll. 170ff.)

To this the poet's rejoinder is a passionate plea for renewal. Characteristically, this plea is couched in imagery of water signifying, as before, rejuvenescence and creativity and, with it, the acceptance of flux in all its weal and woe:

> So gib mir auch die Zeiten wieder,
> Da ich noch selbst im Werden war,
> Da sich ein Quell gedrängter Lieder
> Ununterbrochen neu gebar,
> . . .
> Gib ungebändigt jene Triebe,
> Das tiefe, schmerzenvolle Glück,
> Des Hasses Kraft, die Macht der Liebe,
> Gib meine Jugend mir zurück!   (ll. 184ff.)[23]

The last prologue, *Prolog im Himmel*, takes up the images used by the poets of the preceding prologues to characterise their creativity. But this time such images are associated with the divine Creator and thence with his highest creation – Faust, representative of man. The archangels praise the mystery of creation, which is permanence in the midst of transience: 'Dauer im Wechsel'. Enduring, yet resplendent with fresh glory – 'herrlich wie am ersten Tag' – creation flowers above the flux and fury of the elemental forces which sustain it, however much such forces are themselves beholden to time and transience:

Es schäumt das Meer in breiten Flüssen
Am tiefen Grund der Felsen auf,
Und Fels und Meer wird fortgerissen
In ewig schnellem Sphärenlauf.

Und Stürme brausen um die Wette,
Vom Meer aufs Land, vom Land aufs Meer,
Und bilden wütend eine Kette
Der tiefsten Wirkung rings umher.   (ll. 255ff.)

It is in such a context of the enduring born of flux, that the hero
of the drama about to begin, Faust himself, is introduced to us.
The very first we learn about him, from the lips of Mephistopheles, are the words:

Nicht irdisch ist des Toren Trank noch Speise.   (l. 301)

And the Lord himself takes the Devil up on his image in the terms
of the wager he proposes to him:

Zieh diesen Geist von seinem Urquell ab,
Und führ' ihn, kannst du ihn erfassen,
Auf deinem Wege mit herab . . .   (ll. 324ff.)

Thus, whatever we may find in the drama itself by way of the
symbolism associated with water, it is from the outset embedded
in a highly significant context: fluid has come to signify a
rejuvenating if risky return to the source of creativeness, and this
source is conceived as inexhaustible. Moreover, whatever images
of fluid we shall find associated with the hero of the drama will
link him with the two poets, with the speaker of *Zueignung* as well
as with the poet of the *Vorspiel auf dem Theater*, and thereby with
the creative mode which is the distinguishing characteristic of the
artist.

The possibility of a connecting link between the two poets of
the prologues and the hero of the drama suggests itself all the
more strongly in view of the obverse link between the 'lustige
Person' and Mephistopheles. Goethe himself hinted at a continuity between these two figures in the Paralipomena to the
Vorspiel auf dem Theater which declares:

Und wenn der Narr durch alle Szenen läuft,
So ist das Stück genug verbunden.[24]

If Mephisto's denial of creation and creativeness is a thread which runs through the piece as a whole, prologues and all, is it too much to hazard, in view of the imagery of water sounded so early and so specifically, that the firmest thread connecting its diverse parts is the quest for creativeness which is centred in its hero?

II

One of the most striking things about the first part of *Faust*, in all its versions, is the fact that, at every turning point, the action is carried forward through the administration of liquid in some form or another, whether the event be recollected or enacted before our eyes. The first indication of this comes when Faust, after his short-lived elation, turns to his phial in the hope that a draught of its 'braune Flut' may dispatch him to the 'hohe Meer' of eternity. His rebirth on Easter Sunday is palpably symbolised in the 'Erquickungstrank' offered him by the old peasant. The wager with the Devil comes into effect as Faust signs his name with 'that very special juice', a drop of his blood. The first lap of his trip into the world, out of the dusty desiccation of his study 'wo Sinnen und Säfte stocken,' finds him at 'Auerbachs Keller' where Mephistopheles hallucinates wine and the hallucinatory gratifications thereof. In the final version of the drama, a more potent drink is prepared for the hero in the 'Hexenküche', a brew of which the Devil predicts:

> Du siehst, mit diesem Trank im Leibe,
> Bald Helenen in jedem Weibe.   (l. 2603f.)

And thus begins the second half of Part I and the thread on which the action hangs continues unbroken. And if here, in the *Urfaust* at least, the distinction between plot and inner action cannot at all times be maintained, the reason for this is to be found in Goethe's technique of compressing and discharging dramatic tension in single episodes of lyrical intensity and merely hinting at the intervening events.[25] Thus, Faust's impact on Gretchen is rendered by the ballad she sings of the 'König in Thule', old lover and 'Zecher' who, dying, commits his goblet to the sea, whilst the coarseness of Faust's desire mellows into tenderness as Gretchen tells him how she nursed her little sister in her mother's place:

> Da konnte sie nun nicht dran denken,
> Das arme Würmchen selbst zu tränken,
> Und so erzog ich's ganz allein,
> Mit Milch und Wasser; so ward's mein.   (ll. 3130ff.)

It is the sleeping potion administered to Gretchen's mother which enables the lovers to enter into sexual communion. The tears bedewing the flowers Gretchen offers to the *Mater Dolorosa* bespeak the anguish born of her heedless surrender. Later, in church, the mother's sleeping draught, the threshold drenched with her brother's blood and the 'quillende' life that stirs in her womb are woven into a single fabric of despair. The *Fragment* of 1790 we may remember, ends with Gretchen's cry: 'Nachbarinn! Euer Fläschchen!–' impotent medicine against a sickness unto death! The crumbling of Gretchen's mind is poetically projected into the rotten dampness of her prison walls, and by and by her fantasies give way to a piercing flash of the truth: her lover's hand is moist with blood and her baby is drowned

> Am Bach hinauf,
> Über den Steg,
> In den Wald hinein,
> Links, wo die Planke steht,
> Im Teich. (ll. 4554ff.)

Such continuity on the level of the external action is indicative of an inner continuity that is more striking yet. This continuity is due to the fact that 'the earnest, young professor in his study' and Gretchen's 'übersinnlicher sinnlicher Freier' speak the same language. Both express their aspirations and desires through the self-same symbolism – the symbolism of liquid. Or perhaps it is wiser from the start to resist the temptation to operate with such schizoid constructs as are implied in the word 'both', notwithstanding the fact that the hero himself, in his lament 'Zwei Seelen wohnen, ach! in meiner Brust', is inviting critics to use them,[26] and to say instead that, whether he is cogitating or making love, Faust expresses the intensity of his experience in terms of the same imagery, the imagery of fluid.

Goethe's *Faust* reverses the age-old pattern of Western tragedy. It begins with the hero's near-death and ends with what we might assume to be his last birth. The learned professor of the opening monologue has all but died. The sterility of learning has dried up the springs of his life, and he thirsts for renewal as desperately as does Werther towards the end of his days. He is desiccated and parched. 'Habe nun, ach! . . . studiert'; 'mit **heissem** Bemühn'; 'mit **sauerm** Schweiss'; '**trocknes** Sinnen'; 'das will mir schier das Herz **verbrennen**'; – these are the keynotes that are sounded time and again in the early pages of the tragedy. His prayer is for a return to the springs of life;[27] yet he has nothing but scorn for the 'Quellen' which Wagner, 'der **trockne** Schleicher,' has in mind:

> Das Pergament, ist das der heil'ge Bronnen,
> Woraus ein Trunk den Durst auf ewig stillt?
> Erquickung hast du nicht gewonnen,
> Wenn sie dir nicht aus eigner Seele quillt.   (ll. 566ff.)

'In Worten kramen' does not bring him the refreshment he craves; not even rummaging in the sacred words of the bible. True, he sits down to translate the *Logos* after his Easter Sunday walk, saying:

> Man sehnt sich nach des Lebens Bächen,
> Ach! nach des Lebens Quelle hin.   (l. 1200f.)

But before even he has put pen to paper he knows that the 'Wort', for him, is not the way to the origins:

> Aber ach! schon fühl' ich, bei dem besten Willen,
> Befriedigung nicht mehr aus dem Busen quillen.
> Aber warum muss der Strom so bald versiegen,
> Und wir wieder im Durste liegen?   (ll. 1210ff.)

Oddly enough Faust here, in an intellectual context, uses the same imagery which Mephistopheles will use in circumstances of a very different kind. For when, in *Wald und Höhle*, the Devil taunts him for leaving Gretchen, he uses the identical terms to describe the waxing and waning of Faust's sexual desire:

> Erst kam deine Liebeswut übergeflossen,
> Wie vom geschmolznen Schnee ein Bächlein übersteigt;
> Du hast sie ihr ins Herz gegossen,
> Nun ist dein Bächlein wieder seicht.   (ll. 3307ff.)

Such an overlap makes one wonder. Perhaps the two spheres, the intellectual and the physical, are after all not so far apart as is commonly assumed. How physical is the imagery in which this scholar expresses his spiritual yearning! It is nothing less than a bodily immersion in the sources of life he seeks: first an immersion in the dewy light of the moon – 'in deinem Tau gesund mich baden', then an immersion in the secrets of nature as revealed through the sign of the Macrocosm:

> Auf, bade, Schüler, unverdrossen
> Die ird'sche Brust im Morgenrot!   (l. 445f.)

The mere contemplation of the mystic symbols sets up an overpowering physical experience. Faust drinks in renewal. At the sign
of the Macrocosm he exclaims:

> Ha! welche Wonne fliesst in diesem Blick
> Auf einmal mir durch alle meine Sinnen!
> Ich fühle junges, heil'ges Lebensglück
> Neuglühend mir durch Nerv' und Adern rinnen. (ll. 430ff.)

As he turns to the sign of the Erdgeist, he reiterates:

> Schon fühl' ich meine Kräfte höher,
> Schon glüh' ich wie von neuem Wein . . .   (l. 462f.)

But no contemplation can give to this professor what he wants. As
he turns away from the spectacle of the Macrocosm and woos the
elemental spirit of the Erdgeist – a spirit who describes himself as
living 'in Lebensfluten' and indeed as being, himself, 'ein ewig
Meer' – the imagery used by the hero and of him becomes ever
more physical:

> Welch Schauspiel! Aber ach! ein Schauspiel nur!
> Wo fass' ich dich, unendliche Natur?
> Euch Brüste, wo? Ihr Quellen alles Lebens,
> An denen Himmel und Erde hängt,
> Dahin die welke Brust sich drängt –
> Ihr quellt, ihr tränkt, und schmacht' ich so vergebens?
>   (ll. 455ff.)

And indeed, when the Erdgeist does reply to Faust, he echoes the
hero's own image – the image of the infant suckling at its mother's
breast. He answers

> Du hast mich mächtig angezogen,
> An meiner Sphäre lang' gesogen . . .   (l. 483f.)

The literalness of Faust's 'Wo fass' ich dich?' echoes the language of the 'Künstlergedichte' and the 'Dreingreifen, packen' of
Goethe's letter to Herder: documents, both, testifying indeed not
to intellectual concerns, however passionately pursued, but to the
young poet's preoccupation with artistic creation and its roots in
biological process.[28] What is more, the directness of Faust's language here is underpinned by its take-off, later on in the play,
when Mephistopheles interviews the young freshman. Faust
literally wants to 'fassen' Nature, to seize her by her breasts. The

freshman is content to *er-fassen* 'was auf der Erden und in dem Himmel ist'; and Mephisto's simile of the breasts of wisdom which will in time become acceptable to the wayward infant merely serves as a foil to point up, retrospectively, the unconscious immediacy of Faust's metaphor. Here again the threads of the verbal fabric ply across from the scholar's tragedy to the tragedy of love. For the very lament which the scholar had addressed to Mother Nature is echoed in the lament the lover will presently address to his beloved:

> Ach, kann ich nie
> Ein Stündchen ruhig dir am Busen hängen,
> Und Brust an Brust und Seel' in Seele drängen?   (ll. 3503ff.)

And this plea so moves Gretchen's maternal instinct that she agrees to leave her door unbolted for her lover; Gretchen who had stolen Faust's heart in the first place by her account of how she nursed her baby sister, who, in her madness, fantasises suckling her own dead infant – 'lass mich nur erst das Kind noch tränken' – and who will ask to be buried, 'das Kleine mir an die rechte Brust.'

Oddly enough the fluctuation, on the part of the lovers, between oral eroticism and adult sexuality is adumbrated in Faust's encounter with the Erdgeist, in the seclusion of his study. For there we may observe a similar fluidity within the imagery deployed by the poet. As Faust flinches before the impact of the elemental force he had sucked – 'gesogen' – into his orbit, the Spirit taunts him, asking:

> Wo ist die Brust, die eine Welt in sich erschuf
> Und trug und hegte, die mit Freudebeben
> Erschwoll, sich'uns, den Geistern, gleich zu heben? (ll. 491ff.)

The bisexual overtones of these words are striking.[29] Any doubts we may have as to such implications are dispersed once we perceive the similarity of the images used by Mephisto, emissary of the Erdgeist, this time in a strictly physical context. In *Wald und Höhle*, Mephistopheles jeers at Gretchen's 'übersinnlicher sinnlicher Freier' for his sexual ambivalence in the same terms in which the Erdgeist had taunted the solemn young professor for his ambivalence in the face of his overpowering force. Only here the imagery of fluid, implicit in the earlier 'erschwoll', and the passage from the female to the male pole of sexuality, become explicit:

> Ein überirdisches Vergnügen!

Mephisto sneers as he finds his companion communing with nature, drenched in nature, drinking in 'neue Lebenskraft' 'aus dumpfem Moor und triefendem Gestein,' like a toad; and he continues:

> In Nacht und Tau auf den Gebirgen liegen,
> Und Erd' und Himmel wonniglich umfassen,
> Zu einer Gottheit sich aufschwellen lassen,
> Der Erde Mark mit Ahnungsdrang durchwühlen,
> Alle sechs Tagewerk' im Busen fühlen,
> In stolzer Kraft ich weiss nicht was geniessen,
> Bald liebewonniglich in alles überfliessen,
> Verschwunden ganz der Erdensohn,
> Und dann die hohe Intuition –
> _(mit einer Gebärde)_
> Ich darf nicht sagen, wie – zu schliessen. (ll. 3283ff.)

Such crossthreads interlacing the scholars' and the lovers' tragedy deserve serious consideration. They imply a unity of the drama on a deep level which we may only deny at our peril. This unity is rooted in the fact that the _quality_ of Faust's experiencing remains the same, regardless of the specific _area_ of experience in which he happens to move. Admittedly, the range and intensity of his experiencing is extreme, and he oscillates violently between one pole and the other, between heaven and earth and bible and bed. But to say this does not signify that at any point the two poles of his being, the mental and the physical, fly asunder and that he is the dissociated self which the famous lament about his two souls would suggest him to be. On the contrary: the verbal texture of the drama and, in particular, the imagery of fluid with which we are here concerned, leave no doubt but that _all_ of Faust, mind _and_ body, psyche _and_ soma, is involved in a mode of experiencing which is from the first distinguished by its potential totality as much as by its dynamism and polarity. This is his glory, this is his greatness, and this, most of all, is the basis of his claim to creativity. Earnest though he be, this professor does not approach the mysteries of Nature in any intellectual frame of mind. In fact, he does not desire to know her by any act of cognition. He assaults her 'in derber Liebeslust' and, like a lusty infant, clings to her 'mit klammernden Organen'. Indeed, the experience he seeks is basically not on a verbal level at all. Hence his inability to translate 'Im Anfang war das **Wort!**'[30] The _Logos_, for him, is not the spring of life. The lover, on the other hand, is at all times 'ein übersinnlicher sinnlicher Freier'; not a libertine

like Mephistopheles but one in whom head and heart act in
unison, who is moved in all honesty to testify to the Divine and
to ask:

> Und drängt nicht alles
> Nach Haupt und Herzen dir . . . ?   (l. 3447f.)

as the blood rushes to his loins; one who would

> Brust an Brust und Seel' in Seele drängen   (l. 3504)

in the conviction that 'Brust' and 'Seele' together are
complements of one experiential whole.

It is this totality of motivation, in all manner of situations,
which marks Faust's mode of experiencing as quintessentially
creative. Mephisto means to insult Faust when he points out the
bodiliness of a creative urge which begins with intimations of 'alle
sechs Tagewerk' im Busen' and suggests that it ends – 'ich darf
nicht sagen, wie . . . ' As a matter of fact, he is paying him a
compliment. For only the union of the earthly and the divine, the
activation of mental concepts by biological drives and the
translation of vital energies into concerns of the mind gives birth
to creative Eros. This quest for creative Eros, in changing and ever
more sublimated forms, is the motivating power of Faust's life.
True, it culminates late, in his union with Helena, but the search
for creative wholeness of experience, though still unconscious,
already pervades the first part of the tragedy. It is the propelling
force in Faust's encounter with the Erdgeist, in the seclusion of his
study, as well as in *Wald und Höhle* which marks the water-shed
between a predominantly mental and a predominantly physical
participation in life, as well as in the final stages of the lovers' tragedy.
And everywhere it is articulated through the symbolism of water,
with its associations of renewal through flux and its overtones of
renunciation and the transcendence of what has been renounced in a
symbolic mode of experiencing.

Even at the nadir of Faust's existence, when he is about to take
his life, the imagery that springs to his lips tells us that the resolve
to die is in fact a positive decision; an attempt, however puerile
and regressive, to break through the aridity of his intellectual
world to the springs of life. As he reaches out for his phial, he says:

> Ich fasse dich, das Streben wird gemindert,
> Des Geistes Flutstrom ebbet nach und nach.
> Ins hohe Meer werd' ich hinausgewiesen,
> Die Spiegelflut erglänzt zu meinen Füssen,
> Zu neuen Ufern lockt ein neuer Tag.   (ll. 697ff.)

Even as he raises the poison to his lips, he greets the rising day in ecstasy:

> Der letzte Trunk sei nun, mit ganzer Seele,
> Als festlich hoher Gruss, dem Morgen zugebracht! (l. 735f.)

True, he envisages the risk 'ins Nichts dahin zu fliessen'. But here, as later on, in the invectives against life he will hurl at Mephisto in the Wager Scene, the images which rise unbidden to his lips themselves prove that nothingness, for one like him, is as inconceivable as shipwreck or eternal empty craving, and that already now he has the unconscious trust in his own creativeness which will make him say to Mephisto, much later on in the play:

> In deinem Nichts hoff' ich das All zu finden. (l. 6256)

For all the forms of failure which he envisages are formulated in terms of the imagery of water; and thus they become associated with the rejuvenating return to the elemental origins which makes him immune against despair and extinction.

And indeed, creative renewal does come to him 'aus eigner Seele', long before the rejuvenating draught has been prepared for him in the 'Hexenküche'.[31] It comes, as it comes to the poet of the first prologue, of *Hochbild, Äolsharfen,* and *Trilogie der Leidenschaft,* and as indeed it had come to the young poet of *Wonne der Wehmut*: through the solvent of tears. As, at the sound of the Easter bells, he recalls the fermentation of youth when

> . . . unter tausend heissen Tränen
> Fühlt' ich mir eine Welt entstehn . . . (l. 777f.)

he taps the springs of his creativeness and, in the act of doing so, is restored:

> Die Träne quillt, die Erde hat mich wieder! (l. 784)

It is this thawing of what had been brittle and congealed which meets his eye in *Vor dem Tor*:

> Vom Eise befreit sind Strom und Bäche
> Durch des Frühlings holden, belebenden Blick; (l. 903f.)

this renewed fluidity which finds expression in the vision of the setting sun where colours and contours run liquid into one another and he sees

> Den Silberbach in goldne Ströme fliessen. (l. 1079)

Again, in the crucial avowal of the Wager Scene Faust's creativity *a priori* cheats Mephistopheles of his part of the bargain:

> Aus dieser Erde quillen meine Freuden . . .   (l. 1663)

he declares, unmindful of the future; and we know that as long as there is fluidity, there is that incessant circulation of life[32] which the young Goethe had celebrated in *Mahomets-Gesang* and *Gesang der Geister über den Wassern* – a circulation which is proof against extinction and makes a mockery of Mephisto's nihilism, as indeed the Devil knows:

> Und immer zirkuliert ein neues, frisches Blut.
> So geht es fort, man möchte rasend werden!   (l. 1372f.)

It is true, the imagery of liquid is also associated with error, conflict and guilt. This link is struck early on in the tragedy, before Faust signs himself away to the Devil, long before the witch prepares the magic potion for the hero and the lovers administer the fatal sleeping draught to Gretchen's mother for their own desire's sake. Significantly, this connection with evil is forged at the moment when Faust steps forth from the seclusion of his study into a seemingly innocuous world. It is on their Easter walk 'vor dem Tor', that Faust tells Wagner of the drugs he brewed, with dubious aims and doubtful luck, together with his father, 'ein dunkler Ehrenmann',

> Der, in Gesellschaft von Adepten,
> Sich in die schwarze Küche schloss
> Und, nach unendlichen Rezepten,
> Das Widrige zusammengoss.   (ll. 1038ff.)

To be in league with the elements means to be alive, but also to flounder, 'ohne Ziel, noch Richte.' This is a danger of which the classical Goethe was keenly aware and indeed Faust and the Devil know it, too: Faust, when he reflects on the darker aspects of his past, musing:

> O glücklich, wer noch hoffen kann
> Aus diesem Meer des Irrtums aufzutauchen!   (l. 1064f.)

And Mephisto when, his puritanical client lulled to sleep by a song of the Spirits which is all fluid sensuality, he reveals the true purpose of the exercise, saying:

> Versenkt ihn in ein Meer des Wahns . . .   (l. 1511)

Faust himself dreads the surrender to the elemental weal and woe of living he so passionately seeks. He knows that to make a pact with what by its nature is transient, is bound to lead into dishonesty and guilt. He dreads to pledge himself, on the impulse of the moment, to the lure of the moment, in the measure in which he desires it. For how is it possible to be faithful to the moment – any moment, even the most fulfilled – when that moment is faithlessly speeding past? When, through the very intensity with which it is experienced, it threatens to become discontinuous? It is because he knows this danger that he is so unwilling to seal the pact with the Devil with his signature in blood as convention would have it:

> Ist's nicht genug, dass mein gesprochnes Wort
> Auf ewig soll mit meinen Tagen schalten?

he asks, and continues:

> Rast nicht die Welt in allen Strömen fort,
> Und mich soll ein Versprechen halten?   (ll. 1718ff.)

These are terrifying words. They bespeak the danger that lurks behind the uncommitted quest for sensibility and feeling: the lability and ultimate disintegration of experience which is sought, and prized, for its own sake. It is an artist's danger, the danger of dissolution – ever the price of living form – which threatens Tasso and Epimetheus and, in another way, the Brahmin woman of the *Paria* trilogy. They know it and Goethe knew it too, from early on in his life. Much later, he exposed it in the gruesome fragmentation of Epimetheus's grief even as it rises to his heart and lips:

> Pflückend geh ich und verliere
> Das Gepflückte. Schnell entschwindet's.
> Rose, brech' ich deine Schöne,
> Lilie, bist du schon dahin.

The earnest young professor, too, knows all about the fickleness of feeling. He knows, and dreads, the evanescence of the inspired moment:

> Das Wort erstirbt schon in der Feder . . .   (l. 1728)

He encounters it in his solitary quest for experience, long before he has loved and left Gretchen; and it is here and here alone, in the seclusion of his study that, for a few brief moments, he approaches the anguished cynicism of the libertine.

Thus, when Faust finally breaks with his past and takes the plunge into the elemental depths of time and life, when he exclaims:

> Lass in den Tiefen der Sinnlichkeit
> Uns glühende Leidenschaften stillen!
> In undurchdrungnen Zauberhüllen
> Sei jedes Wunder gleich bereit!
> Stürzen wir uns in das Rauschen der Zeit . . . (ll. 1750ff.)

we know, as indeed he does, that this leap will bring, not only a renewal, but a dying; not only the fullness of life, but also the wretchedness of betrayal and guilt.

Thus, the imagery he uses before ever he sets out onto his journey into life foreshadows the dissolution of selfhood he will experience as he enters Gretchen's little world:

> Mich drang's, so grade zu geniessen,
> Und fühle mich in Liebestraum zerfliessen!
> Sind wir ein Spiel von jedem Druck der Luft?
>
> Und träte sie den Augenblick herein,
> Wie würdest du für deinen Frevel büssen!
> Der grosse Hans, ach wie so klein!
> Läg', hingeschmolzen, ihr zu Füssen.   (ll. 2722ff.)

But it also adumbrates the verdict of guilt he will pronounce upon himself at the end of *Wald und Höhle* when he has found his separate identity again:

> Bin ich der Flüchtling nicht? der Unbehauste?
> Der Unmensch ohne Zweck und Ruh',
> Der wie ein Wassersturz von Fels zu Felsen brauste
> Begierig wütend nach dem Abgrund zu?   (ll. 3348ff.)

Indeed, the language Faust uses at the beginning of the drama already contains Gretchen's agony and his own, at its very end:

> Jammer! Jammer! Von keiner Menschenseele zu fassen,
> dass mehr als ein Geschöpf in die Tiefe dieses Elendes versank . . .
> *(Trüber Tag Feld,* ll. 23ff.)

III

At the beginning of Part II, the sleeping 'Unglücksmann' is washed clean of guilt and restored to life by 'Der Blüten

Frühlingsregen' and by a long immersion 'im Tau aus Lethes Flut'. And then the sight of the waterfall and the arc of the rainbow does something more for him. It raises him to a level of living which is altogether 'edler, würdiger, höher'[33] than the catastrophic immediacy of his existence in the first part of the tragedy had been. Faust no longer *is* the 'Wassersturz' as which he had seen himself in *Wald und Höhle*, rushing to wreck and ruin. He now *perceives* it from afar, and perceives it as a symbol of the life he feels pulsing in his own veins. For, as the torrent falls earthward and foams heavenward, it replenishes itself in a continual circulation:

> Von Sturz zu Sturzen wälzt er jetzt in tausend,
> Dann abertausend Strömen sich ergiessend,
> Hoch in die Lüfte Schaum an Schäume sausend. (ll. 4718ff.)

But high above this elemental cycle, more ethereal still,

> Wölbt sich des bunten Bogens Wechseldauer,
> Bald rein gezeichnet, bald in Luft zerfliessend,
> Umher verbreitend duftig kühle Schauer.   (ll. 4722ff.)

'Wechseldauer' – what a wonderful evocation of the creative mode with its fluctuating rhythm of form and transience and the freshness exuding from such fluidity! Time and again, in *Iphigenie* and *Wilhelm Meister* and in such late poems as *Phänomen, Hochbild* and *Äolsharfen* as well as here, Goethe has turned to the symbol of the rainbow to say the ultimate that poetic language can express about the creative mode of experiencing. Born where sun and water meet, the rainbow is element in its most spiritualised form. Not only does its arc form a bridge between heaven and earth, between the infinite and the finite, between the eternal and the ephemeral. Each drop of water, suffused with light, is a reflection of the colour spectrum in all but its totality.[34] And as it mirrors the spectrum upon the tiny area of its surface, each drop within the arc becomes a symbol of the infinite. Indeed, it is the symbol of the symbol. For is not the symbol 'ein im geistigen Spiegel zusammengezogenes Bild'?[35] More than that: the drop of water which reflects the spectrum symbolises the inborn creativity of human perception, and that in turn is symbolic of our spiritual creativity. Whenever the eye is affected by a given colour, we read in the *Farbenlehre*, it spontaneously produces its complement and thus, virtually, the spectrum in its totality.[36] This innate striving for totality on the part of the eye[37] mirrors, and reminds us of, a corresponding psychic tendency. It is 'der Wink, dass uns die

Natur durch Totalität zur Freiheit heraufzuheben angelegt ist'.[38]
Because eye and soul share a disposition towards totality, because
the eye, like the soul, resists the pathological one-sidedness of any
single affection, perception – and the perception at that of the
rainbow which so abundantly meets the eye's need for wholeness
– is fitted to be the archetypal symbol of creative totality.

Faust is able to perceive infinity in the raindrop because his
own eye is 'sonnenhaft'. And in the perceptual totality of 'des
bunten Bogens Wechseldauer' he is ready, now, to apprehend the
kindred phenomenon of his own creative totality, and in it 'das
menschliche Bestreben' *per se*. Now he can 'supplieren' wholeness
of experience where before he saw nothing but the here and now
of the blinkered moment. Now he can understand himself and the
world as a transparent symbol of the infinite:

> Am farbigen Abglanz haben wir das Leben.   (l. 4727)

But what, in the context of this phrase, does the word 'haben'
mean? We cannot grasp or hold life reflected any more than we
can grasp or hold the moonbeam or the rainbow. Creative
experiencing betokens an altogether new mode of 'having',
adumbrated in the final lines of *Zueignung* –

> Was ich besitze, seh' ich wie im Weiten,
> Und was verschwand, wird mir zu Wirklichkeiten.

and finally realised in Faust's union with Helena: a union neither
distant nor devouring, neither unreal nor real, but transcending
possession and renunciation alike in the transparency of the
symbolic 'Augenblick'.

Thus, by an organic development, the act which begins with a
Faust born into a symbolic mode of experiencing ends with his
invocation of Helena from the shades; and here, for the first time,
his figure is brought into open association with the aesthetic
sphere. To call up Helena, he must descend to the realm of the
'Mothers'. It is a return to the same solitude to which Faust had
already dispatched Knabe Lenker, allegorical representative of
poetry, bidding his 'dear son' there to create a world of his own.
As befits a mystic experience, which is ineffable, this solitude is
described in terms that come near to it yet fall short of it. And the
images in which Mephisto circumlocutes the experience which lies
ahead of Faust are the familiar ones of water:

> Und hättest du den Ozean durchschwommen,
> Das Grenzenlose dort geschaut,
> So sähst du dort doch Well' auf Welle kommen,
> Selbst wenn es dir vorm Untergange graut.

> Du sähst doch etwas. Sähst wohl in der Grüne
> Gestillter Meere streichende Delphine;
> Sähst Wolken ziehen, Sonne, Mond und Sterne –
> Nichts wirst du sehn in ewig leerer Ferne,
> Den Schritt nicht hören, den du tust,
> Nichts Festes finden, wo du ruhst.   (ll. 6239ff.)

Later on, Faust relates that his 'Schreckensgang' did indeed lead him

> . . . durch Graus und Wog' und Welle
> Der Einsamkeiten, her zum festen Strand.   (l. 6551f.)

But long before he says so we know that his voyage signifies an immersion into elemental depths. For his reply to Mephisto's ominous picture of the void he will face – 'in deinem Nichts hoff' ich das All zu finden' – takes us back to another journey he had attempted at the outset of the tragedy, when he had sought to die. There too he had faced the threat 'ins Nichts dahinzufliessen'; and his language had shown that nothingness, to him, in fact meant a rejuvenating surrender to the sustaining element. And indeed, a closer comparison of Faust's two voyages, the contemplated voyage into death at the beginning of Part I and the voyage to the Mothers here, at the beginning of Part II, may help us determine the meaning of this mysterious enterprise.

Thirsting for the breasts of nature and rejected by the Erdgeist, Faust decides to take his life. Reason and science, with all their complicated apparatus, have failed to open the door into the mysteries of nature:

> Ich stand am Tor, ihr solltet Schlüssel sein;
> Zwar euer Bart ist kraus, doch hebt ihr nicht die Riegel.
>
>   (l. 670f.)

Thus defeated, Faust resolves to break into the inner sanctuary of life through the doors of death:

> Vermesse dich, die Pforten aufzureissen,
> Vor denen jeder gern vorüberschleicht.
> Hier ist es Zeit . . .
> . . .
> Nach jenem Durchgang hinzustreben,
> Um dessen engen Mund die ganze Hölle flammt;   (ll. 710ff.)

The symbolism of this passage is transparent. Death is, as it were, a birth process in reverse. Faust is trying to force his way back into the womb of nature, in a desperate attempt to gain direct access to life. When, later on, he does find this access, it is through sexual communion with Gretchen.

> Mein Schoss, Gott! drängt
> Sich nach ihm hin.

sings Gretchen in the *Urfaust* (l. 1098f.); and presently she confesses: 'ich liess' dir gern heut nacht den Riegel offen' (l. 3506).

These simple words are crucial to the tragic action; they are also pregnant with all manner of association. They recall Faust's crude and vain attempt to force his way through the gates of life by intellectual means or even by suicide; they echo the 'Soldatenlied' he hears as he first emerges into life, 'Vor dem Tor', as well as the ribaldries he witnesses in 'Auerbachs Keller' – the first station on his journey:

> Riegel auf! in stiller Nacht.
> Riegel auf! der Liebste wacht.
> Riegel zu! des Morgens früh.   (ll. 2105ff.)

and they adumbrate Mephisto's serenade which results in the death of Gretchen's brother Valentin.[39] The deployment of the images 'Riegel' and 'Pforten', in fact, follows the same pattern which we have observed in connection with the imagery of water; it is first sounded in an intellectual context in the solitude of Faust's study, to become ever more erotically charged.

When Mephisto tells Faust about the realm of the Mothers, he resorts to the same imagery. He equips Faust with a key, a little thing which grows as he holds it in his hand and mysteriously strengthens and emboldens him:

> Wohl! fest ihn fassend fühl' ich neue Stärke,
> Die Brust erweitert, hin zum grossen Werke.   (l. 6281f.)

He tells him:

> Nach ihrer Wohnung magst ins Tiefste schürfen;   (l. 6220)

and bids him descend until he finds himself ' . . . im tiefsten, allertiefsten Grund' (l. 6284). But on *this* journey Faust will not encounter any bolted doors. Expressly Mephisto tells him:

> Nicht Schlösser sind, nicht Riegel wegzuschieben   (l. 6225)

and this modification both links the hero's present venture with his earlier ones and distinguishes it from them. For now the direction and the quality of Faust's quest have changed. He no longer seeks 'das Ewig-Weibliche' outside himself, through spiritual communion with Mother Nature or through sexual communion with Gretchen. He seeks it at its source,[40] in his own creative depth, and on *this* journey there are no walls left to penetrate, no doors to be unbolted and unlocked. At this moment, as he dares delve into the depths of his own being, the intellectual and the physical, the masculine and the feminine poles of his own being fuse and from the union of opposites springs 'ein Drittes, Neues, Höheres, Unerwartetes'[41]: creative Eros.

'The true analogy for creative process is not parthenogenesis, but bisexual creation.'[42] These words by Samuel Alexander apply as truly to Goethe's account of the creative act here as to his formulation of it in the 'Künstlergedichte' and in *Tasso*. As, in the poem *Sprache*, the poet's sword pierces 'der Urne Bauch'; as in *Künstlers Morgenlied* the style is both the impregnating organ and the organ of conception; as Tasso rests within his inner world and then breaks out, into the world of relationship, so it is here: conception and impregnation are united in one person and in one act. Armed with his glowing key Faust penetrates into the depths of his own being and there touches the glowing bowl of the tripod, a female symbol associated with the female personage of Pythia:

> Ein glühnder Dreifuss tut dir endlich kund,
> Du seist im tiefsten, allertiefsten Grund.
> . . .
> Da fass ein Herz, denn die Gefahr ist gross,
> Und gehe grad' auf jenen Dreifuss los,
> Berühr ihn mit dem Schlüssel! (ll. 6283ff.)

Thus Mephisto. And his instructions are borne out in the invocation scene which is visible to all:

> Der glühnde Schlüssel rührt die Schale kaum,
> Ein dunstiger Nebel deckt sogleich den Raum;
> Er schleicht sich ein, er wogt nach Wolkenart,
> Gedehnt, geballt, verschränkt, geteilt, gepaart.
> . . .
> Das Dunstige senkt sich; aus dem leichten Flor
> Ein schöner Jüngling tritt im Takt hervor. (ll. 6439ff.)

Similarly, a little later, from the same vapours, there emerges Helena herself.

We must not overlook, either in Mephistopheles's description of the voyage to the Mothers, or indeed in the invocation scene, the importance attaching to imagery of vapours, mists and clouds. All these are manifestations of water; what is more, they are manifestations of the element which most vividly testify to its capacity for metamorphosis: formation, transformation and the dissolution of what has formed, in an unending cycle. And mist and clouds, throughout Goethe's poetry – and certainly from the poem *Zueignung* onwards – signify, not only as Trunz suggests, 'das Leichteste des Irdischen, das Geistigste, Lichtdurchflossenste,'[43] but more specifically the creative state: on the one hand its fluidity, on the other the engrossment of the artist in his medium and the condensation, and clarification, of what was nebulous before.

Thus Faust's voyage to the Mothers is an immersion into his own elemental depths – 'in Graus und Wog' und Welle'; and this journey into himself initiates a long process of creation. When Helena's form has materialised from the drifting mists, he exclaims:

> Hab' ich noch Augen? Zeigt sich tief im Sinn
> Der Schönheit Quelle reichlichstens ergossen?   (l. 6487f.)

'Tief im Sinn': these words confirm what Mephisto's travel instructions had intimated – that Faust has descended into his own depth, to the creative matrix of his being where all is fertile flux, 'Gestaltung Umgestaltung', organic process waiting to invade matter so as to animate it into living form.

To retrieve 'die Schöngestalt' –

> Die Gestalt aller Gestalten,
> Welche die Sonne jemals beschien   (l. 8907f.)

– Faust must venture into the chaos that lies beyond the realm of forms, into the elemental flux which is the womb of life. But no sooner has he wrested form from flux than he must surrender it again, if he would stay alive. Faust knows it in advance when he says:

> Doch im Erstarren such' ich nicht mein Heil,
> Das Schaudern ist der Menschheit bestes Teil;
> Wie auch die Welt ihm das Gefühl verteure,
> Ergriffen, fühlt er tief das Ungeheure.   (ll. 6271ff.)

He has to learn it again, and more painfully, when Helena

vanishes from his grasp, both here and at the end of the third act. The lesson which Faust learns is the bitter truth of the artist, a truth which Tasso and Epimetheus endure, which Epimetheus' brother Prometheus rejects. It is the insight which came to Goethe in Italy and had to be relearned time and again, until the crisis of Marienbad and, indeed, until the last lines of Faust were written 'in einer Art von Wahnsinn'. By the inexorable law of creativeness, living form cannot be had, or held, in perpetuity.[44] Always it must be snatched from transience and elemental chaos and offered up again, and always the artist must endure the threat of disintegration and loss of identity which, at each reiteration of the word 'Mütter', strikes the hero with the force of a cudgel blow.

This emergence of living form from the elements and its return to the elements is the commanding theme of the second and third acts of *Faust II*. Indeed, one might say that the *Klassische Walpurgisnacht* celebrates the apotheosis of the element which up to now has been the hidden source of Faust's creativeness. For here, at last, the 'Lebensfeuchte' emerges as the hero of the cosmic pageant which is enacted before our eyes.

In this cosmogenic myth, the act of creation which had begun in the innermost recesses of Faust is projected outward and continues, visibly enacted in the hero's phantasy, in Homunculus and in a multitude of figures who seethe around these two searchers and help them in their quest.[45] In the phantasmagoria of this second act we do not see much of Faust; but the glimpses we get of him are sufficient to supply the thread of the inner action.

At first we see Faust unconscious in his study, scene of his long past intellectual endeavours. His place is taken by Wagner of whom Mephistopheles sardonically says:

> Die Schlüssel übt er wie Sankt Peter,
> Das Untre so das Obre schliesst er auf.   (l. 6650f.)

Thus, even before we witness the act, the imagery tells us that the Professor must be trying his hand at creation; and, indeed, presently we hear that

> Türpfosten bebten, Riegel sprangen . . .   (l. 6669)

And whilst, by dint of an awe-inspiring intellectual effort, Wagner produces his brain-child, Homunculus, we see the act of fullblooded creation bodied forth in two sensuous dream images. First, in the depth of Faust's unconscious there takes place the conception of Helena. Leda is visited by the swan:

> Sie setzt den Fuss in das durchsichtige Helle;
> Des edlen Körpers holde Lebensflamme
> Kühlt sich im schmiegsamen Kristall der Welle.   (ll. 6908ff.)

Conception begins with the willing immersion in fluid depths
which promise to engender form: 'Schmiegsames Kristall' – these
words spring from the same creative trust which was to find
unsurpassed utterance in the poem *Lied und Gebilde*. Here and
there the poet seems to indicate that form is latent in elemental
flux: 'Wasser wird sich ballen.'

Later on the act of conception is complemented by the act of
impregnation. In a trance-like vision, Faust sees the continuation
of his earlier dream. He sees Zeus immerse himself in wave and
woman:

> Einer aber scheint vor allen
> Brüstend kühn sich zu gefallen,
> Segelnd rasch durch alle fort;
> Sein Gefieder bläht sich schwellend,
> Welle selbst, auf Wogen wellend,
> Dringt er zu dem heiligen Ort . . .   (ll. 7301ff.)

It is from this twofold, bisexual experience – foreshadowed in
the attachment of bowl to key – that the creative Eros springs
which emboldens Faust to ask:

> Und sollt' ich nicht, sehnsüchtigster Gewalt,
> Ins Leben ziehn die einzigste Gestalt?   (l. 7438f.)

– which empowers him to bring Helena to life from her
shadow-like existence in the realm of archetypal forms. To a
symbolic life, certainly: neither real nor unreal, neither distant nor
near, but timelessly true – the life of a work of art.

This process of aesthetic creation is paralleled in the process of
organic re-creation which Homunculus has to undergo. Sprung
from an intellectual act, Homunculus himself has remained a
sexually indeterminate, disembodied spirit. In Wagner's cerebra-
tions sex has been discounted:

> Der zarte Punkt, aus dem das Leben sprang,
> Die holde Kraft, die aus dem Innern drang
> Und nahm und gab, bestimmt sich selbst zu zeichnen,
> Erst Nächstes, dann sich Fremdes anzueignen,
> Die ist von ihrer Würde nun entsetzt;   (l. 6840ff.)

But however much Wagner rails against sex and relegates it to the
realm of brutes, the delicacy of the words the poet has put onto

his lips tells us that he has left out of account more than he knows. 'Der zarte Punkt' – what a wonderful evocation this is of the act of love: the fusing, in *one* shared sentience, of male and female and even of the incipient life that springs from such togetherness. In endeavouring to bypass the organic ways of nature and to create life by dint of intellect alone, Wagner has fooled himself. He has *made* Homunculus, but he has not *created* him. And it is Homunculus himself who must now achieve his own creation, precisely as Faust must create Helena within himself. The child must become the father – and the mother – of the man; and Mephistopheles well knows this when he cuts short Wagner's farewell from his offspring, remarking *ad spectatores*:

> Am Ende hängen wir doch ab
> Von Kreaturen, die wir machten. (l. 7003f.)

But, however wanting Wagner's achievement be, is he not here enduring the fate of every creator, be it Tasso or Epimetheus or Nereus, or, indeed, Faust: to be bereft of his creation?

As Faust must re-experience the union of Leda and the swan in order to conceive Helena, so Homunculus must re-create the very antecedents of his life in order to 'become': he must achieve his own conception – breath-taking phantasy of a genius, who, born too late and under Northern skies, had to give birth to himself again in the classical South, and himself had to create the cosmos he was to inhabit. Like Faust on his way 'durch Graus und Wog' und Welle', and Leda stepping into the 'schmiegsamen Kristall der Welle', Homunculus must give himself up to the element, there to dissolve and be conceived; the flame of his spirit, like Leda's 'holde Körperflamme', must enter the 'Lebensfeuchte' to be bodied forth: for

> Alles ist aus dem Wasser entsprungen!!
> Alles wird durch das Wasser erhalten!
> Ozean, gönn uns dein ewiges Walten.
> Wenn du nicht Wolken sendetest,
> Nicht reiche Bäche spendetest,
> Hin und her nicht Flüsse wendetest,
> Die Ströme nicht vollendetest,
> Was wären Gebirge, was Ebnen und Welt?
> Du bist's, der das frischeste Leben erhält. (ll. 8435ff.)

But, like Faust and Zeus, Homunculus's spirit must be drawn by the sight of beauty born of the elements to entice him into such a *Stirb und Werde*.

As Faust's inner creation of Helena comprises both poles, masculine and feminine, of his being, so Homunculus's creation of himself is twofold and bisexual: it means Homunculus *and* Galatea, flame *and* water, impregnatory excitement *and* conception, the piercing of his glassy self *and* its inception in the element. For only from the merging of male and female, of the mental and the physical poles of life, does creative Eros spring. The intellectuality of the study – Faust's study as much as Wagner's – remains barren, Homunculus remains a construct and Helena a chimera until the full force of physical experience, fused with all the powers of the spirit, issues in a true begetting and conceiving. On the other hand, even biological 'becoming' cannot be achieved without that *Selige Sehnsucht* which tempts the footloose spirit into the finality of conception and embodiment. This continuum of the physical and the mental aspects of experiencing, this secret identity of the laws which govern aesthetic and organic 'becoming' is the overarching theme of the first three acts of *Faust II*.[46] Of these, Act II, written last, is the structural centre, for it is here that the several threads meet and interweave. In this act the biological basis of Faust's creative quest is reflected, and magnified, in Homunculus's search for embodiment; on the other hand, the Eros which is operative in Homunculus's bid to 'become' is reflected and magnified in Faust, who 'mit verrückten Sinnen' wanders through the orgiastic night, inflamed with the 'einzigste Gestalt' he has glimpsed.

To celebrate organic and artistic creation as one mystery was natural for a poet who believed 'dass die höchste und einzige Operation der Natur und Kunst die Gestaltung sei',[47] who at the sight of classical works of art could exclaim, overwhelmed: 'Diese hohen Kunstwerke sind zugleich als die höchsten Naturwerke von Menschen nach wahren und natürlichen Gesetzen hervorgebracht worden. Alles Willkürliche, Eingebildete fällt zusammen, da ist die Notwendigkeit, da ist Gott.'[48] Artistic creation has its roots deep in natural process. Like Helena's and Homunculus's conception, it depends on the surrender of form to the flux of elemental forces. Such dissolution issues in a 'becoming.' But it is also a dying. Nereus loses Galatea no sooner than he has glimpsed her; Homunculus, his glassy shell dissolved, vanishes out of our sight and Faust will once again lose his creation to the element whence he retrieved her, after a timeless moment of fulfilment.

None the less, Goethe, at the end of the *Klassische Walpurgisnacht*, was able to give praise to the elemental force which dissolves as it creates and to Eros who inflames the living with *Selige Sehnsucht* and entices them into the 'seltne Abenteuer' of creation:

So herrsche denn Eros, der alles begonnen!
Heil dem Meere! Heil den Wogen,
Von dem heiligen Feuer umzogen!
Heil dem Wasser! Heil dem Feuer!
Heil dem seltnen Abenteuer!   (ll. 8479ff.)

IV

Helena, pinnacle of art and nature, steps into life moist from the element:

Vom Strande komm' ich, wo wir erst gelandet sind,
Noch immer trunken von des Gewoges regsamem
Geschaukel, das vom phrygischen Blachgefild uns her
Auf sträubig-hohem Rücken, durch Poseidons Gunst
Und Euros' Kraft, in vaterländische Buchten trug.   (ll. 8489ff.)

Gradually, out of the welter of figures and forms that had drifted through the *Klassische Walpurgisnacht,* the 'Gestalt aller Gestalten' crystallises: the Grecian queen, self-sufficient and composed, in speech and bearing alike. Yet from the beginning she is surrounded by uncertainty and forebodings of sacrifice; and before long Phorkyas has undermined her sense of her own reality until, after an annihilating crisis, not unlike that of Faust at the beginning of *Part II,* she accepts the symbolic status of her experience and her very being. Now she is ready for Faust as Faust is ready for her. The transformation she has undergone is perhaps illuminated more clearly by the words which she speaks as she embarks on her encounter with Faust than by her famous cry –

Ich schwinde hin und werde selbst mir ein Idol.   (l. 8881)

Following Phorkyas, although she knows her to be a 'Wider-dämon', she says:

was die Königin dabei
Im tiefen Busen geheimnisvoll verbergen mag,
Sei jedem unzugänglich.   (ll. 9075ff.)

These words bring to mind the lines from the Paria Legend:

Was ich denke, was ich fühle,
Ein Geheimnis bleibe das.

And indeed, they betoken a similar change: the breakthrough to a

metaphysical dimension of life, brought about by the encounter
with elemental chaos; the shuddering recognition, even before
Helena has met Faust and merged her being in his, that life will
disturb the inviolateness of its containment.

The reckless lyricism of Lynkeus, the watchman, ushers in a
symbolic merging of two separate personalities, ages, and cultures;
and this is reflected in the loosening up of the classical metres, first
into blank verse and then into increasingly musical cadences. It is
significant that the flowing over into one another's being which is
symbolised by the lovers' use of rhyme should be accomplished
when Faust, true to his Faustian self and his creativeness, asks the
question:

> Und wenn die Brust von Sehnsucht überfliesst,
> Man sieht sich um und fragt –   (l. 9379f.)

It is in reply to Faust's 'überfliesst' that Helena discovers her
own answering rhyme and, with it, the communion of love. She
completes his question, continuing for him:

> wer mitgeniesst.

The fusion is completed, and articulated in terms of the dominant
symbolism. Perhaps nowhere else in the whole drama do we find
such a delicate interweaving of related imports. Which is the
symbol here, and which is the thing symbolised? Is it enough to
say, as critics have done, that the marriage between rhyming
words symbolises the marriage between Faust and Helena which
is being consummated, almost, before our very eyes? Or does not
this passage derive its resonance from the fact that Helena's and
Faust's discovery of one another equally serve to symbolise the
solitary bliss of the poet as he experiences sound yielding to sound
and word to word? At such a peak of poetry, 'how can we know
the dancer from the dance?'

As one would expect, imagery of fluid pervades the description
of Arcady and of the cave in which Faust's and Helena's marriage
is consummated:

> Tust du doch, als ob da drinnen ganze Weltenräume wären,
> Wald und Wiese, Bäche, Seen; welche Märchen spinnst du ab!
>
> (l. 9594f.)

the Chorus asks; to which Phorkyas replies:

> Allerdings, ihr Unerfahrnen! das sind unerforschte Tiefen . . .
>
> (l. 9596)

But immersion in elemental depths means creation and dissolution in one. It means the birth and death of Euphorion,
epitome of the genius of poetry, means his surrender to elemental
passion and his self-destruction. The identity of Euphorion, son of
Faust and Helena, with Knabe Lenker and his association with
Lord Byron has been spelt out by Goethe and is a critical
stock-in-trade. What seems to have escaped critics is the association of Euphorion and Knabe Lenker with Goethe's own Tasso,
through the caterpillar symbolism shared by all three and extended even to Helena; for when, in Arcady, Faust for the third
and last time returns to the mystery of Helena's birth, he recalls
how

> . . . mit Eurotas' Schilfgeflüster
> Sie leuchtend aus der Schale brach . . .   (l. 9518f.)

The gifts tossed into the air by Knabe Lenker –

> . . . der Poet, der sich vollendet,
> Wenn er sein eigenst Gut verschwendet   (l. 5574f.)

– turn into 'frevle Schmetterlinge' when they are caught. And of
Euphorion we are told that, no sooner than he was born, he
disentangled his limbs from the constriction of his swaddling
clothes, as Hermes had done before him,

> .   . . . die purpurne,
> Ängstlich drückende Schale
> Lassend ruhig an seiner Statt;
> Gleich dem fertigen Schmetterling,
> Der aus starrem Puppenzwang
> Flügel entfaltend behendig schlüpft,
> Sonnedurchstrahlten Äther kühn
> Und mutwillig durchflatternd.   (ll. 9654ff.)

Thus the three figures closest to the hero are linked with a
symbol which unequivocally associates them with the aesthetic
mode. In the chapter on *Tasso*, we have observed the crucial
importance attaching to the caterpillar symbol.[49] Through it, more
than through any other image complex, the poet-hero articulates
the nature and tragedy of the creative artist. It signifies the
rooting of artistic creativity in elemental drive, the sacrifice, in the
making of art, of a stable human form and, last but not least, the
independence of the created product from its creator. Here, the
association of this symbol with Helena and Faust's two 'sons'
bespeaks their loss, long before Euphorion cries the fatal words:

> Doch! – und ein Flügelpaar
> Faltet sich los!
> Dorthin! Ich muss! ich muss!
> Gönnt mir den Flug!   (ll. 9897ff.)

– words so reminiscent of Tasso's wish

> Im neuen Sonnental die Flügel rasch
> Und freudig zu entfalten –

and spoken long before Helena disappears.

The creator is doomed to suffer a *Stirb und Werde*, to surrender back to the elements the form he has wrested from the elements: as Tasso is bereft of the Princess and of the poem which had been his shelter and his strength, so too Helena vanishes from the sight of Faust, her garments dissolve into clouds, 'Gestaltenreiche, bald Gestaltenlose,' and her servants return to the fluid element there to live on as sap and wave and stream and wine.

But the most significant aspect of the caterpillar symbolism is its association with Faust himself. Not only does he become linked with the sphere of artistic creativity in that his most cherished creations are linked with it. He himself is explicitly connected with it, both at the outset of his creative phase, at the beginning of *Part II,* and at the very end: in *Anmutige Gegend,* the spirits had sung to him

> Schlaf ist Schale, wirf sie fort!   (l. 4661)

and in the last scene of all the Selige Knaben will welcome Faust, in words which take us back to Euphorion's birth:

> Freudig empfangen wir
> Diesen im Puppenstand;
> Also erlangen wir
> Englisches Unterpfand.
> Löset die Flocken los,
> Die ihn umgeben!
> Schon ist er schön und gross
> Von heiligem Leben.   (ll. 11981ff.)

And, indeed, the symbolism is taken up in Gretchen's final words:

> Sieh, wie er jedem Erdenbande
> Der alten Hülle sich entrafft
> Und aus ätherischem Gewande
> Hervortritt erste Jugendkraft.   (ll. 12088ff.)

Thus, at the very last, Faust is once again associated with the mode of artistic creativity and its *Stirb und Werde*. But that is after the end of his mortal span. And it is to his dying that we must now turn.

V

When Helena vanishes from the sight of Faust, her veil and her garments stay behind. Presently, they dissolve into clouds which surround Faust and, drawing him upward, disappear with him. Mephistopheles interprets the true meaning of this event when he says:

> Die Göttin ist's nicht mehr, die du verlorst,
> Doch göttlich ist's. (l. 9949f.)

Faust has lost his creation, it is true. But he has not lost his creativeness.[50] The symbols of veil and cloud, for Goethe always associated with the creative state, tell us so. A solitary and even tragic figure, he is none the less enveloped in the element and sustained by contact with it; he is sheltered, like the poet in *Harzreise im Winter* for whom the speaker pleads:

> Aber den Einsamen hüll
> In deine Goldwolken!
> Umgib mit Wintergrün,
> Bis die Rose wieder heranreift,
> Die feuchten Haare,
> O Liebe, deines Dichters!

like the young Tasso who says:

> Still ruhet noch
> Der Zukunft goldne Wolke mir ums Haupt. (II, 3)

like the speaker of *Zueignung* for whom poetry is a veil

> aus Morgenduft gewebt und Sonnenklarheit.

It is not necessary to be young as these poets are to be wrapped in a golden cloud of creativeness. Rather the obverse is true. It is contact with the creative element which rejuvenates and even conquers death. Has Faust not summoned up a cloud-wreathed Helena twice, from death and from antiquity? And does not the force of creative Eros empower Euphrosyne to return from the shades, enveloped in a cloud, to instil her desire for living form into the poet? Both, she and he, are symbols of the brief and grievous passage of the artist from formlessness to formlessness, like the 'bewegte Gebilde' of the clouds which announce Euphrosyne's coming and her going.

Euphrosyne leaves the poet beneath the 'höchsten Gebirgs beeisten zackigen Gipfeln', distraught, yet creative. When, at the beginning of Act IV, Faust appears once again, he too finds himself face to face with the 'starre, zackige Felsengipfel' of the 'Hochgebirg'. But he steps out of the sheltering cloud,

> Entlassend meiner Wolke Tragewerk, die mich sanft
> An klaren Tagen über Land und Meer geführt.   (l. 10041f.)

Once more, 'der Einsamkeiten tiefste schauend unter meinem Fuss', he, like the poet in the elegy *Euphrosyne,* sees love and loveliness pass by in the changing forms of clouds, 'sich wandelnd, wogenhaft, veränderlich': first the sculpted splendour of Helena, then the frail beauty of Gretchen. Once more, at the memory of his first loving, he is renewed:

> Des tiefsten Herzens frühste Schätze quellen auf . . .   (l. 10060)

but then the cirrus cloud rises upward into the ether

> Und zieht das Beste meines Innern mit sich fort.   (l. 10066)

To be sure, these lines point forward to the last words of the play, and thus to Faust's final rebirth. But for the time being they intimate a separation. Even as he has dismissed the carrying cloud, so he now dismisses 'das Beste meines Innern': the 'Ewig-Weibliche' within him. The speaker in *Euphrosyne* had given himself over to the fructifying influx of love and grief. Faust, standing on the same granite, opts for what is permanent. As he feels *terra firma* once more, his heart – the heart 'des jüngsten, mannigfaltigsten, beweglichsten, veränderlichsten, erschütterlich-sten Teiles der Schöpfung' – turns to the security 'des ältesten, festesten, tiefsten, unerschütterlichsten Sohnes der Natur.' As he takes leave of the cloudy shapes which have borne him to this spot, it is as if one heard him say words spoken much earlier by his creator when he was emerging from the fertile flux of youth: '. . . man gönne mir, der ich durch die Abwechslungen der menschlichen Gesinnungen, durch die schnellen Bewegungen derselben in mir selbst und in andern manches gelitten habe und leide, die erhabene Ruhe, die jene einsame stumme Nähe der **grossen, leise sprechenden Natur** gewährt, und wer davon eine Ahnung hat, folge mir.'[51]

It is the last time that we see Faust thus, 'ausgesetzt auf den **Bergen des Herzens'.**[52] It is also the last time that he uses the symbolism of water to evoke those ranges of experience with which it has been linked throughout the tragedy: love and creativeness, entwined from the beginning and, at the peak of the drama, fusing into that creative Eros which has empowered him to summon up 'die einzigste Gestalt'.

No sooner has Faust dismissed the cloud, than he conceives his next and final ambition which he duly confides to Mephistopheles. It is his ambition to conquer the sea:

> Mein Auge war aufs hohe Meer gezogen;
> Es schwoll empor, sich in sich selbst zu türmen,
> Dann liess es nach und schüttete die Wogen,
> Des flachen Ufers Breite zu bestürmen.
> Und das verdross mich; wie der Übermut
> Den freien Geist, der alle Rechte schätzt,
> Durch leidenschaftlich aufgeregtes Blut
> Ins Missbehagen des Gefühls versetzt. (ll. 10198ff.)

The simile he uses confirms what we already know from the cumulative force of meaning that has accrued to the imagery of water at this stage of the drama: the surging of the sea has an inner significance for Faust, 'den freien Geist, der alle Rechte schätzt'. This self-characterisation strikes a new, and strange, note. One thinks one hears Antonio taunting Tasso when the young poet approaches the older man, ready

> sich dem Bessern
> Vertrauend ohne Rückhalt hinzugeben!

only to receive the retort: 'Du gehst mit vollen Segeln!' And indeed, as we look more closely, the association begins to gain in significance and weight. A similarity in the movement of the two dramas begins to reveal itself. For just as Tasso, having defined the nature and destiny of the artist in terms of the symbol of the caterpillar, veers in the face of catastrophe and restates them in terms of the uncontrollable sea,[53] so here, in *Faust.* Faust too had been associated with the caterpillar symbol both directly (at the very beginning and the very end of the second part) and indirectly, through his connection with his most cherished creations:

Knabe Lenker, Helena and Euphorion. But now he has lost
Helena and Euphorion, as Tasso has lost his poem; and as Tasso
has relinquished his cocoon so he has dismissed the sheltering
cloud; and now, the catastrophic potentialities of the creative
mode burst on him, the trauma of disintegration which is the
conditio sine qua non of creativeness; and at this point Faust veers
exactly as Tasso had done before him. The disastrousness of
elemental chaos is what has gripped his mind and his dread of it
has become epitomised in the senseless surging of the sea.[54]
'Leidenschaftlich,' the hero continues his description of what so
perturbs him:

> Sie schleicht heran, an abertausend Enden,
> Unfruchtbar selbst, Unfruchtbarkeit zu spenden;
> Nun schwillt's und wächst und rollt und überzieht
> Der wüsten Strecke widerlich Gebiet.
> Da herrschet Well' auf Welle kraftbegeistet,
> Zieht sich zurück, und es ist nichts geleistet,
> Was zur Verzweiflung mich beängstigen könnte!
> Zwecklose Kraft unbändiger Elemente!   (ll. 10212ff.)

And thus it is that he conceives his plan:

> Erlange dir das köstliche Geniessen,
> Das herrische Meer vom Ufer auszuschliessen,
> Der feuchten Breite Grenzen zu verengen
> Und, weit hinein, sie in sich selbst zu drängen.
>
>   (ll. 10228ff.)

Can we believe it: Faust here denounces as 'unfruchtbar' and
'zwecklos' the element which has been the sustaining power of his
creativeness, the element Goethe had extolled in 'Felsbuchten des
Ägäischen Meers,' written in 1830, only a few months before Act
IV was finally taken in hand. 'Die Lebensfeuchte', 'diese holde
Feuchte' in which Gretchen's child was born, in which Helena was
conceived, in which Homunculus achieved embodiment, is now
rejected. It has become 'der wüsten Strecke widerlich Gebiet'; and
the aged hero whose creativeness throughout the play had been
associated with the fluidity of the element now craves only one
thing: to constrict and conquer that no man's land which
stretches between the peaks of creativity and which, for all its
amorphousness, is the breeding ground of life:

> Das herrische Meer vom Ufer auszuschliessen,
> Der feuchten Breite Grenzen zu verengen
> Und, weit hinein, sie in sich selbst zu drängen.

Only a few times in his life did Goethe speak of water with the unconcealed revulsion which informs these lines; perhaps on half a dozen occasions in all. Each is significant in itself and each is linked, moreover, with a definite stage in the development of the theme with which we are here concerned. Water and its associated forms becomes the epitome of the destructive forces at work in *Die Natürliche Tochter*, a tragedy conceived under the impact of the French Revolution and concerned more urgently than any other work of Goethe's with the creative trauma of loss and disintegration. In this unfinished drama, written around the turn of the century, we find the following description of the islands to which Eugenie is to be banished:

> Der Sonne glühendes Geschoss durchdringt
> Ein feuchtes, kaum der Flut entrissnes Land,
> Um Niederungen schwebet, giftgen Brodems,
> Blaudunstger Streifen angeschwollne Pest. (IV, 2)

To these words Eugenie replies:

> Entsetzen rufst du mir hervor! Dorthin?
> Dorthin verstösst man mich! In jenes Land,
> Als Höllenwinkel mir von Kindheit auf
> In grauenvollen Zügen dargestellt.
> Dorthin, wo sich in Sümpfen Schlang und Tiger
> Durch Rohr und Dorngeflechte tückisch drängen,
> Wo, peinlich quälend, als belebte Wolken
> Um Wandrer sich Insektenscharen ziehn,
> Wo jeder Hauch des Windes, unbequem
> Und schädlich, Stunden raubt und Leben kürzt. *(Ibid.)*

Does not such imagery – there is plenty of it and it is not any one character's, but the poet's own – bespeak the deeper reason why this tragedy defied completion? The very sources of creativity are poisoned because, in a paroxysm of rigidity, the poet shunned the fluidity which is the price of living form. True, this most resolutely classical of Goethe's dramas was written at a time when he was undermined by grave illness and still shaken by the terrors of the French Revolution. But this is not what it is 'about'. It is 'about' the trauma of being creative in the face of cataclysmic events, both within and without, conditions which made the exposure exacted by the creative act too hazardous.

Never has Goethe expressed such terror at vital process as here, in *Die Natürliche Tochter*. The anguish at a precious creation *stepping forth* into being and appearing in the world when such a step is tantamount to being delivered over to the forces of disintegration – this is the essence of the play. The anguish experienced in that play by the Duke, Eugenies' father, reflects Tasso's twofold anguish: anguish at his creation relinquishing him, its creator, and at the inexorable breaking up, within himself, of the creative configuration from which it had sprung.

Here is the central conception of Goethe's unfinished tragedy – a tragedy concerned, ultimately, with the hazards of the aesthetic mode; and it is nothing separate from or outside of the precarious frame in which it was envisaged. If ever a work of literature was 'about' itself, that is to say about the creative constellation in which it was conceived and – in this instance – aborted, this is. Can we wonder that the ensuing work of art was fragile in the extreme and doomed to remain a fragment? Why should we not accept Goethe's own retrospective explanation that he could not nurse the tragedy to completion because he had committed the unforgivable blunder 'mit dem ersten Teil **hervorzutreten,** eh' das Ganze vollendet war'?[55] This explanation is satisfying in that, with unerring verbal precision, the poet links the total import of this work – which *is* about the implications of *stepping forth* – with the creative mould in which it took shape, reminding us of the dancer in the dance;[56] and indeed, in the tragedy itself, this connection is confirmed by the slant given to the imagery with which we are here concerned.[57]

The link with Faust? We may remember that, at that very time, that is to say around 1800, Goethe claims to have first conceived those scenes of Act V which are concerned with Faust's conquest of the sea and which culminate in the hero's death;[58] and, more striking still, that at that time the poet envisaged Faust as planning to drain some inland marshes rather than to give battle to the open sea. His last speech, in that earlier version, began thus:

> Dem Graben, der durch Sümpfe schleicht
> Und endlich doch das Meer erreicht,
> Gewinn ich Platz für viele Millionen.

And, indeed, a trace of this earlier plan is discernible in Faust's final speech as we know it. For here, too, his culminating ambition is not to tame the open seas but to cleanse the land of the very last remnants of contaminated waters:

> Ein Sumpf zieht am Gebirge hin,
> Verpestet alles schon Errungene;
> Den faulen Pfuhl auch abzuziehn,
> Das Letzte wär' das Höchsterrungene.   (ll. 11559ff.)

Does not a link between these two conceptions suggest itself? Again, the crisis of Marienbad precipitated verse imbued with the same agonised abhorrence which Faust expresses at the sight of the sea. Not only the *Paria* trilogy in which water comes to symbolise recesses of the soul that are tragically and grotesquely at odds with the 'obere Leitende', disruptive of the very human form. There is also the tormented outcry, towards the end of the *Marienbader Elegie*, as the poet discovers that, in the agony of parting from his beloved, everything disintegrates, even his image of her:

> Wie könnte dies geringstem Troste frommen,
> Die Ebb und Flut, das Gehen wie das Kommen?

Just over a year later – at the beginning of 1825 – while the memory of this was still fresh, floods disastrously swept the coasts of the North Sea. With scarce-concealed excitement, the poet refers to this catastrophe in his *Versuch einer Witterungslehre*. 'Es ist offenbar', he writes

> dass das, was wir Elemente nennen, seinen eigenen wilden wüsten Gang zu nehmen immerhin den Trieb hat. Insofern sich nun der Mensch den Besitz der Erde ergriffen hat und ihn zu erhalten verpflichtet ist, muss er sich zum Widerstand bereiten und wachsam erhalten. Aber einzelne Vorsichtsmassregeln sind keineswegs so wirksam, als wenn man dem Regellosen das Gesetz entgegenzustellen vermöchte, und hier hat uns die Natur aufs herrlichste vorgearbeitet, und zwar indem sie ein gestaltetes Leben dem Gestaltlosen entgegensetzt.
> Die Elemente daher sind als kolossale Gegner zu betrachten, mit denen wir ewig zu kämpfen haben . . . Die Elemente sind die Willkür selbst zu nennen.[59]

During the very days in which he wrote these reflections, Goethe's diary records his preoccupation with *Faust II*; and indeed we know that it was in 1825 that the plan to have his hero drain inland marshes finally gave way to the plan to have him give battle to the open sea.[60]

Thus we may say that Goethe's rare allusions to water in an entirely negative vein stem from the dread of elemental forces within and without he felt at moments of personal crisis or in the face of natural or political upheaval; and the connection of such references with the changing character of Faust's 'kolossale Gegner' seems assured.

But what, in the *Faust*-tragedy itself, can be the meaning of the

abrupt reversal of significance the symbolism of water has undergone?

We stand on the threshold of the *Herrschertragödie*. Faust's
ambition to rule the waves is enunciated in a wider context. He
wants to rule, and rule for the sake of ruling. Expressly he says to
Mephistopheles:

> Wer befehlen soll,
> Muss im Befehlen Seligkeit empfinden.   (l. 10252f.)

And indeed, the whole of Act IV with its confused and seemingly
irrelevant action – the war for supremacy waged between 'Kaiser'
and 'Gegenkaiser' – is the externalisation of a struggle that is
waged within the hero's soul. Here, as in Act II – these were the
last two acts to be written – the poet relied on the reader 'der sich
auf Miene, Wink und leise Hindeutung versteht'.[61] In these acts,
more than anywhere else, he left his meaning implicit, resorting to
the technique ' . . . durch einander gegenüber gestellte und sich
gleichsam ineinander abspiegelnde Gebilde den geheimeren Sinn
dem Aufmerkenden zu offenbaren.'[62] The political scene is a
mirror magnifying Faust's endeavour to enthrone within himself
the rule of consciousness and will. Such correspondence between
inner and outward events is illuminated in an interesting way.
The state is likened to an organism, within which every individual
and party are the constituent organs or limbs. Faust himself
resorts to this metaphor in the speech in which he dissuades the
Emperor, as the head of the *corpus commune*, from fighting his battle
in person.[63] By the use of such metaphors the diffuse political
whole is scaled down to the dimension of the single organism, and
its large destinies are seen to be the reflections of individual
psychic events. The fact that Faust sides with the Emperor, with
the help of the 'drei Gewaltigen' – 'aus Urgebirgs Ur-
menschenkraft' – signifies the change that has come over him. It
reflects his identification with 'das obere Leitende' in himself, and
his endeavour to establish the conscious rule of the will over what
is elemental and defies control. Symbolically to represent Faust's
reconstitution of himself after the Helena tragedy, to show the
re-organisation of his psyche – so exposed in its creativeness – ,
and to hint at a final hardening, indicated by his association with
the 'allegorische Lumpen' from their volcanic depth: this is the
main business of Act IV; for only in the light of such an inner *tour
de force* could the hero's death become explicable. And beside the
urgency of that task, the importance of the contemplated *Beleh-
nungsszene*, in which Faust was formally to receive the coastal strip
from the Emperor, was bound to pale; it was never written.

VI

Faust, a hundred years old as we encounter him in the final act, has achieved his ambition. He is an autocratic ruler. He has conquered chaos within and without. He has claimed an empire from the rule of the sea and has colonised and peopled it. His palace, set in ornamental gardens intersected by a large and linear canal, is the geometrical centre of a world-wide net of power. Everything terminates there. Ships from the farthest horizon enter his harbour laden with his goods. Faust, it seems, has achieved his goal.

But he has lost something, and we know what it is before he himself puts his finger on what is missing in his life. We know it – and critics have pointed this out – from the very setting in which we find him, juxtaposed as it is to the setting and at- mosphere of the opening scene of the act. It has been well ob- served that 'Offene Gegend', with its open sea, its dunes and the archaic simplicity of its figures contrasts with Faust's 'Ziergarten' and its competent and straight canal in the same way as the archetypal world of *Die wunderlichen Nachbarskinder* contrasts with the petrified mode of life and the artificiality of park and ponds in *Die Wahlverwandtschaften*.[64] In the plot of that novel, as in Faust's coastal empire, we see nature 'als Garten . . . behandelt,' as Philemon so innocently puts it.[65] The three ponds, once upon a time arbitrarily sliced off a mountain lake, are arbitrarily restored to their natural appearance. And the elements strike back. Mocking the precautions of the ever-busy landscape gardeners, the pond, in the end, swallows up Charlotte's son, fruit of a passion that has become alienated from the natural order of things. Neither the child Otto nor indeed the two men whose name. it shares are renewed through their contact with the element. No one in this world has the capacity to be reborn, except Ottilie, 'das himmlische Kind', whose dying, by the purity of her acceptance, does become a creative *Stirb und Werde* in its most sublimated form; least of all the Major to whom such a rebirth was granted in his youth.

And just as, in *Die wunderlichen Nachbarskinder,* contact with the strongly flowing and dangerous stream is life-giving where in the main body of *Die Wahlverwandtschaften* the stagnant waters of the pond signify death, so it is here, in Faust. Only exposure to the elemental strata of life will yield life, and such a return is denied to those who approach them in the spirit of a controlled experiment. Faust has removed himself from the elemental force with which Philemon and Baucis live. It is a perilous sea – the

figure of the once ship-wrecked Wanderer reminds us of that –
and yet it is to that very sea that the Wanderer turns as he gives
thanks for his rescue:

> Und nun lasst hervor mich treten,
> Schaun das grenzenlose Meer;
> Lasst mich knieen, lasst mich beten,
> Mich bedrängt die Brust so sehr.   (ll. 11075ff.)

And rightly so. For does not his 'grauses Abenteuer' recall the
young Faust's own readiness to surrender himself to the elemental,
even at the risk of ship-wreck and, if necessary, death? Does it not
recall Faust's 'Schreckensgang' to the Mothers, 'durch Graus und
Wog' und Welle', and indeed does it not recall the 'seltne Abenteuer' of creation, Homunculus's conception and the conception of
Helena in Faust which is hailed at the end of the *Klassische
Walpurgisnacht*? Intercourse with elemental nature is perilous but
life-giving and the three figures of *Offene Gegend* know it. True,
Philemon praises Faust's achievement:

> Das Euch grimmig missgehandelt,
> Wog' auf Woge, schäumend wild,
> Seht als Garten Ihr behandelt,
> Seht ein paradiesisch Bild.   (ll. 11083ff.)

But the irony of this 'behandelt' is patent. What mortal dare
manipulate nature as Faust does? Besides, Philemon is an old
man, all passion spent. His remaining span is short and his vitality
is on the wane. So old is he indeed that even when Faust came,
he was too enfeebled to help him claim the land from the sea:

> Und wie meine Kräfte schwanden,
> War auch schon die Woge weit.   (l. 11089f.)

By their unconscious ambiguity, these words hint at a connection,
other than of simultaneity, between the ebbing of strength and
the retreating of the element. They are puzzling and they linger
on in the mind.

   And yet, in every deeper sense, the old couple have remained
close to nature. Not only the old woman who, more conscious of
her natural heritage than Philemon and more sceptical of Faust's
technological wonders, distrusts the 'Wasserboden' and exhorts
her husband to remain true to their age-old values and their
simple ways: but Philemon himself just as much. Baucis's first
words to the Wanderer are about him:

> Lieber Kömmling! Leise! Leise!
> Ruhe! lass den Gatten ruhn!
> Langer Schlaf verleiht dem Greise
> Kurzen Wachens rasches Tun. (ll. 11059ff.)

These lines, written by an old man close to death about an old man close to death, take us across the span of half a century, back to Goethe's early manhood and to the most radiant image of youthful splendour he ever wrought. They take us to the words Egmont speaks to his secretary, a young man old at heart:

> Kind! Kind! nicht weiter! Wie von unsichtbaren Geistern gepeitscht, gehen die Sonnenpferde der Zeit mit unsers Schicksals leichtem Wagen durch; und uns bleibt nichts, als mutig gefasst die Zügel festzuhalten und bald rechts, bald links, vom Steine hier, vom Sturze da, die Räder wegzulenken. Wohin es geht, wer weiss es? Erinnert er sich doch kaum, woher er kam. (II, *Egmonts Wohnung*)

Egmont knows that we come from unconsciousness and return to unconsciousness. And not only from the unconsciousness of birth and infancy to the unconsciousness of senility and death. Every day we emerge from the unconsciousness of sleep and dream and every night we return there. Every morning, Apollo's chariot, on its cosmic course, drawn by the sun-steeds of time and whipped along by invisible spirits, arises out of the vastness of the sea, every evening to immerse itself in its depths. Sleep and unconsciousness, the sun-steeds, the invisible spirits and the sea – these are different cyphers for one and the same thing: the elemental forces that carry our lives and yet elude our conscious will. It is his very acknowledgement of these forces which assures Egmont's mastery of life, to the point where mastery is possible. Margarete and Alba chafe at the elements they would control. And this is why they fail to be the masters of their destiny. Margarete hopes 'dass sich alles unter ihr sanftes Joch gelassen schmiegte, dass . . . die widrigsten Elemente sich zu ihren Füssen in sanfter Eintracht vereinigten' *(ibid.)*. Yet she knows that elements cannot be controlled, and there is abdication in her words: 'O was sind wir Grossen auf der Woge der Menschheit? Wir glauben sie zu beherrschen, und sie treibt uns auf und nieder, hin und her' (I, *Palast der Regentin*). Alba dreams that he can chart 'weite Meere nach einer vorgezognen Linie,' but reality refuses to match his blueprint. Oranien does not walk into his trap, and Alba must concede defeat:

> So zwingt dich das Geschick denn auch, du Unbezwinglicher! Wie lang gedacht! Wie wohl bereitet! Wie gross, wie schön der Plan! . . . Wie in einen Lostopf greifst du in die dunkle Zukunft: was du fassest, ist noch zugerollt, dir unbewusst, sei's Treffer oder Fehler!
>
> (IV, *Der Culenburgische Palast*)

By his own admission Egmont is a sleepwalker, 'welcher' –
Goethe loved this description by Angelika Kauffman – 'durch sein
ganzes Leben gleichsam wachend geträumt . . . [und] zuletzt
noch gleichsam träumend wache'[66]: and it is because he lives from
the resources of his unconscious and entrusts himself to the
carrying element of his life – to sleep and dreams, to the power of
love, even to his horse – because he knows when it is time to think
and to see and when it is time to stop thinking and seeing, that
he lives strongly and swiftly and, above all, creatively. He knows,
and accepts, that

> We are such stuff
> As dreams are made on, and our little life
> Is rounded with a sleep.[67]

It is because of this vitalising interaction between his conscious
and unconscious drives that he can say, at the end: 'Ich höre auf
zu leben, aber ich habe gelebt'; words by an artist at living which,
from afar, echo Lynkeus's praise of the poetry of life.

In the Faust of Act V this balance is destroyed, a development
for which the previous act has prepared us. The Faust who has
banished the sea in which Egmont's sun-steeds nightly refresh
themselves is a figure in whom the synthesis between conscious
and unconscious forces has been tragically disrupted. He has
deprived himself of the carrying force of his creativeness.[68] He now
craves to be all-seeing, all-conscious and all-controlling. He is
masculine consciousness personified. That is why he grudges
Philemon and Baucis their little home:

> Dort wollt' ich, **weit umherzuschauen,**
> Von Ast zu Ast Gerüste bauen,
> Dem **Blick** eröffnen weite Bahn,
> Zu **sehn,** was alles ich getan,
> Zu **überschaun mit einem Blick**
> Des Menschengeistes Meisterstück . . .   (ll. 11243ff.)

What an obsessional emphasis on perception! And how far we
have moved from the 'Geistermeisterstück' of an earlier Faust
who, out of musical mists, summoned up Helena's perfection, and
indeed from the 'Webermeisterstück' of the beginning,

> Wo *ein* Tritt tausend Fäden regt,
> Die Schifflein herüber hinüber schiessen,
> Die Fäden **ungesehen** fliessen,
> *Ein* Schlag tausend Verbindungen schlägt . . .[69]   (ll. 1924ff.)

This is creation: the weaving together of a thousand unseen threads in the fluid depths of the unconscious mind; and we may note in passing that Goethe was once again to use this, his favourite image of the warp and the weft, a year after he composed the ominous opening of Act V, in the last letter of his life in which he deals with the interlacing of conscious and unconscious in the creative act. But of that presently.

Faust knows that his all too conscious 'Menschengeistes Meisterstück' is *vanitas vanitatum*. There is something beyond his dominion and it eludes 'des allgewaltigen Willens Kür' (l. 11255). The fragrance of the lime-trees and the chiming of the churchbell from across the dunes torment him as the surging of the sea had done: 'was zur Verzweiflung mich beängstigen könnte!' They torment him because they remind him of what he has lost: the renewing power of the tears he had wept at the sound of the Easter bells, long ago, the power to refresh himself in the flux of feeling, the perilous and creative contact with the springs of his being which had sustained his life: the capacity and the courage for a *Stirb und Werde*.

It is this Faust, brittle and cut off from the sources of his vitality in the endeavour indefinitely to push back the frontiers of consciousness and will, who is destined to encounter Sorge. He had met her before, that Easter Sunday in his youth, and he had recognised her nature and the secret of her power;

> Die uns das Leben gaben, herrliche Gefühle,
> Erstarren in dem irdischen Gewühle.   (l. 638f.)

But then she had not been able to touch him. His tears, and the renewal they had brought, had washed her clean away. In that Easter night, he had intuitively known – as Egmont knows – that Sorge is the incapacity to surrender the self and to be resurrected through such a surrender. With an insight strange in one so young, he had diagnosed this blighting of the soul:

> Und was du nie verlierst, das musst du stets beweinen.
>
>   (l. 651)

But then, this had not been a real danger. He had been ready to surrender himself to death, to the Devil, to the joys and sorrows of loving Gretchen and Helena and Euphorion, their son. And he had stayed creative and alive. Now, after their loss, 'der Einsamkeiten tiefste schauend unter meinem Fuss', Faust has ceased to expose himself to the perilous flux of feeling. In the name of safety, peace and permanence – a permanence which grows ever more precarious as the clock is ticking away and the sands of time are running out – he has sealed off the source of his creativeness. He has conquered the ocean, and ringed all around by his possessions, the centenarian stands before us, unwilling to yield to transience, barren, brutal and bereft of love. He is all masculine consciousness[70] and the world around him, creation of his conscious will, is barren too. There is nothing left to surrender, and nothing to surrender to. He has succeeded in conquering the sea, in pushing it back 'far into itself':

> Und, weit hinein, sie in sich selbst zu drängen.   (l. 10231)

But in doing so, he has dug his own grave. By a supreme irony the 'Graben' which is to extract the last bit of moisture from the last bit of marsh turns out to be his 'Grab'.

Thus, drained of his resources and drawn off from his 'Urquell', Sorge can strike at his roots[71] and he is ready for death. But not for the Devil. For the first breath of extinction restores him, not indeed to creativeness, but to a creative vision of the world. As Sorge blinds him, he once again perceives the truth by which he had abided all his life: intercourse with the elemental forces within us and without is the condition of any existence that deserves to be called human and creative.[72] The spaces he has opened up will enable millions

> **Nicht sicher** zwar, doch tätig-frei zu wohnen
>
> . . .
>
> Das ist der Weisheit letzter Schluss:
> Nur der verdient sich Freiheit wie das Leben,
> Der **täglich sie erobern** muss.
> Und so verbringt, **umrungen von Gefahr,**
> Hier Kindheit, Mann und Greis sein tüchtig Jahr.
>
> (ll. 11564ff.)

In the end, Faust transcends the delusion that consciousness is all. He returns to a creative vision of life which, on its heroic scale, echoes Egmont's acceptance, and reflects the wisdom of old age voiced at the outset of the act:

> Langer Schlaf verleiht dem Greise
> Kurzen Wachens rasches Tun.

Wakeful activity, ringed by the elemental, on the alert against its inroads, yes; but also in creative contact with it: for the elements are the cradle of life.

As he dies, Faust is already preparing for another *Werde*. In accepting the life-giving power of the elements, at the very last, he is well on the way to shedding his 'Puppenstand',[73] a form grown so brittle that he must truly die; he is ready to be rejuvenated in the give and take of heavenly love. 'Wie gut ists dass der Mensch sterbe um nur die Eindrücke auszulöschen und gebadet wieder zu kommen',[74] Goethe had written to Charlotte von Stein from Ilmenau, years before, in an image which links death as a release from consciousness with the renewal that submergence in the elemental flux brings; and now *die Liebe von oben* can redeem Faust, because he has redeemed 'das Ewig-Weibliche' within his depths.

Goethe composed the unearthly poetry of the last choruses in December 1830, some four months before he wrote the opening scenes of the final act. He wrote those ominous scenes with his eyes wide open. He wrote them, not so much to supply the crime that would fit the punishment meted out to Faust in the encounter with Sorge. As Kommerell and Staiger have convincingly argued,[75] neither remorse nor a sense of guilt in any ordinary meaning of that word play any part in that reckoning. The opening scenes of the act, rather, are concerned with formulating the biological trauma of aging, the inexorable waning of creative vitality and the endeavour to protect what life there is left against the threat of disintegration; they portray man's hardening in the face of extinction, the fight for preservation at any cost, even at the risk of inner death. Of this trauma Sorge, and Death whose approach she heralds, are but the organic symptoms.[76]

This death of creativeness the poet, close to death himself, fashioned into poetry in the dying of Faust. It is a near-death he himself had experienced many times in his life; and at times he had barely survived. He had experienced it before his flight to Italy, after Schiller's death and perhaps even during the time of their friendship; and then again after the disaster with Ulrike von Levetzow.

It is perhaps the surpassing miracle of Goethe's life, that, for all the vulnerableness of his psychic organisation and for all the complexity of his inner world, a cosmos needful of order and peaceful stability if it was to be preserved, the poet dared, to the last, to expose himself to the elemental strata whence his creativeness sprang. As Max Kommerell says: 'Dichterisch ist es, sich zu bergen, indem man sich grenzenlos aussetzt.'[77] Others besides Goethe have done this. What is uniquely Goethean is that he enlisted the help of consciousness to achieve this creative venture. He developed consciousness to a degree unknown in any artist of his rank; to a pitch where the man could admonish the poet in him, saying:

> Gebt ihr euch einmal für Poeten,
> So kommandiert die Poesie . . .   (l. 220f.)

and, remembering that he had once said so, get on with the job and finish *Faust* before time ran out. But unlike Faust in the opening scenes of the final act, he never wielded consciousness as a destructive weapon. He used it to guard, guide and to enhance the unconscious activity of his inborn genius. He used it to foster the mystery of that elemental force, but never to supplant it.

This is the burden of Goethe's last two letters to Wilhelm von Humboldt, which incessantly circle around the interlacing of conscious and unconscious in the creative act, or as he calls it, in the last words to flow from his pen, around 'diese Geheimnisse des Lebens'. The first of these letters is written at the end of his work on *Faust,* towards the close of the year which had seen the composition of the final choruses, had yielded Act IV and had ended with the writing of the opening scenes of Act V – the Philemon and Baucis sequence.[78] Goethe begins by expressing his joy at his friend's recovery from serious illness. 'Schon durch die öffentlichen Blätter, verehrter Freund, unterrichtet', he writes, 'dass der Wellenschlag jener wilden Ostsee auf die Organisation des teuersten Freundes einen so glücklichen Einfluss geübt, hab ich mich höchlich erfreut und dem so oft verderblichen Gewässer alle Ehre und Reverenz erwiesen.' 'Von meinem Faust', he writes later on in the same letter,

> ist viel und wenig zu sagen; gerade zu einer günstigen Zeit fiel mir das Diktum ein:
>
> > Gebt ihr euch einmal für Poeten,
> > So kommandiert die Poesie;
>
> und durch eine geheime psychologische Wendung, welche vielleicht näher studiert zu werden verdiente, glaube ich mich zu einer Art von Produktion erhoben zu haben, welche bei völligem Bewusstsein dasjenige hervorbrachte, was ich jetzt noch selbst billige, ohne vielleicht jemals in diesem Flusse wieder schwimmen zu können, ja was Aristoteles und andere Prosaisten einer Art von Wahnsinn zuschreiben würden.

The poet then recounts the difficulties of rounding into a coherent whole a work conceived so many decades back and composed so intermittently, and especially the difficulty of finding the right moment to part with it:

> . . . bis ich endlich für rätlich hielt auszurufen:
> Schliesset den Wässrungskanal, genugsam tranken die Wiesen.

Some fifteen weeks later, in what was to be the last letter from Goethe's hand, the poet once more addresses himself to his friend.[79] He recapitulates the themes which over the past year have cropped up time and again, in his letters and in his conversations. He speaks of his spasmodic mode of production and the resultant gaps between the 'most interesting parts' of Faust on which he had concentrated; at his friend's request, he once again returns to the mode of productivity of which he had spoken in his earlier letter. He explains that this is the result of a life-long schooling, enabling him, at last, to interlace 'Bewusstsein und Bewusstlosigkeit . . . wie Zettel und Einschlag, ein Gleichnis das ich so gerne brauche', and to blend 'in einer freien Tätigkeit', yet 'ohne Bewusstsein', 'das Erworbene mit dem Angebornen, so dass es eine Einheit hervorbringt welche die Welt in Erstaunen setzt.' In the case of his *Faust* he confesses that he was forced, in the end, to achieve 'dasjenige durch Vorsatz und Charakter . . . , was eigentlich der freiwillig tätigen Natur allein zukommen sollte'. Yet so perfectly attuned to one another's needs are genius and skill that he feels sure that no one will be able to tell where spontaneity ended and effort began. Once again he refers to his bitter-sweet resolve to leave his *Faust* manuscript sealed, thus denying himself the pleasure of sharing it with his friends; for 'meine redlichen, lange verfolgten Bemühungen um dieses seltsame Gebäu würden schlecht belohnt und an den Strand getrieben, wie ein Wrack in Trümmern daliegen und von dem Dünenschutt der Stunden zunächst überschüttet werden.'

These last documents are inestimable for the light they shed on Goethe's mode of productivity; to us they are of especial importance for the hints they supply towards the understanding of the colonisatory activities of the centenarian hero and his dying. For images of water recur no less than four times in these two letters; and they point to the very areas of experience with which we have found them to be associated all along in *Faust,* up to the point where Helena vanishes and the hero resolves to give battle to the sea. Here, too, water means renewal: like the Wanderer at the opening of the fifth act of *Faust II,* the poet gives reverence and praise to the 'so oft verderblichen Gewässer' of the sea. They have restored his friend to life and health. Here, too, water signifies creation. The word itself implies what the context states explicitly: 'hervorbringen' presupposes an immersion into the changing element; and although to Aristotle and other prose writers, such an immersion might appear as a kind of madness, it yet leads to something of enduring value and is as indispensable to productiveness as 'Bewusstlosigkeit' is to 'Bewusstsein,' and as the warp is to the weft. And here, too, images of water tell us something about the life of the created product: life springs from a saturation with moisture; indeed, its very permanence rests on the depth of its immersion in the fluid element. Prematurely remove it from its native environment and cast it ashore, and it will be choked beneath the barren sands of time.

These letters were written at the very time when Goethe completed the last portions to be written of *Faust II* – the fourth act in which Faust conceives the ambition to conquer the sea and fights for the land from which he will wage war on it, and the first scenes of the fifth act which show him as master of the element. Is it coincidence that, during the weeks in which the sea emerged as the true antagonist of the centenarian hero, the poet should speak of his own creativity in terms of the self-same images, the images of water, and use them with all the weight and reverence which has accrued to them throughout *Faust* and, indeed, throughout his poetry? To the end of his life, water, for Goethe, remained what it had always been – the sustaining element of his creativeness. It was only when he had given his life to his creation and equipped it, 'wie ein ausgestattetes Kind',[80] that he weaned it from his waning strength and tenderly decreed:

Schliesset den Wässrungskanal, genugsam tranken die Wiesen.

Perspectives

It is time to draw some tentative conclusions from the materials I have laid before my readers and to ask the question on which I touched in the introductory remarks, a question around which every single chapter in this book has more or less openly revolved: what were the artistic conditions under which Lessing's genius was sparked off creatively in such a manner that his own misgivings about his creative status were allayed, at least in the act of writing? And analogously, what was the artistic configuration most apt to release Goethe's genius to the full?

As one would expect, this liberation took place in radically different configurations of external and internal circumstances. What emerges from the preceding pages is that Lessing achieved the breakthrough to his genius when, undeflected by the wave of irrationality which swept him off his course in *Emilia Galotti,* he found his true poetic inspiration in the values of the conscious mind to which he was committed. It is paradoxically the vision, passionately embraced, of human reason answering divine reason, which set his language on fire and generated that creative white heat in which ideas and images, inspiration and expression, meet, melt and merge to be forged into one henceforth indivisible whole. Lessing, it seems, needed the reassuring framework of a reasonable subject-matter approached in a reasonable cast of mind to achieve a full release of his creativity. *Emilia Galotti* has less fire than *Laokoon,* and it took the unprepossessing subject of an elderly Jew pledged to sweet reason to make the creative sparks fly and to accomplish that rare literary phenomenon – charm. It would seem that only when Lessing approached the creative act with such inner safeguards, could he allow himself as it were to fall, without his knowledge, into an intuitive and even unconscious mode of art-making. The congruence, in *Minna* as well as in *Nathan,* between *Gehalt* and *Gestalt* – in both plays both are circular; the wealth of formal relations through which *Nathan der Weise* articulates the deeper strata of its import; last but not least, the concreteness of the insights gleaned through the poet's encounter with his verbal medium, insights often foreign to the author's own intellectual temper: all these would suggest that the formative processes kindled in Lessing by the 'right' kind of material were of

a highly intuitional order and, in part at least, unconscious. To
the eternal gain of posterity Lessing proved not to be correct when
he said, in the epilogue to the *Hamburgische Dramaturgie*: 'Ich bin weder
Schauspieler, noch Dichter. Man erweiset mir zwar manchmal die
Ehre, mich für den letztern zu erkennen. Aber nur, weil man mich
verkennt . . . Ich fühle die lebendige Quelle nicht in mir, die durch
eigene Kraft sich empor arbeitet, durch eigene Kraft in so reichen, so
frischen, so reinen Strahlen aufschiesst: ich muss alles durch Druck-
werk und Röhren aus mir herauf pressen.' Let W. B. Yeats make the
responses to this hard-pressed poet. 'Art', he writes, ' . . . shrinks
from all that is of the brain only, from all that is not a fountain
jetting from the entire hopes, memories, and sensations of the
body.' We have seen this fountain spouting with a jet that is
strong and pure; we have overheard the soliloquy Lessing held
with himself in creative moments, a soliloquy conducted through
operational symbols such as rings and riches and love and, indeed,
water, going out into the world and returning, enriched, to their
source, in an effortless and abundant circulation. We know that
he was wrong, and it is one of the aims of this book to disprove
his harsh self-characterisation from the most intimate evidence at
the critic's disposal – the poet's words in the poet's works.

Goethe, on the other hand, accomplished the decisive breakthrough to his creative depths when he learned to handle
materials that welled up from his subconscious mind, and learned
to handle them in an intuitive and even unconscious fashion. This
is the way – we have seen it – in which he transcended what he
knew to be the creative defect of his first *Götz*. This is the burden
of the sentence which concludes his letter to Herder: ' . . . wenn
Schönheit und Grösse sich mehr in dein Gefühl webt, wirst du
Gutes und Schönes thun, reden und schreiben, **ohne dass du's
weisst, warum.**' From that early point of his career onward to the
end of the second *Faust*, he never wavered in the conviction that
the creative act is essentially unconscious, 'dass alles, was das
Genie als Genie tut, unbewusst geschehe.' This knowledge is
implicit in work upon work and it is overtly expressed in innumerable statements ranging over every phase of his development. His whole relation to Schiller, both during the years of their
friendship and in the retrospect of age, derives its complexion
from this inner sureness. Goethe fended off his friend's over-
consciousness with the same poise and protectiveness, both of his
own and the other's best interests, of which he had already shown
himself capable in his youthful contacts with Herder.

Nevertheless, to say that Goethe came into his own when he
allowed himself to be unconscious would amount, at the best, to

a half-truth. Such a description would not begin to account for the daring feats of intellect which went into the making, not only of such openly didactic works as *Die Metamorphose der Pflanzen, Die Metamorphose der Tiere* or *Wilhelm Meisters Wanderjahre,* but also of *Die Wahlverwandtschaften, Der West-Östliche Divan, Faust II,* and even of a relatively early poem such as *Wandrers Nachtlied II.* The fascination and the essential modernity of the idiom of much of Goethe's later work are inseparable from the high degree of reflective consciousness which is the very warp of its fabric: psychological and scientific knowledge, knowledge of different cultures, manners, literatures and religions. But all such knowledge the poet allowed to lapse into unconsciousness when it was necessary. He was able to 'forget' it so that his creative energies could seize upon it afresh and weave it into a many-coloured texture, intimate and objective, simple and strange, lyrical and urbane in one. This is why his poetic personality is as fraught with 'world' as it is, and why its frontiers seem to expand beyond the bounds of any one individual, however catholic.

The movement of these two writers' minds then seems to proceed in opposite directions: Lessing's from an uneasy flirtation with unconsciousness to an unashamedly conscious stance in which, at the last, he found true creative spontaneity; Goethe's from initial consciousness to an unconsciousness strong and secure enough to carry an ever more formidable intellectual freight.

Comparisons are at best problematic; they become offensive when they labour the obvious. In the case of Lessing and Goethe, it need hardly be said that Goethe's genius emerges as incomparably the greater of the two, both in the quantity of his output and in its poetic quality. I would suggest that the difference between the two poets lies in the depth from which their poetic experience springs and in the depth at which language itself becomes imbued with this experience. To make this dual statement is really to say one and the same thing. For the quality of conception and the quality of expression in art are, as I have tried to show all along, interdependent factors within one and the same creative configuration. To say this implies a modification of the hypothesis I put forward towards the end of Chapter 10. As a corrective to wrong-headed aesthetic thinking, we are well advised to term an experience an *Urerlebnis* if only it springs from an intense involvement of the artist with his artistic medium; but the extent of such an involvement will in fact be interdependent with the kind of conception to which the poet exposes himself in the first place. We saw that in the second *Götz* it took the conception of organic being, pursued to its psychosomatic depth, to release a poetic language itself structured at an organic level. Equally, it took an organically structured idiom to release, and articulate, the poet's conception as it finally emerged. This 'somatic' character of Goethe's language was henceforth to remain the mark of his greatest poetry, and this is a quality which Lessing's language never remotely approached. Nevertheless, with different and less sensitive tools, Lessing too, in *Minna von Barnhelm* and *Nathan der Weise,* succeeded in creating that autonomous semblance of life which is the hallmark of art. It is for this reason not inappropriate to speak of genius in the case of both poets, however differing in calibre, to seek to define the distinctive character of each and to identify the creative configuration most conducive to its functioning.

But there is yet another reason for treating of Lessing and Goethe in one volume, side by side. Let me try to put my point like this. Herder has argued that the mark of poetry is its untranslatability. Its specific virtue lies in its form. This insight flowed from his conception of language as an organically structured body. You cannot reassemble a body in another substance without violating its life. As Susanne Langer well puts it, it is the 'many-sided involvement of any element with the total fabric of the poem . . . [which] gives it a semblance of organic structure; like living substance, a work of art is inviolable; break its elements apart, and they no longer are what they were – the whole image is gone.' In one sense then we may say, as Herder said two hundred years ago, that the test of a work of art is that it does *not* survive translation, that is to say, the dismemberment of its linguistic body and the breaking up of such innumerable links as language establishes between every part and every other part, and indeed between every part and the whole. So fine an organisation could not survive so radical an operation. On the other hand it has been argued, and rightly, that the measure of a certain kind of greatness in art is precisely that it *will* survive translation into a foreign tongue. T. S. Eliot writes: ' . . . the European poet is not necessarily a poet whose work is easier to translate into another language than that of poets whose work has significance to their fellow-countrymen.' But he adds the rider: 'his work is more translateable only in this way: that whereas in the translating of such a poet as Shakespeare, into another language, just as much of the original significance is lost, as is lost when we translate a lesser English poet, there is also more saved – for more was there.' Indeed, Goethe took up an even more radical stance, and the value judgement he makes is of especial relevance to Lessing whose verse is so easily translated – into another language or, indeed, into German prose. In *Dichtung und Wahrheit* he writes: 'Ich ehre den Rhythmus wie den Reim, wodurch Poesie erst zur Poesie wird, aber das eigentlich tief und gründlich Wirksame, das wahrhaft Ausbildende und Fördernde ist dasjenige was vom Dichter übrig bleibt, wenn er in Prose übersetzt wird. Dann bleibt der reine vollkommene Gehalt*, den uns ein blendendes Äussere oft, wenn er fehlt, vorzuspiegeln weiss, und wenn er gegenwärtig ıst, verdeckt.' (III, 11.)

I would suggest that 'more' of the kind that survives translation 'was there' both in the case of Lessing's *Nathan* and of Goethe's *Faust* than in the instance, say, of Kleist or even Hölderlin. And this is the deepest reason why I treat of these two authors in one book – a volume which really clamours to be complemented by a study, along similar lines, of Schiller.† These three most luminous stars in the firmament of German letters are classical, and reach European stature, by no means only because of the richness of their innate artistic endowment. In the case of Lessing this is patently not so. Hölderlin and Kleist were blessed with much more prodigious poetic gifts than Lessing could ever muster; and Schiller, too, would fare badly on such a count alone, with the possible exception of his great tragic trilogy. But Hölderlin and Kleist did not invest their talents usuriously and so, in the end, for all their staggering genius, they remain parochial, outside the main stream of the great European tradition. Lessing, Goethe and Schiller, on the other hand, exploited what they were given; like Lessing's own Nathan, they did so by engaging in a vigorous two-way traffic, between self and world and also between art and life. That they could do so is due, in no mean measure, to a felicitous historical configuration permitting each to realise his full creative potential. And about this it is necessary still to say a word or two.

These three men were heirs to the Age of Enlightenment, with its unshakeable faith in the primacy of universal reason and in a will geared to its persuasions. They were also heirs to a cult of feeling, quietly practised at first by the Pietists who kept the mainsprings of creativity flowing beneath the sands of the Enlightenment, and then becoming itself a religion in the *Sturm und Drang*. Thus they had a double legacy, one intellectual and the other emotional. Lessing, Goethe and Schiller were at their height at the point of confluence of these two streams. At this historical moment the burning task felt by the best was the education and

---

* AGA (x, p. 540) misprints this word as *Gestalt*.
† *Cf.* my forthcoming books *Schiller's Drama: Talent and Integrity* and *Schiller: A Master of the Tragic Form. His Theory in His Practice.*

enlightenment of feeling and impulse, in an endeavour to make their vitality available to the purpose of mature living. It is no accident that some of the most acclaimed manifestos of the humanistic era – *Iphigenie, Nathan der Weise, Fidelio* and *The Magic Flute* – should circle around the theme of deep yet essentially non-erotic feeling-relationships leading to the betterment of humanity. But education and enlightenment of feeling, what is this if not the central challenge facing the artist? As Susanne Langer puts it: 'What discursive symbolism . . . does for our awareness of things about us and our own relation to them, the arts do for our awareness of subjective reality, feeling and emo-tion; they give inward experiences form and thus make them conceivable.' And, more sweepingly still: 'Art education is the education of feeling . . . ' whilst 'Bad art is corruption of feeling'. Susanne Langer here stands firm and square on ground mapped out and won by the German classicists, and she would be the last to deny her dependence upon the pioneer work of Schiller in his letters *Über die ästhetische Erziehung des Menschen.* But Schiller, although the most theoretically explicit of the great triad, himself stood upon ground claimed and prepared by his two elders. We have seen how Lessing's *Nathan* draws its fire from the knowledge that depth of feeling is inseparable from enlightenment of the spirit; and I hope I have convinced my readers that it is not only the fire of its ideas but of its words which springs from this liberating experience. And we have seen how Goethe's whole life, from the first to the last, circled around the problem, posed to him by his time, of reconciling in a creative synthesis the claims of reason and instinct, of deliberation and spontaneity, of conscious and unconscious.

Thus, Lessing, Goethe and Schiller wrote within an unques-tioned frame of moral endeavour. The historical hour demanded the integration of man's intellectual and emotional drives. Young and vigorous impulses, uncovered by the *Sturm und Drang,* were clamouring to be integrated with the rationality cultivated by the Enlightenment. Within this frame, art had a definite role to play and a definite place to occupy. The deepest moral promptings of the age coincided with the prompting which makes men produce art – the impulse to understand and formulate the inner life of feeling: and from this coincidence the best drew their strength.

It is because Schiller recognised the monistic implications of art-making that he felt compelled to put forward a theory of art which is at the same time a moral theory of education: and the enlargement of vision he thus gained in turn fructified the import and structure of his mature poetry. It is because Goethe felt organic process to lie at the root of art-making that he burrowed out the laws of organic process in nature, and such scientific insight in turn fertilised his mature art. And finally, it is because Lessing, like Schiller, divined the unitary message at the heart of the creative experience, that he was able to conceive of art as an exemplar of divine Creation; and the knowledge of such significance was instrumental in creating the incomparable serenity which informs every page of *Nathan der Weise,* a play which Goethe himself did not tire of praising as 'das höchste Meisterstück menschlicher Kunst'.

That these poets did not live in an aesthetic vacuum is attested by the range and integration of their activities. Lessing was a critic, aesthetician and theologian side by side with being a poet; Goethe a man of action and a highly original scientist; and Schiller an aesthetician of the first rank and a historian. In every case, their art-making enhanced their other activities and was enhanced by them in turn. There is nothing compartmentalised about their poetry. For all their keen awareness of the creative process and for all the fact that this process itself was precipitated into their art and preserved in it, there is no sign of effeteness about this intercourse between creator and creation. To be sure, they wrote about their art; but they had something beside their art to write about, because their art-making itself was fed by energies geared and committed to the ideal of a mature humanity. Such a commitment resulted in an invigorating circulation between life and art which kept both sound and whole. This integration of life qualities and aesthetic qualities it is which puts these writers into a class all on their own and makes them great figures on the European scene. They instilled into their art a human substance born of the sturdy interaction of life and art. It is this which survives any translation of *Nathan* as surely as it survives, together with much besides, any translation of *Faust.* Such substance is the fruit of an inner maturity which perhaps could only ripen in the sun of a rare and fortunate historical configuration. It is in virtue of this human displacement that *Nathan der Weise,* for all its evident poetic shortcomings, stands as a solitary sublime peak next to Goethe's *Faust*; as Jaspers and Dilthey have recognised, the two wisest dramatic poems which Germany has given to the world.

NOTES

NOTES

AGA   Artemis Gedenkausgabe   ⎫

HA   Hamburger Ausgabe   ⎬ of Goethe's works

Ak   Akademie-Ausgabe   ⎭

LM   Lachmann-Muncker Ausgabe (3rd ed.) of Lessing's works

DVLG	*Deutsche Vierteljahrsschrift für Literaturwissenschaft und Geistesgeschichte*
GLL	*German Life and Letters*
GR	*Germanic Review*
JbdGS	*Jahrbuch der Goethegesellschaft*
JbdDSG	*Jahrbuch der Deutschen Schillergesellschaft*
JEGP	*Journal of English and Germanic Philology*
JFDH	*Jahrbuch des Freien Deutschen Hochstifts*
MH	*Monatshefte* (Wisconsin)
MLN	*Modern Language Notes*
MLR	*Modern Language Review*
Mod. Phil.	*Modern Philology*
N	*Neophilologus*
NRu	*Die Neue Rundschau*
PEGS	*Publications of the English Goethe Society*

1. *'Emilia Galotti:* The Vision and the Way'

1. This, however, is by no means the universally accepted view. W. Oehlke interprets Conti's words as the credo of the Southern artist, saying: 'denn dieses [i.e. das Licht] malt, tief in die Seele blickend, nicht die Hand' *(Lessing und seine Zeit,* Munich, 1919, Vol. II, p.155). W. Kraft sees 'eine tiefsinnige Auffassung der Kunst' in these words. He argues that Conti does not intend to say that Raphael would have become the greatest painterly genius, had he been born without hands: ' . . . diese paradox formulierte Bedingung entspringt dem Paroxysmus der Begeisterung, die da zu wissen glaubt: für den, der sich bemüht, kommt es nicht auf die Hand an, sondern auf den Maler . . . nicht auf die Technik, sondern auf das Urbild der Kunst . . . Denn im Urbild ist alles vorhanden, wovon die durch Technik bewirkte Ausführung der Spiegel und doch nicht die Entsprechung ist.' ('Emilia Galotti', *NRu 1961, Vol. 72,* p.229)

2. This was pointed out by Ernst Feise *('Emilia Galotti* and Goethe's *Werther', Mod. Phil.* 75, 1917-18, p.332) and Julius Petersen ('Goethe und Lessing', *Euphorion 30,* 1929, p.182).

3. This significance, however, has often been denied. The presence of *Emilia Galotti* on Werther's desk has been accounted for by the fact that Jerusalem – on the description of whose death Goethe modelled the closing pages of *Werther* – was found dead with the book by his side. *Cf.* Max Herrmann, *Goethes Sämtliche*

Werke, JA, XV, p.395; Oskar Walzel, *Festausgabe,* ed.Petsch, Leipzig, 1926, IX, p.23. Many critics consider the final allusion to *Emilia Galotti* to be unmotivated. *Cf.* Julius Petersen (*loc.cit.,* p.182); Walter Silz ('Ambivalences in Goethe's Tasso', *GR 31,* 1956, p.24, n.8); G. Fittbogen, who suggests that Goethe forgot to cross the reference out ('Die Charaktere in den beiden Fassungen von Werthers Leiden,' *Euphorion 17,* 1910, p.557); and Ernst Feise (*Werther,* New York, 1914 and 1942, p.230, and 'Entstehung, Problem und Technik von Goethe's *Werther',* *JEGP XIII,* 1914, p.35). In *'Emilia Galotti* and Goethe's *Werther',* however, Feise substantially modifies his original thesis (*Mod.Phil. XV,* 1917-18, p.332).

More recently, critics have tended to argue that Goethe's allusion is meaningful. *Cf.* R. T. Ittner, 'Werther und Emilia Galotti', *JEGP XLI,* 1942, p.418; Leonard Forster, 'Werther's Reading of *Emilia Galotti',* *PEGS XXVII,* 1958, p.35; E. Dvoretzky, 'Goethe's *Werther* and Lessing's *Emilia Galotti',* *GLL XVI,* 1962; and Erich Trunz, ed., *Goethes Werke,* HA, VI, p.586.

4.   *Cf.* Chapter 2, p.23f. and Chapters 8 and 9.

5.   The thematic import of *Emilia Galotti* for Goethe's *Werther* is illuminated by the similarity of Werther's reaction on the point of dying to that of Emilia. He kisses the pistols with which he will shoot himself, rapturously exclaiming: 'Sie sind durch ihre Hände gegangen.' This is not a superficial likeness: it points up the catastrophic consequences of repudiating the material side of life. How deeply this terrible and touching gesture of Emilia imprinted itself upon Goethe's mind may be seen from the fact that the passage from which I have quoted above was the first snatch of the novel he ever wrote, and, by all appearances, its poetic nucleus. (*Cf.* AGA IV, p.267 and p.1062.)

6.   The recurrence of the Plotinian motif at the peak of the tragedy would seem to prove conclusively that through it the poet, from the beginning, is concerned to formulate the metaphysical basis of his tragic theme.

7.   *Cf.* Chapter 5, pp.94ff.

8.   In this connection, *cf.* W. Dilthey who writes convincingly: 'Der Despotismus übt einen lähmenden Einfluss auf sie aus. Sie trauen weder sich noch dem Weltlauf. In dieser engen und schlimmen Welt, in der sie existieren sollen, sind sie zur Passivität verurteilt. Sie haben das Handeln verlernt. So zögern sie ungeschickt und handeln vorschnell.' (*Das Erlebnis und die Dichtung,* Berlin, 1907, p.64.)

If *Emilia Galotti* is to be called a biological tragedy, as has repeatedly been done, then surely only in the negative sense that living time, in which life may organically exfoliate, is murdered. 'Eine Rose gebrochen, ehe der Sturm sie entblättert . . . ' (V,7) – what else does this 'ehe' mean? *Emilia Galotti* ends where *Philotas* begins: with the denial of biological process and of time which is its matrix. *Cf.* H. Schneider, 'Emilia Galotti's Tragic Guilt', *MLN 1956,* Vol.71; also Günther Müller, *Geschichte der Deutschen Seele: Vom Faustbuch zu Goethes Faust,* Freiburg i.B., 1939. Müller writes: 'Denn auch dies Werk, in dem Lessings tragische Lebensüberzeugung den strengsten Ausdruck gefunden hat, lebt unter der rationalen Oberfläche von der Unentrinnbarkeit der Leidenschaften und ihrer biologischen Folgen' (p.269). I would contend that Müller's 'lebt' is singularly misleading in its implications. The experience of the 'Unentrinnbarkeit der Leidenschaften und ihrer biologischen Folgen', in the form that it takes here, does not feed the deeper life of the drama: it blights it.

For the handling of time in *Philotas, cf.* Chapter 2 and Chapter 10, II. For a comparison with Goethe's handling of time, *cf.* Chapter 3, pp.44ff., and for his own developing experience of time, *cf.* Chapter 5, especially p.98.

9.   *Cf.* Chapter 10.

10.   For a divergent appraisal of the import of the identical poetic structures,

notably the symbol of the hand, *cf.* E. M. Wilkinson, 'The Blind Man and The
Poet' (in: *German Studies Presented to W. H. Bruford,* London, 1962, p.42f.).

2.   *'Philotas:* A Price for Purity'

1.   Leonello Vincenti, 'Lessings *Philotas'* (in: *Gotthold Ephraim Lessing,* ed. G. and
S. Bauer, Wege der Forschung, Band CCXI, Darmstadt, 1968, p.202).
2.   *Ibid.,* p.204.
3.   The glib assumption that the drama owes its existence and its theme to a
patriotic upsurge on the part of its creator is disproved by Lessing's own letters
of the time in which he sharply dissociates himself from the nationalistic
sentiments aroused by the Seven Years War. In this connection *cf.* Lessing's
letters to Gleim of December 16, 1758, and February 14, 1759. *Cf.* E. Schmidt,
Lessing, Berlin, 1909, Vol. I, p.354f. A. Strodtmann *(G. E. Lessing, Ein Lebensbild,*
Berlin, 1878, p.132) and W. Oehlke *(op.cit.* I, p.281) take a more critical view
than E. Schmidt of the immaturity of his heroism. W. Dilthey accords the play
an interpretation on Schillerian lines. It articulates 'das Grundgefühl Lessings,
die Independenz des Willens'. Its heroic temper stems from the 'Manifestation
der grossen, moralischen Person, die eben nur dem Tode gegenüber ihr Wesen
erweist.' *(Op.cit.,* p.53.) The present interpretation should enable the reader to
re-examine for himself the validity of the categories with which Dilthey operates
in a brilliant essay written, however, more than sixty years ago.
4.   *Cf.* L. Vincenti, 'Lessings *Philotas',* in: *G. E. Lessing,* ed.Bauer, p.202.
5.   *Cf.* Chapter 10 pp.240ff.
6.   Goethe, *Warum gabst du uns die tiefen Blicke.*
7.   *Cf.* Chapter 1.
8.   *Cf.* Chapters 8 and 9.
9.   Critics have often noted the resemblance between Philotas's own 'wütende
Schwermut' and the melancholy temperament of Lessing's friend Ewald von
Kleist who sought death in the battle of Kunersdorf. On hearing the news of von
Kleist's death, Lessing writes to Gleim, in a 'sehr wilde Traurigkeit': 'Er hatte
drey, vier Wunden schon; warum ging er nicht? Es haben sich Generals mit
wenigern und kleinern Wunden unschimpflich bey Seite gemacht. Er hat sterben
wollen.' (September 6, 1759.) A few days before, he had reported: 'Er soll nicht
mehr als sechs Wunden haben; der rechtschaffne Mann!' (to Gleim, Sep. 1,
1759). The connection between Lessing's ambivalence *vis-à-vis* his friend's injuries
and Philotas's own greed for more scars and wounds than he has, is obvious; less
obvious, and more important, is the relationship between heroism and death
which Lessing expresses in the words: 'er hat sterben *wollen.'* For Ewald von
Kleist as well as for Lessing's own Philotas, the desire to die is not the
consequence of a warrior's heroism. On the contrary: the youth's heroism is the
consequence of his deepseated desire to die. How is it possible that critical
opinion has overwhelmingly regarded this most personally rooted of tragedies as
an academic exercise in classical succinctness?
10.   King Aridäus's last words bear a striking resemblance to the last words of
Emilia Galotti, spoken by the Prince, '– Gott! Gott! –' he exclaims in horror. 'Ist
es, zum Unglücke so mancher, nicht genug, dass Fürsten Menschen sind: müssen
sich auch noch Teufel in ihren Freund verstellen?' (V,8). This horror-stricken
echo alone should put us on our guard against conceding to the young Prince
himself the 'idealen Vorrang' in the moral conflict he has engendered, as does L.
Vincenti ('Lessing's *Philotas',* in: *G. E. Lessing,* ed.Bauer, p.209).

11. *Cf.* Chapter 10, pp.214ff.
12. *Cf.* Chapter 10, pp.218ff.

3. 'Götz von Berlichingen's Dead Hand'

1. This reading is culled from both versions of the play in so far as they articulate one common theme. Quotations are from the early version. Formulations of the final version are cited if and when they serve to make Goethe's overall intention clearer. More far-reaching deviations from the earlier text such as tend to modify its total import will be discussed in Chapter 4. Quotations here and in Chapter 4 are based on the text as given in *Werke Goethes,* Akademie-Verlag, Berlin, 1958, Vol. I, which conveniently prints the two versions side by side.
2. *Dichtung und Wahrheit,* III, 13, AGA X, p.623.
3. *Cf.* Chapter 1, pp.8ff. and 12.
4. Quoted in Max Morris, *Der Junge Goethe,* Leipzig, 1909, Vol. II, p.284.
5. How deepseated this conception was may be seen from the fact that as late as 1815, in a scenario of *Götz von Berlichingen,* Goethe still introduces the figure of Weislingen as 'des Bischofs rechte Hand'. *Cf.* H. G. Gräf (ed.), *Goethe über seine Dichtungen,* Frankfurt, 1906, Vol. V, p.91, No.2269.
6. Gottfried's autobiography reads: 'und sein Göttliche Gnad und Hülff mir nicht wohl wöllt'; the 'fruchten' is Goethe's. *Cf.* Morris, *op.cit.,* Vol. VI, p.199.
7. By E. Staiger, in *Goethe,* Zurich, 1956, Vol. I, p.94.
8. Already here Goethe intuitively grasped the weakness of the Idealist position which rates the execution of an intention as morally secondary to the intention itself and as in no way able to detract from its value. Later, in *Die Leiden des jungen Werther,* Goethe was to show up the same weakness on the aesthetic plane. The failure of Werther's powers of execution – his 'Darstellungskraft' – so far from being taken lightly, is shown to be the *cause* of the gradual decline of his powers of conception – his 'Vorstellungskraft'. This last point is stressed by E. M. Wilkinson in 'The Blind Man and the Poet' (in: *German Studies Presented to W. H. Bruford,* London, 1962, p.45).
9. This view is argued by W. Kayser (ed., HA IV, p.488f.). As against that, H. Meyer-Benfey takes the line that the Weislingen action is fully integrated into the main action centred in Götz and strictly subordinated to it *(Goethes Götz von Berlichingen,* Weimar, 1929).
10. *Cf.* also the remarkably frank account Goethe gives of his relationship with his sister Cornelia in *Dichtung und Wahrheit,* II, 6 (AGA X, pp. 252ff., especially pp.253 and 255).
11. H. Meyer-Benfey writes: 'Auf das Verhältnis zwischen Götz und Weislingen ist das ganze Drama gegründet; es beherrscht ihrer beider Leben . . . Die Liebe [zu Maria] ist bei Weislingen . . . eine Abzweigung des neuerwachten Freundschaftsgefühls für Götz' *(op.cit.,* p.107).
12. III, 13, AGA X, p.624.
13. W. Kayser, ed., HA IV, p.487; also H. Meyer-Benfey, *op.cit.,* pp.136ff.
14. W. Kayser, ed., HA IV, p.487f; E. Staiger, *op.cit.,* I, p.92; H. Meyer-Benfey, *op.cit.,* pp.136ff; and M. Morris, *op.cit.,* Vol. VI, p.197.
15. *Cf.* H. Meyer-Benfey, *op.cit.,* pp.79ff; and W. Kayser, ed., HA IV, p.491, and in: *Das Sprachliche Kunstwerk,* Berlin, 1956, p.396.
16. Meyer-Benfey states quite frankly: 'Götzens Tod ist lyrisch begründet, nicht dramatisch' *(op.cit.,* p.67). ' . . . ebensowenig wie ein ethisches, ist ein

psychologisches Problem in Götz verkörpert. In ihm vollzieht sich . . . kein seelisches Geschick . . . Nur seine Kraft ist verfallen, aber auch das eben nur infolge jener äusseren Unfälle und Enttäuschungen, nicht infolge innerer Zersetzung und Brüchigkeit. Sein Schicksal . . . kommt ihm ausschliesslich von aussen' (p.75). Kayser, similarly, adduces lyrical features which prepare us for a death which remains basically unexplained. 'Keine Handlung, kein Geschehen macht Götzens Untergang notwendig' (ed., HA IV, p.489). Staiger so completely denies the tragic in *Götz* that he does not feel any need to come to terms with the hero's death. According to him, the whole 'trübe Konzept' springs from Goethe's unsuccessful endeavour to incorporate Herder's philosophy of history into his play (*op.cit.*, I, p.92).

17.   Meyer-Benfey, *op.cit.*, p.92.
18.   Staiger, *op.cit.*, I, p.89.
19.   Kayser, ed., HA IV, p.489.
20.   Nothing could be more misleading than to see Götz's avowal of total independence ('[Ein freier Rittersmann], der nur abhängt von Gott, Seinem Kaiser und sich selbst') as a simple reflection of his creator's infatuation with the heroic German past. Here, on the broad historical plane no less than on any other level of the drama, Goethe is consistently articulating a mode of being which for all its lovableness and vitality is tragically unviable.
21.   Critics frequently sense some biological necessity in Götz's dying, without, however, being able to account for this impression. *Cf.* Müller, *Kleine Goethebiographie*, Bonn, 1948, pp.55 and 57; Meyer-Benfey, *op.cit.*, pp.75 and 95; and W. Kayser, ed., HA IV, p.489.
22.   For a comparison with the experience and handling of time in Lessing's tragedies, *cf.* Chapter 1, pp.10ff. and note 8, Chapter 2, pp.28f. and Chapter 10, pp.217ff. and 220f.
23.   *Cf.* Chapter 5.

4.   'From *Urgötz* to *Götz*: A Torso Grown Whole?'

1.   Critical opinion has varied in its assessment of Goethe's achievement. T. Minor and A. Sauer concur with Goethe's own judgment. Emphasising the rapidity of Goethe's artistic development during the months that followed the production of the *Urgötz*, they conclude: ' . . . der deutlichste Beweis derselben ist die neue Fassung des *Götz von Berlichingen*' (*Studien zur Goethe-Philologie*, Vienna, 1880, p.123.) H. Meyer-Benfey, in his full length study of the work, comes to similar conclusions. He judges the revised version of 1773 to be 'nicht nur eine Verbesserung des ersten Entwurfs, sondern auch eine reinere Durchführung und Ausgestaltung der dichterischen Intention. Ihr Ergebnis ist nicht ein neues Werk, sondern das ursprüngliche in reinerer und vollkommenerer Gestalt' (*Goethes Götz von Berlichingen*, Weimar, 1929, p.141.) Kayser, on the other hand, comes to a predominantly negative conclusion. In his letter to Herder of July 1772, he says, Goethe promised 'eine gänzliche Umarbeitung. Die Druckfassung von 1773 hat das weder in sprachlicher noch in anderer Hinsicht gebracht.' . . . ' . . . Wenn Goethe in *Dichtung und Wahrheit* hinzufügte, er habe die Umarbeitung so gründlich betrieben, *dass in wenigen Wochen ein ganz erneutes Stück vor mir lag*, so erweckt er falsche Vorstellungen von dem Ergebnis.' (Ed., HA IV, pp.492ff.) J. M. Clark stresses the dramatic hopelessness even of the revised version: 'But in spite of all efforts to improve, the tragedy remained intractable from the point of view of production . . . Try as he would, he could do nothing

with it.' (J. M. Clark, [ed.] *Nelson,* London and Edinburgh, 1961, p.xix). Eduard von der Hellen emphasises 'eine entschiedene Einheit der inneren Handlung' in the second version and rates it as the best of Goethe's dramas in respect of its objectivity *(Goethes Sämtliche Werke,* JA X, p.xviii).

2.   Goethe to Herder, Frankfurt, beginning of 1772.
3.   Goethe to Herder, July 1772.
4.   *Ibid.*
5.   Goethe to Kestner, Frankfurt, middle to 21 August 1773.
6.   Goethe to Jacobi, Frankfurt, August 21, 1774.
7   III, 13 (AGA X, p.625).
8.   *Cf.* Chapter 3, pp.36ff. and 45.
9.   See M. Morris, *Der junge Goethe,* Vol. II, *loc.cit.*
10. F. Nolte in *Lessing's Laokoon,* Lancaster, Pa., 1940, p.46.
11. *Cf.* Chapter 5, section I.
12. The intention to point up the symmetry between the destinies of the protagonists underlies the greater part of the changes the poet made in the order of scenes in Act V. In the first version, the scenes dealing with Weislingen's sickness and death had been interspersed between scenes given over to Adelheid. They are now removed from this context and in their entirety shifted to offset Götz's sickness and death. The description Elisabeth gives to Lerse of Götz's state (V, pp.263ff.) is now followed by the revelation of Weislingen's corresponding state, first in his monologue (V, p.270) and then in the scene with Maria (*ibid.,* pp.271ff.). And this, in turn, leads on to the dying scene of Götz. Such structural rearrangement is borne out by new formal links in the verbal texture. Elisabeth now refers to Götz's 'schleichend Fieber' (V, p.263), anticipating the 'elendes Fieber' of which Weislingen will speak (V, p.270). Similarly, Weislingen's statement 'Meine Kraft sinkt nach dem Grabe' (V, p.271) is now reiterated verbatim by Götz (V, p.291). If such links are intended to underscore the parallelism of their fate, the changes the poet made in the motivation of Franz's death are designed to underscore differences between the protagonists which are perhaps more basic yet. Franz no longer dies, as he had done in the first version, at the hands of Adelheid, his erstwhile mistress. He kills himself out of remorse for having caused his master's death. Thus he reflects Weislingen's own prevailing pattern of treacherousness coupled with devotion, and his death both reflects and offsets the death of Georg who dies for his 'getreuherzigen' master in unswerving dedication.
13. III, 13, AGA X, p.624f.
14. Thus, the poet sacrificed Adelheid's love relation with Sickingen which had contained much first-rate poetry, and also her love scenes with Franz. Both these ramifications of the action had cluttered up the main line of Act V, not only by obscuring the fate of the hero – as has often been observed – but also by obscuring the parallelism of Götz's and Weislingen's fate which is central to the theme of the play. Another sacrifice was the deletion of the scene showing Adelheid with the Gipsies. In choosing, instead, to let Götz be tended by the Gipsies, the poet turned his original invention to excellent account. For the scene not only shows the hopelessness and humiliation of the hero, but also his nearness to the vital and healing forces of nature. Thus, what had been a romantic digression in connection with Adelheid becomes a contribution to the main theme of the play when transferred to Götz.
15. *Italienische Reise,* Venice, October 9, 1786.
16. Sievers is 'der Nimmersatt'. The Bamberger are so cross 'sie mögten **schwarz werden.** Götz wird sie [die Bamberger] lausen.' He 'wolt ihm [dem

Bischof] **das Bad gesegnet** und ihn **ausgerieben** haben.' Sievers calls a Bamberg horseman **'den Fratzen'**, Metzler calls him **'den Hund'**. He threatens the innkeeper, saying: 'Nur nit viel geschimpft Hänsel, sonst kommen wir dir über die Glazze.' There is reference to **plauen, ausprügeln.** Götz's horseman greets the news of Weislingen's whereabouts with the words 'das ist ein **gefundenes Fressen.'** The relation between nobles and peasants is summed up in the words: 'Dürfen wir nur so einmal an die Fürsten, **die uns die Haut über die Ohren ziehen.'**

17.   *Cf.* also the report given by Götz's man to Elisabeth. The details of Götz's encounter with Weislingen have gone. Instead Weislingen, casually, is said to have gone another way and to have been sitting 'geruhig beym Grafen auf Schwarzenberg' (p.34).

18.   Minor and Sauer have remarked on the recasting of wearisome chunks of narrative in the form of dialogue and on the increase of the number of questions without, however, analysing the nature and function of such changes, beyond saying 'die schöne Scene hat um Vieles gewonnen' *(op.cit.,* p.219).

19.   For an opposite view, *cf.* Minor and Sauer, who consider that the changes in the dialogue are largely determined by the poet's ' . . . Streben nach schärferer *Motivirung' (op.cit.,* p.151). In their view, Goethe modelled the idiom of the revised version on Lessing's *Emilia Galotti,* the result of this influence being a dialogue that is governed by the 'Forderungen einer strengen Logik.' *(ibid.,* p.219).

20.   E. Dvoretzky, *The Enigma of Emilia Galotti,* The Hague, 1963.

21.   For a detailed discussion of this problem, *cf.* Chapter 10.

22.   There are many instances of suffering articulated poetically by the evocation and subsequent denial of purposiveness. *Cf.* e.g. Lersee's response to Maria's intimation of good news in Act V: 'Wenn ihr ein Engel des himmels wärt und ein Wunderevangelium verkündigtet, Dann wollt ich sagen willkommen. Solang euer Trost auf dieser Erde gebohren ist, so lang ist er ein irdischer Artzt, dessen Kunst iust in dem Augenblick fehlt, wo man seiner Hülfe am meisten bedarf.' (V, p.282f.) *Cf.* also the concluding words of the same scene, spoken by Maria: 'O Gott sind denn die Hoffnungen dieser Erde Irrlichter, die unsrer zu spotten, und uns zu verführen, mutwillig in ängstlicher Finsterniss, einen freundlichen Strahl zu senden, scheinen' (V, p.284).

23.   Letter to Herder, July 1772. For varying assessments of the meaning of this comparison, *cf.* J. Minor and A. Sauer, *op.cit.,* p.260f.; R. Ittner, 'Werther and *Emilia Galotti', JEGP 41,* 1942, p.420; L. A. Willoughby, review of E. Staiger, *Goethe 1749-86,* in: *Germanic Review Vol. 31,* 1956, pp.149ff.; E. Dvoretzky, 'Emilia Galotti and Werther', *GLL (New Series) Vol. XVI,* 1963, p.25; E. M. Wilkinson, 'Goethe to Herder, July 1772', *GLL (New Series) Vol. XV,* 1961, p.117f.; E. M. Wilkinson, 'The Inexpressible and the Un-speakable', *GLL (New Series) Vol. XVI,* 1963, p.316. E. M. Wilkinson asks the question: ' . . . in what sense can "intellectual" be meaningfully applied to the Shakespearian outpourings of an ardent young *Genie?'* (p.316). These observations furnish a considered answer to this question.

24.   Further instances of this tendency are to be found in Act IV, p.179 (ll. 4-14) where Götz amplifies the simile of himself as the 'Böse Geist, den der Capuziner in einen Sack beschwur . . . '. In the *Urgötz* the passage runs on as follows: 'Schlepp Pater, schlepp! Sind deine Zauberformeln stärcker als meine Zähne, so will ich mich schweer machen, will deine Schultern ärger niederdrücken, als die Untreue einer Frau das Herz eines braven Manns . . . ' etc. Similarly, in Act V (p.243, ll. 11-19) Götz commissions Georg to tell the

peasants 'Sagt i[c]h ihnen nicht zu, ihnen zu ihren rechten und Freyheiten behülflich zu seyn, Wenn sie von allen Tähtlichkeiten abstehen, und ihre grundlose unnütze Wuth in zweckmäsigen Zorn verkehren wollen . . . ' etc. Both speeches, in the second version, are freed of all purposive argumentation and reappear in the simplest form.

25.   Other instances of such outbursts are to be found in Act IV when Götz is imprisoned in Heilbronn. *Cf.* especially p.179 (ll. 1-13), p.180 (ll. 18-28), p.181 (ll. 6-12), p.187 (ll. 6-16), p.189 (ll. 6-9), all of which were to be deleted. Practically the whole of the scene showing Metzler in a frenzy of cruelty (V, pp.121-7) was deleted in the version of 1773. Metzler's fury, significantly, had been fanned by his intention of avenging his brother's death, another purpose which is altogether dropped in the final version.

26.   In this connection *cf.* also the imagery in I, p.50 (ll. 1-15), III, p.174 (ll. 14-24); the cruelty of Metzler and his helpmates (V, pp.222-5) has become an elemental orgiastic experience articulated in purely physical terms. For this reason these scenes are much more terrifying than in the first version where the predominance of mental and sentimental elements created a pathos which had seemed altogether contrived. In this context, the increased number of references, throughout Act V, to Götz's wounds is important. They are twice mentioned in the encounter with the Gipsies – 'Meine Wunden verbluten' (p.250, l. 23) and 'Meine Wunden ermatten mich' (p. 251, l. 4); Elisabeth refers to 'Sein Alter, seine Wunden, ein schleichend Fieber' (p.263, l, 16); Maria reiterates: 'Seine schwere Wunden, sein Alter . . . sein graues Haupt' (p.272, ll. 3-4); Götz himself, in the *Kerkerszene,* adds his wounds to the enumeration of the adversities that assail him (p.289, l. 10), and finally adds the image of mutilation 'meine Wurzeln sind abgehauen' (p.291, ll. 23-4). All this is new and combines to form an imagistic pattern of great power. In such a context Elisabeth's simple mention of his wounds, at the opening of the *Kerkerszene,* divested as it now is of all the references to his and her mental state in which it had formerly been embedded, immeasurably gains in depth and poignancy. Seen as a whole, this new image pattern helps prepare the reader for Götz's death and is instrumental in creating the illusion of a long span of time between the beginning of the tragedy and its end, an aesthetic illusion on which critics have frequently remarked. It does so by strengthening our perception that we are witnessing a process of biological decline. Moreover the simple image drawn from the sphere of physical life helps prepare the reader for the non-tragic and conciliatory turn at the end of the drama. It does so in conjunction with other image patterns denoting physical states and activities, by stressing the naturalness of what is happening.

27.   The motif of sleep which is so important in the first scenes, thereafter recedes almost completely. Might it be that the poet's preoccupation with it at the beginning of his rewriting is a projection into Götz's character of his own need to create from the depths of the unconscious, blindly? The need which had found expression in his words to Herder 'Jetzt . . . tue [ich] die Augen zu und tappe' (July 1772; AGA XVIII, p.174)?

28.   This conception of an organic society in which the individuals are inter-dependent parts sharing one common life, has been prepared by the addition, in the second version, of the 'Bauernhochzeit'. This scene, inserted at the end of Act II, implements the conception of a common life and weal much more concretely and powerfully than the *Reichstagsszene* at the beginning of Act III in the first version had done, the place of which it clearly took. What is more, it directly links this conception with the figure of Götz. In it the *Brautvater* and the *Bräutigam* discover that each has gained through the gain of the other. The father

of the bride has ' . . . Ruh und Fried mit meinem Nachbar, und eine Tochter wohl versorgt dazu.' The groom is 'in Besitz des strittigen Stücks, und drüber den hübschten Backfisch im ganzen Dorf' (II, p.119). This directly foreshadows Götz's vision of a community based on reverence for the Emperor and 'Fried und Freundschaft der Nachbarn' in which 'jeder würde das Seinige erhalten und in sich selbst vermehren, statt dass sie jetzo nicht zuzunehmen glauben, wenn sie nicht andere verderben' (III, p.175). This conception of a social community reflects, on the periphery of the drama, the symbiotic community of life and interests between the tragic protagonists. Götz knows that his fate is inseparably linked with that of Weislingen and that neither can gain by opposing the other. Weislingen breaks this law of his life, and therein lies the deepest meaning of his 'Bundbrüchigkeit'.

29. In conversation with Eckermann, January 18, 1827.

30. The beginnings of this change go back further in the play. *Cf.* Götz's first drink with Weislingen (I, p.43) which in the *Urgötz* is accompanied by references to the immediate practical situation. In the final version it becomes an act of sharing, a symbol of their togetherness. *Cf.* also III, p.138. In the *Urgötz* Adelheid had told Franz: 'Wenn ihr gessen habt und [die] Pferde geruht haben wollen wir fort' (IV, p.208). In the final version she admonishes him: 'du musst was essen, trinken, und rasten', to which he replies: 'Wozu das? Ich hab euch ja gesehen. Ich bin nicht müd noch hungrig' (III, p.138). Food and drink here have become interchangeable with emotional satisfaction.

31. For a theoretical discussion of the sense in which it is meaningful to use organic analogies with reference to works of art, *cf.* Susanne K. Langer *(Feeling and Form,* London, 1953), whose incisive formulations have been of great help to me.

32. Besides, Goethe's sharpened dramatic instinct forbade him to leave the scene as it was. In the first version, Elisabeth, the champion of the active life, had been assigned sixty-three lines in a theoretical discourse about the active versus the pious life, as against twenty-four lines given over to Maria. In terms of dramatic envisagement, this was a self-defeating distribution. In *Götz,* Elisabeth is left with twenty-seven lines as against Maria's fifteen. Elisabeth is no longer characterised by talking about activity but by being active. Instead of discussing the merits of Maria's story, she breaks into it with her practical concern for Götz; and if she herself goes on to tell Carl a story of her husband's valour, instead of telling Maria what sort of a story she would tell Carl if she were that sort of person, the reason surely is not primarily that Goethe modelled her on his own mother who was a great storyteller (Minor and Sauer, *op.cit.,* p.160), but that he was now envisaging his characters in more stringently dramatic terms. The same development led to the obviation of the corresponding reflections in Act II (pp.101-5) and to the omission, or recasting in dramatic terms, of a great deal of reflective material: e.g. the *Reichstagsszene (Urgötz* III, pp.124-6), Franz's Hamlet-like speech about reflection being a sickness of the soul *(Urgötz* III, p.169), Sickingen's reflections about Götz's magnanimity *(Urgötz* IV, p.194), the frequently quoted comment of one Reichsknecht about the drowning of the other (III, p.146), to mention only a few instances.

33. Goethe to Salzmann, November 28, 1771.

34. *Cf.* Grete Schaeder, *Gott und Welt,* Hameln, 1947 (p.31f.), also Emil Staiger, *Goethe,* Zurich, 1956, Vol. I (p.93).

35. To say this is not to ignore the biblical allusions which crowd in, particularly towards the end of the play. Indeed, I would add to those noted previously (*cf.* Kayser, ed., HA IV, pp.489 and 501) the evident allusion to the

Passover Meal *(Matthew* 26) in the meal shared by Götz and his friends to which I refer as the 'last supper' scene; also the allusion to Christ's apprehension *(Matthew* 26) in the *Rathausszene* in Heilbronn (IV, pp.182ff.) with its burghers armed with 'Stangen' and 'Wehren', and its reiterated order of 'fangt ihn' (p.189 l. 15) and 'Greift ihn' (p.190, l. 19). These associations are an important preparation for the allusions to the Passion of Christ at the end of the play. A similar association of the hero's sufferings with the Passion can be discerned towards the end of *Werther* and *Egmont,* yet no one would argue that such allusions are expressions of an underlying Christian conception, certainly not in the case of *Egmont.* Goethe feels free to draw on this archetypal account of suffering to lend depth and universality to the destiny of his poetic figures. But such associations remain at all times controlled by his commanding conception and strictly subordinated to it.

36. Edward Bullough, *Aesthetics,* ed. E. M. Wilkinson, London, 1957, p.146.
37. *Dichtung und Wahrheit,* III, 13, AGA X, p.625.
38. This gradual receding of the representational aspects of a work of art has been very aptly described by Pablo Picasso: 'Do you think', he writes, 'it concerns me that a particular picture of mine represents two people? Though these two people once existed for me, they do so no longer. The "vision" of them gave me a preliminary emotion: then little by little their actual presence became blurred; they developed into a picture and then disappeared altogether, or rather they were then transfigured into all kinds of problems. They are no longer two people, you see, but forms and colours; forms and colours that have taken, meanwhile, the idea of two people, and preserve the vibration of their life.' *(Observer,* July 10, 1960.)

5. 'Goethe to Herder, July 1772 and the "Künstlergedichte": An Artist learns about Loving'

Titles of, references to and quotations from the 'Künstlergedichte' are based on HA which throughout prints these poems in their earliest version. These versions are indispensable for a discussion of Goethe's poetic development at that precise point of time.

1. AGA IV, p.123.
2. Weimar, March 17, 1832. *Cf.* Chapter 11, p.305.
3. For Goethe's relation to Pindar, *cf.* especially Ernst Maass, *Goethe und die Antike,* Berlin, 1912, and Otto Regenbogen, *Griechische Gegenwart,* Leipzig, 1942. *Cf.* also E. M. Wilkinson and L. A. Willoughby, 'Wandrers Sturmlied', in: *Goethe Poet and Thinker,* London, 1962; and E. M. Wilkinson, 'The Poet as Thinker', *op.cit.,* p.139f. For Herder's influence on the young Goethe, *cf.* E. M. Wilkinson, 'Goethe to Herder, July 1772', *GLL (New Series),* Vol XV, October 1961, p.116f.: E. M. Wilkinson, 'The Blind Man and the Poet', in: *German Studies presented to W. H. Bruford,* London, 1962, pp.29-57. For some aspects of Herder's theory of language and poetry, *cf.* E. M. Wilkinson, 'The Inexpressible and the Unspeakable, Some Romantic Attitudes to Art and Language', *GLL (New Series), Vol. XVI,* April and July 1963, pp.308ff.
4. *Cf.* especially E. M. Wilkinson, 'The Blind Man and the Poet'.
5. Max Morris records for the first time the use of a seal bearing the imprint of Socrates in connection with this letter *(Der Junge Goethe,* Leipzig, 1912, Vol. VI, p.236, no. 92). Enquiries to the Nationale Forschungs- und Gedenkstätten der klassischen Deutschen Literatur in Weimar and to the Freie Deutsche Hochstift Frankfurter Goethemuseum have confirmed that this was indeed the first

occasion on which this seal was used. Nothing is known of the origin of the seal which represents the head of a bearded man and is universally thought to be a likeness of Socrates.

6. Letter to Herder, Frankfurt, beginning of 1772.

7. Letter to Herder, Wetzlar, July 1772.

8. *Herders Sämtliche Werke,* ed. B. Suphan, Berlin, 1877, Vol. I, p.394.

9. *Ibid.,* p.397.

10. *Ibid.,* p.397f.

11. It is interesting to note that Suphan neither gives the reference to this passage in Plato nor offers any comment on the significance of Herder's analogy.

12. *The Symposium,* translated by W. Hamilton, Penguin, 1951, p.46.

13. *Op.cit.,* p.86.

14. *Op.cit.,* p.90f.

15. Throughout the *Symposium* the notion is held of a kind of latent, chronic pregnancy which precedes actual conception, that is to say, fertilisation by contact with another's beauty. This notion, strange to us, may in part be explained by the rudimentary state of the biological sciences – the Greeks of Plato's time, for instance, imagined the complete child to be contained in the seed of the male – but if we read 'pregnancy' as the active readiness to conceive, we might come closer to the inner truth of Plato's thinking.

16. Suphan, Vol. I, p.45.

17. I have the authority of Professor Gilbert Ryle for making this statement.

18. In this connection, *cf.* pp.95ff. of this chapter.

19. *Ed.cit.,* Act I, p.22.

20. Letter to Herder, probably October 1771.

21. The erotic overtones in this and other letters from Goethe to Herder cannot be overlooked. They become particularly clear here, in the two immediately succeeding letters of October 1771 and the beginning of 1772, revealing the curious correspondence, in the mind of the young poet, between his own relation to Herder and that of Alcibiades to Socrates. Of the, at times, acutely disturbing influence of Herder upon the younger man there can also be no doubt. The frictions between them led to a serious estrangement lasting from May 1773 until January 1775. In this connection, it is interesting to consider Goethe's one-act drama *Satyros* written between spring and autumn 1773, that is to say, at the beginning of their temporary break. The identity of the title figure of this play has been variously interpreted. For a summary, *cf.* HA IV, pp.529ff. I would submit that Goethe's *Satyros* represents a humorous, composite portrait of Herder and Socrates-Eros, as seen through the eyes of Alcibiades. Written at the beginning of his estrangement from Herder, this portrait betrays all the ambivalence which characterises Alcibiades's own portrait of Socrates at the end of the *Symposium.* It is generally recognised that Alcibiades, in his panegyric on his master, all but identifies Socrates with the principle of love as it has emerged from Socrates's immediately preceding panegyric on love: a curiously indeterminate, cosmic force informing alike the most primitive sexual drives in the animal world and the most sublimated manifestations of human creativity. Similarly, in Alcibiades's presentation, Socrates emerges as the most sublime embodiment of spiritual creativity. At the same time, this central assumption is embedded, both at the beginning and at the end of Alcibiades's speech, in a web of highly ambivalent and hostile allusions: Socrates, Alcibiades declares, bears 'a strong resemblance to those figures of Silenus in statuary shops, represented holding pipes and flutes . . . '; also 'he is like Marsias, the satyr' *(Symposium, ed.cit.,* p.100). Socrates's physical ugliness and, even more, his uncanny hypnotic

power as an orator give rise to this comparison, which is taken up at the end of the panegyric where Alcibiades roundly asserts that there is nothing like Socrates 'unless you go beyond humanity altogether, and have recourse to the images of Silenus and Satyr which I am using myself in this speech' (ed.cit., p.110). Silenus and the satyrs in antiquity were universally connected with Dionysius; the one was represented as a bald, dissolute old man with a flat nose, yet regarded as an inspired prophet; the others were represented as uncouth beings with goat-like characteristics, and addicted to every kind of sensuality. It is evident that, in a portrait composed of such conflicting features, Alcibiades, equally admiring and resentful of his master's sublime disinterestedness, is giving expression to his own deeply ambivalent feelings about Socrates; and this ambivalence directly reflects the fundamental ambivalence of the principle of Eros itself, as it has emerged from the *Symposium* as a whole. Indeed, we may say that Alcibiades's panegyric is the Satyr play concluding the two serious sections of this drama in dialogue form.

I would submit that Goethe's own *Satyros*, written in anger yet fully alive to Herder's prophetic genius, envisages Herder much as Alcibiades had envisaged Socrates: uncouth, primitive, hypnotic, yet possessed of an irresistible power and insight: a satirical and often burlesque portrait in which Goethe permits himself to give full rein to his own ambivalence, the ambivalence of Eros.

22. E. M. Wilkinson, 'Goethe to Herder, July 1772', p.116.
23. In *Bedenken und Ergebung*, AGA XVI, p.872f.
24. By E. M. Wilkinson, ('The Blind Man and the Poet', pp.32ff.).
25. *Ibid.*, pp.47ff.
26. Suphan, Vol. I, p.395.
27. Suphan, Vol. VII, p.52.
28. In: *Studies in German Literature of the Eighteenth Century*, London, 1965, p.8.
29. Second Part, II, I, *Suphan*, Vol. XXII, p.8f.
30. Suphan, Vol. VIII, p.170.
31. *Maximen und Reflexionen*, AGA IX, p.571 (554). In this connection, *cf.* E. Staiger, *Stilwandel, Studien zur Vorgeschichte der Goethezeit*, Zurich, 1963, pp.121ff.
32. *Emilia Galotti*, I, 4.
33. Erich Trunz, ed., HA I, p.441.
34. *Lied und Gebilde*, AGA III, p.296.
35. *Maximen und Reflexionen*, AGA IX, p.669, No. 1348.
36. P. Hankammer, *Spiel der Mächte*, Stuttgart, 1960, p.179.
37. Letter to J. Taylor, February 27, 1818.
38. Letter to Herder, July 1772.
39. *Nach Plotins Enneaden*, AGA XV, p.411.
40. S. Alexander, *Beauty and other Forms of Value*, London, 1933, p.125.
41. *Cf.* ' "Psychical Distance" as a Factor in Art and an Aesthetic Principle', in: *Aesthetics, Lectures and Essays*, ed. E. M. Wilkinson, London, 1957, pp.93ff.
42. W. Rasch has noted this point and adduced an interesting parallel in *Harzreise im Winter*. Quoting the lines: 'Winterströme stürzen vom Felsen/In seine Psalmen', he comments: 'Das ist die Dichtung als zweite Schöpfung, das Wirken des "second maker under Jove", der aus allem, was er sieht und hört und erfährt, Poesie macht – wie es Wieland sagt' (*Goethes 'Torquato Tasso'. Die Tragödie des Dichters*, Stuttgart, 1954, p.30).
43. *Cf.* this chapter, pp.107ff.
44. *Cf.* S. Alexander who writes: ' . . . the conception comes through the actual execution . . . The metaphor of conception is indeed misleading. It omits the impregnating excitement which is supplied by the material in which the

artist works when his mind is occupied with a subject matter' *(op.cit.,* p.125). It may be noted in passing that Goethe's use of 'Griffel' here is strikingly similar to Herder's use of 'Werkzeug', *(cf.* p.87 above).

45. 'Heutige Lyrik und der dichterische Prozess', in: *Gespräch über Lyrik,* ed. W. Urbanek, Bamberg, 1961, p.69.

46. *The Symposium, ed.cit.,* p.45f.; *cf.* also note 12, p.118.

47. *Op.cit.,* p.54f.

48. In: *Über Charaktere im Roman und im Drama,* Hofmannsthal lets Balzac tell his story of the painter Frenhofer *(Le Chef d'oeuvre inconnu),* who has for ten years worked on the picture of a nude without letting anyone see it. Poussin offers him his own mistress, a singularly beautiful girl, as a model. 'Und der Alte? Er bemerkt sie kaum. Seit zehn Jahren lebt er in seinem Bild. In einem Delirium, das kaum mehr Pausen macht, fühlt er diesen gemalten Körper leben, fühlt die Luft ihn umspülen, fühlt diese Nacktheir atmen, schlafen, sich beseelen, dem Lebendig-Heraustreten sich nähern. Was könnte ihm eine lebende Frau, ein wirklicher Körper noch geben? Er sieht diesen wirklichen Frauenkörper, er sieht alle Formen und Farben, alle Schatten und Halbschatten und Harmonien der Welt überhaupt nur mehr als Negativ, in einem geheimen, nur ihm begreiflichen Bezug auf sein Werk.' (H. v. Hofmannsthal, *Gesammelte Werke,* Frankfurt, 1959, Prosa II, p.42).

49. S. Alexander makes this point on art in general: 'The poem is not the translation of the poet's state of mind, for he does not know till he has said it either what he wants to say or how he shall say it . . . When the artist has achieved his product he knows from seeing it or hearing it what the purpose of his artistic effort was. He makes the discovery of what were the real directive forces of his action.' *(Op.cit.,* p.59.) Similarly: 'the work of art . . . however much it owes its form to the artist, reveals to him his own meaning, and the artistic experience is not so much invention as discovery' *(op.cit.,* p.73).

50. *Die Schönen Künste,* AGA XIII, p.31.

51. For the Goethe of this time, so deeply engrossed in the kinaesthetic exploration of his medium in all its bodiliness, this opposition is summed up in the words 'tappen' and 'gaffen', *cf.* letter to J. G. Röderer, Frankfurt, September 21, 1772; letter to Herder, Wetzlar, July 1772, and *Zum Shäkespears Tag* (AGA IV, p.122).

52. In: *Aus Goethes Brieftasche,* AGA XIII, p.50. Goethe is not quite as disinterested in Falconet's thesis as E. Trunz suggests (HA XII, p.572). He sympathises with those who feel that the beauty of marble as a material by its very harmonious radiance inspires the sculptor with those feeling imports he finally expresses in it. Only he goes further: the true artist, he argues, finds such harmonies everywhere: 'Er mag die Werkstätte eines Schusters betreten, oder einen Stall, er mag das Gesicht seiner Geliebten, seine Stiefel, oder die Antike ansehn, überall sieht er die heiligen Schwingungen und leise Töne, womit die Natur alle Gegenstände verbindet.' *(Ibid.)* By the very audacity of its juxtapositions, this passage demonstrates the poet's extraordinary and unfailing susceptibility to medium wherever he encounters it; an acute sensitiveness to the intimately physical aspect of things – to the way they smell, to their feel, their very grain. These words point forward to one of the younger Goethe's most revealing statements about the relationship between mind and medium: 'Gedancken über den Instinckt zu irgend einer Sache . . . ' Goethe writes in his diary, on July 14, 1779: 'Jedes Werck was der Mensch treibt, hat möcht ich sagen einen Geruch. Wie im groben Sinn der Reuter nach Pferden riecht, der Buchladen nach leichtem Moder und um den Jäger nach Hunden. So ists auch im Feinern. Die Materie woraus einer formt, die Werckzeuge die einer braucht, die

Glieder die er dazu anstrengt das alles zusammen giebt eine gewisse Häuslichkeit und Ehstand dem Künstler mit seinem Instrument. Diese Nähe zu allen Saiten der Harfe, die Gewissheit und Sicherheit wo mit er sie rührt mag den Meister anzeigen in ieder Art.' (AGA *Tagebücher*, p.81).

53.   *Aus Goethes Brieftasche*, AGA XIII, p.53.

54.   As R. G. Collingwood has it: 'A painter may be interested either in the volumes of a woman or in her femininity.' (*Journal of Philosophical Studies*, Vol. IV, 'Form and Content in Art', July 1929.)

55.   *Aus Goethes Brieftasche*, AGA XIII, p.51f.

56.   *Dichtung und Wahrheit*, III, 13, AGA X, p.648.

57.   Letter to Zelter, March 27, 1830.

58.   I am here building upon the theory of art put forward by Susanne K. Langer. Mrs Langer argues that the artist imprints the universal rhythms of sentience upon the very structure of his work of which indeed it is the overall symbolic expression. This is no doubt so. But she has not dealt with the question how the artist, in the first place, comes by these universal forms of feeling in their abstract purity. My observations here and elsewhere in this book are concerned with precisely this point. I would suggest that the artist has access to the universal rhythms of sentience precisely because his relation to his medium is erotically charged, thereby predisposing him to experiencing at a deep organic level. *Through* this relation to his medium, and *within* the creative cycle, he responds to the whole spectrum of organic experiencing with undiminished immediacy and in psychosomatic depth – to birth, efflorescence, maturity, decline, death, and – of course – passion. At the same time, such experiencing being displaced from its native context and transferred to a foreign arena, from the very start involves those processes of abstraction which lie at the root of all our symbolising activities. Thus, all along, the artist is in immediate touch with, so to speak, models or analogues of universal sentient experience which are, however, entirely private to him. Such models he exhibits in his symbolic structures, often – as in the representational arts – alongside more readily accessible imports furnished by his subject matter and merging with them. Such analogues can be absorbed 'ohne weiteres' by the recipient's sensibility, because their logical structure is congruent with that of the universal rhythms of sentience as experienced by him. (S. K. Langer, *Philosophy in a New Key* (Mentor), New York, 1951; *Feeling and•Form*, London, 1953; *Problems of Art*, London, 1957.)

59.   Frankfurt, March 1774.

60.   Fischer Bücherei, Frankfurt und Hamburg, 1960, p.258.

61.   *Aus Goethes Brieftasche*, AGA XIII, p.48.

62.   AGA XIII, p.141.

63.   Letter to Goethe, Jena, August 23, 1794.

64.   *Propyläen-Einleitung*, AGA XIII, p.141f.

65.   Letter to Friedrich H. Jacobi, Frankfurt, August 21, 1774.

66.   Letter to Schiller, Weimar, January 18, 1797.

67.   Elizabeth Sewell, *The Orphic Voice*, London, 1960, p.222.

6.   *'Die Leiden des jungen Werther*: A Requiem for Inwardness'

1.   III, 13, AGA X, p.642.

2.   *Cf.* Chapter 5, p.89.

3.   Caroline Sartorius in a letter to her brother, October 27, 1808 (in: Gräf (ed.), *Goethe über seine Dichtungen*, I, 2, p.584).

4.   Friedrich Gottlieb Welcker, reporting a conversation with Goethe, autumn 1805 (Gräf, I, 2, p.574).

5.   Letter to Zelter, December 3, 1812.

6.   To Eckermann, January 2, 1824.

7.   *An Werther.*

8.   III, 13, AGA X, p.639.

9.   Caroline Sartorius in a letter to her brother, October 27, 1808 (in: Gräf, *op.cit.*, I, 2, p.584).

10.   To Eckermann, January 2, 1824.

11.   For a detailed appraisal of the biblical background of *Werther cf.* Herbert Schöffler, *Die Leiden des jungen Werther. Ihr geistesgeschichtlicher Hintergrund,* Frankfurt, 1938.

12.   III, 12, AGA X, p.591.

13.   III, 13, AGA X, p.642. The extent of Goethe's identification with water and its lability may be seen from the poem the infuriated young poet wrote in reply to Nicolai's skit *Die Freuden des jungen Werther*: 'Mag jener dünkelhafte Mann/ Mich als gefährlich preisen;/Der Plumpe, der nicht schwimmen kann,/Er will's dem Wasser verweisen!' In contrast to his clumsy opponent, Goethe does not envisage himself as a swimmer *in* the element; he is the swimming element! There is a dangerous depersonalisation in these words, but over and above it, an awareness of virtuosity in exposure which sets Goethe apart from Nicolai and, indeed, from his own Werther.

14.   III, 12, AGA X, p.597. This motif of conflicting pressures is introduced in the novel as early as Book I, letter of May 22. It culminates in the simile Werther uses when, socially slighted, he imagines driving a knife, or sword, through his body 'um diesem gedrängten Herzen Luft zu machen' and continues: 'Man erzählt von einer edlen Art Pferde, die, wenn sie schrecklich erhitzt und aufgejagt sind, sich selbst aus Instinkt eine Ader aufbeissen, um sich zum Atem zu helfen. So ist mir's oft, ich möchte mir eine Ader öffnen, die mir die ewige Freiheit schaffte.' (II, March 16.)

15.   III, 13, AGA X, pp.638 and 644; and III, 14, AGA X, p.654.

16.   Goethe's *Ganymed* is almost universally cited as expressing Werther's pantheistic *Naturgefühl* and thus, by extension, his *Lebensgefühl* as a whole. Whilst there is an obvious basis for this comparison in the letter, say, of May 10, the unqualified analogy between the hero of a full-length novel and the speaker in a lyric is misleading. Not even on that single occasion referred to in the letter of May 10 does Werther achieve that *unio mystica* in which the poem so effortlessly culminates. Taken in its entirety, the novel portrays Werther's tragic failure 'in regelmässigen Pulsen uns zu entselbstigen', a capacity epitomised by Ganymed which Goethe, in *Dichtung und Wahrheit,* sees as the indispensable condition of inner balance.

17.   Goethe introduces this motif in the letter of July 6, in the characteristically veiled and tactful manner demanded by the I-form of the novel. In this letter Werther recounts how, on a sudden impulse, he kissed Lotte's small sister Malchen as she was bringing her sister a glass of water from the well. The sense of pollution experienced by the child – and understood by Lotte – is significant and points to the future. By obtruding his own emotions, Werther has destroyed a chaste gesture and the refreshment he might have derived from it; and this is something he will do over and over again. This incident should put us on our guard against accepting too readily Werther's own interpretation of his relationship with children as has been done by critics as discerning as G. Schaeder (*Gott und Welt,* Hameln, 1947, p.79) and E. Staiger (*Goethe,* Zurich, 1957, I, p.157). The single epithet 'sehr beschäftigt' by which Goethe characterises

Malchen's act shows that the child is object-oriented and cannot, without violence, be swallowed up in the 'sentimentalische' subjectivity of a Werther.

18.   The best proof of that is the steady recurrence, in the earlier portions of the novel, of gustatory images such as *essen, trinken, schmecken, kosten, laben* and others which are gradually superseded by images expressing physical deprivation such as *lechzen, schmachten, darben, hungrig, durstig, trocken, versiegt,* etc. This seemingly paradoxical tie-up between acquisitive greed and impoverishment is retrospectively illuminated, towards the end of the novel. Here, the Editor contrasts the moderation of an Albert intent upon *preserving* his long desired happiness with the rapaciousness of a Werther, 'der gleichsam mit jedem Tage sein ganzes Vermögen verzehrte, um an dem Abend zu leiden und zu darben' (AGA IV, p.477). Werther lives beyond his means; and it is precisely the ability to do so without being caught out which fascinates him at the beginning of the novel (I, letter of July 11). This strange anecdote has been mistakenly cited as evidence of Goethe's tendency to utilise materials which are inadequately assimilated into the total structure of the work of art in which they figure (*cf.* W. Silz, 'Ambivalences in Goethe's Tasso', *GR 31,* 1956, p.244, n.8). Goethe frequently employs the image of a household to express a state of inner balance or imbalance (*cf.* his diary entries of February 8 or 9, 1778 and July 14, 1779).

19.   *Cf.* Chapter 3, pp.36ff. and 45, and Chapter 4, p.74.

20.   It is interesting that Christian Friedrich von Blankenberg, himself concerned with the theory of the novel, should have been the first to appreciate this aspect of Goethe's *Werther* (*cf.* in *Neue Bibliothek der schönen Wissenschaften und der freien Künste,* Leipzig, 1775, Band 18, 1.Stück). Goethe himself was deeply disappointed at the overwhelmingly emotive response of his contemporaries to his novel. Its reception, throughout his life-time, considerably contributed to his sense of isolation. In *Dichtung und Wahrheit* he writes: 'Man kann von dem Publikum nicht verlangen, dass es ein geistiges Werk geistig aufnehmen solle. Eigentlich ward nur der Inhalt, der Stoff beachtet, wie ich schon an meinen Freunden erfahren hatte . . . ' (III, 13, AGA X, p.644). The present-day picture has not substantially changed. But *cf.* Victor Lange, 'Goethe's Craft of Fiction', *PEGS, New Series, Vol. XXII,* 1953 which is concerned with the formal aspects of the novel and stresses the narrator's irony enabling the poet 'to transpose the experienced reality from a mere confession to a symbolic design' (p.39f.).

21.   *Cf.* Chapter 5, pp.83ff.

22.   *Aus Goethes Brieftasche,* AGA XIII, p.48.

23.   *Aesthetics,* ed. E. M. Wilkinson, London, 1957, pp.98ff.

24.   *Cf.* E. Trunz, ed., HA VI, p.545.

25.   To Eckermann, February 17, 1830.

26.   Letter to F. Jacobi, Frankfurt, August 21, 1774.

27.   *Ibid.*

28.   III, 13, AGA X, p.630f.

29.   In: *Bedeutende Fördernis durch ein einziges geistreiches Wort,* AGA XVI, pp.879ff.

30.   In Goethe's own view, in *Dichtung und Wahrheit* (III, 13, AGA X, p.631), this artistic stratagem resulted in a piece of fiction which, in point of objectivity, approximates to the dramatic form. Even allowing for the fact that this account was written in retrospect and may have been coloured by his later development, one cannot help seeing in this extraordinary artistic circumspection on the part of a very young and involved poet the lineaments of a scientific method he was to formulate, nearly twenty years later, in the essay *Der Versuch als Vermittler von Objekt und Subjekt* (AGA XVI, pp.844ff.).

31.   *Torquato Tasso,* V, 5.

32.   *cf.* Chapter 1, notes 2 and 3.

33.   To say this is by no means to underrate the importance attached to the silhouette as an artistic genre in Goethe's day, and its importance for Goethe himself, especially during the period of his active interest in Lavater's work. But in this particular context Goethe does use the silhouette as a symbol of inarticulateness, much as the poet felt the silhouette of himself he sent to Lotte to be essentially inexpressive. Much can be seen on it, he writes to her: 'Aber meine Liebe siehst du nicht.'

34.   This rift between Werther's intellectual and emotional responses on the one hand and his sensory perception on the other assumes a special significance on those occasions when the poet's focus is on Werther's creativity. It does, however, characterise his letters throughout. The generalised statement, emotional or intellectual as the case may be, tends to frame his highly particularised perceptions. 'Dass das Leben des Menschen nur ein Traum sei . . . ' (I, May 22); 'Was man ein Kind ist!' (I, July 8); 'Es ist doch gewiss, dass in der Welt den Menschen nichts notwendig macht als die Liebe' (I, August 15); 'Musste denn das so sein, dass das, was des Menschen Glückseligkeit macht, wieder die Quelle seines Elendes würde?' (I, August 18). The general and the particular do not meet, merge and modify one another, together to bring forth the symbolic. This essentially uncreative mode is radically opposed to what Goethe himself was to term his 'exakte sinnliche Phantasie' – that creative mode which Schiller so sensitively identified when he wrote to Goethe: 'Ihr Geist wirkt in einem ausserordentlichen Grade intutiv, und alle Ihre denkenden Kräfte scheinen auf die Imagination, als ihre gemeinschaftliche Repräsentantin, gleichsam kompromittiert zu haben' (August 31, 1794).

35.   It need hardly be said that Goethe was fully alive to the absurdity of Werther's posture. Not only did he know better in his capacity as a visual artist; even as a poet he is so deeply inured with the sense of working in a quasi-material medium that he will use spatial distance as a handy metaphor for psychical distance. *Cf.* his letter to Herder, Frankfurt, beginning of 1772.

36.   II, *Herausgeberbericht,* AGA IV, p.480.

37.   Is this not an echo of *Laokoon,* Chapter XI, where Lessing argues that descriptive poetry can arouse in our imagination nothing more than the 'schwanken und schwachen Vorstellungen willkürlicher Zeichen'? This formulation and the argument in which it is embedded betray that unsensuousness of the poet in relation to his verbal medium which disturbed Goethe in Lessing's handling of language in *Emilia Galotti.* It is the same unsensuousness in relation to his own material medium which is shown here as blighting Werther's creativity at its very root: for it is the very power of conception which is failing him. *Cf.* Chapter 3, p.38f. and note 8; also Chapter 4, p.50.

38.   Goethe has traced this characteristic response into the smallest 'Zäserchen' of the novel's verbal fabric. For Werther the joy of being a farmer lies not merely, or even principally, in eating 'den Kohl allein' which he had planted. As he eats his cabbage he savours ' . . . all die guten Tage, den schönen Morgen, da er ihn pflanzte, die lieblichen Abende, da er ihn begoss, und da er an dem fortschreitenden Wachstum seine Freude hatte, alle in **einem** Augenblicke wieder mit . . . ' (I, June 21). This passage is vital, and not only because it reveals the whole apparatus of seeming productivity as a thinly veiled mechanism of greed. More importantly, it illuminates Werther's claim that he is able, without affectation, to weave 'die Züge des patriarchalischen Lebens' into his mode of being. This assertion has often been accepted at its face value (*cf.* E. Staiger, *Goethe,* I, p.156). But the true farmer is no more likely to react with such intensity to a cabbage than he is likely to read 'his' Homer while podding 'his' peas. He is too busy for either. It is precisely the 'stille, wahre Empfindung' and the

'simple, harmlose Wonne' Werther insists on feeling when he should not be feeling at all, but doing, which eventually drives him into exhaustion and death. (And perhaps the foreign *simpel* instead of its German equivalent is a verbal pointer to the fact that Werther is fooling himself.)

The critic's task vis-à-vis Goethe's novel is not to minimise Werther's short-comings as both E. Staiger and V. Lange do, by interpreting him as a sensitive modern man who becomes alienated from an environment too petrified to sustain him. It is to recognise his deep disturbance and *yet* to account for the majestic stature to which he rises at the end, and for the awareness – shared alike by reader and author – that his suffering becomes increasingly representative. In no small measure, this achievement is the result of the shift of perspective in the *Herausgeberbericht.* It is only when his inwardness becomes concealed from our view and we are placed at a distance from him that his figure, like a mountain range seen from an appropriate distance, begins to stand free and to reveal its full and formidable height. And in the measure in which the poet makes him enact his suffering rather than articulate it verbally – in that nocturnal rock climb for instance, of which, incredibly, his hat is the sole evidence – he regains the dimension of mystery of which our too close insight into him had threatened to deprive him.

39. *Cf.* Chapter 5, pp.102ff.
40. Letter to Kestner, Frankfurt, December 25, 1772.
41. *As You Like It,* II, 1.
42. AGA IX, p.508 (No. 92).
43. AGA IX, p.528 (No. 277).
44. III, 13, AGA X, pp.631ff.
45. III, 13, AGA X, p.614.
46. III, 13, AGA X, p.648.
47. Letter to Kestner, Frankfurt, November 21, 1774. The religious tenor of this letter cannot be overlooked. The work that has wrung itself from the poet's depths is sacred, and that aura has communicated itself to all involved in the mystery – to Lotte and Kestner as well as to himself – and has made them into beings 'apart'. And mingled with religious awe there is, in the poet's faith in the power and goodness of his creation, all the tenderness of the lover for his beloved. Assuring his friend that all the personal embarrassment created by the ap-pearance of the novel will be smoothed out in the shortest of times, presumably by a revision he proposes to undertake, he writes: ' . . . und dann – binnen hier und einem Jahr versprech ich auch auf die **lieblichste einzigste innigste** Weise alles was noch übrig seyn mögte von Verdacht, Missdeutung pp. im schwäz-zenden Publikum . . . auszulöschen . . . '. As Keats has it, he 'looks upon fine phrases like a lover.' (To Benjamin Bailey, August 14, 1819.)
48. Letter to Karl F. von Reinhard, Weimar, December 31, 1809.
49. *A Midsummer Night's Dream,* V, 1.
50. III, 13, AGA X, p.639.
51. III, 13, AGA X, p.642.
52. Weimar, September 1, 1780. It is interesting to note the occasion of this letter. Goethe writes to Sophie that he is now studying mineralogy 'mit ganzer Seele' and asks her to let him have some specimens of metals and stones. Plainly, his mind has been transported back to the process of crystallisation he had experienced when he composed *Werther,* more than six years earlier. The practical request, the characterisation of himself as 'die warme Kälte' as well as the stance he adopts of the mysterious and slightly resigned outsider – in all these the poet re-lives the inner situation associated with the writing of his novel.
53. Quoted in Max Morris, *Der Junge Goethe,* IV, p.78.

7.   'Torquato Tasso : A Poet's No Man's Land'

1.   *Cf.* Chapter 11, p.261f., p.276 and note 44.
2.   J. Kunz stresses the importance of Plato's philosophy at the Academy of
Ferrara (ed., HA V, p.453, note to p.222) and, more generally, within the universe of
discourse of Goethe's drama (*ibid.,* pp.447 and 456).
3.   *Cf.* Chapter 5, p.85.
4.   Plato, *The Phaedrus, Lysis, and Protagoras,* ed. J. Wright, London, 1929,
pp.46ff., Section 246.
5.   This repetition is cited as an instance of the kind of oversight which resulted
from the fact that Goethe used portions of an earlier version – the *Urtasso. Cf.
Torquato Tasso,* ed. J. G. Robertson, Manchester, 1918, p.xxix and note to
ll.1802ff. and 1824ff.
6.   *Cf.* Chapter 5, p.98f.
7.   *Kenner und Künstler.*
8.   *Cf.* the interpretation of this passage by W. Rasch. *(Goethes 'Torquato Tasso'.
Die Tragödie des Dichters,* Stuttgart, 1954, p.49f.) L. Ryan, too, accords this
speech a central place in the drama ('Die Tragödie des Dichters in Goethes
Torquato Tasso', JbddSG IX, 1965, p.316).
9.   *Die schönen Künste in ihrem Ursprung, ihrer wahren Natur und besten Anwendung,*
betrachtet von J. G. Sulzer (1772), review by Goethe, AGA XIII, p.29.
10.   However, it must be said that the poem *Die Nektartropfen,* written in 1781,
places the constructional instinct of the higher animals alongside human art,
while such early poems as the first ode to Behrisch and *Der Wandrer* view this
phenomenon with a high degree of ambivalence.
11.   Caroline Herder to Herder, middle of March 1789.
12.   'Über Charaktere im Roman und im Drama', *Gesammelte Werke, ed.cit.,*
Prosa II, Frankfurt, 1959, p.38f.
13.   *Italienische Reise,* March 30, 1787, AGA XI, p.247.
14.   *Ibid.,* April 2, 1787, AGA XI, p.249.
15.   True, Giambattista Manso's biography of Tasso, which Goethe certainly
knew in Heinse's translation, sports no less than three Leonoras, and makes great
play of the fact that Tasso used this plurality to cloak his clandestine passion for
Leonora da Este. But Goethe had no hesitation in bending plot and characters
as he found them recorded, to his own purposes. Besides, the opening conversation between the two Leonoras leaves no doubt of the fact that he is essentially
concerned with precisely this plurality. It hardly needs to be said that Tasso's
relation to the Princess is incomparably deeper than that to her namesake.
Nonetheless, for all his ambivalence towards Leonora Sanvitale, the sense of hurt
disappointment he evinces in IV, 3 suggests that he is not quite so proof against
her charms as is usually assumed. *Cf.* especially ll.2498 to 2503. It is interesting
to note that H. von Hofmannsthal is fully alive to 'das an Tasso Tadelnswerte,
Verführerhafte' ('Unterhaltung über den *Tasso', ed.cit.,* Prosa II, p.188).
16.   Letter to Kestner, Frankfurt, November 21, 1774.
17.   *Cf.* Chapter 5, p.89f. The cardinal importance of these images for Goethe's
current conception of artistic creativity and their entirely positive associations
are illuminated by the extract from K. P. Moritz's *Über die bildende Nachahmung
des Schönen* which Goethe printed in his own *Italienische Reise.* Goethe, at the time,
wholeheartedly subscribed to his friend's views; and it is interesting to note that
he made him stay at his house in Weimar throughout the winter months of the
year 1788-9 while he finished his *Tasso.*
18.   Book II, Chapter 3, AGA IX, p.151f.
19.   To see the figure of Antonio thus, dynamically, obviates a great many of

the difficulties critics have encountered in their reading of this character. It is neither necessary to interpret him as a villain, as Bielschowsky has done (*Goethe: Sein Leben und seine Werke*, I, Munich, 1896, pp.476ff.), nor to reconstruct a hypothetical *Ur-Antonio* vastly different in point of character and dramatic function from the representative figure Goethe clearly intended to depict in the final version of the play, as J. G. Robertson and F. Gundolf have done (J. G. Robertson, *op.cit.*, p.xxxvi and F. Gundolf, *Goethe*, Berlin, 1920, p.326). Wolf-dietrich Rasch, too, is forced to concede that Antonio's handling of Tasso in II, 3 is 'eine Quälerei perfider Art' and to argue that Goethe needed Tasso to be innocently provoked so as to point up the inevitability of the collision between 'Dichter' and 'Staatsmann'. To argue thus is to reduce Antonio, in this phase of the action, to a *deus ex machina*, rather than to account for his 'Entgleisung' as a phenomenon in its own right. If we see Antonio as a figure admittedly less finely strung than either Tasso or the Princess, yet subject to the same pressures to which they are all exposed, this strange 'crumbling up' at a transitional moment when discipline is relaxed and before he has found himself again, is not only devoid of inconsistency: it is superbly in keeping with the grain of which the man is made. H. von Hofmannsthal, in his 'Unterhaltung über den *Tasso* von Goethe', sees the organic necessity of Antonio's temporary aberration from his norm when he writes: 'Wie wahr ist der Zustand vergegenwärtigt, der sich einstellen muss, wenn ein älterer Freund nach langer Abwesenheit zurückkehrt und seinen Platz von einem Neuen, Jüngeren besetzt findet' *(ed.cit.,* Prosa II, p.187). What else does Antonio express when he complains to Leonore Sanvitale: 'Ja, mich verdriesst – und ich bekenn es gern – / Dass ich mich heut so ohne Mass verlor. / Allein gestehe, wenn ein wackrer Mann / Mit heisser Stirn von saurer Arbeit kommt/Und spät am Abend in ersehntem Schatten/Zu neuer Mühe auszuruhen denkt/Und findet dann von einem Müssiggänger/Den Schatten breit besessen, soll er nicht / Auch etwas Menschlichs in dem Busen fühlen?' (III, 4).

20.   *Über Laokoon*, AGA XIII, pp.161ff.
21.   Paul Valéry writes: ' . . . A work of art is never *finished* . . . but abandoned; and this abandonment, whether to the flames or to the public (and whether as the result of fatigue or obligation) is . . . a kind of *accident*, comparable to the interruption of a train of thought which fatigue, annoyance, or some external event happens to obliterate' ('Concerning *Le Cimetière Marin*' reprinted in *The Creative Vision, Modern European Writers on their Art*, ed. H. M. Block and H. Salinger, New York, London, 1960, p.29f.). For a similar view, *cf.* also R. G. Collingwood who writes: 'I learned what some critics and aestheticians never know to the end of their lives, that no "work of art" is ever finished, so that in that sense of the phrase there is no such thing as a "work of art" at all. Work ceases upon the picture or manuscript not because it is finished but because sending-in day is at hand, or because the printer is clamorous for copy, or because "I am sick of working at this thing" or "I can't see what more I can do to it".' *(An Autobiography*, London, 1939 (Pelican, 1944), p.8.)
22.   W. H. Auden, *Twelve Songs* (V).
23.   This is the position taken up by Rasch. He sees Tasso's danger as lying in the 'Verflüchtigung des eigenen Daseins', 'das Gefühl, nur zu einer Art gleich-nishafter, symbolischer, ästhetischer Existenz zugelassen zu sein' *(op.cit.,* p.58). According to Rasch, Tasso's behaviour towards the Princess, in the later stages of the action, springs from the poet's desire to prove to himself that he is 'real'. Nowhere does Rasch touch upon the poet's alienation from his creative self which I regard as Tasso's central problem, given Goethe's starting point.
24.   *Cf.* p.152 of this chapter.

25. *Problem und Erwiderung*: 'Zur Morphologie', Band II, Heft 1, 1823; AGA XVII, p.177.
26. *Cf.* Chapter 11, p.303.
27. *Bildung und Umbildung Organischer Naturen*: 'Die Absicht eingeleitet', AGA XVII, p.13f.
28. For a different view, *cf.* E. M. Wilkinson, 'Goethe's *Torquato Tasso*. The Tragedy of the Poet', who considers Tasso as being in the middle of his creative cycle rather than at the end of it, as, in my view, the plot constrains us to assume. Accordingly, she regards the poet's visions as artistically viable conceptions, 'the drafts of poems'. Needless to say, I do not deny the possibility that the poet may at any time enter upon a new creative cycle. He most probably will. But the 'visions' Goethe shows us here are after-tremors of a sustained creative effort rather than the beginnings of a new one. (In: E. M. Wilkinson and L. A. Willoughby, *Goethe Poet and Thinker*, pp.75ff.)
29. *Cf.* E. M. Wilkinson and L. A. Willoughby, *op.cit.*, p.127.
30. *Cf.* Chapter 5, p.101 and Chapter 11, pp.268, 279ff., 290 and 300ff.
31. Letter to Schiller, Weimar, June 24, 1797.
32. An unusual state of stress caused by conflicting pulls is expressed in the juxtaposition of 'unwiderstehlich' and 'unwiderruflich'. What these pulls were is perhaps best illustrated by a quotation from the *Italienische Reise,* taken from the correspondence of April 1788. On April 14 Goethe writes: 'Die Verwirrung kann wohl nicht grösser werden! Indem ich nicht abliess an jenem Fuss fort zu modellieren, ging mir auf, dass ich nunmehr Tasso unmittelbar angreifen müsste, zu dem sich denn auch meine Gedanken hinwendeten, ein willkommener Gefährte zur bevorstehenden Reise. Dazwischen wird eingepackt, und man sieht in solchem Augenblicke erst, was man alles um sich versammelt und zusammengeschleppt hat.' (AGA XI, p.598.) The following pages relate the agony of disbanding the plaster casts of classical statues he had collected and the temptation to purchase an original which, at the last moment, was unexpectedly offered to him – an opportunity he regarded ' . . . als einen Wink höherer Dämonen . . . die mich in Rom festzuhalten und alle Gründe, die mich zum Entschluss der Abreise vermocht, auf das tätigste niederzuschlagen gedächten' *(ibid.,* p.607f.).

Clearly, Goethe's conflict is as between the visual arts the poet is 'irretrievably' leaving behind and poetry which 'irresistibly' draws him into his inwardness. W. D. Robson-Scott excellently sums up the significance of classical art for Goethe at this time. 'Classical art . . .', he writes, 'was the most effective bulwark against the restless demonic tendencies in his own nature. It was . . . a kind of reaction-formation to his own dynamism, to his own emphasis on change, metamorphosis, eternal flux. In the formal perfection of classical art, especially in the noble forms of Greek sculpture and architecture, Goethe found a serenity, an assurance and stability, which satisfied some of the deepest needs of his personality.' (*Goethe and the Visual Arts,* Inaugural Lecture delivered at Birkbeck College, May 17, 1967.) One must, however, add that in the long run the cure did not work. *Cf.* I. Graham, *Schiller's Drama. Talent and Integrity,* Chapter 11 (in press, 1973).

33. AGA XI, p.971f.
34. Letter to the Duke Karl August, February 19, 1789.

8. 'The Currency of Love: *Minna von Barnhelm'*

1. The frequent references to money in this play and the importance it assumes

as a stage property have been noted by a number of critics. These facts have been variously interpreted. In no case, however, has money been recognised as the principal poetic symbol of the play. E. Staiger notes the frequent allusions in passing but assigns a negative significance to them. 'Die Unzulänglichkeit des Rechnens wird uns damit eingeprägt, wie in den zugespitzten Gesprächen die Unzulänglichkeit der Logik, die zarte menschliche Verhältnisse auf Begriffe zu bringen versucht' (*Die Kunst der Interpretation*, Zurich, 1957, p.85). H. Cohn rightly stresses the presence of money as a stage requisite and regards Tellheim's 'Geldnot' as a 'Vokabel', i.e., as a symbol of a deeper failure to meet Minna's claim to love and happiness ('Die beiden Schwierigen im deutschen Lustspiel; Lessing, *Minna von Barnhelm* – Hofmannsthal, *Der Schwierige*', *Monatshefte*, Wisconsin, 1952, p.258).

2.   Tellheim's generosity and his unwillingness to take have been widely noted and have by and large been accepted as a sign of his nobility of character. *Cf.* G. Fricke, *Studien und Interpretationen*, Frankfurt, 1956, p.30f.; Otto Mann, 'Lessing, *Minna von Barnhelm*', in: *Das Deutsche Drama vom Barock bis zur Gegenwart*, ed. B. v. Wiese, Düsseldorf, 1960, I, p.92; and Erich Schmidt, *Lessing*, Berlin, 1901, Vol. I, p.480f. On the other hand, W. Schlegel commented: 'Gezerre mit übertriebener Delikatesse, die wieder keine ist' (*Berliner Vorlesungen* I, quoted by E. Schmidt, *op.cit.*, Vol. I, notes p.725). Schopenhauer, too, had criticised the play on this count, saying 'das Stücke triefe von Edelmut, also sei es unwahr' (quoted by E. Schmidt, *op.cit.*, Vol. I, p.480). Needless to say, such emotive condemnation does not do any more justice to the character of Tellheim or the theme of the play than the uncritical acceptance of Tellheim's magnanimity. But Schlegel's 'übertriebene Delikatesse, die wieder keine ist' does at least, by implication, touch on the central problem revealed by Tellheim's behaviour: the inadequacy of a giving which is rooted in a refusal to receive. It suggests that Tellheim's tortuousness has a bearing on the real value of his giving. The indissoluble interpenetration of giving and taking in relationship, rather than the conflict between love and honour with which this play has been traditionally associated, is, I submit, the central issue of *Minna von Barnhelm*, and the symbolism of money is the central poetic structure through which this theme is articulated. G. Fricke has advanced the most consistent reading of the play in terms of a conflict between the claims of honour and the claims of love. But by treating the claims of honour upon Tellheim as absolute and objectively binding, he has also introduced two irreconcilable standards of value. Tellheim, in this reading, remains precariously perched between the 'kategorische Imperativ der inneren sittlichen Forderung' and the claims of human relationship. So strong is his response to the moral aspects of the situation that it threatens to separate him from 'jeder natürlichen und echten Gemeinschaft mit dem Du' and to encapsulate him 'in die Abstraktheit des sittlichen Subjekts . . . das mit sich und seiner Ehre allein ist' (*op.cit.*, p.33). As long as each of these two incommensurable demands is regarded as absolute, they are mutually exclusive. Like many other critics, Fricke fails to recognise that Tellheim's notion of honour, looked at more closely, lacks the nimbus of Kant's categorical imperative with which it has been surrounded. Tellheim is not beholden to the 'kategorische Imperativ der inneren sittlichen Forderung', that is to say, to the integrity of his motive, the actual consequences springing from such motivation notwithstanding. If he were, he could be well satisfied with his magnanimous deed which was right in itself and won him Minna's heart. Expressly he says: 'Die Ehre ist nicht die Stimme unsers Gewissens, nicht das Zeugniss weniger Rechtschaffenen – ' and completes this quite un-Kantian statement, saying: ' . . . ich bin es **in den Augen der Welt** nicht werth, [der Ihrige] zu seyn' (IV, 6). It is because Fricke – like so many

others – does not appreciate the conventionality of Tellheim's conception of honour that he gets himself entangled in a tortuous philosophical argument such as the following which is false to the basic temper of the play. 'Tellheim,' he writes, ' . . . ist in Gefahr, nur noch der schweren sittlichen Forderung, dem unbestechlichen Ruf der Ehre, zu folgen und so, eingesperrt in die Innerlichkeit des Gewissens . . . die unmittelbare Verbindung mit dem Du zu verlieren . . . **und Recht und Anspruch des Du . . . auf** *seine* **Ehre zu verkennen**' (*op.cit.,* *p.39*). Neither Just, nor Werner, nor Minna is exercised about 'his' or 'her' honour in relation to Tellheim – that would signify yet more encapsulation, at yet another remove – they are quite simply concerned with the man they want to be allowed to love and help.

3.   E. Schmidt takes this self-characterisation literally and without a trace of humour, arguing: 'seine Weigerung, als ein schnöd verabschiedeter Invalide die Braut zu freien, ist doch keine Grille, sondern sittlicher Zwang . . . ' (*op.cit.,* Vol. I, p.488). This attitude is understandable since Schmidt has nothing but condemnation for Minna and thus deprives himself of the corrective to Tellheim's own exaggerated notions which Lessing has built into his comedy, to wit, the temperament and actions of Minna herself.

4.   Goethe criticised this act (to Riemer, August 31, 1806), and scholars have deplored its lengthiness and episodic character. From the point of view adopted here, however, it appears as absolutely central to the development of Lessing's poetic theme. For a detailed and interesting appraisal of the Riccaut scene and its function in the comedy *cf.* Fritz Martini, 'Riccaut, die Sprache und das Spiel in Lessings Lustspiel *Minna von Barnhelm*', in: *G. E. Lessing,* ed. G. and S. Bauer, Darmstadt, 1968).

5.   E. Staiger comments: ' . . . das Gespräch, das wir vernehmen, bezieht sich auf die Theodizee, auf jene Frage, die seit Leibniz die Gemüter beschäftigt und das Denken der Zeit zusammenschliesst' (*op.cit.,* p.87). *Cf.* Chapter 2, p.26 and Chapter 10, pp.226, 237 and 240.

6.   *Hamburgische Dramaturgie,* 79 Stück.

7.   *Cf.* Chapter 1, pp.8ff.

8.   H. Cohn perceptively writes: 'Armut und Unglück stehen ihm zu, solange er nicht von *der* Instanz rehabilitiert ist, der er seine moralische Existenzberechtigung verdanken will' (*loc.cit.,* p.259).

9.   Lessing has been harshly criticised on this score. *Cf.* Erich Schmidt, *op.cit.,* I, p.490f.; G. Fricke, *op.cit.,* p.42; and E. Staiger, *op.cit.,* p.92. H. Cohn recognises that Minna arouses Tellheim's compassion but at the same time suggests, with implied criticism, that she does not appreciate the depth of his predicament (*loc.cit.,* p.260). The most decisive function of Minna's 'prank' is that it reveals her own depth of empathic compassion. Only because Tellheim feels this can she help him. *Cf.* Chapter 10, p.225.

10.   Otto Mann is the most consistent defender of this position. He argues not only that the King's letter is, in fact, a *deus ex machina,* but also that, Tellheim's moral position being unexceptionable, the King's letter is the only conceivable manner in which the situation can be righted ('Lessing, *Minna von Barnhelm*', in: *Das Deutsche Drama* . . . , ed. B. von Wiese, I, p.91). Mann concludes: 'Insofern bleibt die ganze Geschehensbewegung durch Minna vordergründig . . . sie wird nicht die Kraft, die die Auflösung bewirkt' (*ibid.,* p.98).

11.   G. Fricke seems to me to read Kleist into Lessing when he writes: 'Etwas von der steten Bedrohung des unbedingten und unendlichen Gefühls durch die überall bedingte und endliche Wirklichkeit, aus deren Fragmenten sich die Seele im entscheidenden Augenblick den *ganzen* Vers bilden muss, wird hier sichtbar' (*op.cit.,* p.45). Böckmann, in an excellent chapter on 'das Formprinzip des Witzes

bei Lessing', stays closer to the temper of the play when he writes: 'Indem . . . dauernd spürbar bleibt, dass der Ring die menschliche Beziehung und die Gefühlsinnerlichkeit symbolisiert und also auf die Liebe zielt, fasst sich in dem Spiel um den Ring nur der Kampf um die Liebe selbst zusammen' (in: *Formgeschichte der deutschen Dichtung*, Hamburg, 1949, p.545).

9. *'Nathan der Weise*: The Spoils of Peace'

1. The role of money in this drama was for the first time investigated in Klaus Ziegler's sociologically oriented study 'Das Deutsche Drama der Neuzeit', in: *Deutsche Philologie in Aufriss*, 14. Lieferung, Vol. III, pp.1039ff. Ziegler discerns a secondary, humorous plot centred in Saladin's court and concerned with the economic and social realities of money. This economic theme, Ziegler argues, serves to place the ethical theme of the main action in a factual, empirical nexus, thus depriving it of such unconditional moral relevance as has traditionally been assigned to it. A subtler thesis has been advanced by J. A. Bizet ('Die Weisheit Nathans', in: *G. E. Lessing*, ed. G. and S. Bauer, Darmstadt, 1968). Bizet argues: 'Nathans Reichtum ist die rechtmässige Folge seiner Weisheit, ja noch mehr, er ist ihr Ausdruck und ihre Bestätigung' (p.306; *cf.* also p.309). As the words *Folge, Ausdruck, Bestätigung* and *Entsprechung* imply, money, in this study, is regarded as little more than a symptomatic manifestation of Nathan's wisdom. A far more intimate connection between the two is argued here.
2. The importance of the epithet appended to Nathan in the title of the play is stressed by Bizet ('Die Weisheit Nathans', p.306f.) and by Fritz Brüggemann ('Die Weisheit in Lessings *Nathan'*, ibid., pp.74ff.).
3. This rumour which is presented, discussed and rejected in a definite dramatic context is accepted at its face value by Bizet in the passage referred to in note 2 above.
4. It will be seen that here, as in *Minna von Barnhelm*, the psychological problem is not the inability to give but, on the contrary, the inability to take which masks itself as compulsive giving. To base Nathan's claim to wisdom on his capacity to give, on the lines of the Aristotelian argument that to give is more difficult than to take, is to miss the underlying dialectic of Lessing's position which gives it both its depth and its fascination (*cf.* J. A. Bizet, 'Die Weisheit Nathans', p.309f.).
5. A similar point is forcefully made by B. v. Wiese in *Die Deutsche Tragödie von Lessing bis Hebbel*, Hamburg, 1948, p.67. For the similarity of the ideological temper of Lessing and the younger Kant, *cf.* especially W. Dilthey, *Das Erlebnis und die Dichtung*, Leipzig, 1907, p.135f.
6. Goethe, *Trilogie der Leidenschaft*.
7. Lessing's blank verse is throughout so jagged that it is impossible to base important points of interpretation upon a consideration of his rhythmical and syntactical stance at any given point, as has recently been done. In the case of such verse material any such procedure means over-interpretation (*cf.* H. Politzer, Lessings Parabel von den drei Ringen', in: *G. E. Lessing*, ed. G. and S. Bauer, p.351).
8. *Cf.* Chapter 10, p.225f.
9. ' . . . Naked came I out of my mother's womb, and naked shall I return thither. The Lord gave, and the Lord hath taken away; blessed be the name of the Lord.' (*Job* I, 21.)
10. The beauty of Nathan's response and the fact that it has significance in the

drama as a whole has been pointed out by F. Brüggemann ('Die Weisheit in Lessings *Nathan*', p.81).

11. E. Schmidt has noted that the action of the drama is motivated by 'eine fortlaufende geschlossene Kette' of good deeds (*op.cit.*, II, p.399).

12. For a perceptive account of *Schwärmerei* in *Nathan* and, more generally, as a phenomenon of Lessing's time, *cf.* F. Brüggemann, 'Die Weisheit in Lessing's *Nathan*', pp.76ff. *Cf.* also E. M. Wilkinson, 'The Blind Man and the Poet', in: *German Studies presented to W. H. Bruford*, London, 1962.

13. Although Nathan's practical calling has been emphasised, the intimate verbal connection between his profession – *Handeln* – and the poetic message of the play and, indeed, its author's deepest convictions has, to the best of my knowledge, not been noted.

14. H. Politzer ('Lessings Parabel von den Drei Ringen', p.350f.) objects to Lessing's exclusive emphasis on *Gehorsam* in contrast to Boccaccio who describes the three sons as *belli e virtuosi e molto al padre loro obedienti*, on the ground that Nathan, throughout the play, is associated with a more active and participating humanity than is allowed for by this word. But Nathan's outgoing activity and participation in human affairs presupposes a wholesale act of renunciation – *Gehorsam* – accomplished, first, after the death of his family and then once again through his readiness to give up Recha. Only by the fundamentally religious act of accepting his place in the Theodicy is Nathan freed to give all of himself. Dilthey admirably formulates this basic temper when he writes: 'Nur aus gänzlicher allumfassender Selbstverleugnung entspringt das neue Verhältnis der freien Persönlichkeit zum Unsichtbaren, und dieses macht erst die allgemeine Menschenliebe möglich' (*op.cit.*, p.115f.). *Cf.* also Günter Rohrmoser's formulation: 'Weisheit hat den sehr konkreten inhaltlichen Sinn, sich selbst entsagend der Führung Gottes anheim zu stellen, ohne eigenes Wähnen, Meinen und Wollen. Der Mensch wird damit zum Träger der Theodizee' *(Das Deutsche Drama vom Barock bis zur Gegenwart,* ed. B. v. Wiese, I, p.117).

15. It must be remembered that on the linguistic level adoption – *an Kindes statt annehmen* – is placed within the purview of the poetic theme: *an-nehmen,* like *an-genehm,* are cognate forms of *nehmen* which, together with its correlative *geben,* is the verbal pivot of the play.

16. In this play, Lessing consistently forces us to re-formulate statements of the kind 'x *has* the true ring' or 'x *has* the true God' into statements of the kind 'x *is* a certain kind of person'. Once this is recognised, all questions relating to the uniqueness of the ring, or of God, and the rival claims made to and about either (by the three brothers, or the three monotheistic religions), are revealed as pseudo-questions. But these are precisely the problems with which Politzer concerns himself. He writes that once the Father in the parable has decided to have two imitation rings made, ' . . . ist es . . . völlig gleichgültig geworden, ob einer der drei Ringe der echte sei und welcher es wäre: da die Echtheit des ursprünglichen Opals an seine Einmaligkeit geknüpft ist, verschlägt es nichts mehr, ob er zwei- oder dreimal kopiert wurde: die magische Kraft des Originals ist im Augenblick seiner Vervielfältigung verlorengegangen. Und was nun folgt, des Richters Mahnung an die Söhne, den dreifachen Ring in dreifacher Befolgung seiner ethischen Maxime dreifach in Humanität umzusetzen, hat die Frage endgültig umgangen, welche der Sultan Nathan – und Goeze Lessing – stellte, wie nämlich die Existenz *eines* Religionsstifters mit der *dreier* Monotheismen vereinbar sei' (*op.cit.*, p.358). Politzer argues that the Father becomes the blind victim of his own forgery when he finds himself incapable of telling the three rings apart. 'Wie mit einem Hexeneinmaleins hat er aus einem Ring drei gemacht, hat aber dabei sein Wissen um die Einmaligkeit des einen Ringes

eingebüsst und ist damit recht eigentlich das geworden, was der Richter seinen Söhnen vorwerfen wird, ein "betrogener Betrieger". Im Kern dieser Fabel ruht nicht mehr eine einfache Maxime, sondern ein Paradox" (p.353). I would argue that, by having three indistinguishable rings made, the Father, so far from being fooled and fooling his sons, is opening their eyes to the true nature of the issue before them. He knows that, once they discover that there is not one ring but three, the material object and the mere fact of its possession will be shown up for what it is – a worthless criterion for the settlement of their rival claims. Instead, he forces them into the recognition that their intrinsic value can only be adjudged by reference to what they *are* – to the quality of their being as it is manifested in their doing. To *have* the ring means nothing. To *be* a certain kind of person – like the ring, outgoing, in love – means everything. In a moral context the one criterion is proven to be quantitative and worthless, whilst the other one is qualitative and true. This incommensurability of the two criteria is underscored by the only true paradox in the parable which has escaped Politzer: the paradox that only the son who *forgoes* his claim to having the true ring, by loving his brother better than himself, 'has' it.

17. This homogeneity is denied by Stuart Atkins ('The Parable of the Rings in Lessing's *Nathan der Weise*', *GR XXVI*, 1951), W. E. Maurer ('The Integration of the Ring Parable in Lessing's *Nathan der Weise*', *MH (Wisconsin)* LIV, 1962), and H. Politzer who argues that Lessing could not dramatically implement the conception of tolerance developed in the parable. W. Dilthey (*op.cit.*, p.117), H. Schmidt (*op.cit.*, II, p.344) and W. Oehlke (*op.cit.*, II, p.382) take the view upheld here that parable and drama are fully integrated.

18. *Cf.* Chapter 10, p.254.

19. *Cf.* Chapter 10, p.242 and Perspectives, p.307f.

10. 'The Prose of Passion and the Poetry of Reason: Lessing's Creativity'

1. Critical opinion on this point may be classified under three headings: those who believe that Emilia is in fact not erotically involved with the Prince; those who concede that she is but consider her death to be determined by other motives; and those who regard her death as motivated by the fear that she would in fact be seduced by the Prince if she fell into his hands. The first group is represented by H. Steinhauer who sets himself the aim 'Emilias Ehre wiederherzustellen . . . und eine ganz "reine" Emilia dar[zu]stellen, die dennoch einer Verfehlung schuldig ist,' her failing being her excessive respect for royal power ('The Guilt of Emilia Galotti', *JEGP 48,* 1949; translated in *Deutsche Dramen von Gryphius bis Brecht,* Frankfurt and Hamburg, 1965, p.49). For the second approach, *cf.* H. W. Weigand, 'Warum stirbt Emilia Galotti?', *JEGP,* *XXVIII,* 1929 and H. Hatfield: 'Emilia's Guilt once more', *MLN Vol. 71,* 1956. For the third approach, *cf.* H. Schneider, *loc.cit.;* Günther Müller, *op.cit.;* E. L. Stahl, *ed.cit.* and 'Lessing, *Emilia Galotti*', in: *Das Deutsche Drama vom Barock bis zur Gegenwart,* ed. B. v. Wiese, *ed.cit.;* and F. O. Nolte, 'Lessings *Emilia Galotti* im Lichte seiner *Hamburgischen Dramaturgie*', in: *Gotthold Ephraim Lessing,* ed. Bauer, *ed.cit.*

2. *Cf.* Chapter 1, pp.10ff.

3. Karl Lessing to G. E. Lessing, February 3, 1772.

4. F. Nolte rightly notes: 'Odoardo und Appiani sind fast identische Gestalten, nur durch einen Abstand von Jahren voneinander getrennt' (*loc.cit.*, p.234).

5. *Kabale und Liebe* (I, 3).

6. This is, indeed, how two critics at least have seen her. W. Dilthey writes: 'Sie

ist das Geschöpf eines heissen südlichen Naturells, frühreifer Erfahrungen des Beichtstuhls und der Träume, die Guastala und sein Hof in einer so gearteten Natur hervorbrachten . . . ' (*Das Erlebnis und die Dichtung*, Leipzig, 1907, p.64). Oehlke stresses the southern atmosphere and temperament of the characters: 'Italiens Sonne kocht fast allen diesen Menschen im Blut; der heissblütigen Emilia wie dem leidenschaftlichen Prinzen, der geschäftigen Quecksilbernatur Marinellis . . . wie dem unklar-schwermütigen Bräutigam Appiani . . . wie dem Maler Conti mit seinem südländischen Esprit und seiner leichten Sorglosigkeit . . . ' (*op.cit.*, II, p.154). Oehlke's fanciful and cliché-ridden account is hardly worth quoting for its own sake; it does, however, demonstrate the gulf that may lie between an author's conscious intentions, that is to say, the discursive meaning carried by his words (which have gone some way to suggesting Oehlke's picture) and the import that is in fact poetically implemented. To assess the width of this gulf is our task; it begins where the task of Oehlke ends.

7. This link has been noted by Oehlke (*op.cit.*, II, p.183) and E. L. Stahl ('Lessing, *Emilia Galotti*', in: *Das Deutsche Drama vom Barock bis zur Gegenwart*, ed. B.v.Wiese, p.102).

8. *Sämtliche Schriften*, LM Vol. IX, p.120f.

9. *Sämtliche Schriften*, LM Vol. IX, p.128.

10. In this connection, *cf.* F. O. Nolte, *Lessing's Laokoon*, Lancaster, Pa., 1940, especially Chapter 6. The following summary is an apt comment on the weakness of Lessing's theoretical position and practical achievement here: 'What, then – to be general – does the artist represent? Apropos of a subject, he concretely and vividly represents certain virtues which are inherent in his medium, thoroughly becoming to his medium, and utterly indefinable apart from his medium' (p.60).

11. *Sämtliche Schriften*, LM Vol. IX, p.129.

12. February 10, 1772.

13. F. O. Nolte justly stresses the excessive self-control of all the characters in the play and buttresses his argument by an impressive catalogue of the reminders – addressed by characters to another or even to themselves – to keep calm. He summarises: 'Das, was die Personen der *Emilia* in Worten und Taten am meisten wünschen, ist eben jene Gemütsverfassung, die tragische Erregung und Intensität von vornherein ausschliessen würde – : Mässigung, Gelassenheit, *Ruhe*' ('Lessings *Emilia Galotti* im Lichte seiner *Hamburgischen Dramaturgie*', p.233). In this connection, *cf.* Chapter 1, pp.10ff. The observations made there regarding the characters' progressive experience of time as standing still accord well with Nolte's conclusions; *cf.* also W. Dilthey, *op.cit.*, p.64.

14. *Cf.* Chapter 10, p.207f.

15. This result differs radically from the conclusions drawn by H. Weigand ('Warum stirbt Emilia Galotti?') and by H. Steinhauer ('The Guilt of Emilia Galotti', in: *Deutsche Dramen von Gryphius bis Brecht*) in Weigand's wake. Weigand rightly observes that Emilia speaks 'die Sprache der Logik, nicht der Leidenschaft . . . Immer nimmt die Wirkung dieser Sprache auf unser Gefühl den Umweg über den Verstand . . . Ob diese Stilisierung der Form auch das Wesen des Seelischen beeinträchtigt, ob das Elementar-Triebhafte der Leidenschaft tatsächlich ausgeschaltet wird zugunsten einer logischen vielmehr als psychologischen Spannung – diese Frage möchte ich entschieden verneinen. Wäre es anders, so müsste der Versuch eines tieferen Eindringens in die Voraussetzungen der Katastrophe überhaupt versagen.' (P.467). But this is precisely what has happened: the attempt has failed time and again. More important, the basic critical and aesthetic assumptions underlying this argument are untenable. In a work of art, it is impossible to separate 'Form' from 'Wesen'

and to look for ranges of imports which are not articulated in it, through its
medium. A verbal work of art is in its entirety made up of words and its life is
the life of its words. *Cf.* Chapter 4, pp.59f. and 74ff. and Chapter 5, p.80f.
16.   *Cf.* Chapter 2, pp.19ff.
17.   Used by R. D. Laing, *The Divided Self,* London, 1960.
18.   *Fragmente* III, 6, *cf.* Chapter 5, p.83.
19.   In connection with this image, *cf.* Chapter 10, p.234.
20.   I have chosen the word 'end' to render as faithfully to the text as is possible
a number of words which Philotas does, in fact, use interchangeably, such as
'Zweck', 'vollkommen' and 'vollendet'. The following pages will help explain this
multiplicity of terms used to designate a concept which is vital to Philotas's
argument.
21.   Goethe, *Urworte. Orphisch.*
22.   Goethe, letter to Frau von Stein, dated before July 29, 1777.
23.   *Cf.* the experience of time evolved in *Emilia Galotti* (Chapter 1, pp.10ff.). For
contrast with both, *cf.* the experience of time projected by Goethe in *Götz von
Berlichingen* (Chapter 3, p.44f.) and in the poetry of the period (Chapter 5, p.98f.).
24.   *Cf.* Susanne K. Langer, *Feeling and Form,* London, 1953, especially
Chapter 7.
25.   *Cf.* the epigraph to Chapter 5.
26.   Keats, letter to J. H. Reynolds, May 3, 1818.
27.   *Cf.* Oehlke, *op.cit.,* I, p.397.
28.   It is true that Othello's prowess plays a prominent part in Desdemona's
growing passion. He himself testifies to this, saying: 'She lov'd me for the dangers
I had passed;/And I lov'd her that she did pity them' (I, 3). But Desdemona
hears of Othello's exploits from his own lips, and what attracts her is not so
much his goodness but the strange and outlandish flavour of his stories. It is
precisely his exotic presence, so romantically different from her domestic world,
which feeds a growing passion between opposites.
29.   Oehlke notes this point, writing: 'Sie liebt ihn, um seiner Tat willen, ehe sie
ihn kennt. Ihre Liebe hat eine sittliche Wurzel, und von der aus mag man ihre
leidenschaftliche oder 'wollüstige' Seite einschätzen . . . Kann ein Weib mehr
Charakter sein und weniger Sinnlichkeit . . . ?' (*op.cit.,* I, p.408).
30.   Already Goethe stressed Minna's male intellect: 'Im *Tellheim* die Ansicht
seiner Zeit und Welt im Punkt der Ehre, in *Minna* Lessings Verstand' (to Riemer,
August 31, 1806). *Cf.* Oehlke who writes: 'An Klarheit des Geistes nimmt
dieses sächsische Edelfräulein es mit jedem deutschen Philosophen auf . . . '
(*op.cit.,* I, p.406f.).
31.   Lessing writes to his brother: 'Die jungfräulichen Heroinen und
Philosophinnen sind gar nicht nach meinem Geschmacke . . . Ich kenne an
einem unverheiratheten Mädchen keine höhere Tugenden, als Frömmigkeit und
Gehorsam.' (February 10, 1772.)
32.   In: *Die Kunst der Interpretation,* Zurich, 1957.
33.   *Ibid.,* p.83.
34.   *Ibid.,* p.84.
35.   This delight in playing for the sake of playing and its dangers has been
variously noted. *Cf.* H. Meyer-Benfey, *Lessings 'Minna von Barnhelm',* Göttingen,
1915, p.102; Fritz Martini, 'Riccaut, die Sprache und das Spiel . . . ', in: *G. E.
Lessing,* ed. G. and S. Bauer, p.418; H. Cohn, 'Die beiden Schwierigen im
deutschen Lustspiel', p.259f.); E. Staiger, *op.cit.,* p.92. The most critical comment
comes from F. J. Schneider *(Die Deutsche Dichtung der Aufklärungzeit,* Stuttgart,
1948) who wonders whether so frivolous a girl is likely to be 'überhaupt die
rechte Frau für Tellheim . . . ' (p.265).

36.   For a detailed and subtle reading of Minna's play within the play, *cf.* Fritz Martini ('Riccaut, die Sprache und das Spiel . . .') who with great acumen analyses the thematic and the aesthetic function of this play-acting. However, Martini does not go on to consider whether this play – which he himself carefully contradistinguishes from a calculating intrigue – does not also effect an aesthetic catharsis in the recipient, Tellheim.

37.   *Hamburgische Dramaturgie, 79. Stück.*

38.   This consistency is stressed – not without a hint of criticism – by Oehlke (*op.cit.,* I, p.414f.).

39.   *Complete Works,* New York, 1927, V, p.35.

40.   *Aesthetics,* ed. E. M. Wilkinson, London, 1957. Bullough writes: ' "Probability" and "improbability" in Art are not to be measured by their correspondence (or lack of it) with actual experience . . . it is rather a matter of *consistency* of Distance' (p.110).

41.   The passionate sense of bereavement and anger Lessing felt at the untimely death of v. Kleist bears a strong resemblance to the bitter and violent grief he evinced at the death of his wife. No other letters from Lessing's hand can compare with these in the unguardedness of their passion. (*Cf.* the letter to Gleim, Berlin, September 6, 1759, and letters to J. J. Eschenburg, Wolfenbüttel, December 31, 1777 and January 14, 1778; also the letter to Karl Lessing, Wolfenbüttel, January 12, 1778.)

42.   This point is forcefully made by F. O. Nolte in 'Lessings *Emilia Galotti* im Lichte seiner *Hamburgischen Dramaturgie',* pp.231ff. *Cf.* note 13 of this chapter.

43.   *Cf.* W. Dilthey, *op.cit.,* p.127f. and E. Schmidt, *op.cit.,* II, p.369f.

44.   Book of Job, I, 21.

45.   G. Rohrmoser expresses a similar view: 'Wer aber ist der alles auf ein glückhaftes Telos hin durchführende Autor der merkwürdigen Fabel? Ohne Zweifel der Dichter. Aber doch nur in einem sehr vordergründigen Sinn. Es würde zu den Überzeugungen Lessings, in denen der Dramaturg mit dem Theologen in ihm übereinstimmt, sehr wohl passen, wenn wir annehmen, dass es die Vorsehung selbst ist, die dem gewagten und sehr kühnen dramatischen Spiel als Folie zur Abbildung zugrunde liegt.' ('Lessing, *Nathan der Weise',* in: *Das Deutsche Drama . . . ,* I, p.120.)

46.   *Sämtliche Schriften,* LM Vol. XIII, p.88.

47.   *Sämtliche Schriften,* LM Vol. XIII, p.391.

48.   *Cf.* F. Brüggemann, 'Die Weisheit in Lessings Nathan'; also W. Oehlke who makes the impressive statement: 'Die Linien des Herzens und Verstandes laufen nebeneinander her, solange bis sie auf der höchsten Stufe der Entwicklung eins werden. Auf dieser Stufe steht Nathan' (*op.cit.,* II, p.400). As against this, it is startling to find a thinker of W. Dilthey's rank lapse into the following dichotomous judgment: 'Aber auch Nathan zahlt für die Bewusstheit, die in sich und anderen nichts Dunkles lassen will, für das alles betastende, ruhelose Denken mit der Eintönigkeit eines Charakters, in welchem keine naiven Kräfte im Rückhalt sind; die Mutter alles Grossen ist eben die Leidenschaft' (*op.cit.,* p.122f.).

49.   C. E. Schweitzer stresses the point that Nathan is not the 'finished man' critics usually assume him to be, but has himself gone through a process of education. This education is accomplished through the transition from the concept of a physical fatherhood to the more mature one of spiritual fatherhood, a transition first achieved by Nathan and also, independently of him, by other characters in the play. ('Die Erziehung Nathans', *MH (Wisconsin) 1961,* p.53.) G. Rohrmoser, too, stresses the rigorous process of education to which Lessing subjects his characters, in which even their concept of the father-child relation

undergoes a profound revision (in: *Das Deutsche Drama* . . . , ed. B. v. Wiese, p.124f.).

50.   In this connection, *cf.* G. Rohrmoser whose formulation – first seen after the completion of this chapter – I would totally accept: 'Die hier von Nathan vollzogene totale Selbstaufhebung als unbedingtes Sichanheimstellen unter den Willen Gottes, der in allem auch noch so unbegreiflichen und grauenvollen Geschehen in Natur und Geschichte als waltende Macht dankbar anerkannt und hingenommen wird, dürfte die wirkliche Aussage Lessings zum Problem der Religionen sein. Da, wo eine solche Einigung mit Gott vollzogen ist und als Kontinuität eines Lebens durchgehalten wird, ist die religiöse Frage keine Frage mehr, und die Frage nach der Vorsehung selbst wird gegenstandslos. (In: *Das Deutsche Drama* . . . , ed., B. v. Wiese, I, p.123.)

51.   *Sämtliche Schriften,* LM Vol. XIII, p.421f.

52.   *Sämtliche Schriften,* LM Vol. XIII, p.422.

53.   *Sämtliche Schriften,* LM Vol. XIII, p.209.

54.   *Cf.* Chapter 5, pp.106ff. and Chapter 6, pp106 and 131ff. In this connection, *cf.* Susanne K. Langer, *Feeling and Form,* in particular Chapter 3.

55.   *Op.cit.,* I, p.357.

56.   This aspect is largely glossed over in E. Schmidt's study. W. Oehlke, however, and the informative biography by Adolf Strodtmann drive the point home forcefully and unmistakably.

57.   July 29, 1771.

58.   November 20, 1771.

59.   November 25, 1771.

60.   Both Schmidt and Oehlke note how reminiscent this letter is of Lessing's own Tellheim; but neither regards this attitude as being in any way problematic.

61.   November 5, 1775.

62.   August 9, 1778.

63.   Letter to J. J. Eschenburg, December 31, 1777.

64.   Letter to Karl Lessing, December 1, 1776.

65.   In this connection, *cf.* the discussion by E. M. Wilkinson of the poetic categories Staiger adopts in his *Grundbegriffe der Poetik,* Zurich, 1946 *(MLR Vol. 44, 1949, pp. 433-37).*

66.   In: *Über die Ästhetische Erziehung des Menschen in einer Reihe von Briefen,* letter XXV.

67.   *Op.cit.,* p.51.

68.   Letter to J. J. Eschenburg, January 10, 1778.

69.   *Faust,* 'Zueignung', 1.31f.

11.   'Faust's Conquest of the Sea'

Quotations from *Faust* are based on the text of HA, in which lines are numbered throughout.

1.   *Cf.* Chapter 7, p.153 and epigraph to Part Four.

2.   Ernst Cassirer. *Freiheit und Form. Studien zur Deutschen Geistesgeschichte,* Berlin, 1918, 2nd ed., p.310.

3.   *Op.cit.,* p.403.

4.   *Goethes Werke,* HA Vol. III, p.477.

5.   *Ed.cit.,* p.584.

6.   *Ed.cit.,* p.552.

7.   W. Emrich, *Die Symbolik von Faust II,* Frankfurt a.Main, Bonn, 1964, p.34.

8.   *Op.cit.,* p.35

9. *Op.cit.,* p.432.

10. H. Herrmann, 'Faust, der Tragödie zweiter Teil: Studien zur inneren Form des Werkes', *Zeitschrift für Ästhetik und allgemeine Kunstwissenschaft 12,* 1916-17, pp.86-137, 161-78, 311-51.

11. P. Stöcklein, 'Die Sorge in Faust', in: *Wege zum späten Goethe,* Hamburg, 1960.

12. D. Lohmeyer. *Faust und die Welt,* Potsdam, 1940.

13. M. Kommerell, 'Faust II Teil: Zum Verständnis der Form', in: *Geist und Buchstabe der Dichtung,* Frankfurt a.Main, 1962.

14. In: *Goethes Urfaust und Faust, ein Fragment,* ed. L. A. Willoughby, Oxford, 1943, p.XIX.

15. *Ed.çit.,* p.468.

16. *Ed.cit.,* p.469.

17. *Ibid.*

18. AGA IV, pp.267 and 1062.

19. In this connection, *cf.* E. M. Wilkinson and L. A. Willoughby, *Goethe Poet and Thinker,* London, 1962, pp.105ff.

20. *Cf.* Chapter 7, p.158ff.

21. In this connection, *cf.* P. Stöcklein, *op.cit.,* pp.107ff.

22. *Cf.* W. Emrich who very aptly writes: 'Das "Wasser" ist vor allem seit dem Divan und vielen anderen Vorformen bei Goethe Symbole [*sic*] einer Wiedergeburt lange brachliegender oder in allzustrengen Formen gebannter Phantasiekräfte, einer Entfesselung, Steigerung und Befreiung geistig-dichterischer und lebendiger Kräfte . . . ' (*op.cit.,* p.291). Also: 'Element, Wasser, Eros bedeuten für Goethe immer Möglichkeiten der Lösung, Erfüllung, Gestaltung und Reifwerdung "gläsern" gehemmter Produktivkräfte . . . ' (*ibid.*).

23. In contrast to the view implied here, O. Seidlin argues that the *Prolog auf dem Theater* was neither intended for, nor intrinsically belongs to the *Faust*-drama, but was written as a prologue to *Die Zauberflöte (Von Goethe zu Thomas Mann,* Göttingen, 1963, p.56f.).

24. Paralipomena 3, AGA V, p.542. Needless to say, *Der Narr,* i.e. Mephistopheles, in the course of the tragedy takes on a number of roles and performs a number of functions, some of them decidedly constructive. Not the least of them being that he represents, and strengthens, the reality principle in Faust. Analogously, in his role of *Die lustige Person,* before the beginning of the tragedy, he has profound things to say about the artist, the artistic process and the effect of art. But when this is conceded – and to do so is tantamount, merely, to conceding that Mephistopheles is a part of Goethean being as much as Faust or any other character in the play – it remains true to say that his principal function is that of negating, and that this nihilistic stance is inevitably directed against the forces making for creation and indeed against creation itself.

25. *Cf.* L. A. Willoughby, *ed.cit.,* p.XXVII.

26. A similar caution is expressed by G. Storz in *Goethe-Vigilien,* Stuttgart, 1953, pp.175ff.

27. For a detailed study of this image, its ramifications in *Faust,* and its oriental origin, *cf.* R. Mühlher, 'Der Lebensquell. Bildsymbole in Goethes *Faust', DVLG 31,* 1957, pp.38ff.

28. *Cf.* Chapter 5.

29. *Cf.* Chapter 5, pp.101 and 105, Chapter 7, p.261 and Chapter 11, pp.279 and 284.

30. For the historical and theological background of Faust's translation of the Logos, *cf.* R. Mühlher, *loc.cit.,* p.46f. and E. M. Wilkinson, 'The Theological Basis of Faust's Credo', *GLL X, 3,* 1957, p.236f.

31.   B. Fairley makes the point that the theme of rejuvenation is sounded well before Faust is actually rejuvenated in the *Hexenküche,* and argues that this latter episode crept into the drama while Goethe was in Italy and himself experienced a sense of miraculous rejuvenation (*Goethes Faust: 6 Essays,* Oxford, 1965, p.95f.).

32.   For a detailed study of this image, *cf.* E. Loeb, *Die Symbolik des Wasserzyklus bei Goethe,* Paderborn, 1967.

33.   Letter to Karl Ernst Schubarth, November 3, 1820.

34.   *Cf. Farbenlehre. Didaktischer Teil,* Sechste Abteilung, para. 814, AGA XVI, p.215.

35.   *Philostrats Gemälde,* AGA XIII, pp.792ff.; WA I 49, 1, p.142.

36.   *Farbenlehre. Didaktischer Teil,* Sechste Abteilung, para. 805, AGA XVI, p.214.

37.   *Ibid.,* para. 812, p.215.

38.   *Ibid.,* para. 813, p.215.

39.   For a discussion of this image pattern, *cf.* E. M. Wilkinson and L. A. Willoughby, *op.cit.,* p.103f.

40.   In this connection, *cf.* Dorothea Lohmeyer, *Faust und die Welt,* Potsdam, 1940, who writes: 'Der Gang zu den Müttern ist ein inneres Ereignis' (p.83). Hans Kern forcefully sums up the significance of Faust's undertaking, thus: 'Die Sympathie zum weiblichen Pol des Kosmos ist ein Wesensmerkmal des romantischen Eros . . . Der erste aber, der wieder an die dunkle Pforte des Reiches der "Mütter" klopfte, ist Goethe gewesen.' ('Wandlungen des Eros-gedankens', *Goethe-Kalender 1933,* p.121). *Cf.* also E. M. Wilkinson and L. A. Willoughby, *op.cit.,* p.184, and *Goethes Faust,* ed. R. Petsch, Leipzig, 1925, p.47.

41.   *Polarität,* AGA XVI, p.864.

42.   *Cf.* Chapter 5, p.101 and note 40.

43.   *Werke,* HA III, p.603.

44.   In this connection, W. Emrich writes: 'Jede Besitznahme des Schönen hebt seine Unendlichkeit auf, vernichtet sein inneres, unsterbliches Leben.' . . . ' "Lebendig" können schöpferische Kräfte nur bleiben durch Verwandlung des Seienden . . . ' (*op.cit.,* p.300). Max Kommerell approaches the problem similarly, in connection with the *Paria* trilogy: 'Nimmt die Schönheit Gestalt an in einem Menschen des andern Geschlechts, so verwirrt sich die Liebe, die besitzen will, mit dem Gefühl des Schönen, das Distanz schafft. Geistiges wird ergriffen, als ob es ein Leib wäre, Leibliches wird als geisterhaft behandelt. Daher die Beispiele furchtbar vergeblicher Umarmungen: Tasso büsst sie mit dem Tod seiner Seele, der Jüngling des Märchens erstarrt an der schönen Lilie, Faust wird bei der Berührung des Schemens von einem lähmenden Schlag getroffen.' (*Gedanken über Gedichte,* Frankfurt, 1943, p.422f.)

45.   E. Trunz makes this point. *Cf. Werke,* HA III, p.575.

46.   This identity, here, is stressed by G. W. Hertz ('Natur und Geist in Goethes Faust', *Deutsche Forschungen 25,* p.114f.). *Cf.* also D. Lohmeyer, *op.cit.,* pp.85 and 101.

47.   Letter to Zelter, October 30, 1808.

48.   *Italienische Reise,* III. Teil, Rome, September 6, 1787; AGA XI, p.436.

49.   *Cf.* Chapter 7.

50.   This passage is vital since the reading of it tends to be coupled with the interpreter's assessment of the ensuing *Herrschertragödie; cf.* note 71 below. A similar view to the one argued here is held by W. Emrich (*op.cit.,* p.365) and D. Lohmeyer (*op.cit.,* p.120), whilst E. Staiger (*op.cit.,* III, p.396) goes some way towards it. K. Burdach (*Goethes Sprache und Stil im Alter, Vorspiel II,* Halle, 1926, p.436) and M. Kommerell (*op.cit.,* p.396) contend that Mephistopheles is speaking 'in character', and that his words here do not represent the poet's view. For a contrary view to the one expressed here, *cf.* E. Cassirer who writes: 'Die

wahrhafte Befreiung und Erlösung Fausts vollzieht sich nicht in der Welt der Schönheit, sondern in der Welt der Tat' (*op.cit.*, p.413). Similarly F. Gundolf who writes: 'Die Schönheit ist ein Gut, keine Form seines Lebens' (*Goethe*, 9th ed., Berlin, 1920, p.771).

51. *Über den Granit*, AGA XVII, p.480.

52. R. M. Rilke, *Gesammelte Werke*, Leipzig, 1930, Vol. III, p.420.

53. Chapter 7, p.162f.

54. E. Trunz (ed., HA III, p.600f.) stresses the symbolic character of Faust's colonising activity. *Cf.* also P. Stöcklein, *Wege zum späten Goethe*, p.104.

55. *Tag- und Jahreshefte* for 1803, AGA XI, p.719. Josef Kunz rejects Goethe's explanation as a mystification (HA V, p.480).

56. W. B. Yeats, *Among School Children.*

57. Emil Staiger touches on Goethe's awareness of this connection (*Goethe, ed.cit.*, II, p.390f.). A further and telling link between Goethe's retrospective account and the drama itself is the motif of the secret treasure which plays a central part in both. For the aesthetic significance of this motif, *cf.* also Goethe's report on the progress of *Hermann und Dorothea:* 'Es kommt nut noch auf zwei Tage an, so ist der Schatz gehoben, und ist er nur erst einmal über der Erde, so findet sich alsdann das Polieren von selbst' (letter to Schiller, Jena, March 4, 1797). *Cf.* W. Emrich's analysis of this motif and related ones (*op.cit.*, especially pp.192 and 198).

58. To Eckermann, May 2, 1831. Eckermann reports Goethe as saying: 'Die Intention auch dieser Scenen . . . ist über dreyssig Jahre alt; sie war von solcher Bedeutung, dass ich daran das Interesse nicht verloren, allein so schwer aus-zuführen, dass ich mich davor fürchtete'.

59. *Versuch einer Witterungslehre*, AGA XVII, p.642.

60. The connection between these events has been shown by E. Staiger to whose detailed account I am indebted (*op.cit.*, III, p.423f.).

61. Letter to Johann Heinrich Meyer, July 20, 1831; also letter to Sulpiz Boisserée, September 8, 1831.

62. Letter to K. J. L. Iken, September 27, 1827.

63. Lines 10473-10486. It is interesting to note that in the scenario for Act IV Goethe refers to the speech in terms of its dominant metaphor. '[*Am Rande*: Zweikampf. Faustsche Rede dagegen. Haupt, das von den Gliedern verteidigt wird.]' (AGA V, p.590.)

64. E. Staiger, *op.cit.*, III, p.427f.

65. Line 11085.

66. *Italienische Reise*, Rome, December (Bericht), 1787.

67. Shakespeare, *The Tempest*, IV, 1.

68. A similar reading is put forward by W. Emrich (*op.cit.*, p.401f.), E. Staiger (*op.cit.*, III, p.428) and P. Stöcklein (*op.cit.*, pp.132ff.).

69. These words, it is true, are actually spoken by Mephistopheles. But he is in fact parodying typically Faustian attitudes. Moreover, Goethe's own use of them in *Antepirrhema* and as a conclusion to the essay *Bedenken und Ergebung* should leave no doubt but that they represent a crucial statement of the creative mode as such.

70. P. Stöcklein makes this point emphatically (*op.cit.*, p.160).

71. The opposite view is taken by W. Hertz ('Faust und Friedrich der Grosse', *Euphorion 24*, 1922-23, p.382), Karl Burdach ('Faust und die Sorge', *DVLG* I, 1923, p.21), and A. R. Hohlfeld, *(Fifty Years with Goethe*, Madison, 1953, p.90f.). As against this, H. Moenkemeyer writes: 'Wir glauben weder an das "innere Licht" noch an eine wirkliche Wandlung durch die "Sorge" . . . Erst in seiner Todesvision bahnt sich die Wandlung an . . . ' (*Erscheinungsformen der Sorge bei Goethe*, Giessen, 1954, p.145).

72.   *Cf.* E. Staiger (*op.cit.*, III, p.428) for a similar reading.
73.   K. Lohmeyer denies any connection between the image of the 'Puppen-stand' here (and the 'Flocken' in which Faust is enveloped) and the symbolism of cocoon and silkworm, and declares: 'was brauchen wir den Puppenstand der Knaben auf Faust zu beziehen: er ist doch mehr als sie und soll sie lehren!' ('Das Meer und die Wolken in den beiden letzten Akten des *Faust*', *Jahrbuch d. Goethe Gesellschaft 13*, 1927, p.117). I hope to have shown that both parts of this argument are untenable, as indeed is a reading which refers the 'Puppenstand' to the Selige Knaben rather than to Faust himself.
74.   Letter to Charlotte v. Stein, Ilmenau, July 2, 1781.
75.   M. Kommerell, *op.cit.*, pp.93ff. and E. Staiger, *op.cit*, III, p.435. For a contrary view, *cf.* P. Stöcklein, *op.cit.*, pp.117ff.
76.   In this connection *cf.* P. Stöcklein, *op.cit.*, pp.134 and 150, and E. Beutler, ed., AGA V, p.744.
77.   In: *Gedanken über Gedichte*, Frankfurt, 1943, p.173.
78.   December 1, 1831.
79.   March 17, 1832.
80.   *Die Wahlverwandtschaften*, AGA IX, p.152; *cf.* Chapter 7, 156.

INDEX

Italicised page numbers indicate key references

Alexander, S., 101, 251, 279, 327-8
Alienation, 124, 133, 136, 155ff.:
  creative: from world, 134, 136, 151, 153;
  from self, 134, 136f., 158f., 287, 330, 335;
  from created product, *156ff.*, 287, 294,
  335
  See also Artist
Anacreon, 82
Aristotle, 1
Art:
  authenticity and reality, 123, 134, *251*;
  continuum with natural process, 96ff.,
  103ff., 113, 114, 146, *148ff.*, 163, 259, 267,
  287, 313, 334; defence against nature,
  152, 158f., 261, 281f.; dependence on
  exposure, 159, 290, 302, 306; interaction
  of art-experience and life-experience, 72f.,
  102ff., 108, *116ff.*, 123, 146ff., 160f., *246f.*,
  311ff., *313*; as discovery, 108 and note 49,
  250, 328; opposition to nature, 113; art
  not finished, 138, 335; art versus life, 153;
  educates forms and feeling, 311
  See also Creative process, Form, Permanence in flux
Artist:
  a 'second nature', 113; power of abstraction as root of symbol-making, 132, *329*;
  transference of structure of experience to
  different contexts, 102ff., 106ff., 112,
  131f., 133, 242f., *329,* 331; erotic relation
  to medium, 104, 106f., *158ff.*, 327f., *329*;
  lability and ambivalence, 107f., 112,
  132ff., 136, 154, *160ff.*, 327, 334; trauma
  of disintegration of creative configuration, *152*, 168, *158ff.*, 273, 281, *292ff.*, 294,
  296, 303; alienation, 133f., 134, 136, 151,
  155f. (*see also* Alienation); nostalgia for
  permanence, 156f., *158ff.*, 162, 302f., 336
  See also Creative process, Medium,
  Morphology, Permanence in flux
Atkins, S., 341
Auden, W. H., 30, 115, 158

Bauer, G. and S. (ed.), 318, 338, 339, 343
Beethoven, 183, 312
Benn, G., xiii, 106
Beutler, E., 349
Bielschowsky, A., 335

Bildungstrieb, 144ff., *147f.*, *152*, 160f.
  See also Morphology, Weben
Bizet, J. A., 339
Blake, W., 165
Blankenburg, C. von, 331
Böckmann, P., 339
Body and mind: creative oneness of, *xiif.*,
  22ff., 36f., 89, 96, 252, 260, 269f., 284;
  dissociation between, *12f.*, 81, 94, 209ff.
Boisserée, S., 296
Brentano, Maximiliane, 133f., 154
Brüggemann, F., 339, 340, 344
Buff, Charlotte, *see* Kestner, Charlotte
Buff, Henrich Adam, 133
Bullough, E., 75, 122, 228, 325, 344
Burdach, K., 347, 348

Carl August, Duke of Weimar, 19, 163
Cassirer, E., 257, 345, 347-8
Circulation:
  as symbol of natural cycles, xii, 27f., 29,
  218ff., 240, 241; as symbol of creative
  cycle, xii, 241f., 272, 275, 308; as symbol
  of relatedness, 181, *184ff.*, *188f.*; as sym-
  bol of Theodicy, 171f., *239f.*
  See also Creative process, Return,
  Theodicy, Vision and reality
Circularity: of import and form, 197, 307;
  logical, 196f.
Clark, J. M., 320-1
Cohn, H., 337, 338, 343
Coleridge, S., 116, 122
Collingwood, R. G., 329, 335
Compassion: as motivation of characters,
  225; as catharising emotion, 225f., 338
Conception and expression:
  expression modifying conception, xiii, 28,
  74f., 204ff., 229, 319, 321, 322f., 342f.;
  expression as discovery, 55ff., 63, *73f.*,
  108, 114, 251ff.; language as creator of
  meanings, *57ff.*, 123, *244ff.*, 321f.; formal
  relations as creator of meanings, 20, *40ff.*,
  59, 72, 123, 210f., *264ff.*, 307, 321, 323;
  interdependence between conception and
  expression, 309, 310, 332
  See also Vision and reality